D1234201

Roosevelt

WITHDRAWN

The FDR Years

On Roosevelt and His Legacy

THE FDR YEARS

On Roosevelt and His Legacy

WILLIAM E. LEUCHTENBURG

973 .917092
L652f

COLUMBIA UNIVERSITY PRESS   NEW YORK

JUN 2 8 1996
CUYAHOGA COMMUNITY COLLEGE
EASTERN CAMPUS LIBRARY

Columbia University Press
New York   Chichester, West Sussex
Copyright (c) 1995 Columbia University Press
All rights reserved
Library of Congress Cataloging-in-Publication Data
Leuchtenburg, William Edward, 1922-
        The FDR years : on Roosevelt and his legacy / William E. Leuchtenburg.
            p.   cm.
        Includes bibliographical references and index.
        ISBN 0-231-08298-3
        1. Roosevelt, Franklin D. (Franklin Delano), 1882-1945. 2. New
        Deal, 1933-1939. 3. United States—History—1933-1945. I. Title.
        E806.L474 1995
        973.917'092—dc20   95-13282
⊗   CIP

Casebound editions of Columbia University Press books are printed
on permanent and durable acid-free paper.
Printed in the United States of America
c 10 9 8 7 6 5 4 3 2 1

To My Students Who Have Written about the
New Deal Era and Who Have Taught Me So Much

Richard M. Abrams
Jerold S. Auerbach
Catherine A. Barnes
Gloria Barron
Stephen W. Baskerville
James L. Baughman
Alison R. Bernstein
Thomas E. Blantz, C.S.C.
Barbara Blumberg
James Boylan
Allan Brandt
John J. Broesamle
David Burner
Helen C. Camp
Mark Lincoln Chadwin
William H. Chafe
John W. Chambers
Ellen Chesler
Jean Christie
Stanley Coben
Olen Cole, Jr.
Robert Dallek
John D'Emilio
Leonard Dinnerstein
Lowell K. Dyson
Richard M. Fried
Mark I. Gelfand
Richard Gillam
Rita Werner Gordon
Otis L. Graham, Jr.
Lloyd J. Graybar
Cheryl Greenberg
Thomas N. Guinsburg
Jacquelyn Dowd Hall
Alonzo L. Hamby
Howell John Harris
Cynthia Harrison
Robert Harrison
Hazel W. Hertzberg
Jonathan Houghton
Haggai Hurvitz
Robert P. Ingalls
Fred Israel
Travis Beal Jacobs
Robert E. Jakoubek

Harry P. Jeffrey
James P. Johnson
Richard C. Keller
Susan Estabrook Kennedy
Christopher Lasch
Steven F. Lawson
John Lax
Daniel Leab
Linda Lear
Lawrence Levine
Peter B. Levy
Edwin R. Lewinson
Roy Lubove
Maeva Marcus
Anne Mitchell
John Modell
Regina Markell Morantz-Sanchez
John O'Sullivan
William Pencak
Monty Noam Penkower
Richard Polenberg
Davis R. B. Ross
Irving Sandler
Bonnie Fox Schwartz
Jordan A. Schwarz
Holly Cowan Shulman
Barbara Sicherman
Bryant Simon
Daniel Joseph Singal
Harvard Sitkoff
Gilbert E. Smith
Bruce M. Stave
Barbara McDonald Stewart
Duane Tananbaum
Barbara L. Tischler
Charles H. Trout
Nancy Bernkopf Tucker
Melvin I. Urofsky
Sydney Weinberg
Richard Weiss
Sarah Wilkerson-Freeman
Lawrence S. Wittner
Andrew Workman
Howard Zinn

New Deal issues still agitate the contemporary mind. Baptism, the doctrine of the real presence, and the Immaculate Conception may be discussed without passion, but men display emotion at the first mention of federal economic policy, agricultural subsidies, public housing, conservation—even, still, at the name Franklin Delano Roosevelt.

OTIS L. GRAHAM, JR.

Contents

PREFACE

I vividly remember when I first heard the words "Franklin Delano Roosevelt." The year was 1930, and I was seven. Together with my second grade classmates, I had been herded into a capacious study hall in a New York City public school where a board of education honcho had come to call, much like an Anglican bishop on a diocesan visit to a working-class parish. We had no sooner settled in our seats than this forbidding presence popped a question: "What is the first name of the Roosevelt who is our governor and who is being talked about as the next president of the United States?" Silence. Then one youngster piped up, "Theodore." The stranger shook his head grumpily no. Then came a rain of wild guesses, while he stood there glowering. There were a few more cries of "Theodore" or "Teddy," though these were patently the wrong retorts. Then utter and awkward silence. Finally, he told us the answer. It was one, I said to myself on that tense occasion, I had better commit to memory. But little did I realize that morning how the phrase "Franklin Delano Roosevelt" would accompany me all the rest of my days.

Two years later, when I was nine, I knew the name well enough. I was living in a New Jersey suburb during the summer of the 1932 Democratic convention, and I stayed up late listening on the radio to the proceedings from Chicago with the same breathless interest with which I followed the pennant race that season. Indeed, just as I had made out a crude scorecard for the World Series broadcasts the previous fall, with names of players such as Foxx and Cochrane and Bottomley, so did I draw lines on a pad for the roll call of the forty-eight states with space for the names of the candidates, some of them now largely forgotten—including my father's inexplicable favorite, the industrialist Owen D. Young. Ballot after ballot very early one morning, I entered the numbers for Alfred E. Smith, John Nance Garner, Newton D. Baker, and the rest, and that night, way past my usual bedtime, recorded the final reckoning: victory for the man who had been the front-runner all along—FDR.

In the ensuing year, Franklin Roosevelt emerged as a large presence in my life. He had hardly taken office when he put through the Economy Act, which resulted in a furlough for my father, who, for days at a time, stayed home instead of commuting to work in the big post office across from Pennsylvania Station. Despite that worrisome situation, I was caught up in the irresistible pace of the First Hundred Days with headlines of newly created alphabet agencies conveying an unfamiliar and ineluctable excitement about national politics. I have a graphic recollection of my mother pasting in a window the National Recovery Administration Blue Eagle sticker I brought home from school.

The impact of FDR and the New Deal did not end with that halcyon springtime. In 1935 I earned enough tutoring younger children in the neighborhood to go off by myself on a nine-hour Greyhound bus trip to the nation's capital to see New Deal Washington at first hand. A year later, I impressed my best friend by accurately predicting Roosevelt's victory in the 1936 election, a feat achieved only because my family could not afford a subscription to the *Literary Digest* with its faulty poll. The next year, yet another visiting educational bureaucrat stopped by one of my classrooms to inquire whether any of us could state with precision the particulars of the President's Court-packing plan. (We all flunked.) And when I went off to Cornell in the fall of 1939, it was the National Youth Administration, as I have explained elsewhere, that made it possible for me to work my way through college.

When I entered graduate school, it seemed natural to concentrate my research on the FDR years, an inclination that led not only to a number of books—*Flood Control Politics: The Connecticut River Valley Problem* (Harvard University Press, 1953); *The Perils of Prosperity, 1914–32* (University of Chicago Press, 1958), which has a chapter on the Great Depression; *Franklin D. Roosevelt and the New Deal, 1932–1940* (Harper and Row, 1953); *New Deal and Global War* (Time, Inc., 1964), the penultimate volume of the twelve-volume Life History of the United States; *The New Deal* (Harper and Row, 1968), an anthology that is a volume in the Documentary History of the United States; and *In the Shadow of FDR: From Harry Truman to Bill Clinton* (Cornell University Press, 1993)—but also to a good many essays for scholarly journals, popular articles, and lectures. It is these occasional pieces that are the source of almost all of this book.

The idea for the book, although it now seems to be the logical culmination of this series of developments, came fortuitously. At lunch with the editor in chief of the Columbia University Press, Kate Wittenberg, in the dining room of a Chicago hotel in the spring of 1992, Alan Brinkley mentioned to us that he had just come upon one of these essays that he had not known about and suggested that, since there must be others like it, I put together a collection of them. I responded that, though I appreciated his thought, I doubted there were enough to make a book, but afterward, as I walked up windy Michigan Avenue with my wife, mulling over the notion, I realized that there were actually more possibilities than one volume could absorb. In fact, I would have to be selective.

The nine essays I have chosen come from a variety of sources. Five originated as contributions to multiauthor volumes; one was a chapter in my first book; another first appeared as an article in a scholarly journal; and still another was written for a popular audience. All have been revised, most of them substantially, but I have not altered their forms. I have annotated only those pieces that were annotated when they originally appeared. I have attempted to cover a wide range of areas, but I have deliberately not sought to deal with jurisprudence, which is the subject of another collection of my writings: *The Supreme Court Reborn: The Constitutional Revolution in the Age of Roosevelt* (Oxford University Press, 1995).

No words can begin to express adequately my debt to my wife Jean Anne. She was there at the inception of this enterprise; encouraged me to take it on; and has been an unfailing source of inspiration ever since. Editor of the superb journal *Ideas*, published by the National Humanities Center, she has turned her skills unremittingly toward improving this manuscript and has contributed even more by her joyful companionship.

William E. Leuchtenburg
Bailey Island, Maine
July 1994

THE FDR YEARS

On Roosevelt and His Legacy

ONE

Franklin D. Roosevelt: The First Modern President

[This essay began as a paper at a Conference on Leadership in the Modern Presidency at the Woodrow Wilson School of Princeton University on April 3, 1987. The gathering was organized by Fred I. Greenstein, Professor of Politics, who conceived the interesting idea of pairing historians of presidencies from FDR to Ronald Reagan with government officials from the respective administrations. As the opening speaker, I was startled to find, when I went to the podium and looked out at the audience, that I was staring right into the eyes of H. R. Haldeman (part of the duo that day on Richard Nixon) who was seated in the front row just a few feet away. I was fortunate to be paired with the wise and gentle Wilbur J. Cohen, who had first gone to Washington at a precocious age in Franklin Roosevelt's first term. Long before he became Secretary of HEW under Lyndon Johnson, authorities on the Welfare State were fond of saying that an expert on Social Security was someone who had Wilbur Cohen's phone number. Unhappily, he died the very next month. The proceedings of the conference, which were dedicated to Cohen, were published as Fred I. Greenstein, ed., *Leadership in the Modern Presidency* (Cambridge: Harvard University Press, 1988). I have made some modifications of the original essay, which in a few places drew upon my book *New Deal and Global War* (New York: Time, Inc. 1964), vol. 11 of the *Life History of the United States.*]

The presidency as we know it today begins with Franklin Delano Roosevelt. To be sure, many of the rudiments of the executive office date from the earliest years of the republic, and, in the nineteenth century, figures such as Andrew Jackson demonstrated how the president could serve as tribune of the people. In this century, too, both Theodore Roosevelt and Woodrow Wilson showed that the White House could radiate power. Yet, as Fred I. Greenstein has observed, "With Franklin Roosevelt's administration . . . the presidency began to undergo not a shift but rather a metamorphosis." Indeed, so powerful an impression did FDR leave on the office that in the most recent survey of historians he was ranked as the second greatest president in our history, surpassed only by the legendary Abraham Lincoln.[1]

This very high rating would have appalled many of the contemporaries of "that megalomaniac cripple in the White House." In the spring of 1937 an American who had been traveling extensively in the Caribbean confided, "During all the time I was gone, if anybody asked me if I wanted any news, my reply was always—'there is only one bit of news I want to hear and that is the death of Franklin D. Roosevelt. If he is not dead you don't need to tell me anything else.'"[2] One of FDR's Hudson Valley neighbors, who viewed the President as "a swollen headed nit-wit," exiled himself to the Bahamas until Roosevelt was no longer in the White House, and the radio manufacturer Atwater Kent retired because he would not do business while "That Man" was there. It has been said that "J. P. Morgan's family kept newspapers with pictures of Roosevelt out of his sight, and in one Connecticut country club . . . mention of his name was forbidden as a health measure against apoplexy." In Kansas a man went down into his cyclone cellar and announced he would not emerge until Roosevelt was out of office. (While he was there, his wife ran off with a traveling salesman.)[3]

At neither end of the ideological spectrum did respect for civility of discourse restrain the Roosevelt-haters. The Communist leader Earl Browder said that FDR was "carrying out more thoroughly and brutally than even Hoover the capitalist attack against the masses," and the domestic fascist William Dudley Pelley called the President the "lowest form of human worm—according to Gentile standards." One critic accused him of "blathering platitudes like a parson on vacation," and another wrote to him savagely, "If you were a good honest man, Jesus Christ would not have crippled you." It was in a formal address to the Chicago Bar Association, not in a harangue to an extremist rally, that a United States Senator from Minnesota did not hesitate to liken Roosevelt to the beast of the Apocalypse, "who set his slimy mark on everything."[4]

Roosevelt, his critics maintained, had shown himself to be a man without principles. Herbert Hoover called him a "chameleon on plaid," while H. L. Mencken said, "If he became convinced tomorrow that coming out for cannibalism would get him the votes he so sorely needs, he would begin fattening a missionary in the White House backyard come Wednesday." The Sage of Baltimore declared, "I am advocating making him king in order that we may behead him in case he goes too far beyond the limits of the endurable."[5]

A good number of historians as well have found fault with FDR. New Left writers have chided him for offering a "profoundly conservative" response to a situation that had the potential for revolutionary change, while commentators of no particular persuasion have criticized him for failing to bring the country out of the Depression short of war, for maneuvering America into World War II (or for not taking the nation to war soon enough), for refusing to advocate civil rights legislation, for permitting Jews to perish in Hitler's death camps, and for sanctioning the internment of Japanese-Americans. Even a historian who thought well of him, Allan Nevins, wrote that "his mind, compared with that of Woodrow Wilson, sometimes appears superficial, and . . . he possessed no such intellectual versatility as Thomas Jefferson—to say nothing of Winston Churchill." Nevins added: "In respect to character, similarly, he had traits of an admirable kind; but . . . even in combination they fell short of a truly Roman weight of virtue."[6]

Roosevelt has been castigated especially for his inability to develop any grand design. Most great leaders have had an idea they wanted to impose, noted a contemporary critic, "whereas Roosevelt, if he has one, has successfully concealed it." Similarly, the political scientist C. Herman Pritchett later concluded that the New Deal never produced "any consistent social and economic philosophy to give meaning and purpose to its various action programs." He added,

> Priding itself on its experimental approach, guided by a man who thought of himself as a quarterback trying first one play and then another and judging their success by immediate pragmatic tests—the New Deal, along with all its great positive contributions to American life, may well be charged with contributing to the delinquency of American liberalism.[7]

Especially forceful on this point have been two of the original members of the Brain Trust. Raymond Moley wrote:

> To look upon these policies as the result of a unified plan was to believe that the accumulation of stuffed snakes, baseball pictures, school flags, old tennis shoes, carpenter's tools, geometry books, and

chemistry sets in a boy's bedroom could have been put there by an interior decorator.

Or, perhaps it would be more apt to say that the unfolding of the New Deal between 1932 and 1937 suggested the sounds that might be produced by an orchestra which started out with part of a score and which after a time began to improvise. It might all hang together if there were a clear understanding between the players and the conductor as to the sort of music they intended to produce. But nothing was more obvious than that some of the New Deal players believed that the theme was to be the funeral march of capitalism; others, a Wagnerian conflict between Good and Evil; and still others, the triumphant strains of the *Heldenleben*.

Even harsher disapproval has come from a man who in many ways admired FDR, Rexford Tugwell. "The Roosevelt measures were really pitiful patches on agencies he ought to have abandoned forthwith when leadership was conferred on him in such unstinted measure," Tugwell maintained. "He could have emerged from the orthodox progressive chrysalis and led us into a new world." Instead, he busied himself "planting protective shrubbery on the slopes of a volcano."[8]

Given all of this often very bitter censure, both at the time and since, how can one account for FDR's ranking as the second-greatest president ever? In raising that question, it may readily be acknowledged that such polls often say more about the ideological predisposition of scholars than about the nature of presidential performance, and that historians have been scandalously vague about establishing criteria for "greatness." Yet there are in fact significant reasons for Roosevelt's rating, some of them substantial enough to be acknowledged even by skeptics.

One may begin with the most obvious: he has been regarded as one of the greatest of our presidents because he was in the White House longer than anyone else. Alone of American presidents, he broke the taboo against a third term and served part of a fourth term too. Shortly after his death, the country adopted a constitutional amendment limiting a president to two terms. Motivated in no small part by the desire to deliver a posthumous reprimand to FDR, this amendment has had the ironic consequence of assuring that Franklin Roosevelt will be, so far as we can foresee, the only chief executive who has ever served or will ever serve more than two terms.

Roosevelt's high place rests also on his role in leading the nation to accept the far-ranging responsibilities of world power. When he took office, the United States was firmly committed to isolationism; it had refused to participate in either the League of Nations or the World Court. Denied by Congress the discretionary authority he sought, Roosevelt made full use of his executive power in recognizing the USSR, crafting the Good Neighbor Policy, and, late in his second term, providing aid to the Allies and leading the nation toward active involvement in World War II. So far had America come by the end of the Roosevelt era that Henry Stimson was to say that the United States could never again "be an island to herself. No private program and no public policy, in any sector of our national life, can now escape from the compelling fact that if it is not framed with reference to the world, it is framed with perfect futility."[9]

As a wartime president, Roosevelt had wide latitude to demonstrate his executive leadership by guiding the country through a victorious struggle against the fascist powers. Never before had a president been given the opportunity to lead his people to a triumph of these global dimensions, and it seems improbable, given the nature of nuclear weapons, that such a circumstance will ever arise again. As commander-in-chief, a position he was said to prefer to all others, Roosevelt not only supervised the mobilization of men and resources against the Axis but also made a significant contribution to fashioning a postwar settlement and creating the structure of the United Nations. "He overcame both his own and the nation's isolationist inclination to bring a united America into the coalition that saved the world from the danger of totalitarian conquest," Robert Divine has concluded. "His role in insuring the downfall of Adolf Hitler is alone enough to earn him a respected place in history."[10]

For good or ill, also, the United States first became a major military power during Roosevelt's presidency. Under FDR, Congress established peacetime conscription and after Pearl Harbor put millions of men and women into uniform. His long tenure also saw the birth of the Pentagon, the military-industrial complex, and the atomic bomb. By April 1945, one historian has noted, "A Navy superior to the combined fleets of the rest of the world dominated the seven seas; the Air Force commanded greater striking power than that of any other country; and American overseas bases in the . . . Atlantic, the Mediterranean, and the Pacific rimmed the Eurasian continent." The columnist George Will has summed up the historic dimensions of the transformation: "When FDR died in 1945, America was more supreme than Great Britain after Waterloo, than France of Louis XIV—than any power since the Roman Empire. And it had a central government commensurate with that role."[11]

But there is one explanation more important than any of these in accounting for FDR's high ranking: his role in enlarging the presidential office and expanding the domain of the State while leading the American people through the Great Depression.

Roosevelt came to office at a desperate time, in the fourth year of a worldwide depression that raised the gravest doubts about the future of Western civilization. "The year 1931 was distinguished from previous years . . . by one outstanding feature," commented the British historian Arnold Toynbee. "In 1931, men and women all over the world were seriously contemplating and frankly discussing the possibility that the Western system of Society might break down and cease to work."[12] On New Year's Eve 1931 in the United States, an American diplomat noted in his diary, "The last day of a very unhappy year for so many people the world around. Prices at the bottom and failures the rule of the day. A black picture!" And in the summer of 1932 John Maynard Keynes, asked by a journalist whether there had ever been anything before like the Great Depression, replied: "Yes, it was called the Dark Ages, and it lasted four hundred years."[13]

By the time Roosevelt was sworn in, national income had been cut in half and more than fifteen million Americans were unemployed. Every state had closed its banks or severely restricted their operations, and on the very morning of his inauguration the New York Stock Exchange had shut down. For many, hope had gone. "Now is the winter of our discontent the chilliest," wrote the editor of *Nation's Business*. "Fear, bordering on panic, loss of faith in everything, our fellowman, our institutions, private and government. Worst of all, no faith in ourselves, or the future. Almost everyone ready to scuttle the ship, and not even women and children first."[14]

Only a few weeks after Roosevelt took office, the spirit of the country seemed markedly changed. Gone was the torpor of the Hoover years; gone, too, the political paralysis. "The people aren't sure . . . just where they are going," noted one business journal, "but anywhere seems better than where they have been. In the homes, on the streets, in the offices, there is a feeling of hope reborn." Again and again, observers resorted to the imagery of darkness and light to characterize the transformation from the Stygian gloom of Hoover's final winter to the bright springtime of the First Hundred Days. Overnight, one eyewitness later remembered, Washington seemed like Cambridge on the morning of the Harvard-Yale game: "All the shops were on display, everyone was joyous, crowds moved excitedly. There was something in the air that had not been there before, and in the New Deal that continued throughout. It was not just for the day as it was in Cambridge." On the New York Curb Exchange, where trading resumed on March 15, the stock ticker ended the day with the merry message: "Goodnite. . . . Happy days are here again."[15]

It was altogether fitting to choose the words of FDR's theme song, for people of every political persuasion gave full credit for the revival of confidence to one man: the new president. FDR's "conspicuous courage, cheerfulness, energy and resource," noted the British ambassador at Washington, Sir Ronald Lindsay, contrasted so markedly with the "fearful, furtive fumbling of the Great White Feather," Herbert Hoover, that "the starved loyalties and repressed hero-worship of the country have found in him an outlet and a symbol." In March a Hoover appointee from the Oyster Bay branch of the Roosevelt family wrote his mother, "I have followed with much interest and enthusiasm Franklin's start. I think he has done amazingly well, and I am really very pleased. One feels that he has what poor Hoover lacked, and what the country so much needs—leadership." A month later the Republican Senator from California, Hiram Johnson, acknowledged:

> The admirable trait in Roosevelt is that he has the guts to try. . . . He does it all with the rarest good nature. . . . We have exchanged for a frown in the White House a smile. Where there were hesitation and vacillation, weighing always the personal political consequences, feebleness, timidity, and duplicity, there are now courage and boldness and real action.[16]

On the editorial page of *Forum*, Henry Goddard Leach summed up the nation's nearly unanimous verdict: "We have a leader."[17]

The new president had created this impression by a series of actions—delivering his compelling inaugural address, summoning Congress into emergency session, resolving the financial crisis—but even more by his manner. "Roosevelt's voice," the philosopher T. V. Smith said, "knew how to articulate only the everlasting Yea." Supremely confident in his own powers, he could imbue others with a similar self-assurance. He felt altogether comfortable in the world into which he was born, and with good reason. As his aunt said, "*Il a été élevé dans un beau cadre*" (He was brought up in a beautiful frame). Like George Washington, as David Potter suggested, "he was a 'code man' who had fixed himself upon a model (perhaps of Groton, Harvard, and Hudson River society), and who found small place for personal introspection in such a role." Moreover, he had acquired an admirable political education: state senator, junior cabinet officer, his party's vice-presidential nominee, two-term governor of the largest state in the Union.[18]

Roosevelt faced formidable challenges as president, but he never doubted that he would cope with them, for he believed that he belonged in the White House. He had sat on Grover Cleveland's knee, cast his first vote for Uncle Teddy, and seen Woodrow Wilson at close range; but the office seemed peculiarly his almost as a birthright. As Richard Neustadt has observed: "Roosevelt, almost alone among our Presidents, had no conception of the office to live up to; he was it. His image of the office was himself-in-office."[19] He loved the majesty of the position, relished its powers, and rejoiced in the opportunity it offered for achievement. "The essence of Roosevelt's Presidency," Clinton Rossiter later wrote, "was his airy eagerness to meet the age head on. Thanks to his flair for drama, he acted as if never in all history had there been times like our own."[20]

FDR's view of himself and of his world freed him from anxieties that other men would have felt, and would have found intolerable. Not even the weightiest responsibilities seemed to disturb his serenity. One of his associates said, "He must have been psychoanalyzed by God." A Washington correspondent noted in 1933:

No signs of care are visible to his main visitors or at the press conferences. He is amiable, urbane and apparently untroubled. He appears to have a singularly fortunate faculty for not becoming flustered. Those who talk with him informally in the evenings report that he busies himself with his stamp collection, discussing in an illuminating fashion the affairs of state while he waves his shears in the air.

Even after Roosevelt had gone through the trials of two terms of office, *Time* reported:

He has one priceless attribute: a knack of locking up his and the world's worries in some secret mental compartment, and then enjoying himself to the top of his bent. This quality of survival, of physical toughness, of champagne ebullience is one key to the big man. Another key is this: no one has ever heard him admit that he cannot walk.[21]

On the centennial of FDR's birth, George Will wrote:

Anyone who contemplates this century without shivering probably does not understand what is going on. But Franklin Roosevelt was, an aide said, like the fairy-tale prince who did not know how to shiver. Something was missing in FDR. . . . But what FDR lacked made him great. He lacked the capacity even to imagine that things might end up badly. He had a Christian's faith that the universe is well constituted and an American's faith that history is a rising road. . . . Radiating an infectious zest, he did the most important thing a President can do: he gave the nation a hopeful, and hence creative, stance toward the future.[22]

No one can be certain where this equanimity came from, but Eleanor Roosevelt once reflected:

I always felt that my husband's religion had something to do with his confidence in himself. . . . It was a very simple religion. He believed in God and in His guidance. He felt that human beings were given tasks to perform and with those tasks the ability and strength to put them through. He could pray for help and guidance and have faith in his own judgment as a result. The church services that he always insisted on holding on Inauguration Day, anniversaries, and whenever a great crisis impended, were the expression of his religious faith. I think this must not be lost sight of in judging his acceptance of responsibility and his belief in his ability to meet whatever crisis had to be met.[23]

Roosevelt's sangfroid was matched with an experimental temperament. Like his father, he always had his eye out for something new. As Frank Freidel wrote: "James was a plunger in business, Franklin in politics." FDR had twice actually gone on treasure-hunting expeditions. "The innovating spirit . . . was his most striking characteristic as a politician," Henry Fairlie has commented. "The man who took to the radio like a duck to water was the same man who, in his first campaign for the New York Senate in 1910, hired . . . a two-cylinder red Maxwell, with no windshield or top, to dash through (of all places) Dutchess County; and it was the same man who broke all precedents twenty-two years later when he hired a little plane to take him to Chicago to make his acceptance speech. . . . The willingness to try everything was how Roosevelt governed."[24]

Serenity and venturesomeness were precisely the qualities needed in a national leader in the crisis of the Depression, and the country drew reassurance from his buoyant view of the world. Frances Perkins later remarked:

> Overshadowing them all was his feeling that nothing in human judgment is final. One may courageously take the step that seems right today because it can be modified tomorrow if it does not work well. . . . Since it is a normal human reaction, most people felt as he did and gladly followed when he said, "We can do it. At least let's try."[25]

Roosevelt scoffed at the idea that the nation was the passive victim of economic laws. He believed that the country could lift itself out of the Depression by sheer willpower. In one of his fireside chats, he said:

> When Andrew Jackson, "Old Hickory," died, someone asked, "Will he go to Heaven?" and the answer was, "He will if he wants to." If I am asked whether the American people will pull themselves out of this depression, I answer, "They will if they want to." . . . I have no sympathy with the professional economists who insist that things must run their course and that human agencies can have no influence on economic ills.[26]

FDR's self-command, gusto, and bonhomie created an extraordinary bond between himself and the American people. In November 1934 Martha Gellhorn reported to Harry Hopkins from the Carolinas:

> Every house I visited—mill worker or unemployed—had a picture of the President. These ranged from newspaper clippings (in destitute homes) to large coloured prints, framed in gilt cardboard. . . .

And the feeling of these people for the President is one of the most remarkable phenomena I have ever met. He is at once God and their intimate friend; he knows them all by name, knows their little town and mill, their little lives and problems. And though everything else fails, he is there, and will not let them down.[27]

Roosevelt nurtured this relationship by making the most of the advantage his position offered to instruct the citizenry. Shortly after his first election he declared:

The Presidency is not merely an administrative office. That is the least of it. It is pre-eminently a place of moral leadership.

All of our great Presidents were leaders of thought at times when certain historic ideas in the life of the nation had to be clarified. Washington personified the idea of Federal Union. Jefferson practically originated the party system as we now know it by opposing the democratic theory to the republicanism of Hamilton. This theory was reaffirmed by Jackson.

Two great principles of our government were forever put beyond question by Lincoln. Cleveland, coming into office following an era of great political corruption, typified rugged honesty. Theodore Roosevelt and Wilson were both moral leaders, each in his own way and for his own time, who used the Presidency as a pulpit.

That is what the office is—a superb opportunity for reapplying, applying to new conditions, the simple rules of human conduct to which we always go back. Without leadership alert and sensitive to change, we . . . lose our way.[28]

To acquaint the country with new moral imperatives and with his departures in public policy, Roosevelt made conscious use of the media almost from the moment he entered the White House, with his press conferences serving to educate newspaper writers and, through them, the nation on the complex, novel measures he was advocating. He was fond of calling the press meeting room in the White House his "schoolroom," and he often resorted to terms such as "seminar" or the budget "textbook." When in January 1934 he invited thirty-five Washington correspondents to his study, he explained his budget message to them "like a football coach going through skull practice with his squad."[29]

According to Leo Rosten, FDR's comportment at his first press conference as president, on March 8, 1933, became "something of a legend in newspaper circles":

> Mr. Roosevelt was introduced to each correspondent. Many of them he already knew and greeted by name—first name. For each he had a handshake and the Roosevelt smile. When the questioning began, the full virtuosity of the new Chief Executive was demonstrated. Cigarette-holder in mouth at a jaunty angle, he met the reporters on their own grounds. His answers were swift, positive, illuminating. He had exact information at his fingertips. He showed an impressive understanding of public problems and administrative methods. He was lavish in his confidences and "background information." He was informal, communicative, gay. When he evaded a question it was done frankly. He was thoroughly at ease. He made no effort to conceal his pleasure in the give and take of the situation.[30]

Jubilant reporters could scarcely believe the transformation in the White House. So hostile had their relations become with Roosevelt's predecessor that Hoover, who was accused of employing the Secret Service to stop leaks and of launching a campaign of "terrorism" to get publishers to fire certain newspapermen, finally discontinued press conferences altogether. Furthermore, Hoover, like Harding and Coolidge before him, had insisted on written questions submitted in advance. Roosevelt, to the delight of the Washington press corps, immediately abolished that requirement and said that questions could be fired at him without warning. At the end of the first conference, reporters did something they had never done before—gave the man they were covering a spontaneous round of applause. One veteran, and often sardonic, journalist described it as "the most amazing performance the White House has ever seen." He added: "The press barely restrained its whoopees. . . . Here was news—action— drama! Here was a new attitude to the press! . . . The reportorial affection and admiration for the President [are] unprecedented. He has definitely captivated an unusually cynical battalion of correspondents."[31]

The initial euphoria persisted long afterward. Roosevelt could sometimes be testy—he told one reporter to go off to a corner and put on a dunce cap—but, for the most part, especially in the New Deal years, he was jovial and even chummy, in no small part because he regarded himself as a longtime newspaperman, having been "president"—that is, editor-in-chief—of the Harvard *Crimson*.[32] He also saw to it that every nervous newcomer on his first White House assignment was introduced to him with a handshake, and he made clear that members of the Fourth Estate were socially respectable by throwing a spring garden party for them at the White House.

Above all, FDR proved an inexhaustible source of news. Jack Bell, who covered the White House for the Associated Press, observed:

> He talked in headline phrases. He acted, he emoted; he was angry, he was smiling. He was persuasive, he was demanding; he was philosophical, he was elemental. He was sensible, he was unreasonable; he was benevolent, he was malicious. He was satirical, he was soothing; he was funny, he was gloomy. He was exciting. He was human. He was copy.[33]

Another correspondent later said, "We never covered Washington in the twenties. We covered the Senate. You wasted your time downtown." But under FDR "downtown"—the White House—became the best beat in the land. "You are still the most interesting person," the independent Republican editor William Allen White told him near the end of his second term. "For box office attraction you leave Clark Gable gasping for breath."[34]

Reporters came to view their encounters with Roosevelt as the greatest show around. A columnist wrote later, "The doubters among us—and I was one of them—predicted that the free and open conference would last a few weeks and then would be abandoned." But twice a week, with rare exceptions, year after year, the President submitted to the crossfire of interrogation. After sitting in on one of these conferences, John Dos Passos noted that Roosevelt replied to questions "simply and unhurriedly as if he were sitting at a table talking to an old friend"; "his voice is fatherly-friendly, without strain, like the voice of the principal of a first-rate boy's school."[35] So readily did FDR inspire confidence that he felt free at times to suggest, "If I were writing your stories to-day, I should say. . . ." At the end, the words "Thank you, Mr. President" were the signal for a pell-mell scramble for the telephones in the White House press room. Reporters had never seen anything like it. He left independent-minded newspapermen such as Raymond Clapper with the conviction that "the administration from President Roosevelt down has little to conceal and is willing to do business with the doors open." If reporters were 60 percent for the New Deal, Clapper reckoned, they were 90 percent for Roosevelt personally.[36]

Some commentators have seen in the FDR press conference a quasi-constitutional institution like the question hour in the House of Commons.[37] To a degree, it was. But the fact remains that the President had complete control over what he would discuss and what could be published. He intended the press conference not as an instrumentality to accommodate inquisitors but as a public relations device he could manipulate to his own advantage. In particular, the press conferences gave Roosevelt a way of circumventing the hostility of right-wing publishers to his program and of stealing the scene from his opponents in the other branches of government. In his extraordinary "horse-and-buggy" monologue following the Supreme Court's *Schechter* decision, Roosevelt used the press conference as a forum for what amounted to a dissenting opinion delivered to the nation, with reporters reduced to the role of scribes.[38]

Franklin Roosevelt was also the first chief executive to take full advantage of the capacity of radio to project a president's ideas and personality directly into American homes. When FDR got before a microphone, Frances Perkins recalled, "his head would nod and his hands would move in simple, natural, comfortable gestures. His face would smile and light up as though he were actually sitting on the front porch or in the parlor." He appeared, said another observer, to be "talking and toasting marshmallows at the same time." In his first days in office, he gave a radio address that was denominated a "fireside chat" because his intimate, informal delivery made every American think the President was sitting at a hearth alongside him or her. As David Halberstam has pointed out,

> He was the first great American radio voice. For most Americans of this generation, their first memory of politics would be sitting by a radio and hearing *that* voice, strong, confident, totally at ease. If he was going to speak, the idea of doing something else was unthinkable. If they did not yet have a radio, they walked the requisite several hundred yards to the home of a more fortunate neighbor who did. It was in the most direct sense the government reaching out and touching the citizen, bringing Americans into the political process and focusing their attention on the presidency as the source of good. . . . Most Americans in the previous 160 years had never even seen a President; now almost all of them were hearing him, *in their own homes*. It was literally and figuratively electrifying.[39]

By quickening interest in government, Roosevelt became the country's foremost civic educator. Charles A. Beard, often a vehement critic, went so far as to say that Franklin Roosevelt discussed "more fundamental problems of American life and society than all the other Presidents combined." FDR's rousing inaugural address drew 460,000 letters; in contrast, President Taft had received only 200 letters a week. Whereas one man had been able to handle all of Hoover's mail, a staff of fifty had to be hired to take care of Franklin Roosevelt's incoming correspondence. "The mail started coming in by the truckload," a former White House aide said. "They couldn't even get the envelopes open."[40] His chief of mails recalled: "When he advised millions of listeners in one of his fireside chats to 'tell me your troubles,' most of them believed implicitly that he was speaking to them personally and immediately wrote him a letter. It was months before we managed to swim out of *that* flood of mail."[41]

Not only by fireside chats and public addresses but also by his openness to ideas and to people not previously welcomed in Washington, Roosevelt greatly broadened the political agenda and encouraged outsiders to enter the civic arena. One scholar has observed:

> Franklin Roosevelt changed the nature of political contests in this country by drawing new groups into active political participation. Compare the political role of labor under the self-imposed handicap of Samuel Gompers' narrow vision with labor's political activism during and since the Roosevelt years. The long-run results were striking: Roosevelt succeeded in activating people who previously had lacked power; national politics achieved a healthier balance of contending interests; and public policy henceforth was written to meet the needs of those who previously had gone unheard.

"Of course you have fallen into some errors—that is human," a former Supreme Court Justice wrote the President in 1937, "but you have put a new face upon the social and political life of our country."[42]

FDR's role as civic educator frequently took a decidedly partisan turn, for he proved to be an especially effective political leader by building a coalition of lower-income ethnic voters in the great cities tenuously aligned with white voters in the Solid South. The 1936 returns confirmed the emergence of the Democrats as the new majority party in the Fifth American Party System in an election that showed a sharp cleavage along class lines. In tripling the vote received by the Democratic presidential nominee in 1920, Roosevelt carried close to 99 percent of South Carolina ballots, almost all cast by whites, at the very time that blacks were abandoning the party of the Great Emancipator to join the FDR coalition.[43]

Although Roosevelt has been scolded for failing to bring about a full-fledged party realignment, no president has ever done so much to redraw the contours of party conflict. He brought into his administration former Republicans such as Henry Wallace and Harold Ickes; enticed hundreds of thousands of Socialists, such as the future California congressman Jerry Voorhis, to join the Democrats; worked with anti-Tammany leaders such as Fiorello La Guardia in New York; backed the Independent candidate George Norris against the Democrats' official nominee in Nebraska; and forged alliances with third parties such as the American Labor Party.[44] In 1938 he dared attempt, largely unsuccessfully, to "purge" conservative Democrats from the party, and in World War II he may even have sought to unite liberal Republicans of the Wendell Willkie sort with liberal Democrats in a new party, although the details of that putative arrangement are obscure.

Roosevelt won such a huge following both for himself and for his party by putting together the most ambitious legislative program in the history of the country. Although he was not the first chief executive in this century to adopt the role of chief legislator, he developed that function to an unprecedented extent. He made wide use of the special message, and he accompanied these communications with draft bills. He wrote letters to committee chairmen or members of Congress to urge passage of his proposals, summoned the Congressional leadership to White House conferences on legislation, used agents such as Tommy Corcoran on Capitol Hill, and appeared in person before Congress. He made even the hitherto mundane business of bill signing an occasion for political theater; it was he who initiated the custom of giving a presidential pen to a Congressional sponsor of legislation as a memento. In the First Hundred Days, he adroitly dangled promises of patronage before Congressmen, but without delivering on them until he had the legislation he wanted. The result, as one scholar put it, was that "his relations with Congress were to the very end of the session tinged with a shade of expectancy which is the best part of young love."[45]

To the dismay of the Republican leadership, Roosevelt showed himself to be a past master not only at coddling his supporters in Congress but also at disarming would-be opponents. The prominent conservative Congressman Joseph E. Martin, who sought to insulate his fellow Republicans in the House from FDR's charm, complained that the President, "laughing, talking, and poking the air with his long cigarette holder," was so magnetic that he "bamboozled" even members of the opposition. "As he turned on his radiance I could see the face of one of my men lighting up like the moon," Martin recorded resentfully. He had to step swiftly to rescue the man from the perilous "moon glow" and give him a dose of "dire warnings." On another occasion a visitor outside the Oval Office observed Roosevelt just after he had deftly disposed of a mutinous Congressional delegation. The President, unaware that he was being watched, slowly lit up a Camel in his ivory cigarette holder, and, as he settled back, "a smile of complete satisfaction spread over his face."[46]

To be sure, his success with Congress has often been exaggerated. The Congress of the First Hundred Days, it has been said, "did not so much debate the bills it passed . . . as salute them as they went sailing by"[47]; but even in 1933 Roosevelt had to bend to the wishes of legislators more than once. In later years Congress passed the bonus bill over his veto; shelved his "Court-packing" plan; and, on neutrality policy, bound the President like Gulliver. After putting through the Fair Labor Standards Act in 1938, Roosevelt was unable to win approval of any further New Deal legislation. Moreover, some of the most important "New Deal" measures credited to Roosevelt—federal insurance of bank deposits, the Wagner Act, and public housing—originated in Congress as bills that he either opposed outright or accepted only at the last moment. Judged by latter-day standards, his operation on the Hill was almost primitive. He had no Congressional liaison office, and he paid too little attention to rank-and-file members.

Still, Roosevelt's skill as chief legislator is undeniable. One historian concluded that "Franklin Roosevelt's party leadership as an effective instrument of legislation is unparalleled in our party history," and a political scientist has stated:

> The most dramatic transformation in the relationship between the presidency and Congress occurred during the first two terms of Franklin D. Roosevelt. FDR changed the power ratio between Congress and the White House, publicly taking it upon himself to act as the leader of Congress at a time of deepening crisis in the nation. More than any other president, FDR established the model of the powerful legislative presidency on which the public's expectations still are anchored.[48]

Roosevelt achieved so much in good part because of his exquisite sense of timing. No one has captured that trait so well as the political scientist Erwin Hargrove:

> In his leadership of public opinion FDR oscillated from the heroic to the cautious. With his sensitivity to public moods, he was forthright as a leader when crisis was high and public sentiment was ripe for heroic leadership. This was the case when he first entered office and embarked on the dramatic legislative leadership of the first hundred days. . . . At other times he was more cautious and gradually prepared the public for a new departure. For example, he held off on social security legislation in order to . . . educate people that it was not alien to the American tradition of self-reliance. He did this by blending press conferences, a message to Congress, two fireside chats, and a few speeches, in each of which he progressively unfolded the Americanness of the plan. . . . He did this kind of thing with artistry, and the artistry was an extension of his own empathy and ability to act to win others over.[49]

As one aspect of his function as chief legislator, Roosevelt broke all records in making use of the veto power. By the end of his second term, his vetoes already totaled more than 30 percent of all the measures disallowed by presidents since 1792. Unlike the other famous veto president, Grover Cleveland, who limited his disapproval primarily to pension legislation, Roosevelt expressed his will on a range of subjects from homing pigeons to credit for beer wholesalers. Franklin Roosevelt was the first chief executive to read a veto message personally to Congress, and he even defied the unwritten canon against vetoing a revenue measure when in 1944 he turned down a tax bill on the grounds that it benefited the greedy rather than the needy. According to one credible tale, FDR used to ask his aides to look out for a piece of legislation he could veto, in order to remind Congress that it was being watched.[50]

So far did Roosevelt plumb the potentialities of the chief executive as legislative leader that by the end of his first term the columnist Raymond Clapper was writing, "It is scarcely an exaggeration to say that the President, although not a member of Congress, has become almost the equivalent of the prime minister of the British system, because he is both executive and the guiding hand of the legislative branch." And by World War II, FDR's leadership in the lawmaking process was so accepted that a conservative Republican found fault with the President for failing to submit to Congress a detailed list of bills that he expected it to enact.[51]

Roosevelt rested his legislative program on the assumption that government should actively seek social justice for all Americans, not least those who are disadvantaged. Starting in the spectacular First Hundred Days, Roosevelt brought the Welfare State to America, years after it had become a fixture in other lands. Although European theorists had been talking about *der Staat* for decades, the notion of the State got little attention in America before FDR. The historian James T. Patterson, responding to left-wing critiques of FDR, has written:

> Roosevelt was no hard-eyed merchandiser; his opportunism was grounded in social concern and conscience, without which the New Deal would indeed have been mindless and devious. He was also cordial, easy, relaxed—in the words of a perceptive writer, "a thoroughly attractive and engaging man." Part of this attractiveness was his ability to understand what ordinary people wanted. When asked whether artists should qualify for relief work, he replied quickly, "Why not? They're human beings. They have to live. I guess the only thing they can do is paint and surely there must be some public place where paintings are wanted." In January 1935 he expressed to Perkins his commitment on social security: "I see no reason why every child, from the day he is born, shouldn't be a member of the social security system. Cradle to the grave—from the cradle to the grave they ought to be in a social insurance system."[52]

The President moved beyond the notion that "rights" embodied only guarantees against denial of freedom of expression to the conception that government also has an obligation to assure certain economic essentials. In his State of the Union message of January 1944 he declared:

> This Republic had its beginning, and grew to its present strength, under the protection of certain inalienable political rights—among them the right of free speech, free press, free worship, trial by jury, freedom from unreasonable searches and seizures. . . .

As our Nation has grown in size and stature, however—as our industrial economy expanded—these political rights proved inadequate to assure us equality in the pursuit of happiness.

We have come to a clear realization of the fact that true individual freedom cannot exist without economic security and independence. "Necessitous men are not free men." People who are hungry and out of a job are the stuff of which dictatorships are made.

In our day these economic truths have become accepted as self-evident. We have accepted, so to speak, a second Bill of Rights under which a new basis of security and prosperity can be established for all—regardless of station, race, or creed.

Among these are:

The right to a useful and remunerative job in the industries or shops or farms or mines of the Nation;

The right to earn enough to provide adequate food and clothing and recreation;

The right of every farmer to raise and sell his products at a return which will give him and his family a decent living;

The right of every businessman, large or small, to trade in an atmosphere of freedom from unfair competition and domination by monopolies at home or abroad;

The right of every family to a decent home;

The right to adequate medical care and the opportunity to achieve and enjoy good health;

The right to adequate protection from the economic fears of old age, sickness, accident, and unemployment;

The right to a good education.[53]

In expanding the orbit of the State, Roosevelt demanded that business recognize the superior authority of the government in Washington. At the time, that was shocking doctrine. In the pre–New Deal period, government had often been the handmaiden of business, and many presidents had shared the values of businessmen. When FDR made clear that he did not hold the same values, he was denounced as a traitor to his class. But in one way Roosevelt was not of their class. He was a member of the landed gentry and the old mercantile stratum who could claim ancient lineage. Claes Martenzen van Rosenvelt, the first of the clan in the New World, had come to New Amsterdam in the seventeenth century. Both the Roosevelts and the Delanos were prosperous merchant families who had derived much of their fortunes from seafaring. As a landowner with a Hudson River estate, a man from a family that moved easily in the Edith Wharton universe of Knickerbocker society, Roosevelt approached economic problems with different preconceptions from those of the industrialist or the financier on the make.

With a country squire's contempt for the grasping businessman and with a squire's conviction of noblesse oblige, FDR refused to accept the view that business and government were coequal sovereigns. Although the New Deal always operated within a capitalist framework, Roosevelt insisted that there was a national interest that it was the duty of the president to represent and, when the situation called for it, to impose. Consequently, the federal government in the 1930s came to supervise the stock market, establish a central banking system monitored from Washington, and regulate a range of business activities that had hitherto been regarded as private. The historian Ralph De Bedts has pointed out:

> Presidential support for the establishment and continued extension of regulatory powers to benefit every variety of public investor was never forgotten or neglected. Did Senators need a word of explanation on a bill under consideration? They received a "Dear George" letter earnestly stating the public need for such legislation. Were Congressional chairmen hard put to keep their committees from amending legislation to the point of emasculation? They—and the public press—received sternly polite notes that clearly threw the considerable weight of the Chief Executive on the side of their efforts.

When James M. Landis stepped down as chairman of the SEC, he wrote Roosevelt: "Our commission and our work sprang from your mind, your utterances, your ideals."[54]

As a result of these many new measures, Roosevelt gained a reputation as "the great economic emancipator,"[55] but his real contributions, as James MacGregor Burns has said, were "far more important than any possible set 'solution'—a willingness to take charge, a faith in the people, and an acceptance of the responsibility of the federal government to act." Burns added:

> While Roosevelt's symbolic leadership was related to definite, concrete acts of government, his interpretation of the situation, in the broadest sense, was more important than any specific program. For

he established then and later that the federal government must and could be accountable for the nation's economic well being. . . . Roosevelt accomplished a decisive interpretation of events: he dramatized the role of the federal government so that people would see it not as a remote and passive power but as a force that could salvage them and shape the nation's economy.[56]

After a historic confrontation with the Supreme Court, Roosevelt secured the legitimation of this enormous expansion of the State. In 1935 and 1936 the Court struck down more important national legislation than in any other comparable period in our history. Roosevelt responded in February 1937 with an audacious scheme to "pack" the Court with as many as six additional Justices. Although he did not get his plan through, the Court never again disallowed a New Deal law. In fact, as a consequence of "the Constitutional Revolution of 1937," the Supreme Court has never since invalidated any significant statute regulating the economy.[57]

Roosevelt quickly learned that enacting a program was an altogether different matter from getting it implemented and that he had to turn his thoughts to being not only chief legislator but also chief administrator. The former Assistant Secretary of the Navy once complained:

> The Treasury is so large and far-flung and ingrained in its practices that I find it almost impossible to get the action and results I want—even with Henry [Morgenthau] there. But the Treasury is not to be compared with the State Department. You should go through the experience of trying to get any changes in the thinking, policy, and action of the career diplomats and then you'd know what a real problem was. But the Treasury and the State Department put together are nothing compared with the Na-a-vy. The admirals are really something to cope with—and I should know. To change something in the Na-a-vy is like punching a feather bed. You punch it with your right and you punch it with your left until you are finally exhausted, and then you find the damn bed just as it was before you started punching.[58]

To overcome resistance to his policies in the old-line departments, Roosevelt resorted to the creation of emergency agencies. "We have new and complex problems," he once said. "Why not establish a new agency to take over the new duty rather than saddle it on an old institution? . . . If it is not permanent, we don't get bad precedents." This tactic often turned out wonderfully well, for those who engaged in freewheeling ventures such as the TVA had a sense of liberation and an élan missing in the encrusted bureaucracies. Still, as Arthur Schlesinger, Jr., the ablest defender of FDR as an administrator, has acknowledged, the President sometimes "acted as if a new agency were almost a new solution. His addiction to new organizations became a kind of nervous tic which disturbed even avid New Dealers."[59]

Roosevelt also departed from orthodoxy in another way. In flat defiance of the cardinal rule of public administration textbooks—that every administrator ought to appear on a chart with a clearly stated assignment—the President not only deliberately disarranged spheres of authority, but also appointed men of clashing attitudes and temperaments. Although the squabbling of a Harry Hopkins with a Harold Ickes left the impression of a government in disarray, this procedure had the advantage of alerting Roosevelt to policy conflicts and permitting him to resolve them when they were ripe. Schlesinger has maintained:

> His favorite technique was to keep grants of authority incomplete, jurisdictions uncertain, charters overlapping. The result of this competitive theory of administration was often confusion and exasperation on the operating level; but no other method could so reliably insure that in a large bureaucracy filled with ambitious men eager for power the decisions, and the power to make them, would remain with the President.[60]

To secure trustworthy information, Roosevelt relied on a congeries of informants and personal envoys. Though there were times when one man enjoyed his close confidence—Louis Howe early in the New Deal, Harry Hopkins in the war years—Roosevelt never had a chief of staff, and no individual was ever permitted to take the place of the "countless lieutenants and supporters" who served "virtually as roving ambassadors collecting intelligence through the Executive Branch," often unaware that more than one person had the same assignment. "He would call you in, and he'd ask you to get the story on some complicated business," one of FDR's aides later said, "and you'd come back after a couple of days of hard labor and present the juicy morsel you'd uncovered under a stone somewhere, and *then* you'd find out he knew all about it, along with something else you *didn't* know. Where he got his information from he wouldn't mention, usually, but after he had done this to you once or twice you got damn careful about *your* information."[61]

So evident were the costs of FDR's competitive style—not only bruised feelings but also, at times, a want of coherence in policy—and so "harum-scarum" did his methods seem, that it became commonplace to speak of Roosevelt as a poor administrator. Grant McConnell has stated bluntly: "Usually there is . . . something intensely personal, whether inborn or not, in the capacity to manage a complex organization. Obviously, the talent for administration may be cultivated and improved. Some presidents, Franklin Roosevelt for example, had neither talent nor taste in this direction." And a British analyst has commented that although the "mishmash" Roosevelt put together was "inspired," it resulted not in a "true bureaucracy" but in "an ill-organized flock of agencies, with the sheep dogs in the White House snapping at their heels as the President whistled the signals."[62]

Roosevelt himself appeared to believe that these charges were not without foundation. Over cocktails at the White House in the fall of 1936 he mused, "You know, I just had a lovely thought. I've just been thinking what fun it would have been if I could have run against Roosevelt. I don't know whether I could have beaten him but I'd have given him a close race." He explained:

> First off in the campaign I would have repudiated Hearst. Second, I would have repudiated the DuPonts etc. Then I'd have said "we want Security, relief, etc. etc." But here's the story: "the Democrats can't be trusted with the administration of these fine ideals." I'd have cited chapter and verse on WPA inefficiency (and there's plenty of it). You know the more I think about it the more I believe I could have licked myself.[63]

Not a few commentators, though, have concluded that Roosevelt was a superior administrator. They point out that he vastly improved staffing and that he broke new ground when he assigned Henry Wallace to chair a series of wartime agencies, for no vice president had ever held administrative responsibilities before. Granted, there was no end of friction between subordinates such as Hopkins and Ickes, or Cordell Hull and Sumner Welles, but Wallace once observed, in a rare witticism, that FDR "could keep all the balls in the air without losing his own." In Abe Fortas's words: "Roosevelt was a master at controlling friction and making it constructive. He was a real Toscanini. He knew how to conduct an orchestra and when to favor the first fiddles and when to favor the trombones. He knew how to employ and manipulate people. As you go through life you see giants become men, but in the New Deal days men became giants."[64]

Furthermore, his admirers contend, if the test of a great administrator is whether he can inspire devotion in his subordinates, FDR passes with flying colors. Three years after Roosevelt got rid of him as head of the NRA, General Hugh Johnson wrote:

> I so disagree with many of the things he has done and is doing that I think I would resist them in the last ditch. And yet, I fear that if he called me in tomorrow to ask me to do something outside that cate-gory . . .—turned on the famous charm and said: "You've got to do this for me; I need it"—I'd be in there next day as busy as a bird dog in a covert full of quail tracks trying to do what he asked.

Even Ickes, the most notorious grumbler of the Roosevelt circle, noted in his diary, "You go into Cabinet meetings tired and discouraged and out of sorts and the President puts new life into you. You come out like a fighting cock."[65]

An even better test of an administrator is whether he can recruit exceptional talent, and Roosevelt broke new ground by giving an unprecedented opportunity to a new corps of officials: the university-trained experts. Save for a brief period in World War I, professors had not had much of a place in Washington; but in his 1932 presidential campaign FDR enlisted several academic advisers, most of them from Morningside Heights, to offer their thoughts and to test his own ideas. The press called this group "the Brain Trust." During the First Hundred Days, droves of professors, inspired by that example, descended on Washington to take part in the New Deal. So, too, did their students—young attorneys fresh out of law school and social scientists with recent graduate degrees who received an open-arms reception from the federal government that had never been extended before.

This influx of New Dealers upset all the traditional assumptions about who was supposed to be running the government. As Raymond Moley recalled:

We stood in the city of Washington on March 4th like a handful of marauders in hostile territory. . . . The Republican party had close to a monopoly of skillful, experienced administrators. To make matters worse, the business managers, established lawyers, and engineers from whose ranks top-drawer governmental executives so often come were, by and large, so partisan in their opposition to Roosevelt that he could scarcely be expected to tap those sources to the customary degree.[66]

His improvisational style notwithstanding, Roosevelt also made significant institutional changes. When FDR took office, the historian Otis Graham has noted, he had no executive organization to call upon, save for "a handful of secretaries," "two southern newspapermen," and a Navy doctor—in sum, "no institutional capacity to see social problems and policy responses as a whole." Consequently, Graham adds, "Franklin Roosevelt was occupied for his thirteen years as President in a series of resourceful efforts to adapt or invent such an institutional capacity." In November 1933 he established the National Emergency Council to coordinate the work of the New Deal field agencies, and his first term also saw the creation of a National Planning Board and its successors, the National Resources Board and the National Resources Committee. From the very outset, he had a keen interest in reorganizing the government, and over time that concern developed from a desire to cut costs, which had been the traditional rationale, to a determination to strengthen the president's managerial capacity.[67]

Roosevelt took an initiative with important long-range consequences when he named three of the country's foremost scholars of public administration—Louis Brownlow (chairman), Charles E. Merriam, and Luther Gulick—to a President's Committee on Administrative Management, and in response to their report created the Executive Office of the President, which has become "the nerve center of the federal administrative system." By an executive order of 1939, he moved several agencies, notably the Bureau of the Budget, under the wing of the White House and provided for a cadre of presidential assistants. This Executive Order 8248 has been called a "nearly unnoticed but none the less epoch-making event in the history of American institutions" and "perhaps the most important single step in the institutionalization of the Presidency."[68]

Harold Smith, who served in the prewar era and throughout the war years as FDR's budget director, later reflected:

When I worked with Roosevelt—for six years—I thought as did many others that he was a very erratic administrator. But now, when I look back, I can really begin to see the size of his programs. They were by far the largest and most complex programs that any President ever put through. People like me who had the responsibility of watching the pennies could only see the five or six or seven percent of the programs that went wrong, through inefficient organization or direction. But now I can see in perspective the ninety-three or -four or -five percent that went right—including the winning of the biggest war in history—because of unbelievably skillful organization and direction. And if I were to write that article now, I think I'd say that Roosevelt must have been one of the greatest geniuses as an administrator that ever lived. What we couldn't appreciate at the time was the fact that he was a real *artist* in government.[69]

The amount of attention drawn by the New Deal intellectuals has, in some respects, served to diminish FDR's reputation, for commentators have implied that national programs owed less to the President than to those who wrote his speeches and drafted his bills. It has become commonplace, even among his admirers, to view the President as an intellectual lightweight. He read few books, and these not very seriously. Roosevelt, the historian Hugh Gallagher has said, "was no Thomas Jefferson, and neither a scholar nor an intellectual in the usual sense of the word. He had a magpie mind, and many interests, but he was not deep." He had small talent for abstract reasoning, though perhaps no less than most men in public life. He loved brilliant people, commented one of his former aides, but not profound ones. Raymond Moley has observed that the picture of Teddy Roosevelt "regaling a group of his friends with judgments on Goya, Flaubert, Dickens, and Jung, and discussions of Louis the Fat or the number of men at arms seasick in the fleet of Medina Sidonia—this could never be mistaken for one of Franklin Roosevelt. F.D.R.'s interests have always been more circumscribed. His moments of relaxation are given over exclusively to simpler pleasures—to the stamp album, to the Currier and Ives naval prints, to a movie or to good-humored horseplay."[70]

Roosevelt kept himself informed not by applied study but by observation and conversation (the historian James MacGregor Burns has described Roosevelt as "voracious and prehensile in his quest for information"), and his particular qualities of mind served him reasonably well in the 1930s. True, he was not well versed in economic theory, but had he accepted the greater part of what went for economic wisdom in 1932, he would have been badly misguided. Furthermore, contrary to the general notion, he knew far more about economic matters—utilities regulation, agriculture, banking, corporate structure, public finance—than was usually recognized.

He impressed almost everyone who worked with him with his retention of detail. The publisher J. David Stern recalled an occasion when the President recited the average price of ten commodities in 1933 and ten years before and was correct on nine of them. Another observer, a sharp critic of FDR, reported on a 1936 conversation with him on judicial review: "As our talk went on, I was amazed by his reading on the subject and by the grip of his mind. . . . For example, he quoted at length from Madison's *Journal* and Elliot's *Debates*." Similarly, in June 1940 *Time* reported:

> For three weeks he had discussed battlefield contours in military detail with U.S. experts; again and again they have whistled respectfully at his apparent knowledge of Flanders—hills, creeks, towns, bridges. The President's particular forte is islands; he is said to know every one in the world, its peoples, habits, population, geography, economic life. When a ship sank off Scotland several months ago, experts argued: had the ship hit a rock or had it been torpedoed? The President pondered latitude and longitude, said: "It hit a rock. They ought to have seen that rock." Naval Aide Daniel J. Callaghan recalled the rock, disagreed. "At high tide, Mr. President, that rock is submerged." No such thing, said the President, even at high tide that rock is 20 feet out of the water.

Far more important, though, than his knowledge of particulars was his grasp of the interrelationship of the larger aspects of public policy. "Never, at least since Jefferson," a prominent jurist wrote to Justice Brandeis in 1937, "have we had a President of such constructive mind as Roosevelt."[71]

Indeed, so manifest has been FDR's mastery of the affairs of state and so palpable his impact on the office as chief administrator, chief legislator, and tribune of the people that in recent years an altogether different, and disturbing, line of inquiry has surfaced: Does the imperial presidency have its roots in the 1930s, and is FDR the godfather of Watergate? For four decades much of the controversy over the New Deal centered on the issue of whether Roosevelt had done enough. Abruptly, in the

Watergate crisis, the obverse question was raised: Had he done too much? Had there been excessive aggrandizement of the executive office under FDR? In an address on Watergate, Senator Alan Cranston of California, a liberal Democrat, declared: "Those who tried to warn us back at the beginnings of the New Deal of the dangers of one-man rule that lay ahead on the path we were taking toward strong, centralized government may not have been so wrong."[72]

The notion that the origins of the Watergate scandal lie in the age of Roosevelt has a certain plausibility.[73] In the First Hundred Days of 1933, Roosevelt initiated an enormous expansion of the federal government, with proliferating alphabet agencies lodged under the executive wing. Vast powers were delegated to presidential appointees, with little or no Congressional oversight. In foreign affairs Roosevelt bent the law in order to speed aid to the Allies, and in World War II he cut a wide swath in exercising his prerogatives. FDR was the only president to break the barrier against election to a third term, and for good measure he won a fourth term too. Only death cut short his protracted reign.[74]

Those captivated by the historical antecedents of the Watergate era allege that Roosevelt showed no more concern for the sensitivity of Congress than did Nixon. When Roosevelt was asked in 1931 how much authority he expected from Congress if he became president, he snapped, "Plenty." While in office, he experienced so much conflict with Congress that on one occasion he said he would like to turn sixteen lions loose on the body. But, it was objected, the lions might make a mistake. "Not," Roosevelt answered, "if they stayed there long enough."[75]

Many have found Roosevelt's behavior on the eve of America's intervention in World War II especially reprehensible. Edward S. Corwin and Louis W. Koenig protested that, in the destroyer deal, "what President Roosevelt did was to take over for the nonce Congress's power to dispose of property of the United States . . . and to repeal at least two statutes," while Senator William Fulbright accused Roosevelt of having "usurped the treaty power of the Senate" and of having "circumvented the war powers of the Congress." His detractors point out that six months before Pearl Harbor, on shaky statutory authority, he used federal power to end strikes, most notably in sending troops to occupy the strikebound North American Aviation plant in California, and that in the same period he dispatched U.S. forces to occupy Iceland and Greenland, provided convoys of vessels carrying arms to Britain, and ordered destroyers to shoot Nazi U-boats on sight, all acts that infringed upon Congress's war-making authority.[76]

After the United States entered the war, Roosevelt raised the ire of his critics once more by his audacious Labor Day message of September 7, 1942, "one of the strangest episodes in the history of the presidency." In a bold—many thought brazen—assertion of inherent executive prerogative, the President demanded an effective price and wage control statute in the following terms:

> I ask the Congress to take . . . action by the first of October. Inaction on your part by that date will leave me with an inescapable responsibility to the people of this country to see to it that the war effort is no longer imperiled by threat of economic chaos.
>
> In the event that the Congress should fail to act, and act adequately, I shall accept the responsibility, and I will act. . . .
>
> The President has the powers, under the Constitution and under Congressional acts, to take measures necessary to avert a disaster which would interfere with the winning of the war. . . .
>
> The American people can be sure that I will use my powers with a full sense of my responsibility to the Constitution and to my country. The American people can also be sure that I shall not hesitate to use every power vested in me to accomplish the defeat of our enemies in any part of the world where our own safety demands such a defeat.
>
> When the war is won, the powers under which I act automatically revert to the people—to whom they belong.

Congress quickly fell into line, and Roosevelt never had to make use of this threat, which has been likened to the "claim . . . advanced by Locke in the seventeenth century on behalf of royal prerogative"; but the bad aftertaste lingered.[77]

It has also been argued that Nixon's overweening privy councillors wielded such power as a consequence of a reform implemented by Roosevelt. The 1937 report of the President's Committee on Administrative Management called for staffing the Executive Office with administrative assistants "possessed of . . . a passion for anonymity."[78] That job description sounded tailor-made for the faceless men around Nixon, for Haldeman and Ehrlichman seemed so indistinguishable that they were likened to Rosencrantz and Guildenstern.

Even historians well-disposed toward FDR have found aspects of his character and behavior disconcerting. The journalist John Gunther, in a generally adulatory treatment, catalogued some of the President's failings: "dilatoriness, two-sidedness (some would say plain dishonesty), pettiness in some personal relationships, a cardinal lack of frankness, . . . garrulousness, amateurism, and what has been called 'cheerful vindictiveness.'" Similarly, the historian Robert S. McElvaine, in a fair-minded and often approving assessment, has said that Roosevelt "did things in his personal and political life that were simply despicable." In the 1940 campaign, he notes, FDR was not above urging that "way, way down the line" his campaign workers noise it about that his Republican opponent, Wendell Willkie, was carrying on an extramarital affair. He got still uglier when he recommended that they should also spread the rumor that Mrs. Willkie had been paid to pretend that nothing was going on. "*Now, now*," he quickly added, "Mrs. Willkie may not have been *hired*, but in effect she's been hired to return to Wendell and smile and make this campaign with him. Now whether there was a money price behind it, *I don't know*, but it's the same idea."[79]

Yet the parallels between Roosevelt and Nixon have to be set against the dissimilarities. "To Roosevelt, the communications of a President had to be . . . lively, intimate, and open," Emmet Hughes has observed. "He practiced an almost promiscuous curiosity." In marked contrast to the obsessionally reclusive Nixon regime, the New Deal government went out of its way to learn what the nation was thinking and to open itself to questioning. Each morning the President and other top officials found a digest of clippings from some 750 newspapers, many of them hostile, on their desks, and before Roosevelt retired for the night he went through a bedtime folder of letters from ordinary citizens. During the First Hundred Days, he urged the press to offer criticism so that he might avoid missteps, and both then and later he solicited everyone from old friends to chance acquaintances outside the government to provide information that would serve as a check on what his White House lieutenants were telling him and that would give him points of view at variance with those in Washington officialdom.[80]

Roosevelt differed from Nixon, too, in creating a heterogeneous administration and in encouraging dissenting voices within the government. His cabinet included Republicans as well as Democrats; progressives and conservatives; Catholic, Protestant, and Jew. Whereas Nixon fired Secretary of the Interior Wally Hickel and eased out Secretary of Housing and Urban Development George Romney, FDR mollified cantankerous mavericks such as Harold Ickes when they threatened to leave. "What impresses me most vividly about the men around Roosevelt," wrote Clinton Rossiter, "is the number of flinty 'no-sayers' who served him, loyally but not obsequiously."[81]

Furthermore, even in the crisis of World War II, Roosevelt most often acted within constitutional bounds, and any transgressions must be placed in the context of the dire challenge raised by Hitler. Despite his recognition that, after the fall of France, Britain stood alone, he did not conclude the destroyer deal until he had first consulted with the Republican presidential candidate, and his determination to undertake peacetime conscription was one of many that required Congressional approval. Indeed, the biggest cache of discretionary power the President drew upon in the period before Pearl Harbor came from a decision freely taken by Congress in passing the Lend-Lease Act. Winston Churchill was to tell the House of Commons: "Of Roosevelt . . . it must be said that had he not acted when he did, in the way he did, had he not . . . resolved to give aid to Britain, and to Europe in the supreme crisis through which we have passed, a hideous fate might well have overwhelmed mankind and made its whole future for centuries sink into shame and ruin."[82]

Such defenses of Roosevelt, however impressive, fall short of being fully persuasive. As well-disposed a commentator as Schlesinger has said that FDR, "though his better instincts generally won out in the end, was a flawed, willful and, with time, increasingly arbitrary man."[83] Unhappily, of FDR's many legacies, one is a certain lack of appropriate restraint with respect to the exercise of executive power.

The historian confronts a final—and quite different—question: How much of an innovator was Roosevelt? Both admirers and detractors have asked whether FDR's methods were as original as they have commonly been regarded. Grant McConnell has remarked: "His opponents claimed that he arrogated entirely new sources of power; even some of his supporters believed that this was true. In actuality, however, Roosevelt did no more than follow the examples of his predecessors." Even FDR's reputation as a precedent-breaking Chief Legislator has been called into doubt. In focusing the special message on a single issue, Roosevelt has been said to have been merely the "apt pupil" of Woodrow Wilson, and in sending actual drafts of bills to Congress to have been "again the sedulous ape," imitating both Wilson and Teddy Roosevelt. "While President Franklin D. Roosevelt's accomplishment as legislator has surpassed all previous records," Corwin wrote, "the story of it, so far as it is of interest to the student of constitutional practice, offers little of novelty. . . . The pleasure afforded by its study is—to employ Henry James's classification—that of recognition rather than of surprise."[84]

Some skeptics have even asked: Would not all of the changes from 1933 to 1945 have happened if there had been no Roosevelt, if someone else had been president? Historians have long been wary of "the presidential synthesis" and of chronicles that assign larger importance to great men than to social forces. Certainly, secular trends toward the concentration of power in Washington, and more particularly in the White House, were in motion well before 1933. Furthermore, Roosevelt would not have had nearly so large a stage if he had been elected in 1928, before the crisis of the Great Depression.

FDR himself always refused to answer iffy questions, but this one invites a reply, for it came very close to being a reality. In February 1933, a few months before he was to take office, he ended a fishing cruise by coming to Bay Front Park in Miami. That night an unemployed bricklayer, Giuseppe Zangara, fired a gun at him from point-blank range, but the wife of a Miami physician deflected the assassin's arm just enough that the bullets missed the President-elect and instead struck the mayor of Chicago, fatally wounding him.[85] Suppose Zangara had not been jostled, and the bullets had found their mark. Would our history have been different if John Nance Garner rather than FDR had become president? No doubt some of the New Deal would have taken place anyway, as a response to the Great Depression. Yet it seems inconceivable that many of the more imaginative features of the Roosevelt years—such as the Federal Arts Project—would have come into being under Garner, or that the conduct of foreign affairs would have followed the same course, or that the institution of the presidency would have been so greatly affected. As Fred Greenstein has observed: "Crisis was a necessary but far from sufficient condition for the modern presidency that began to evolve under Roosevelt."[86]

That conclusion is one with which most scholars would agree—that Franklin Roosevelt was, to use Sidney Hook's terminology, an "event-making man" who was not only shaped by, but also shaped, his age. He comprehended both what kind of opportunity the Great Depression offered to alter the direction of American politics and what kind of menace Hitler posed that the nation had to be mobilized to confront. As a consequence of both perceptions, America, and indeed the world, differed markedly in 1945 from what it had been in 1933, to no small degree because of FDR's actions. Roosevelt is one of the few American presidents who looms large not just in the history of the United States but also in the history of the world. John Kenneth Galbraith has spoken of the "Bismarck-Lloyd George-Roosevelt Revolution," and Lloyd George himself called FDR "the greatest reforming statesman of the age."[87] To a character in a contemporary novel by an Australian writer, he was "the Daniel of our days."[88]

Roosevelt, who affected so many of the institutions and attitudes in the United States, left an especially deep mark on the institution of the presidency. The historian Herbert Nicholas has said that Roosevelt "discovered in his office possibilities of leadership which even Lincoln had ignored," and the former cabinet secretary Joseph A. Califano, Jr., has written:

> The foundations of the presidency for the final decades of the twentieth century were set more in the terms of Franklin D. Roosevelt than in the terms of George Washington or any of his intervening successors. . . . The combination of domestic crisis (depression) and global war focused ever-increasing power in the White House during his unprecedented four-term presidency. The presidency would never be the same again.

Not all would accept Rossiter's judgment that "the verdict of history will surely be that he left the Presidency a more splendid instrument of democracy than he found it."[89] Not a few analysts have expressed concern that Roosevelt may have come perilously close to creating a plebiscitary presidency and may have raised unrealistic expectations about what a chief executive can deliver.[90] But few would deny that Franklin Delano Roosevelt continues to provide the standard by which every successor has been, and may well continue to be, measured.

TWO

The New Deal and the Analogue of War

[In the course of research for *Franklin D. Roosevelt and the New Deal, 1932–1940*, I repeatedly came upon examples of war as a metaphor for the struggle against the Great Depression and upon references to the World War I mobilization as an antecedent for the New Deal. Both phenomena surprised me because they were almost nowhere mentioned in the literature of the Roosevelt years, which customarily traced the sources of the New Deal to populism and progressivism. These allusions to war were not topics that could be addressed directly—how could you ask an archivist to locate metaphors for you?—but over a period of years I accumulated a cache of these items and sought to comprehend their significance. I first presented my findings at the annual convention of the American Historical Association in New York City in December 1960 and, after substantially revising that paper while I was a Fellow at the Center for Advanced Study in the Behavioral Sciences in Stanford, California in 1961–62, published it as an essay in John Braeman, Robert H. Bremner, and Everett Walters, eds., *Change and Continuity in Twentieth-Century America* (Columbus: Ohio State University Press, 1964). At that time, I expressed my gratitude to those who had read and commented upon an early draft: David Brody, Clarke Chambers, Bernard Cohen, Paul Conkin, Robert Cross, Bertram Gross, Charles Hirschfeld, Richard Hofstadter, Robert Holt, Henry Kaiser, Val Lorwin, Warren Miller, Carl Resek, James Shideler, and Rexford Tugwell. In the three decades that have elapsed since the essay first appeared, the analogue of war has become a staple of accounts both on the New Deal and on the World War I mobilization, and for the latest version of my essay I have taken account of this scholarship as well as of considerably more research in manuscripts sources.]

I

The metaphors a nation employs reveal much about how it perceives reality. The words people use bare the bedrock of its beliefs. Moreover, they are not neutral artifacts; they shape ideas and behavior. Just as the psychoanalyst listens for slips of the tongue or strange incongruities of ideas to help him understand the patient, or the literary critic studies the symbols in a poem or novel, so the historian finds it rewarding to explore the imagery a particular period has used, consciously or unconsciously, to interpret its experience.

II

In the months and years that followed the stock market crash of 1929, America searched for some way to make comprehensible what was happening. Sometimes people thought of the Great Depression as the breakdown of a system, sometimes as the product of the machinations of evil or stupid men, sometimes as the visitation of a plague like the Black Death. But from the very first, many conceived the Depression to be a calamity like war or, more specifically, like the menace of a foreign enemy who had to be defeated in combat. Occasionally, the analogue of war was a general one; more often, it referred specifically to World War I. When Herbert Hoover summoned the leading industrialists to meet in Washington, one financial journal commented: "'Order up the Moors!' was Marshal Foch's reply at the first battle of the Marne. . . . 'Order up the business reserves,' directed President Hoover as pessimistic reports flowed in from all quarters, following the stock market crash."[1]

For the rest of his years in office, Hoover resorted constantly to the idiom of war to describe the Depression.[2] In one of his addresses, he claimed that the country had just won its "battle of Chateau-Thierry" and must "reform [its] forces for the battle of Soissons." "Again and again he used military terms in describing the struggle in which he was engaged," recalled one of his aides. "He was the commanding officer at general headquarters, so visualized himself."[3] Hoover's advisers perceived the crisis in the same terms. In June 1931, after the President unfolded his reparations plan, Secretary of State Henry Stimson confided to his diary: "We have all been saying to each other the situation is quite like war."[4]

In addition to employing the metaphor of war to explain the meaning of the Depression, officials drew on the economic mobilization of World War I for instrumentalities to combat hard times. As the historian Otis

Graham has written, "The most compelling idea in 1933 was the one recent experience in comparable crisis . . .—national planning, as in wartime. In the 1917–18 crisis, when it was clear that the marketplace would not serve the needs of mobilization, the nation turned to planning through various forms of government-industry-labor cooperation. The men of 1933 found the analogy irresistible."[5]

These twin themes are discrete but related. Some who resorted to the analogue of war had no interest in the precedent of the wartime mobilization, and a few who turned to the example of the mobilization did not employ the imagery of war. Hence, it would be possible to examine these strands separately. But so closely did most Americans associate the metaphor of war with the legacy of the 1917 mobilization that it is fruitful to discuss both aspects in a single context. In the New Deal years, the two strands were inseparable. As early as his "forgotten man" speech in the 1932 campaign, Franklin Roosevelt manipulated the analogue of war to his advantage. In that address, he referred to the operations of the war mobilization, a heritage he was to acknowledge on many occasions after his election to the presidency. But the legacy of war was to prove a mixed blessing. Useful as a justification for New Deal actions, it also served to limit and divert the reformers in ways that had not been anticipated.

III

In tracing the genealogy of the New Deal, historians initially paid little attention to the mobilization of World War I. Instead, they centered their interest on two movements: populism and progressivism. Both were important antecedents—a reasonably straight line may be drawn from the Populist subtreasury plan to the Commodity Credit Corporation, from the Pujo committee to the Securities and Exchange Commission. Yet in concentrating on populism and progressivism, writers gave too little attention to the influence of the wartime mobilization, which may have been as great as the example of the Progressive era, or greater, and certainly was more important than populism.[6]

Much of the experience of the prewar generation proved irrelevant to the task facing Roosevelt in 1933, since very little in the Populist and Progressive periods offered a precedent for massive federal intervention in the economy. Many of the activities of that earlier time were modest ventures in regulation or attempts to liberate business enterprise rather than ambitious national programs. Moreover, in these years, reformers thought the state and the city more important arenas than the national capital.

World War I marked a bold departure. It occasioned the abandonment of laissez-faire precepts and raised the federal government to director, even dictator, of the economy. The War Industries Board mobilized production; the War Trade Board licensed imports and exports; the Capital Issues Committee regulated investment; the War Finance Corporation lent funds to munitions industries; the Railroad Administration unified the nation's railways; the Fuel Administration fixed the price of coal and imposed "coal holidays" on Eastern industry; and the Food Administration controlled production and consumption. The Lever Food and Fuel Control Act of 1917 gave the president sweeping powers: to take over factories and operate them, to fix a maximum price for wheat, and to license businesses in necessaries. By a generous interpretation of its powers, the War Industries Board supervised pricing, compelled corporations to accept government priorities, and forced companies to obey federal edicts on how to dispose of their products. "This is a crisis," a War Industries Board representative scolded steel industry leaders, "and commercialism, gentlemen, must be absolutely sidetracked." Actions of this character, as well as the proliferation of public institutions ranging from the United States Housing Corporation to the Spruce Production Corporation, proved important precedents for New Deal enterprises fifteen years later.[7]

The field of labor relations may serve as a single example of the difference in importance of the Populist and Progressive experience from that of World War I. Prior to the war, no serious attempt had ever been made to empower the federal government to uphold the right of collective bargaining. Federal action was limited to peripheral areas. When class divisions were drawn in labor disputes, progressives frequently aligned themselves against the unions.[8] But in World War I, the War Labor Board proclaimed its support of union rights and, to the discomfiture of businessmen, enforced these rights. Many of the labor policies pursued in the war months would have been inconceivable a short while before. When the Smith & Wesson Arms Company of Springfield, Massachusetts, insisted on its prerogative to require workers to sign yellow-dog contracts, the War Department commandeered the plant, even though the Supreme Court had upheld the legality of such contracts. The government even dared to seize Western Union when the president of the firm denied his employees the right to join the Commercial Telegraphers Union.[9] The panoply of procedures developed by the War Labor Board and the War Labor Policies

Board provided the basis in later years for a series of enactments culminating in the National Labor Relations Act of 1935.

The war also gave a home to the new class of university-trained intellectuals that had emerged in the generation before the war. Though some of them had found a career in public service in state governments before 1917, few had worked in the national government, chiefly because there was so little in Washington for them to do. After the United States intervened, Washington swarmed with professors, until, one writer noted, "the Cosmos Club was little better than a faculty meeting of all the universities." In all countries, he observed, professors "fought, and they managed affairs, thus refuting the ancient libelous assumption that they constituted an absent-minded third sex."[10]

Public administrators of this type represented a new force in American politics. They were functionaries and technicians but, more than that, men of influence and even of power. At a time when class conflicts were sharpening, they did not reflect particular classes so much as the thrust for recognition of *novi homines* who had a significant role to play on the national stage. Some, such as Gifford Pinchot, had made their appearance in Washington before the war, and still more, like Charles McCarthy, had been active in such reform capitals as Madison and Albany, but it was the war that offered them an unparalleled opportunity. Randolph Bourne noted sardonically the "peculiar congeniality between the war and these men. It is as if the war and they had been waiting for each other."[11] Phenomena almost wholly of the twentieth century, they came by the 1930s to have a critical part in shaping legislation and in manning the new agencies that their legislation developed. The passage of the Wagner Act in 1935, for example, resulted less from such traditional elements as presidential initiative or the play of "social forces" than from the conjunction of university-trained administrators such as Lloyd Garrison inside the New Deal bureaucracy with their counterparts on Senatorial staffs such as Leon Keyserling in Senator Wagner's office.

This new class of administrators, and the social theorists who had been advocating a rationally planned economy, found the war an exciting adventure. The *New Republic* liberals rejoiced that the war was creating a radical new polity based on the democratization of industry. "During the war we revolutionized our society," the *New Republic* boasted. These liberals distinguished themselves sharply from the New Freedom reformers who sought only modest changes in the nineteenth-century tradition. Nationalists and collectivists, they looked toward a centralized state that would use its powers to reshape the economy in the interests of workers and other disadvantaged groups.[12]

Many of the more collectivist progressives regarded Wilson's war measures as both a fulfillment of their hopes and a happy augury for the future. Enormously impressed by "the social possibilities of war," John Dewey observed that, in every combatant country, production for profit had been subordinated to production for use. "The old conception of the absoluteness of private property has received the world over a blow from which it will never wholly recover." Thorstein Veblen, who worked for the Food Administration in 1918, thought the war had created new opportunities for far-reaching social change. Economists who viewed the War Industries Board as "a notable demonstration of the power of war to force concert of effort and collective planning" anticipated that lessons from the war could be applied in times of peace. When Wesley C. Mitchell closed his lectures at Columbia University in May 1918, he remarked that peace would bring new problems, but "it seems impossible that the countries concerned will attempt to solve them without utilizing the same sort of centralized directing now employed to kill their enemies abroad for the new purpose of reconstructing their own life at home." "What we have learned in war we shall hardly forget in peace," commented Walter Weyl. "The new economic solidarity, once gained, can never again be surrendered."[13]

The end of the war left the administrators with a sense of interruptus. One writer noted unmistakable shadows of annoyance at the Cosmos Club when "the dark cloud of peace" lowered in October 1918. After the war, to the chagrin of the planners, the economic machinery was quickly dismantled. Still, the lesson that the war had taught—that the federal government could mobilize the nation's resources in a planned economy— was not forgotten.[14] Throughout the 1920s, the more advanced progressives looked back fondly toward the war mobilization that seemed to have drawn a blueprint for America's future. In 1927 Rexford Tugwell lauded the war as "an industrial engineer's Utopia." He wanted to coordinate the economy as it had been under the War Industries Board in "America's wartime socialism." "We were on the verge of having an international industrial machine when peace broke," he wrote ruefully. "Only the Armistice," he lamented, "prevented a great experiment in control of production, control of price, and control of consumption."[15]

The fascination the war example held for the progressives owed not a little to the fusion of nationalism and reform in the previous generation. Heralded by Bismarck in Germany and Joseph Chamberlain in Great

Britain, this conjunction appeared in America in the martial fantasies of Edward Bellamy, in Francis Walker's critique of classical economics, in the "industrial armies" of men such as Jacob Coxey, in the military milieu of the Salvation Army, and in the response of certain reformers to the imperialist surge of the 1890s.[16] In the Progressive era, this association was starkly revealed in the career of Theodore Roosevelt, who thought social justice and military preparedness two aspects of a common program.

Though the confluence of nationalism and reform fascinated a number of progressive theorists, notably Brooks Adams, it was Herbert Croly who, in his seminal *The Promise of American Life*, explored the relationship most extensively. Croly set down the deep dissatisfaction of the progressives with the quality of life in America. The homogeneity of the early republic, he wrote, had been fragmented by a century of individualism run riot. So long as the marketplace determined values, so long as each individual or interest was permitted to pursue its own ends with no commitment to a common ideal, the result could not help but be unsatisfying. Reform had foundered because it lacked a sense of national purpose. "In this country," Croly observed, "the solution of the social problem demands the substitution of a conscious social ideal for the earlier instinctive homogeneity of the American nation."[17]

The war offered just such a "conscious social ideal." Through war priorities, as Bernard Baruch later explained, the economy could be "made to move in response to a national purpose rather than in response to the wills of those who had money to buy." The nationalistic demands of war denied, if only for a time, the claims of the profit system. "When production and distribution became really a matter of life and death, immediate and dramatic, every warring nation, after a few months of appalling waste, threw laissez-faire out of the window," noted Stuart Chase in his book *A New Deal* in 1933. "Wars must be won, and it was painfully obvious that laissez-faire was no help in winning them." The individualistic, competitive economy of the prewar years had to submit to the discipline of conscious government direction. Not business profit but the national interest determined how resources were to be allocated. The old system of competition, Tugwell wrote jubilantly, "melted away in the fierce new heat of nationalistic vision."[18]

IV

When the stock market crash of 1929 precipitated the Great Depression, progressives turned instinctively to the war mobilization as a design for recovery. The War Industries Board, Stuart Chase pointed out, had, like the Soviet *Gosplan*, demonstrated that "super-management" could replace "industrial anarchy." George Soule contended that the war had shown that planning was neither beyond human capacity nor alien to American values. "Many of those who now advocate economic planning have been doing so, in one way or another, ever since the experiences of 1917–18, and mainly as result of the possibilities which those experiences suggested for better performance in times of peace." The same "deliberate collective effort" that had made possible a tremendous expansion of production could be turned to peacetime ends, he argued. "If that military and industrial army had been mobilized, not to kill, burn and shatter, but to substitute garden cities for slums, to restore soil fertility and reforest our waste regions, to carry out flood control, to increase the necessities of life available for those in the lower income groups, we could have achieved in a short time a large number of really desirable objectives."[19]

Men such as Gerard Swope of General Electric, a veteran of the 1917 mobilization, and the Wisconsin economist Richard T. Ely drew upon memories of World War I to address this new crisis. Swope wrote Hoover:

> If we were faced with war, the President would immediately call a special session of Congress to declare war and to raise armies. This unemployment situation in many ways is more serious even than war. Therefore it is suggested that an extra session of Congress be called and the President request it to issue a billion dollars of bonds, bearing a low interest rate, and that then a campaign be organized to sell these bonds, much as the Liberty Bond campaigns were organized when we entered the war thirteen years ago.

Ely went a step farther. He proposed the creation of a peacetime army that, when a depression struck, could be expanded by recruiting from the ranks of the unemployed. Under the direction of an economic general staff, the army, Ely declared, "should go to work to relieve distress with all the vigor and resources of brain and brawn that we employed in the World War."[20]

By the middle of 1931, both businessmen and politicians were calling on Hoover to adopt the procedures of the War Industries Board to pull the country out of the Depression. When William McAdoo, who had headed the wartime Railroad Administration, proposed a Peace Industries Board in June 1931, he found ready support. The War Industries Board, one correspondent wrote him, "accomplished wonders during the war, and there is no question but that a board established now to coordinate things in our national industries will also do wonders. This historical precedent is a great asset and ought to guide us in our national planning for the benefit of all." A month later, Charles Beard recommended a National Economic Council with a Board of Strategy and Planning that would follow the pattern of "the War Industries Board and other federal agencies created during the titanic effort to mobilize men and materials for the World War."[21] The following month, Representative Chester Bolton of Ohio advanced a similar proposal. "If we could have another body like the old War Industries Board," he wrote the head of Hoover's voluntary relief agency, "I believe the situation today could be greatly bettered." In September 1931 Swope came forth with the most influential of all the pre–New Deal proposals: the "Swope Plan" to stabilize employment and prices through a constellation of trade associations under a national economic council. Early in 1932, a group of more than a hundred businessmen requested the President to declare a two-year truce on destructive competition and urged him "to consider a return to war-time experience by bringing into existence a National Economic Truce Board."[22]

The cornucopia of proposals included suggestions with widely differing ideological implications. Some cited the war example to support radical recommendations; others used the war precedent simply as a *modus operandi* to free business of the encumbrance of the trust laws. Most of them had in common a demand for greater initiative by the federal government, and many of them—especially the public works proposals—called for a sharp increase in spending.

Such innovations ran far ahead of anything Hoover and his followers would countenance. Most businessmen seemed chary of taking the War Industries Board as a model for peacetime.[23] The President himself gave little indication of a readiness to have the federal government assume a larger role. To be sure, he signed an Employment Stabilization Bill in 1931 and gave a major share of credit for the measure to Otto T. Mallery, the leading advocate of public works in the World War I era.[24] But he deplored recommendations for lavish federal spending. Ventures of this sort, he contended, would unbalance the budget and destroy business confidence in public credit.[25]

These demurrers received small credence from men who recalled war spending. "If it is permissible for government to expend billions in wartime in the organization of production, it is no less legitimate for government in a great emergency of peacetime to do what it is also impossible for private individuals to accomplish," reasoned the distinguished economist Edwin R. A. Seligman.[26] The popular economics writer William Trufant Foster scolded:

> If any one still doubts that our economic troubles are mainly mental, let him consider what would happen if the United States declared war today. Everybody knows what would happen. Congress would immediately stop this interminable talk and appropriate three billion dollars—five billion—ten billion—any necessary amount. . . .
>
> Some day we shall realize that if money is available for a blood-and-bullets war, just as much money is available for a food-and-famine war. We shall see that if it is fitting to use collective action on a large scale to kill men abroad, it is fitting to use collective action on an equally large scale to save men at home.[27]

Although Hoover rejected the demand that he draw on the war legacy to mount a program of public works, he could not resist for long the clamor for government initiative to expand relief to the jobless, who by the summer of 1931 totaled eight million. The Republican editor William Allen White wrote:

> Hundreds of thousands of men, women and children are going to suffer terribly this winter in spite of all that the natural laws of economic change can do, however soon change may start, however rapidly it may move. Yet the situation is not hopeless, for if we can recreate the dynamic altruism outside of government which moved us during the war, we can harness forces that will bring relief and make us a better and nobler people.

If the President could arouse the "latent altruism" of the people, White believed, great sums could be raised for relief, "as we raised the Liberty Loan, Red Cross and Y drive funds during the war."[28]

On August 19, 1931 Hoover named Walter S. Gifford, president of the American Telephone and Telegraph Company, to head the President's Organization on Unemployment Relief. A week later Wilson's Secretary of

War, Newton D. Baker, a member of the Advisory Committee of the POUR, noted that Gifford seemed to be planning to organize the country along the lines of the wartime Council of National Defense, and added: "I am going a step farther and suggest that as far as possible men with military experience in the World War be used. They have had lessons in effective and disciplined action which will be valuable." That fall the Gifford Committee launched a "mobilization" to win support for local fundraising drives. National advertisements proclaimed: "Between October 19 and November 25 America will feel the thrill of a great spiritual experience." A few weeks later, when Senator Edward Costigan of Colorado questioned the advisability of employing such techniques, Gifford responded: "We certainly did it in the war. I do not know that I like it, but, as I say, it is more or less the established practice."[29]

Hoover also turned to the war precedent to meet the financial crisis of the autumn of 1931. In December he asked Congress to create a Reconstruction Finance Corporation frankly modeled on the War Finance Corporation. So little did the draftsmen of the new legislation seek to disguise what they were doing that Section 6 of the new law read: "Section 5202 of the Revised Statutes of the United States, as amended, is hereby amended by striking out the words 'War Finance Corporation Act' and inserting in lieu thereof the words 'Reconstruction Finance Corporation Act.'" The proposal appeared to originate at about the same time in the minds of several different men: Hoover; Federal Reserve Governor Eugene Meyer, who had been managing director of the WFC; Louis Wehle, who had been the WFC's general counsel; and Senator Joseph T. Robinson of Arkansas.[30] All drew their inspiration from the WFC. "The RFC was a revival of the War Finance Corporation, that's all, but with expanded powers," Meyer recalled.[31] When the RFC began operations, it employed many of the WFC's old staff, followed its pattern and that of the wartime Treasury in financing, and even took over, with slight modifications, the old WFC forms for loan applications.[32]

Though one periodical depicted the RFC as the "spearhead of the economic A.E.F. [American Expeditionary Force],"[33] the President and his aides insisted that intervention be held to a minimum. Hoover's reluctance to use the RFC as an agency in a new kind of mobilization suggested that the war analogy meant different things to different men and that it could be turned to conservative purposes as readily as to those envisaged by the progressives. While the progressives thought of the war as a paradigm for national planning, Hoover remembered it as a time when the government had encouraged a maximum of voluntary action and a minimum of disturbance of the profit system.[34] He wanted the crucial decisions to be made, as they often had been in wartime, by corporation leaders. He employed the metaphor of war to serve a conservative function: that of draining internal antagonisms onto a common national enemy.[35] In his address to the Republican National Convention in 1932, the permanent chairman, Bertrand Snell, declared in defense of Hoover: "He solidified labor and capital against the enemy."[36]

Hoover's circumscribed efforts could not silence the persistent drumbeat of martial parallels. In an editorial in the *Philadelphia Record* in the spring of 1932, J. David Stern argued: "It is time that we acted with our full strength as we did in the war. Overnight Congress should give the President the right to declare a gold embargo, just as it gave that right to Woodrow Wilson in 1917." A month later, at its annual meeting in Detroit, the U.S. Conference of Mayors began its report by stating: "The world and the nation are at war. The enemy is hunger. . . . Such a situation calls for prompt, vigorous, and intelligent measures which war always makes imperative. . . . In the face of this threat against human welfare and human life measures must be employed as drastic as those of military authority in times of actual physical warfare."[37]

In his campaign for the Democratic presidential nomination in 1932, New York's Governor Franklin D. Roosevelt sought to reap political advantage from the more militant perception of the war experience by contrasting Hoover's performance with the achievements of the war mobilization.[38] In his "forgotten man" address in Albany on April 7, 1932 Roosevelt declared that American success in the Great War had been due to "generalship" that had not been satisfied with "the timorous and futile gesture" of sending a small army and navy overseas, but that "conceived of a whole Nation mobilized for war, economic, industrial, social and military resources gathered into a vast unit." The United States in 1932, he asserted, faced "a more grave emergency than in 1917," and in meeting that emergency the Hoover administration, like Napoleon who had "lost the Battle of Waterloo because he forgot his infantry," had "either forgotten or . . . does not want to remember the infantry of our economic army." "These unhappy times," he maintained, "call for the building of plans that rest upon the forgotten, the unorganized but the indispensable units of economic power, for plans like those of 1917 that build from the bottom up and not from the top down, that put their faith once more in the forgotten man at the bottom of the economic pyramid."[39]

Less than two weeks later, at the Jefferson Day Dinner in St. Paul on April 18, the Governor repeated that the nation confronted an emergency "more grave than that of war" and once more derided Hoover's efforts to cope with the crisis. He added pointedly: "Compare this panic-stricken policy of delay and improvisation with that devised to meet the emergency of war fifteen years ago. We met specific situations with considered, relevant measures of constructive value. There were the War Industries Board, the Food and Fuel Administration, the War Trade Board, the Shipping Board and many others."[40]

After Roosevelt won the Democratic nomination, the war theme continued to loom large. When Tugwell drafted a statement for him on behalf of creating a national economic council, one passage read: "The Democratic party met one great crisis in the Nation's affairs with administrative imagination and skill which was the admiration of the world. It substituted persuasion and planning then for the use of force. In another great crisis, I now propose that it follow its own historic precedent." During the ensuing campaign, the Washington correspondent Tom Stokes later reflected, Roosevelt "only knew that he faced an enemy known as Depression, that he was ready to enlist whatever weapons and recruits were necessary, and that he was prepared to throw the full force of the national government into the battle."[41]

The 1932 election returned the Democrats to Washington for the first time since Wilson's war administration. It was "only natural," as the historian Carl Swisher later observed, "that some of the World-War leaders should return to federal office and that others should become unofficial advisers of the administration. They, like the President, thought in terms of the dramatic concentration of power in the federal government that they had helped to bring about for the defeat of a foreign enemy. It is not surprising that modes of procedure were carried over from one period to the other."[42] In the interregnum between FDR's election in November 1932 and his inauguration in March 1933, war recollections became even more compelling. The whole political system seemed doomed to self-asphyxiation. The discords of party, the deadlock in Congress, the maxims of the classical economists, the taboos of the Constitution all appeared to inhibit action at a time when action was desperately needed. In contrast, the war was remembered as a time of movement and accomplishment.[43]

During the interregnum the country debated a series of new proposals for using the war experience to vanquish the Depression. Daniel Roper, who was soon to be Roosevelt's Secretary of Commerce, suggested a few days after the election that the new president "appoint one 'super' secretary with the other secretaries assistant to him and organize under this 'super' secretary the plan of the National Council of Defense composed of, say 21 men working without compensation as they did in War times." Three months later, on the eve of the inauguration, Roper was still of the same mind. "Many people," he wrote, "evidently do not realize that we are in a virtual state of war."[44]

A number of political leaders believed the crisis could be met only by vesting in the President the same arbitrary war powers that Woodrow Wilson had been given. The Depression, declared Alfred E. Smith on February 7, 1933, was "doing more damage at home to our own people than the great war of 1917 and 1918 ever did." "And what does a democracy do in a war?" he asked. "It becomes a tyrant, a despot, a real monarch. In the World War we took our Constitution, wrapped it up and laid it on the shelf and left it there until it was over." Four days later Republican Governor Alf Landon of Kansas inquired: "Why not give the President the same powers in this bitter peacetime battle as we would give to him in time of war?"[45]

As Landon's statement suggested, this sentiment cut across party and interest group lines. Less than a week before Inauguration Day as conservative a figure as the head of the Southern Pacific Railroad expressed a desire for the kind of "radical action that was taken by the Government in War time." That same month a prominent New York attorney who had helped draft World War I legislation wrote Hoover's Secretary of State, Henry Stimson, that he "had been in intimate touch with those on the firing line of a wide range of industries," and he regretted that "although there is wide enough recognition that we are in an emergency which is at least comparable to that war, we have not yet got the psychology of unity of action which made what we did in 1917 and 1918 possible." He added:

> We Republicans owe a vital duty to the country, in contrast to the petty spirit which has hamstrung our own administration, to implement the incoming administration with power. As to whether that power will be used and how effectively it will be used we can do little or nothing, but we can help create the power. Circumstances again compel us to play the part we played in 1917–18 of being in many ways the most effective support of placing powers in the hands of the executive.

In the First World War, he remarked, he had seen "the conceptions of the fundamental emergency powers under the constitution clarify and enlarge and be embodied in effective instrumentalities." Hence, he concluded, "Should we not affirmatively lead in measures to meet the national emergency, even though in a minority, as we did in the House Military Affairs Committee of 1917?"[46]

As early as the spring of 1932, weeks before Roosevelt had even been nominated, his Brain Trust had requested Joseph D. McGoldrick and Howard L. McBain to prepare a memorandum on presidential war powers, for they anticipated that Roosevelt would need authority for emergency action. During January 1933 the President-elect asked Rexford G. Tugwell to explore the possibility that the Trading with the Enemy Act of 1917 might provide the basis for an edict embargoing gold exports. Tugwell's research quickly involved him in a comedy of errors in which the New Dealers sought both to obtain the necessary information without letting the Hoover administration learn what they were up to and at the same time to persuade themselves that a statute that had been amended many times gave them the legal authority to do what they intended to do anyway. Governor Roosevelt's legal aides could not have been more cooperative. Senator Thomas Walsh, FDR's choice to be Attorney General, promised that, if the President-elect found he needed the powers, he would quiet his doubts and rule that the old statute gave him the sanction he required. When, after Walsh's death, Roosevelt picked Homer Cummings for the post, he turned over to the new Attorney General the folder on the Trading with the Enemy Act. Cummings obligingly concluded that the statute was still alive.[47]

As the day of Roosevelt's inauguration approached, the epidemic of bank failures drove governors in state after state to proclaim bank holidays and raised fears that the economic system was on the verge of collapse. "A blight has fallen over all American industry," declared the *Akron Beacon-Journal* on March 3. "A foreign invader making easy conquest of our shores could do no worse." As Roosevelt took the oath of office, the atmosphere in Washington, wrote Arthur Krock of the *New York Times*, was like that "in a beleaguered capital in war time."[48]

V

FDR's inaugural address on March 4, 1933, reflected the spirit of wartime crisis. Recruitment of the jobless, he told the anxious throng assembled in

Capitol Plaza, could be accomplished by "treating the task as we would treat the emergency of a war." His program, he explained, comprised "lines of attack." Indeed, he went on:

> If we are to go forward, we must move as a trained and loyal army willing to sacrifice for the good of a common discipline. . . . We are, I know, ready and willing to submit our lives and property to such discipline, because it makes possible a leadership which aims at a larger good. This I propose to offer, pledging that the larger purposes will bind upon us all as a sacred obligation with a unity of duty hitherto evoked only in time of armed strife.
>
> With this pledge taken, I assume unhesitatingly the leadership of this great army of our people dedicated to a disciplined attack upon our common problems.

He would urge Congress to adopt his legislative program, but if Congress failed to act and the emergency continued, the new president announced: "I shall not evade the clear course of duty that will then confront me. I shall ask the Congress for the one remaining instrument to meet the crisis—broad executive power to wage a war against the emergency, as great as the power that would be given to me if we were in fact invaded by a foreign foe."[49]

During the First Hundred Days, Roosevelt sought to restore national confidence by evoking the mood of wartime: the imperative of national unity above any claim of partisan or private interest because the very existence of the country was in danger. The opposition press suspended criticism of the President; corporations, labor unions, and farm organizations pledged their cooperation; and GOP leaders urged the country to rally around the Democratic chief executive. Alf Landon declared: "If there is any way in which a member of that species, thought to be extinct, a Republican Governor of a mid-western state, can aid [the President] in the fight, I now enlist for the duration of the war."[50]

The New Deal hoped to arouse the same sense of devotion to the nation and the same commitment to sacrifice that had been displayed in the war. "It is important," wrote Rexford Tugwell, "that we should again explore the possibilities of what William James called 'the moral equivalents' of war." "The ordeal of war," he told Dartmouth students, "brings out the magnificent resources of youth. . . . The ordeal of depression ought to try your mettle in similar ways. . . . The feeling which shook humanity during the War and which after the War reshaped the entire civilization of mighty nations is called for again."[51]

When the planners of the thirties looked back at the war, they were most impressed by how much had been accomplished once the nation had been unified by allegiance to a common purpose. Writers like Tugwell and George Soule argued that the effective functioning of "a regime of industrial democracy" required the same "loyalty to larger aims" that the War Industries Board had exploited.[52] Nationalistic to the core, they believed that if the country could once again give fealty to a transcendent ideal, the Depression would be conquered as the armies of the Kaiser had been. Charles Beard proposed a "heroic national effort" that would leave people "richer in goods—and still more important, in patriotic spirit." Many conceived the New Deal not simply as a new kind of economic mobilization but also, as the war had been, a venture in "nation-saving."[53] One of the New Deal experiments was later to be lauded because it had led to "a new baptism of patriotism and an increased consciousness of national unity."[54]

Roosevelt's first important official acts were to call Congress back into special session and to use the authority of the Trading with the Enemy Act of 1917 to proclaim a national bank holiday.[55] On March 9 the *New York Times* reported from Washington:

> It was a grim Congress which met today, the most momentous gathering of the country's legislators since war was declared in 1917. It is trite to say that they declared war, but it is nevertheless true that they hurled against the enemy of depression and despondency a weapon which they hoped would penetrate the subtle armor of an allegorical or Bunyan-like antagonist.

The House received FDR's banking bill with much the same ardor with which it had greeted Woodrow Wilson's war legislation. Speaker Henry Rainey said the situation reminded him of the time when "on both sides of this Chamber the great war measures suggested by the administration were supported with practical unanimity. . . . Today we are engaged in another war, more serious even in its character and presenting greater dangers to the Republic." After only thirty-eight minutes, the House passed the Administration's banking bill, sight unseen.[56]

On March 10 the President sent his second message to Congress, a plea for plenary powers to slash government spending. To the dismay of progressive Republicans and liberal Democrats, he proved to be as orthodox on fiscal matters as his predecessor. When Senator Tom Connally of Texas talked to him in December 1932, the President-elect had stressed the importance of balancing the budget by cutting federal spending and had dwelt upon the constitutional restraints on the presidency. "If it was constitutional to spend forty million dollars in a war," Connally responded angrily, "isn't it just as constitutional to spend a little money to relieve the hunger and misery of our citizens?" Roosevelt had brushed aside such remonstrances and chose instead to heed the counsel of his conservative choice for Budget Director, Lewis Douglas. After studying the wartime authority Congress had granted Wilson, he decided to ask the new Congress to renew those powers—but in order to enable him to balance the budget.[57]

The spirit of war crisis sped the economy bill through, though it slashed veterans' pensions, hitherto regarded as untouchable. "It is true this bill grants a great deal of power," conceded Representative John McDuffie of Alabama, "but this country is in a state of war—not against a foreign enemy but war against economic evils that demand some sacrifice on your part and mine." Representative John Young Brown of Kentucky spoke even more bluntly when he lectured fellow Democrats:

I may say to you that we are at war today, and the veterans of this country do not want you, in their name, to desert the standards of the President of the United States.

I had as soon start a mutiny in the face of a foreign foe as start a mutiny today against the program of the President of the United States. [Applause] And if someone must shoot down, in this hour of battle, the Commander in Chief of our forces, God grant that the assassin's bullet shall not be fired from the Democratic side of this House. [Applause][58]

Many Congressmen disliked the Administration's economy bill but feared to oppose Roosevelt. When Wallace H. White, Jr., spoke out against the proposal, a Maine constituent warned him that he was "riding out to certain death." He agreed that White's position was logically sound, yet he cautioned that since "a state of war does exist," the Senator would be foolish to sacrifice himself by disregarding the war atmosphere. After only two days of debate, Congress voted the Economy Act. Senator Henry Fountain Ashurst of Arizona explained: "The conditions are as serious as war and we must follow the flag."[59]

VI

Almost every New Deal act or agency derived, to some extent, from the experience of World War I, not least the Tennessee Valley Authority—the most ambitious New Deal experiment in regional planning. The TVA grew out of the establishment of a government-operated nitrate and electric power project at Muscle Shoals during and after the war. In his message asking for creation of the TVA, Roosevelt concluded: "In short, this power development of war days leads logically to national planning."[60] When the bill was introduced in April 1933, it seemed appropriate to refer it to the House Military Affairs Committee. Although war considerations played an inconsequential part in the birth of the Authority, the TVA Act of 1933 stipulated that in case of war or national emergency, any or all of the property entrusted to the Authority should be available to the government for manufacturing explosives or for other war purposes. The original World War I nitrate plant, which was turned over to the TVA, was to be held as a standby that might be needed in a future war. When foes of the TVA challenged it in the courts, Chief Justice Charles Evans Hughes found constitutional authority for the construction of the Wilson Dam by resting his opinion, in part, on the war power. The TVA was only one of a number of resources operations—from soil conservation to public power development—that employed war rhetoric or drew upon the World War I experience.[61]

The public-housing movement of the thirties had come of age during the war, at which time Congress had authorized the Emergency Fleet Corporation and the United States Housing Corporation to provide shelter for war workers. The war established the principle of federal intervention in housing, and it trained architects such as Robert Kohn, who served as chief of production of the housing division of the U.S. Shipping Board. After the armistice, Kohn observed: "The war has put housing 'on the map' in this country."[62] In 1933 President Roosevelt named Kohn to head the New Deal's first public-housing venture.

Imaginative wartime experiments with garden city ideas paved the way for the greenbelt towns of the thirties, while the rural resettlement and subsistence homestead projects of the New Deal reaped the harvest of seeds planted by Elwood Mead and Franklin K. Lane in the war years. The historian Roy Lubove has pointed out:

> In such residential communities as Yorkship Village (New Jersey), Union Park Gardens (Delaware) and the Black Rock and Crane Tracts (Bridgeport, Connecticut), the Emergency Fleet Corporation and the United States Housing Corporation offered American architects and planners their first opportunity to apply garden city principles in comprehensive fashion: curvilinear street systems and street sizes adapted to function; park and play facilities; row-house design; the skillful spacing of mass and volume for maximum aesthetic effect and maximum sunlight and ventilation. The memory of the federal war-housing program persisted over the next two decades, a reminder of the potentialities of non-speculative, large-scale site planning for working-class housing.[63]

The New Deal's program of farm price supports owed something to the wartime Food Administration and even more to a decade of proselytizing by George Peek, a hard-bitten farm-belt agitator who had served as "a sort of generalissimo of industry" under the War Industries Board. Peek's recollection of how the war had benefited business had led him to argue that the peacetime government should give the same measure of aid to the distressed farmer. Frustrated in the twenties by Republican presidents, Peek pinned his hopes on the election of FDR in 1932. "It looks to me as though in the campaign for Roosevelt for President we are in the last line of trenches and if he is not elected that agriculture is doomed to peasantry," Peek wrote.[64]

FDR's proposals for crop restriction and farm subsidies shocked orthodox opinion, but the war spirit carried the Agricultural Adjustment Act through. The very conservative Georgia Democrat Eugene Cox, in responding to Republican protests against a "gag rule" imposed to speed passage of the AAA bill, said that the country demanded swift action in this "economic war." He added, "I am a good soldier and will vote for this rule and the bill, and trust that all others, because of the circumstances, will do likewise."[65] To head the new Agricultural Adjustment Administration, Roosevelt named Peek.[66] "To him, with his war experience, this whole thing clicks into shape," Peek's wife noted, "and some of the fine men of the country are coming to his call as they did in 1917, and with the same high purpose."[67]

Consciously devised to provide the moral equivalent of war that men like Tugwell sought, the Civilian Conservation Corps aimed to install martial virtues in the nation's youth.[68] When the CCC enrolled its first recruits, it evoked memories of the mobilization of the AEF. "By the fifteenth of July we shall have 275,000 people all actually at work in the woods," Roosevelt reported a few weeks after Congress adopted the proposal. "It is a pretty good record, one which I think can be compared with the mobilization carried on in 1917."[69] That summer, a writer observed: "America has a new army and has sent it to war. In two brief months 300,000 men have enlisted, been trained, transferred to the front, and have started the attack. The battle is on in earnest."[70]

Though the agency was under civilian direction, the Army ran the camps.[71] The CCCers convened at Army recruiting stations; traveled to an Army camp where they were outfitted in World War I clothing; were transported to the woods by troop train; fell asleep in Army tents to the strain of "Taps" and woke to "Reveille." A stanza of a poem by a CCC worker made clear the role of the military:

> "Uncle," he says to his Army,
> "You did a good job before
> When you took three million rookies
> And polished 'em up for war,
> Now if you can handle the civvies
> Like the Doughboys and the Gob,
> And stiffen their ranks till they're tough as the Yanks
> I'll give 'em a great big job."[72]

The CCC newspaper, modeled on *Stars and Stripes*, offered a prize for the best nickname for a CCC worker: "You know—some word that has caught on in your camp—the way the word 'doughboy' was used to describe the American soldier in France." *Happy Days* recounted the work of the "Tree Army" in the language of military communiqués: "Company 217 at Beachy Bottoms, N.Y. has been filled to full Gypsy-moth-fighting strength," or, in Montana, "Depression Warriors Holding Western Front." On July 1 *Happy Days* reported:

The big drive has begun. Uncle Sam has thrown his full C.C.C. strength into the front lines of the forest. . . . The entire reforestation army has landed in the woods—and has the situation well in hand.

In all sectors the reforestation troops are moving ahead. Battle lines of the Gypsy moth are beginning to crack and fall back in New

York and New England. Yellow pine beetles are retreating from the mountains of Colorado and California before the onslaught of the C.C.C. Forest fires . . . are being repulsed on all flanks the moment they show their smudgy red heads through the trees.[73]

Of all the New Deal agencies, the CCC was easily the most popular because it united two objectives: "the conservation of America's natural resources and the conservation of its young manhood." Many observers believed that the "forestry army" embodied James's proposal for an army of youth engaged in a "warfare against nature," although Roosevelt himself may not have been directly affected by James.[74] The Corps, it was claimed, rescued young men from meaninglessness, rebuilt bodies and character, and gave men a soldier's pride of accomplishment.[75] Speaker Rainey wrote: "They are also under military training and as they come out of it they come out improved in health and developed mentally and physically and are more useful citizens and if ever we should become involved in another war they would furnish a very valuable nucleus for our army."[76]

While the CCC, the AAA, the TVA, housing, economy, and banking legislation all shared in the war legacy, it was the National Recovery Administration that was the keystone of the early New Deal, and the NRA rested squarely on the War Industries Board example. The National Industrial Recovery bill, patterned on WIB procedures, wove together a series of schemes for government-business coordination of the kind that had prevailed in the war.[77] One of the most influential designs, sponsored by Meyer Jacobstein, a Rochester, New York banker, and H. G. Moulton, president of the Brookings Institution, recommended creation of "a National Board for Industrial Recovery, with powers similar to those so effectively utilized during the World War by the War Industries Board." When the President commissioned Raymond Moley to frame legislation for industrial recovery, Moley asked General Hugh Johnson, who in World War I had functioned as a liaison between the Army and the WIB, to take over for him. "Nobody can do it better than you," Moley coaxed. "You're familiar with the only comparable thing that's ever been done—the work of the War Industries Board."[78]

The recovery bill, drafted by Johnson and others, won Senate approval by only the narrowest of margins; conservatives foresaw that the measure would enhance the power of the State and progressives feared that it would encourage cartelization, but Roosevelt was more sanguine. When he signed the measure on June 16, he commented: "Many good men voted this new charter with misgivings. I do not share these doubts. I had part in the great cooperation of 1917 and 1918 and it is my faith that we can count on our industry once more to join in our general purpose to lift this new threat."[79]

Before labor would agree to the industrial recovery program, it insisted on the same government recognition of the right to organize that it had enjoyed in World War I. In December 1932, shortly after he learned that Frances Perkins would be the new Secretary of Labor, Sidney Hillman of the Amalgamated Clothing Workers sent her a memorandum urging the government to pursue the kinds of policies the War Labor Board had initiated.[80] In framing the recovery legislation, the WLB's onetime secretary W. Jett Lauck, who served as spokesman for John L. Lewis's United Mine Workers, sponsored a plan for "a national board composed of labor modeled after the War Labor Board." When the national industrial recovery bill emerged from the drafting room, it incorporated the pivotal section 7(a) granting labor's demand for recognition of the right of collective bargaining. The essential provisions of 7(a), noted the economist Edwin Witte, were "but restatements" of principles first recognized by the National War Labor Board.[81]

Roosevelt, as the historian Gerald Nash has pointed out, "sketched . . . the blueprint for the War Labor Policies Board which was modeled on his directive,"[82] and to staff the National Labor Board of 1933, he turned to men he had first encountered in developing war labor programs. William Leiserson, executive secretary of the board, had been FDR's personal adviser on labor affairs in 1918. In formulating labor policy—from interpreting 7(a) through the adoption and administration of the Wagner Act—Roosevelt and his lieutenants drew heavily on war precedents. The war agencies had established the basic principles of the New Deal labor program: that workers had the right to unionize, that they must not be discharged for union activity, and that national boards could restrain employers from denying such rights. In addition, they had evolved the procedure of plant elections to determine bargaining representatives, which was to be the crucial instrumentality employed by the President's labor boards.[83]

A few critics questioned whether all of the panoply of legislation enacted in the spring of 1933 was constitutional, but Homer Cummings acknowledged no doubts. Near the end of the First Hundred Days, the Attorney General gave a radio address in which he said:

The constitutional difficulties inherent in the recent legislation, I think, are grossly magnified. Our fundamental law is faced with no unusual stress or strain. During the World War, we put it to a far more radical test in emergency laws like those relating to selective service, espionage, the War Industries Board, Industrial Mobilization, and the like. Now, as then, we face a war—a war to win the peace, a war to win back prosperity.[84]

Wall Street found some of these New Deal policies hard to accept, but during the Hundred Days War it rallied around. When Roosevelt forbade the hoarding of gold, the *Wall Street Journal* responded that it was necessary for the government to take such action "to protect the public welfare . . . just as it might and should in a time of war prevent any help being given the enemy." At the end of May *Business Week* headlined one story, "Industries Enlist," and in its June issue the *American Bankers Association Journal,* the organ of the group Roosevelt, in his inaugural address, had denounced as "money-changers," declared, "The will to cooperate to the fullest degree exists in every officer and private in this army of workers."[85]

Business stood by Roosevelt in no small part because it sensed that it had no choice, since the nation was placing its hopes in the new president to so great an extent that contrary behavior seemed no more tolerable than it would on a battlefield. As early as mid-March, Senator Robert M. La Follette, Jr., recognized "that something akin to a war psychology has been created and . . . the people generally are critical of all who do not 'stand back of the President,'" and Congressman Robert L. Doughton told a constituent: "We are now at war with poverty, distress and suffering, and unless we have some leadership, we will never end the war. I think the entire country has faith in President Roosevelt . . . and I am therefore following his leadership."[86]

When the historic Hundred Days Congress came to an end in June, commentators seeking to explain what had transpired drew again and again upon the analogue of war and, more particularly, on the experience of the Great War. In an article published that summer, the historian Henry Steele Commager pointed out that it was in World War I "that there was revealed, for the first time, the far-reaching powers of the Federal Government over every process of our industrial life and the astonishing flexibility of our constitutional system," and, subsequently, a journalist friendly to Roosevelt wrote of the procedures of the New Deal: "Above all, they were the methods of the World War, with its truce on partisan politics, its enlistment of non-political experts in responsibility for national reconstruction, its spawning of emergency inter-Departmental Committees, Boards and Administrations, and its wholesale use of publicity and propaganda to win and hold popular support for a prolonged national effort."[87]

After the distinguished Royal Institute in Great Britain directed by Arnold J. Toynbee surveyed the United States in 1933 for its annual review of international affairs, it concluded:

> The foreign observer of the American state of mind in that year could merely take note of its likeness to the war-time state of mind in the European belligerent countries during the General War of 1914–18. During these four years of extreme tribulation, the European belligerent peoples had sought relief from their psychological tension by perpetually demanding of their war-time rulers that they should do some new thing—and what thing mattered little, so long as it was something drastic and sensational and ostensibly directed towards "winning the War." In the United States of 1933, which was a country psychologically at war with the Economic Depression, a similar demand was perpetually being made upon the President by the public, and was perpetually being satisfied by the President in the war-time manner.[88]

VII

In carrying the legislation of the First Hundred Days into effect, Roosevelt took full advantage of the receptivity of the country to wartime appeals. In a fireside chat in July 1933, he requested employers to launch a "great summer offensive against unemployment," and a small-town Oklahoma Chamber of Commerce received a wire from him saying, "The public will be asked to renew its war time patriotism and support only those who join in this program." The country, at least at first, could hardly have been more responsive. In Oklahoma, to foster the NRA, volunteers marched off in two divisions—the Blue Eagle Army and the Loyalty Army—and a minister told his parishioners, "Wars can only be won by unlimited faith in leaders. . . . Upon you devolves the duty of giving your moral support at all times . . . to the government which is seeking to bring about the harmony of the laws of God and the laws of man." To promote the NRA in its Massachusetts community during the summer of 1933, the Dorchester Board of Trade created a "combat unit" officered by a general and colonels, made four-minute talks on behalf of compliance at movie houses in imitation of the World War I practice, and stigmatized those who did not adhere to the government's program as shirkers.[89]

The war rhetoric reverberated throughout Roosevelt's first term and even into his second term when the sense of crisis was not nearly so acute. In 1934 Lord Beaverbrook's *Daily Express* commented on FDR's budget message: "What a lesson President Roosevelt, the hero of the nation, teaches the rulers of this country! President Roosevelt goes to war against the slump with warlike daring and wartime finance. His budget is in the Armageddon of 1918 class." That same year the novelist Martha Gellhorn reported to Harry Hopkins from North Carolina that the federal relief operation was "a kind of desperate job like getting the wounded off the battlefield so that they can die quietly at a base hospital," but Roosevelt told workmen at Norris Dam, "Some day you probably will be known as veterans, veterans of a new kind of war—a war to improve the conditions of millions of our American people." In 1935 Congressman David J. Lewis called for curbs on the Supreme Court because its actions had left Congress, "alone among parliaments, stripped of power to defend the nation against an economic depression more devastating than ordinary war," and the *Oregon Daily Journal* called a fireside chat "a great message from the war front against depression." As late as 1937 a bank president in Hattiesburg, Mississippi wrote: "Whatever the President wants, I am for it. I believe in going over the top according to orders, jumping over with quickness, no hesitation, entering No Man's Land without thought or concern for return."[90]

To head the NRA, Roosevelt named the fiery General Johnson, who could boast pertinent experience not only with the War Industries Board but also in organizing the draft. The war mobilization, Johnson later said, "was a great schooling for the new national effort to which NRA was a part."[91] In mid-July he launched an emotional campaign dramatized by the symbol of the Blue Eagle.[92] "In war, in the gloom of night attack, soldiers wear a bright badge on their shoulders to be sure that comrades do not fire on comrades," explained the President. "On that principle, those who cooperate in this program must know each other at a glance. That is why we have provided a badge of honor for this purpose."[93]

Cabinet members greeted with skepticism Johnson's proposal for a mass movement to muster the nation behind the NRA. Homer Cummings pointed out that the country was not at war, and it might be difficult to get everyone to sign a pledge. Johnson replied that the plan of attack could be put through, for the Depression was more real than the war had been to most Americans. He explained: "Almost every individual has either suffered terribly, or knows of friends and relatives who have; so there is waiting here to be appealed to what I regard as the most fertile psychology that you could imagine. . . . I think this has anything that happened during the War backed off the board."[94]

To enforce the Blue Eagle, Johnson enlisted the housewives of the country. "It is women in homes—and not soldiers in uniform—who will this time save our country," he proclaimed. "They will go over the top to as great a victory as the Argonne. It is zero hour for housewives. Their battle cry is 'Buy now under the Blue Eagle!'"[95] By kindling the mood of the Liberty Loan drives and the draft registration of World War I, Johnson kept alive the intense spirit of the Hundred Days through another season. "There is a unity in this country," the President declared, "which I have not seen and you have not seen since April, 1917."[96]

That fall, as the first enthusiasm began to wane a bit, an NRA handbook in Portland, Oregon, instructed speakers for the Recovery Program:

There has been some scoffing when NRA executives declared that this national emergency was just as grave as the last war. There have been no colorful battles, true enough, to capture the imagination, yet the suffering has been just as great as during the late conflict. Merely as one example, there have been more suicides in the United States in the past four years than ever before in history. Last week the coroner at Portland grew so alarmed at the mounting number of suicides, most of them despondent over unemployment and financial reverses, that he issued a public statement urging relatives of despondent persons to watch them carefully to prevent other tragedies. Suffering among children whose parents have been unemployed is greater than during the past war. Women and children have had to bear the brunt of the depression, something that never occurs during war time. The social ills of the depression . . . are far in excess of the suffering endured during the last war, when there was employment for all, wages were high, and social conditions were excellent. Speakers can draw a startling parallel between the economic waste of the last war, when industrial sections were laid waste by cannonading, and the economic waste in the depression, where block after block of factories stand silent.[97]

The Recovery Administration conceived of the Depression as, in part, a crisis in character. The New Dealers hoped that businessmen would place the public weal above their private interests, just as the copper magnates had responded to Bernard Baruch's appeal in 1917 by supplying metal to the Army and Navy at less than half the market price. In 1933 businessmen were asked to accept as a patriotic duty the assignment to raise wages and agree to a "truce" on price-cutting. The recovery drive, it was argued, would succeed only if it aroused the same kind of "spiritual" fervor that World War I had awakened. Morris Cooke, who would head the Rural Electrification Administration, wrote:

> Conversations with a good many different kinds of people convince me that there is needed to expedite industrial recovery a talk by the President in which he would read into our 57 varieties of effort an ethical and moral quality and call on us individually and collectively to put our shoulders to the wheel just as if we were at war. . . .
> Everywhere I get the impression of our people wanting to be told that the main purpose of the Recovery Administration is not exclusively the rehabilitation of our material wellbeing but a reaffirmation of the spiritual values in life.[98]

To staff the New Deal agencies, Roosevelt turned to the veterans of the war mobilization.[99] Top NRA officials included Johnson's chief of staff, John Hancock, who had managed the War Industries Board's naval industrial program; Charles F. Horner, the genius of the Liberty Loan drive; Leo Wolman, who had headed the section on production statistics of the War Industries Board; and Major General Clarence Charles Williams, who had been Chief of Ordnance in charge of the vast war purchasing. The Works Progress Administration, too, made a lot of use of army officers, who possessed several advantages: having years of experience as administrators—some of them in the World War I mobilization; constituting no financial burden, since they continued to draw salaries from the military; and being, at least ostensibly, removed from politics. Roosevelt, in fact, eventually chose as Harry Hopkins's successor a colonel who was so nonpolitical he had never voted.[100]

Many in New Deal circles had gotten their first taste of government service during the war. The first Administrator for Public Works, Colonel Donald H. Sawyer, had built cantonments; Felix Frankfurter had chaired the War Labor Policies Board; Captain Leon Henderson of Ordnance had served with the War Industries Board; and Senator Joseph Guffey had worked in the WIB on the conservation of oil.[101] For such people, the summer of 1933 seemed like old times. "Washington is a hectic place," wrote Isador Lubin in August. "The hotels are filled, and the restaurants remind me very much of war times. One cannot go into the Cosmos Club without meeting half a dozen persons whom he knew during the war."[102]

The commandants of New Deal agencies thought of themselves as soldiers in a war against depression, with Hugh Johnson particularly fond of the rhetoric of conflict. Early in 1934 he wrote an official, "This is war—lethal and more menacing than any other crisis in our history." In an article published that year entitled "The General," Matthew Josephson reported, "Even today he likens the various phases of the NRA campaigns to the movements of Napoleon, his ideal warrior, or to the battles of World War I."[103]

The young men who came to Washington said they had "volunteered in peacetime." Jerome Frank confided to Frankfurter, "I know you know Roosevelt very well. I want to get out of this Wall Street racket. . . . This crisis seems to be the equivalent of a war and I'd like to join up for the duration." Frankfurter himself told Donald Richberg, "It is heartening to know that you are on the firing line." In accounting for how he came to be involved in the New Deal, Tommy Corcoran explained, "Holmes suggested I might do my country and myself a service in staying on to fight a war as threatening to the nation's survival as one he'd waged to save the Union three score years before." For the New Dealers, doughboy lingo became common parlance. At one point William O. Douglas wrote Leon Henderson, "Thanks a lot—from one front trench veteran to another."[104]

Some even claimed they were conscripts. When Holger Cahill expressed reluctance about a bid to head the Federal Art Project, an associate advised him that he had no alternative: "An invitation from the Government to a job like that is tantamount to an order. It's like being drafted." Another New Dealer, resistant to being chosen to chair the FCC, relented, saying, "I felt that I had no moral right to refuse to accept the commission and I go as a good soldier to the assignment by the Chief Executive."[105]

This martial chord became so commonplace that it even affected agencies not directly involved in the economic mobilization. From his "general headquarters in Washington, D.C.," reported one writer, "General" Harry Hopkins had organized the Federal Emergency Relief Administration as "only one division of the 'American Army' in the War on Want." One of Hopkins's "noncoms," a relief worker in northern Michigan, observed: "We were like an army, drafted into service during a war." She wrote of the FERA Field Director: "He had been in the front-line trenches with the rest of us when the battle raged at its worst." When the FERA gave way to the Works Progress Administration late in 1935, her staff was broken up. "At this time," she commented, "I lost the other two members of my shock troops."[106]

Roosevelt, too, continued to employ this jargon. In his address at Franklin Field in June 1936 accepting nomination for a second term, the President, after noting that in other parts of the world there were people who had once fought for freedom but had given up the struggle, said:

I believe in my heart that only our success can stir their ancient hope. They begin to know that here in America we are waging a great and successful war. It is not alone a war against want and destitution and economic demoralization. It is more than that; it is a war for the survival of democracy. We are fighting to save a great and precious form of government for ourselves and for the world.

I accept the commission you have tendered me. I join with you. I am enlisted for the duration of the war.[107]

The processes of New Deal government also owed much to the war legacy. World War I provided a precedent for the concentration of executive authority, for the responsibility of government for the state of the economy, and for the practice of shunting aside the regular line agencies and creating new organizations with dramatic alphabetical rubrics. When in the Hoover years the RFC, the first of the new agencies, was established, one periodical reported: "R.F.C., of course, is Reconstruction Finance Corporation, and the newspapers have fallen into the war-time habit of using the simple initials instead of the rather cumbersome full name of this anti-hard-times organization." The war offered models, too, for setting up coordinating bodies such as the National Emergency Council headed by Frank Walker.[108] Not least in importance, the war experience was used to justify the New Deal's emergency legislation in the courts.[109]

World War I also saw service as a way to rebut opponents of Roosevelt's economic policies. When critics objected that the country could not afford New Deal reforms, FDR's supporters responded with the familiar retort that if the country could spend as it had in war, it could do so in this new emergency. "When people complain to me of the amount of money that the government has been borrowing," commented Thomas Lamont of the House of Morgan, "I always answer it by saying: 'Well, if the country was willing to spend thirty billion dollars in a year's time to try to lick the Germans, I don't see why people should complain about spending five or six billion dollars to keep people from starving.'"[110]

In 1936 when Roosevelt returned to Forbes Field in Pittsburgh, where, four years before, he had promised to slash federal spending, he concluded that this argument offered the best response to critics who accused him of a profligate disregard of campaign promises. "National defense and the future of America were involved in 1917. National defense and the future of America were also involved in 1933," he asserted. "Don't you believe that the saving of America has been cheap at that price?"[111]

The President's argument would have been more compelling if he had spent at anywhere near the rate that both he and his conservative foes implied he had. For a time in the winter of 1933–34, the Administration gave a fillip to the economy when it embarked on lavish expenditures through the Civil Works Administration, but early in 1934 the President, alarmed by mounting deficits, decreed the death of the CWA. Distressed by Roosevelt's verdict, Senator La Follette inquired: "In 1917, Mr. President, what Senator would have dared to rise on the floor of the Senate and suggest that we could not fight the war against Germany and her allies because it would unbalance the Budget?" *The Nation* voiced a similar protest: "The country is confronted with a vastly greater crisis than it had to meet in the World War but has not yet extended itself financially as it did at that time."[112] Progressives warned that unless the President began to disburse funds at a wartime pace the country might take years to pull out of the Depression. The progressive Cassandras proved correct. The New Deal mobilization of 1933–34, from which so much had been expected, brought disappointing economic returns.

VIII

As a model for economic action, World War I proved unsatisfactory, for the problems confronting Roosevelt in 1933 were quite unlike those Woodrow Wilson had been called on to meet in 1917. As the Harvard economist Edwin Gay wrote: "War stimulates the full expansion of productive energy, but the deep depression cripples every economic process and discourages even the most sanguine business leaders." Some who recalled the war activity hoped that it could provide a prototype in the 1930s for the stepped-up output that had been achieved in 1917–18. But the aims of the New Deal mobilization were not the same as those of the war; General Johnson even called for "an armistice on increasing producing capacity." FDR's biographer Frank Freidel later pointed out: "Unlike wartime measures, the new agencies were to reduce output in most areas rather than raise it, and encourage price increases rather than restrain them. Thus, waging a war on the depression was in some ways the reverse of waging one on a foreign foe."[113]

The economist John M. Clark made a similar observation. The war, he noted, offered precedents for emergency controls, deficit spending, and expanded powers for the Federal Reserve System, but the problems of war and of depression "were radically different; in fact, they were in some respects opposite to one another." The task of determining priorities in a war economy, Clark observed, could not be equated with that of reinvigorating sick industries. He concluded: "All the machinery for allocating limited supplies of essential resources among conflicting uses, which played so large a part in the wartime controls, had no application to the depression. Where the actuating motives of private industry fail and the result is partial paralysis, the problem is essentially opposite to that of war."[114]

These misgivings did not result simply from hindsight. In the midst of the First Hundred Days, the economist Paul Douglas warned that the country did not face the wartime task of rationing scarce resources but the quite different problem of stimulating production. "Industry must get some business before it can proceed to ration it out," he remarked. Disconcerted by the New Deal's obsession with the menace of overproduction when the critical question was how to increase purchasing power, he declared: "Certainly those who are arguing from the analogy of the War Industries Board miss the point. That body had behind it the gigantic purchasing power of the government, and with this weapon it was able to instill some order in the industrial system. But unless the government creates such purchasing power in the present emergency, the regulatory body will be operating in a void."[115]

The NRA invited comparison to the 1917–18 mobilization, but it was an awkward fit. As the historian Jordan Schwarz subsequently observed:

Hugh Johnson, Baruch's unhappy contribution to the New Deal, modeled the National Recovery Administration after Baruch's War

Industries Board. But Johnson knew that he lacked the leverage of war needed to win cooperation from individual enterprises—which the power of patriotism conferred upon Baruch. Also, Baruch used the leverage of military purchasing; poor Johnson lacked control over the parsimonious Public Works Administration. His failure was foreordained.[116]

The war analogy proved mischievous in an even more significant respect. The Tugwells thought of the war as a time when intellectuals had exercised unprecedented power over the economy, and when the feasibility of a planned society had been brilliantly demonstrated. Yet, although intellectuals did wield some power, agencies such as the War Industries Board had been run chiefly by business executives. If they learned anything from the war, it was not the virtues of collectivism but the potentialities of trade associations, the usefulness of the state in economic warfare with the traders of other nations, and the good-housekeeping practices of eliminating duplication and waste. "From the war," David Kennedy has concluded, "can be dated the origins of the modern practice of massive informal collusion between government and organized private enterprise." The immediate consequence of the war was not the New Jerusalem of the planners but the boosterism of Herbert Hoover as Secretary of Commerce. Though the war mobilization did establish meaningful precedents for New Deal reforms, it was hardly the "war socialism" some theorists thought it to be. Perhaps the outstanding characteristic of the war organization of industry was that it showed how to achieve massive government intervention without any permanent diminution in the power of corporations. Furthermore, the historian Robert Cuff has cautioned, "treating the war period as essentially a paradigm for future historical development . . . both diminishes the uniqueness and exaggerates the modernity of America's response to the crisis of World War I."[117]

Confusion over the meaning of the war experience helped conceal the ambiguities of the so-called "First New Deal." The architects of the early New Deal appeared to be in fundamental agreement, since they were united in rejecting the New Freedom goal of a competitive society in favor of business-government coordination in the 1917 style. In fact, they differed sharply. Tugwell hoped that the coordination authorized by the NRA would enable the Recovery Administration to become an agency for centralized government direction of the economy, a possibility that could be fostered by the NRA's licensing power. Most of the other "First New

Dealers," however, meant by business-government coordination an economy in which businessmen would make the crucial decisions. As administrator of the NRA, General Johnson gave small scope to the government initiative Tugwell had envisaged. He never used the licensing power, but relied instead on negotiation with business and on the force of social pressure. Like Moley and Richberg and the President, Johnson placed his faith not in a planned economy but in inducing voluntary business cooperation with government.[118]

The New Deal administrators shared, too, the conviction of the war bureaucrats that progress would be achieved not through worker or farmer insurgency but through government programs, conceived and executed by agency officials. A month after the armistice, Wesley Mitchell had voiced the need for "intelligent experimenting and detailed planning rather than for agitation or class struggle."[119] The war approach that the New Dealers adopted rejected mass action and assumed a community of interest among the managers of business corporations and the directors of government agencies. FDR's lieutenants believed that the great danger to such an experiment lay not in the recalcitrance of conservatives, who were discredited, but in the menace of antiplutocratic movements. Yet in damping the fires of popular dissent, they also snuffed out support they would need to keep the reform spirit alive.

The New Dealers, distrustful of the politics of group conflict, sought, at the beginning, to effect a truce like that of 1917 when, to some extent, class and sectional animosities abated. Perhaps no other approach could have accomplished so much in the spring of 1933; yet it was a tactic with obvious perils for the cause of reform. By presenting the Depression not as the collapse of a system but as a personalized foreign enemy, Roosevelt as much as Hoover sought to mend the social fabric. In doing so, he, like his predecessor, deflected blame away from business leaders many thought responsible for hard times, and diverted attention from the reality that the Depression was not the consequence of an assault by a foreign foe but evidence of an internal breakdown in capitalism.

In their quest for national solidarity, the New Dealers tried on occasion to suppress anti-business expressions of discontent. Roosevelt warned the American Federation of Labor convention in 1933: "The whole of the country has a common enemy; industry, agriculture, capital, labor are all engaged in fighting it. Just as in 1917 we are seeking to pull in harness; just as in 1917 horses that kick over the traces will have to be put in a corral."[120] General Johnson left no doubt of the intent of the President's words: "Labor does not need to strike under the Roosevelt plan. . . . The plain stark truth is that you cannot tolerate strikes. Public opinion . . . will break down and destroy every subversive influence." Far from operating a "labor government," as conservatives charged, the New Dealers in 1933 deeply resented strikes as acts of "aggression" that sabotaged the drive for recovery. Frances Perkins recalled Johnson's belief that "during the period when NRA was attempting to revive industry no stoppage of work could be tolerated under any circumstances. It was like a stoppage of work in war time. Anything had to be done to prevent that."[121]

The World War I experience suggested that if an administrator spurned direct government sanctions but was determined to have his way, the only methods left to him were bluster or vigilantism.[122] On one occasion, the War Industries Board's price-fixing committee had warned a producer to cooperate, or become "such an object of contempt and scorn in your home town that you will not dare to show your face there." Ray Lyman Wilbur, chief of the conservation division of the Food Administration, recalled: "Indiana I found the best organized state for food conservation that I had yet seen. The people were approaching rapidly the stage where violations of wheatless days, etc., were looked upon as unpatriotic enough to require that inquiries as to the loyalty of the guilty citizen, baker or hotel-keeper be made."[123]

The New Dealers never ran to such excesses, and FDR's program, happily, differed in important respects from the World War I administration. As the historian Ronald Schaffer has pointed out:

> Wilson relied on dollar-a-year men, who after the Armistice returned to private employment. Roosevelt constructed a standing bureaucracy. During the Depression years, the federal government had no central propaganda agency like the Creel Committee. It was considerably more tolerant of dissent from the left and showed almost no interest at all in managing the morals of the American people. Unlike Wilson's war administration, the New Deal, particularly after 1934, projected an image of hostility toward big business and, instead of building public esteem for businessmen as wartime agencies had done, occasionally attacked and always overshadowed them.[124]

Yet they were not beyond resorting to social coercion, and they matched the war administrators in bluster. "I have no patience with people who fol-

low a course which in war time would class them as slackers," declared
Attorney General Homer Cummings with regard to the alleged hoarders
of gold. "If I have to make an example of some people, I'll do it cheer-
fully."[125] When Frances Perkins hit out at the effort of the steel industry
to elude the intent of section 7(a) of the National Industrial Recovery Act
by setting up company unions, she denounced these subterfuges as "war
bridegrooms," the popular epithet for matrimonial draft-dodging during
the war. In like manner, after the economist Oliver W. M. Sprague
resigned in protest at the Administration's gold-buying policy, Hugh
Johnson accused him of "deserting with a shot in the flank of the army in
which he had enlisted." During the Blue Eagle drive, Donald Richberg
maintained that in a time of crisis there could be "no honorable excuse for
the slacker who wastes these precious moments with doubting and debate,
who palsies the national purpose with legalistic arguments." A *New
Republic* columnist remarked: "What administration officials—half-con-
sciously, half-unconsciously—want to do is to create a war psychosis in
which any corporation head attempting to defy Mr. Roosevelt and the
N.R.A. will be at once identified by the country with Kaiser Bill,
Hindenburg, Ludendorff and Grover Bergdoll."[126]

Such statements infuriated conservatives. Senator Carter Glass of
Virginia found particularly galling Richberg's denunciation of NRA opponents as "slackers who deserved to have white feathers pinned on them by
the women of the country." Glass wrote of Richberg's war record: "He
never heard a percussion cap pop; he did not know the smell of gun pow-
der; he did not even reach a training camp to learn the difference between
'Forward March' and 'Parade Rest.' When asked by a responsible newspaperman to give his war record in justification of his vituperative assault on
other people, he could do no better than allege he had helped sell some
Liberty bonds." Glass's resentment was shared by other right-wing critics.
"The man who lives well within his income," protested Lewis Douglas,
"has come to be regarded as unpatriotic and as a slacker in the fight against
the depression."[127]

The rhetoric of coercion also troubled a number of the New Dealers. In
the summer of 1933 a group of AAA officials protested:

General Johnson, in picturing the results of his campaign, has frequently used the analogy of the war-time "gasless Sundays." Then,
General Johnson recalls, if a man drove a car on Sunday, his neigh-

bors pushed the car into the ditch. Popular opinion at that time was so inflamed that it expressed itself by violence.

General Johnson's analogy is profoundly significant and disturbing. If his program is adopted, professional drive organizations will soon reappear in full force. Agitators may take advantage of the possible resulting hysteria to set group against group, such as farmers against wage earners, and thus defeat the real progress toward cooperation already made by the Roosevelt Administration.[128]

Some even thought they detected in Johnson's administration of the NRA the glimmerings of a corporate state.[129] But if such was Johnson's purpose—and the grounds for supposing that are unsubstantial—the General received no encouragement. When Harry Woodring, Assistant Secretary of War, wrote early in 1934 that the Army stood prepared to organize the CCC, veterans of World War I, and reliefers into a corps of "economic storm troops," the White House reprimanded him. In late 1934 the authoritarian-minded Johnson was let go. That same year Henry Wallace, seeking to pursue a "middle course," wrote: "There is something wooden and inhuman about the government interfering in a definite, precise way with the details of our private and business lives. It suggests a time of war with generals and captains telling every individual exactly what he must do each day and hour."[130]

Most of all, the Brandeisian faction of the New Dealers objected to the crisis exhortations. Felix Frankfurter wrote Louis Brandeis: "Much too much of 'slacker' talk & old coercions."[131] For the Brandeisians, the "enemy" was not the Depression but big business, and they also distrusted autocratic government. They were uncommunicative in 1933, though, when the New Dealers were emphasizing a war spirit of cooperation and coordination, in part because they feared that the bonds that held society together might be snapped. By 1935 the crisis had been weathered, and the mood of war seemed inappropriate. Brandeisians felt free to assault concentrated corporate power; other New Dealers lost faith in their ability to convert businessmen; and corporation executives increasingly viewed Roosevelt as their foe.

As in wartime, the first enthusiasm when the troops marched to the front had given way to the realization that the army was not invincible, the casualty lists would be long, and the prospect of early victory was no longer promising. Yet the danger of annihilation had been averted too, and as the sense of urgency lessened, the spirit of national solidarity slackened. After a time the New Deal no longer had anything resembling, in the economist Richard Adelstein's phrase, "the lubricating consensus and cooperation on which the success of wartime planning had been based." And "the enemies who began to emerge in the eyes or the imagination of men," as the historian Paul Conkin has observed of the end of the "wartime effort" in 1935, "were not such as could demand the hostility of all Americans, for these enemies were not natural, or providential, or foreign, but human and native. A class and group consciousness was forming."[132]

IX

Yet the rhetoric of war persisted, even when the agencies of mobilization such as the NRA died. In the summer of 1936 Representative Doughton observed: "Of course in every War, if it has a chance at all to be successful, there must be a leader, and this Administration and the Congress have been engaged in a war on hunger, destitute [sic], unemployment, bankruptcy and every evil incident to the economic life of our people." In his presidential campaign that year, Roosevelt told a Massachusetts crowd that, like Marshal Joffre at the First Battle of the Marne, he bore the blame for victory or defeat. "Three and a half years ago we declared war on the depression," the President asserted. "You and I know today that war is being won." But he was quick to point out that the victory had not yet been gained. The country still needed the services of its commander-in-chief. By then, however, references to war had become purely rhetorical.[133] When, that very year, the Administration explored the possibility of using the war power, and especially the precedent of Wilson's War Labor Policies Board, to justify federal regulation of the hours of labor, it concluded that the idea was not feasible.[134]

Only the New Dealers committed to a planned economy held fast to the earlier vision. As late as the summer of 1939 Tugwell looked back wistfully toward the war collectivism. He pleaded for a reorientation of progressive thought away from the traditional emphases on freedom for business, a change that only a crisis like that of 1917 or 1929 would produce. Of the two, Tugwell thought that war offered the better hope, for 1929 had yielded only "atomistic reforms" while World War I had resulted in "national organization on a unitary scheme." "How different it was in 1917!" Tugwell wrote. "It was possible . . . to make immense advances toward industrial unity. . . . That great wartime release of energy was achieved by freeing men's minds. Quantities and qualities could be thought of rather than profits." No sane person would wish a war in order to bring about a "purposive national organization," he acknowledged. "Yet the fact is that only war has up to now proved to be such a transcending objective that doctrine is willingly sacrificed for efficiency in its service."[135]

With each passing year, as the challenge of the Fascist powers became more blatant, the demands of foreign affairs superseded the claims of domestic issues, and New Deal agencies increasingly directed their attention to preparing for the eventuality of war with the Axis. In 1938 the TVA boasted that it was "developing the power necessary for the large-scale operation of war industries in this well-protected strategic area." The furnaces at Muscle Shoals, it reported, were being utilized to turn out phosphorus, a material "used in war for smoke screens and incendiary shells," and the TVA's electric furnaces, the agency foresaw, "might be converted to the electrolytic manufacture of aluminum or of chlorine—used in war gases."[136]

Henry Wallace had long believed that the AAA was an "adjustment" program whose machinery could be used to increase output as well as to limit it. If there were a conflict beyond the ocean, a prospect he dreaded, the United States, he observed as early as 1934, could, through the Triple A, "provision a war . . . with far less of that plunging, uninformed and altogether unorganized overplanting which got us into so much trouble during and after the last great war." A week before the outbreak of hostilities in Europe in September 1939, Wallace wrote the President that if war came, the government might consider developing plans modeled on the Food Administration with which Wallace had worked in World War I. "When we set up County Committees in AAA in 1933, I couldn't help thinking what a splendid mechanism we would have, if we ever got into a war, to meet the food problem. . . . Again when we set up the Ever Normal Granary System, I thought how marvelously this mechanism with its reserve supplies would help the country in case of war."[137]

In 1939 James V. Forrestal, who was shortly to become Undersecretary of the Navy, tried to persuade New Dealers that the way to put across their program was to sell it as preparedness rather than reform; after all, the TVA had originated in the Defense Act of 1916.[138] He won few converts—most liberals refused to adopt a strategy that surrendered the theology of liberalism—but when the war in Europe led to a new emphasis on defense, the New Dealers were quick enough to adapt. A month after Hitler's invasion of Poland, Roosevelt instructed Wallace to phone all bureau chiefs to ask what their experience had been in World War I, and how the new emergency would affect them.[139]

Many soon found themselves running the new defense agencies. Leon Henderson controlled prices; AAA Administrator Chester Davis coordinated agriculture with defense requirements; and Brehon Somervell, who had directed the WPA in New York, took charge of military construction. Under such leadership, the NYA began to train aircraft mechanics; CCC workers developed target ranges and airports for the Army; TVA dams produced the energy for aluminum needed in bomber production; and REA electricity powered army camps and naval installations. New Dealers charged with developing labor policies turned repeatedly to the War Labor Board's precedents. When war came, the historian Arthur Schlesinger, Jr., has written, it "almost seemed an NRA reunion. The child of the War Industries Board, NRA was the father of the War Production Board. Leon Henderson, Donald Nelson, Sidney Hillman, Averell Harriman, William H. Davis, Isador Lubin, Edward R. Stettinius, Jr.—all had their training in national mobilization in the breathless days of 1933 and 1934."[140] Many of these men, it might be added, had first entered government service in World War I.

Precisely as the Keynesians had foreseen, defense and war demands detonated an economic boom. In the summer of 1940 Keynes noted that the United States had failed to achieve recovery because the volume of investment had been "hopelessly inadequate." The "dreadful experience" of war might teach the United States what it had failed to learn in peacetime. He predicted: "Your war preparation, so far from requiring a sacrifice, will be the stimulus, which neither the victory nor the defeat of the New Deal could give you, to greater individual consumption and a higher standard of life." Keynes observed sadly: "It is, it seems, politically impossible for a capitalistic democracy to organize expenditure on the scale necessary to make the grand experiment which would prove my case—except in war conditions."[141]

Keynes's remark was on target. The "grand experiment" of the New Deal had achieved much. But it had not created, or indeed in any serious sense even attempted to create, a new model for American society. The New Dealers resorted to the analogue of war because in the United States the sense of community is weak, the distrust of the State strong.

Up to a point, the metaphor of war and the precedent of World War I proved invaluable. They helped provide a feeling of national solidarity that made possible the New Deal's greatest achievement: its success in "nation-saving," in mending the social fabric. Furthermore, the heritage of World War I legitimated the New Deal's claim to represent an overarching national interest to which business and other parochial interests must conform. The war had proved that, at a time of crisis, the power of individuals with money to turn the nation's resources to their own benefit could be limited by the superior claim of the need to provide a "social minimum."[142] Since the war mobilization had brought to fruition much of progressivism, it offered a useful example for the New Dealers, and since wartime control of industry went much further than earlier efforts in acknowledging the place of the twentieth-century state, it was pertinent for challenges the New Deal confronted.

Yet in other respects the war analogue proved either treacherous or inadequate. The very need to employ imagery that was so often inappropriate revealed both an impoverished tradition of reform and the reluctance of the nation to come to terms with the leviathan state. Only in war or in a crisis likened to war was it possible to put aside inhibiting doctrines, create a sense of common purpose, and permit the government to act in the national interest. But once the war ended, or the sense of crisis dissipated, traditional doctrines once again prevailed. The country still had to find a way to organize collective action without resorting to war or its surrogate, and to face up to the problem of the relation of order to liberty that the power of the twentieth-century state entails.

World War II rescued the New Deal from some of its dilemmas and obscured others. In the war years, many of the New Deal programs were set aside—the WPA, the President said, had earned an "honorable discharge"—[143] and the New Dealers turned their talents to "manning the production line." The AAA helped increase farm production instead of restricting crops; the new industrial agencies sought to speed factory output rather than curtail it. Perhaps the greatest irony of the age of Roosevelt is the most familiar. Only in war was recovery achieved. Only in war did the country finally rescue that one-third of a nation ill-housed, illclad, and illnourished. Only in war was the "army of the unemployed" disbanded.

THREE

FDR and the Kingfish

[This essay evolved over a good many years. I first lectured on Huey Long in a course I taught at Harvard University in the spring of 1952, and he has been the subject of public lectures I have given at venues as distant as the University of Washington in Seattle and the U.S. Embassy at Grosvenor Square in London. I made the talk available to Ken Burns for his film on the Kingfish, and I learned a good deal from serving as a consultant on that excellent documentary. I also have profited from two generations of scholarship, notably the searching analysis of Alan Brinkley, which helped shape the article I published on this topic in *American Heritage* in its October–November issue, 1985. Since that piece appeared, I have made further changes, drawing upon manuscripts research and the most recent work by historians, particularly Anthony J. Badger, Betty Field, Glen Jeansonne, and William Ivy Hair.]

In May 1932 Louisiana's picaresque Senator, Huey Pierce Long, ended a train journey in Atlanta by telling a throng of newspapermen who awaited him at the depot to prepare for a headline-making announcement. After months of temporizing, he was finally ready to reveal whom he would support for his party's presidential nomination at the Democratic National Convention not many weeks away: the patrician governor of New York, Franklin Delano Roosevelt. They were an odd couple, and the choice was not one Huey had come to easily. Five months earlier, he had said of FDR: "He ran too poorly with Cox in 1920 and he would be certain to be beat." Even now he told a pro-Roosevelt Senator, "I didn't like your son of a bitch, but I'll be for him." In this unpromising fashion began an improbable alliance that soon would be transformed into the stormiest political rivalry of the decade: the conflict between FDR and the Kingfish (a sobriquet that derived from the immensely popular radio show "Amos 'n' Andy").

By the time his train pulled into the Atlanta station, Long had already established himself as a figure of national consequence, though he had not arrived in Washington until the start of the year. It had been a debut, however, that the capital was still talking about. There is a well-established rule that freshman Senators are supposed to be not only silent but also invisible. But on his first day in the upper house, Huey bounced onto the Senate floor, slapped one distinguished legislator on the back, poked an Old Guard Republican in the ribs, and ran around the chamber telling everyone the Kingfish had arrived—all the while puffing a big black cigar in violation of the rules. By the end of the week, Long had attracted more attention than had been accorded a newcomer in many years.

Some of this attention simply resulted from Huey's remarkable flair for focusing the spotlight on himself by deliberately flouting propriety. In 1930 he had created an international incident when the German consul at New Orleans and the commander of a German cruiser called on him in order to pay their respects to the governor of the state. The consul wore a morning coat; the commander full naval dress uniform, including epaulettes, plumed hat, and sword. Huey received them clad in a blue lounging robe over green silk pajamas and bright red slippers.

Long drew attention, too, because, at a time when twelve million were unemployed in the Great Depression, he was the best-known advocate of an ancient panacea: sharing the wealth. A few weeks after he took his seat in the Senate, he introduced a resolution to limit fortunes to $100,000,000—and divide up the residue. Huey explained: "Rockefeller and Morgan would sleep much safer tonight if they had one hundred million each under their pillow case than with a billion or two."

But perhaps the most important reason reporters crowded around Long was that he could decide who would get Louisiana's votes at the 1932 Democratic convention and would have a lot to say about the ballots of neighboring Mississippi as well. Once Huey decided to back FDR, he went all the way, and a number of observers credit him with making a crucial contribution to winning the presidential nomination for Roosevelt, especially through his frenetic labors to forestall a movement to desert FDR on the critical third ballot. At one point, referring to the rule that at the time would bind a state's entire delegation to one candidate, he told Mississippi Senator Pat Harrison, "If you break the unit rule, you sonofabitch, I'll go into Mississippi and break you." (Asked about that remark later, the Kingfish conceded, "It is possible that I did make some such statement in the Chicago convention.") "There is no question in my mind," the Bronx County boss, Edward J. Flynn, later declared, "but that without Long's work Roosevelt might not have been nominated."

Long's performance at the convention proved to be the beginning of the end of his brief association with Roosevelt. Imbued with a sense of his own importance, he was determined to play a major role in the campaign and to shape FDR's policies. He even wanted the Democratic National Committee to give him a train outfitted with loudspeakers all for himself, so that he could go off on a romp across the continent that would make him, rather than FDR, the featured star of the 1932 campaign. Instead, the Democratic campaign manager, Jim Farley, shunted him off to the Great Plains, where he could do little harm. As it turned out, he was a sensation. "We never underestimated him again," Farley said. Roosevelt, though, kept him at arm's length.

Distressed at his inability to win from FDR the kinds of commitments he sought, Huey made no secret of his displeasure. On one occasion, shortly after the convention, he was heard yelling over a phone: "God damn it, Frank, don't you know who nominated you? Why do you have . . . those Wall Street blankety blanks up there to see you? How do you think it looks to the country? How can I explain it to my people?"

Roosevelt and Long met for the first time at Hyde Park in October 1932. Garishly dressed, treating the Democratic nominee with condescension, Huey behaved so boorishly that he provoked FDR's doting patrician mother to ask in a voice loud enough to be heard, "Who is that *awful* man?" Afterward, Long commented dismissively on Roosevelt, "He's not a strong man, but he means well." Huey knew, though, that he was getting nowhere with the man destined to be the next president. Following a session at Warm Springs shortly after the election, Long reported, "When I talk to him, he says 'Fine! Fine! Fine!' But [Senate Majority Leader] Joe Robinson goes to see him the next day and again he says 'Fine! Fine! Fine!' Maybe he says 'Fine!' to everybody."

The climactic encounter took place at the end of the First Hundred Days of 1933. Throughout that early springtime of the New Deal, Long had noised his objections to a good number of FDR's proposals and not a few of his appointees. When he arrived at the White House, he was in a cocky, even insolent, mood. He wore a sailor straw hat that he kept on his head, save when he used it to tap the President on the knee or elbow to make a point. Roosevelt never blinked. But by the close of the interview the Senator understood that none of the vast federal patronage destined for Louisiana was going to go to him. By the end of the summer they had parted ways.

In a trenchant paragraph, Alan Brinkley has asked:

Why had it happened? And why so quickly? By any normal standards, there seemed to be every reason for both Long and Roosevelt
to avoid a public falling out. The President, in the first critical days
of an Administration that faced an uncertain future, could hardly
have been eager to win the enmity of a powerful and increasingly
popular member of his own party. And Long, whose national reputation was still in its earliest stages of development, would seem to
have had little to gain from a break with the man who had won the
overwhelming confidence of the American people.

Observers differed about what caused the rupture. Some thought they separated because the Kingfish had been disappointed in patronage. Long
said it was because he disagreed with FDR's policies. Huey never under-
rated Roosevelt's political charm, but he apparently did not have much
respect for his program or his mind. The real reason for the break, though,
was surely more complex.

Few rivalries of the 1930s cut so deeply as the conflict between
Roosevelt and Long. Each held or was bidding for national power at a time
when, in much of the world, totalitarianism was coming to seem the wave
of the future. Roosevelt was one of many who feared that unless certain
social changes were made peacefully, they would ultimately be made vio-
lently. Unless responsible leaders gave new hope to the country, democracy
might not survive. For the President and his circle, the threat to democracy came from two sources: the Old Guard conservatives who resisted
change, and men such as Huey Long who would exploit popular discontent if change were not achieved.

Roosevelt and Long each sensed that, like gunslingers in a Western cow-
town, there was not room enough in Washington for both of them. The
historian T. Harry Williams has contended: "Two great politicians had
come into unavoidable conflict. Each was so constructed that he had to
dominate other and lesser men. Neither could yield to the other without
submerging himself and dimming his destiny. And instinctively each recognized the other's greatness, and feared it."

The Louisiana Senator could not help but be aware of the obstacle FDR
constituted to his ambitions. A contemporary commentator wrote of
Long: "Obviously he cannot succeed while the country still has hopes of

the success of the New Deal and trusts the President. Huey's chances depend on those sands of hope and trust running out." "Long's resentment of the president," Glen Jeansonne has pointed out, "was almost pathological." Indeed, one of Huey's followers observed, "He really believed that anyone with a physical deformity was bad or affected in other ways. He would quote the Bible to the effect God had put his mark on such people. I have heard him . . . say this about FDR."

The President, in turn, recognized that if he stumbled, the Kingfish would be there to pick up the pieces, and he found that prospect frightening. "That is a man totally without principle," he told his son Elliott, who remarked: "The Kingfish was no joke to my parent. To his keen eyes, Huey Long had much in common with Mussolini who, by promising the impossible had made no scruples about the route he would choose to get there." Roosevelt said to an aide: "It's all very well for us to laugh over Huey. But actually we have to remember all the time that he really is one of the two most dangerous men in the country." Long, he noted, was one of a number of demagogues—Father Coughlin was another—who were haranguing the country in a Hitler-like fashion. (Asked if he had Coughlin in mind as the second of the dangerous men, the President answered, "Oh, no, the other is Douglas MacArthur.")

Long's Louisiana served as a model for the kind of despotism the New Dealers feared the country might experience if they did not succeed, for in that state, Huey had come a considerable way toward creating a personal dictatorship. As Brinkley has noted, Long "terrorized the legislature into doing his bidding almost at will. He intimidated the courts and virtually destroyed their independence. He dominated the state bureaucracy so totally that even the lowest level of government employees served only at his pleasure. . . . He surrounded himself constantly with police and armed bodyguards—hard, occasionally brutal men." He carried on vendettas against even the most unimportant of his critics; his bodyguards mauled hecklers; and only the charred remains were left of the printing presses of some of his opponents. To bring the opposition press of New Orleans and Shreveport in line, Long ordered a tax on receipts of newspapers with a large circulation. "The newspapers are the charmed free bull of this country," the Kingfish said. The legislature whooped through this "tax on lying," but the U. S. Supreme Court subsequently struck it down in a unanimous decision.

Even Long's most sympathetic biographer, T. Harry Williams, has conceded:

He wanted to do good, but for that he had to have power. So he took power and then to do more good seized still more power, and finally the means and the ends became so entwined in his mind that he could not distinguish between them, could not tell whether he wanted power as a method or for its own sake. He gave increasing attention to building his power structure, and as he built it, he did strange, ruthless, and cynical things.

Little wonder that readers of *All the King's Men* have seen Huey in Robert Penn Warren's Willie Stark.

"This is my university," Long said of Louisiana State University. "I can fire a thousand of these students and get ten thousand in place of them any time I feel like it." When he learned that a student newspaper planned to carry a letter critical of him, he ordered the presses stopped and the letter deleted. He sent a squad of state troopers to see that the edict was carried out. The University suspended the editor and five members of the staff. Huey explained: "I like students, but this State is puttin' up the money for that college, and I ain't payin' anybody to criticize me."

Long made a point of showing his contempt for the democratic process. Asked how the Kingfish had built his majority in the legislature, one Long leader explained, "They all didn't come for free." Huey, who said of one legislator, "We got that guy so cheap we thought we stole him," boasted that his legislature was "the finest collection of law-makers money can buy." (Years later, his brother Earl, who became a memorable governor of Louisiana, remarked: "Huey used to buy the Legislature like a sack of potatoes. Hell, I never bought one in my life. I just rent 'em. It's cheaper that way.") Everyone has some skeleton in his closet, Huey believed. "I can frighten or buy ninety-nine out of every hundred men," he bragged.

Huey's legislators performed like automatons. When one of them did not vote during the balloting on the newspaper tax, Long, a national official with no authority whatsoever in the state government in Baton Rouge, raced to his seat and cried, "This man votes yes!" While U.S. Senator, he handed one session of the legislature forty-four bills. In little more than two hours, the legislature adopted all forty-four. Told by one lawmaker that his intervention was unconstitutional, Long replied, "I'm the constitution round here."

At a time when democracy on the European continent was going under to totalitarianism, Huey seemed particularly menacing. Many likened him to Hitler and Mussolini, who also seemed preposterous early in their careers, but who gained power nonetheless. One commentator wrote in July 1935, "Unlike the German intelligentsia, who could not judge from experience what Hitler might do, Americans may turn the pages of Louisiana's recent history for . . . insight into the sort of country we would have if Long became our Hitler." A well-respected Washington columnist agreed. "In Huey Long was a potential American Hitler," Thomas Stokes later wrote. "I say that advisedly. I knew the man. I knew the land from which he sprang. I knew his abilities and I knew the desperation to which he appealed."

A number of historians have protested applying the term "fascist" to Long, or regarding him as "the Mississippi valley rendering of Il Duce," and with good reason. He had elaborated no antidemocratic ideology, no conception of a corporate state. "Long's political fantasies," Arthur Schlesinger, Jr., observes, "had no tensions, no conflicts, except of the most banal kind, no heroism or sacrifice, no compelling myths of class or race or nation." Unlike other southern demagogues, Long did not rise to power by racist rhetoric against blacks. (One consequence was that in Monroe, Louisiana, a black family named their newborn after him, Huey P. Newton.) Though there were serious incidents of suppression of civil liberties in Louisiana, Long, to the end of his life, was openly attacked by most of the newspapers of his state. The mayor of New Orleans felt free to address him as "Huey Long, you cringing coward" and to call him "a political degenerate, moral leper, . . . and Al Capone" who "would end in an insane asylum." Long's political beliefs, a number of writers have stressed, were not imported from abroad but were native to American soil, the culmination of a time-honored line of agrarian dissent.

Yet it is also true that Long—far more than has sometimes been acknowledged—did represent a threat to democracy. His hostility to voluntaristic associations—from labor unions to bar organizations—suggested a totalitarian mentality. His contempt for legislatures, his vengeful, even sadistic, politics, and, most of all, his vaulting ambition, constituted a distinct menace. If Long did not engage much in "nigger-baiting," he did resort to racist argot, shunned counsel from black leaders, and indulged racists in his organization such as Leander Perez. That Long's ideas were indigenous to the American tradition of protest made him more rather than less ominous.

Writers interested in the taxonomy of politics, though, have always found Long's ideas hard to categorize. They have been puzzled, in particular, by questions such as whether Long was to the left or the right of Roosevelt. Huey himself viewed all the efforts to classify him with droll detachment. "Hell, I've got a university down in Louisiana that cost me 15,000,000 dollars that can tell you why I do like I do," he once remarked. In the cadence of W. C. Fields, Long instructed a journalist, "Never explain, my boy, never explain. Explanation is the mother of sectarianism." FDR himself had a simpler view—that his struggle with Long represented a contest between democracy and dictatorship. And so it did. But it was something else, also—a conflict between two rival traditions of reform.

Though Roosevelt has sometimes been thought of as a descendant of Populist reformers, it is rather Long who is in the Populist tradition, and FDR is better understood as a foe of the heirs of Populism. Long came from Winn Parish, the birthplace of Populism in Louisiana. His slogan, "Every Man a King," derived from a line in William Jennings Bryan's "Cross of Gold" speech: "Every man a king, but no man wears a crown." While Roosevelt's approach reflected the outlook of an eastern seaboard patrician, Huey voiced the aspirations of rural southerners who had known bitter deprivation. As a consequence, not only his program but also his style differed markedly from FDR's.

Long had come to power by challenging rule by an upper class oligarchy that was arguably the most reactionary and surely the most corrupt in the country. It had three elements: the planters, the corporations (especially oil), and the New Orleans ring headed by the urban boss Martin Behrman. (It was Behrman who, on one occasion, rejected a proposal for a new civic auditorium in the style of a classical Greek theater with the comment, "There aren't enough Greeks living here to make it worthwhile.") This alliance cared for little save its own interests. In literacy, a crucial index of the social rewards of any political system, Louisiana ranked last in the nation, with an illiteracy rate many times higher than in neighboring Mississippi. Anyone who came to power as a consequence of overturning such a regime would inevitably carry with him attitudes toward the establishment vastly different from those of a man like Roosevelt.

In his classic study of southern politics, the political scientist V. O. Key wrote:

As good a supposition as any is that the longer the period of unrestrained exploitation, the more violent will be the reaction when it comes. Louisiana's rulers controlled without check for a long period.

In other states there arose spokesmen for the masses who gave the people at least hope. Louisiana had no Blease [of South Carolina] or Watson [of Georgia] or Vardaman [of Mississippi] to voice the needs and prejudices of ordinary men. . . . Louisiana . . . was a case of arrested political development. Its Populism was repressed with a violence unparalleled in the South, and its neo-Populism was smothered by a potent ruling oligarchy.

When Long overturned the old order in Louisiana, he did more than just win an election; he triggered a political revolution. He gave lower-income rural whites from the forks of the creek, for the first time, their day in the sun. In 1928 fifteen thousand people—sunbonneted women and galloused men—swarmed into Baton Rouge to see one of their own elevated to the governorship. Huey's victory spelled success for a politics of revenge—"a fantastic vengeance upon the Sodom and Gomorrah that was called New Orleans," as Hodding Carter noted. "A squaring of accounts with the big shots, . . . Standard Oil and the bankers, the big planters, the entrenched interests everywhere." Long's strength, noted the novelist Sherwood Anderson, came from "the terrible South that Stark Young and his sort ignore . . . the beaten, ignorant, Bible-ridden, white South. Faulkner occasionally really touches it. It has yet to be paid for."

Franklin Roosevelt derived from a quite different tradition. He felt kinship with those post-Populist reformers, the Progressives, the followers of Theodore Roosevelt and Woodrow Wilson who feared and despised Populism as an uprising of the ignorant, the suspicious, the envious, the unsuccessful. Teddy Roosevelt, not surprisingly, was one of Franklin Roosevelt's childhood heroes, and FDR had been a member of Wilson's junior cabinet. Theodore Roosevelt and Woodrow Wilson had sought to rescue the reform movement from the rural fundamentalists and direct it in channels of respectability that the urban middle class would accept. This legacy—the reform attitude of the Establishment—which Franklin Roosevelt shared with T. R. and Wilson could find no space for the ambitions of a Huey Long.

FDR's conception of politics derived from the gentry. It was nourished by an aristocratic view of the reformer-statesman as the paladin of the lowly. In the novels of Roosevelt's youth—in the political romances of writers like the American novelist Winston Churchill—a Galahad from the ranks of the well-born battles the machine, purifies the corrupt legislature, and routs the evil combine, all the while wooing the heroine who is breathless at the hero's daring in entering the political arena. In the final scene, evil has been undone, and hero and heroine ride off in their coach to live happily forever after—on their inherited income.

Huey shared no such fantasies. His idols came from the pages of Ridpath's *History of the World*—kings, conquerors, potentates—and it was unadorned power, the power of an Alexander, that made the greatest appeal. Long's model was Frederick the Great: "'You can't take Vienna, Your Majesty. The world won't stand for it,' his nit-wit ambassadors said. 'The hell I can't,' said old Fred. 'My soldiers will take Vienna and my professors at Heidelberg will explain the reasons why!'" Unlike FDR, Long had an antiromantic perception of the State. While Roosevelt took pride in his service as Assistant Secretary of the Navy in World War I and genuinely regretted he had not been in combat, Long deliberately evaded participation in the war, an event that held no appeal for him whatsoever. He even sought deferment on the grounds that he was a notary public. Asked why he had not fought for his country, Huey explained, "I was not mad at anybody over there."

From men such as Endicott Peabody at Groton, Roosevelt learned to conceive of public life as a duty the well-born owed to their country. To be sure, FDR could never conceal the gusto with which he took to politics, nor his ardor for social changes many in the Establishment found appalling, but he accepted the gentlemanly precept that the office seeks the man, not the man the office. Huey made no such disclaimer. Politics, for him and for his followers, represented an opportunity for advancement and rewards. Long was admitted to the bar at the age of twenty-one, and, as he himself recounted, "I came out of that courtroom running for office."

Implied in the Endicott Peabody tradition was a high seriousness about politics, and it was against such pretensions that Huey turned the weapon of humor. Long's wit was anti-Establishment. He expressed the derision of the self-educated for the cap and gown, of the laity for the clergy. He jeered at the claims of Roosevelt and the New Dealers to be disinterested public servants. They, like me, Huey insisted, want power. His behavior brings to mind Shakespeare's *Henry IV*, where Falstaff presides over his circle of followers just as Henry does over his court. Henry celebrates the martial, aristocratic virtues such as courage in battle, while Falstaff jeers that it is better to live ignobly than to die, especially to die for impersonal principle.

The values of the Prince must stand the test of Falstaff's disrespect for those values. In like manner, Long played Falstaff to FDR's Henry.

Well before he confronted the New Dealers, Huey had made a point of abusing the notables. As a young man, he nourished the truculent dislike of Winn Parish for planter culture and assumed the role of a country boy gleefully baffling, shocking, and outsmarting the city fellows. He delighted his rural followers by cutting upper-class political leaders down to size. On becoming governor, he took an unknown village doctor from the community of Ville Platte and put him in charge of one of the world's great medical centers. In explaining why he had removed from the post a physician "whose pappy is the Standard Oil's lawyer," Long said, "I'm tired of taking off my hat when I go to New Orleans. . . . The country people can hold the big jobs just like the city man." He sought from city people not just respect but deference. At one point, Governor Long demanded that Shreveport make a public apology to him; that its citizens "bow to him on the street and not scowl at him"; and, above all, that they stop "ignoring" him "from public functions." When Long reached the Senate, he set out purposefully to attack the most elevated persons he could reach. He mimicked the walk of Senators, taunted them to combat. Early in 1933 he deliberately baited the proud and respected Carter Glass until the elderly Virginia Senator rushed at him to thrash him.

Long turned the same weapon of ridicule and disrespect against Roosevelt and his circle. They, no less than the Louisiana planters and oil-men, he insinuated, belonged to the Establishment. He implied that when it came to a critical choice, most members of a privileged class, even reformers, prefer order to justice. He recognized that the progressive tradition had biases of its own—against rural protest and in support of the existing class structure, that even the new caste of professors in government had a stake in the system. The New Dealers, he sensed, were most vulnerable to the charge that they did not represent a new order but sustained the old order. "Maybe you see a little change in the men waiting on tables in the dining room," Huey said, "but back in the kitchen, the same set of old cooks are back there fixing up the vittles and the grub for us that cooked up that mess under Hoover. There has never even been a change of seasoning."

An episode in Washington early in 1933 revealed Huey's approach. Shortly before FDR's inauguration, Long barged into the room of one of the Brain Trusters at the Mayflower Hotel, kicking the door open as he went in. He grabbed an apple, took a big bite, and walked up to Norman

Davis, who epitomized the dignity of the international diplomat close to both Roosevelt and the House of Morgan. Tapping Davis's stark white shirtfront with the half-bitten apple, he shouted: "I don't like you and your Goddamned banker friends!"

After Long broke with the President, he mocked FDR's claim to be the leader of the forces of reform and refused to accord respect to the American chief of state. On a radio broadcast in 1935 he jeered at "Franklin De-lah-no Rosy-felt." The President's most important emergency agency, the National Recovery Administration, he found a particularly inviting target. NRA, the Kingfish said, meant "Nuts Running America." He took the NRA's Blue Eagle off the masthead of the newspaper of his movement, and put in its place "a mangy looking bird turned upside down." Long thumbed his nose, too, at FDR's Cabinet officers. The Secretary of Agriculture he dismissed as "Lord Corn Wallace."

Often his barbs appeared to be fired at random, but they were all aimed at making a single point—that he, not Roosevelt, should be the country's leader. His posthumously published *My First Days in the White House* made that contention explicit by effecting, however good naturedly, a reversal of roles. In that slim literary effort, Huey pictures himself as president, and, after naming Herbert Hoover Secretary of Commerce, demotes FDR to Secretary of the Navy. When Roosevelt protests that he does not regard his new assignment highly, Long asks, "Why not Frank?" Well, it was a terrible fall from the presidency, Roosevelt answers. "You sound just like Hoover," Huey replies, "but he couldn't call to mind any position he held just now." At that riposte, Roosevelt chuckles and promises the new president that he will hear from him.

Though Huey deliberately played the role of clown, he was no fool. "He had, combined with a remarkable capacity for hard, intellectual labor, an extraordinarily powerful, resourceful, clear and retentive mind, an instrument such as is given to very few men," wrote Raymond Moley. His briefs before the Supreme Court were praised by both Chief Justice Taft and Justice Brandeis. When Huey got up to speak at the Democratic National Convention in 1932, the historian Claude Bowers later noted, "there was a general fear that he would mutilate the English language, tear a passion to tatters, make a vulgar exhibition and humiliate the party." Instead, "speaking rapidly in excellent English and with closely knit logic, he made one of the strongest and most dignified speeches of the convention." Bowers added, "It was a revelation to me that there was a Huey Long quite distinct from the frothing demagogue with whom the public was familiar."

The Washington correspondent of the *New York Times* agreed: "His speech in behalf of the legality of his delegates in '32 was the finest legal argument that anybody has ever heard—or that I ever heard—at a National Convention. He dropped all the clowning. He dropped the hillbilly stuff. Huey wasn't the rustic he pretended to be. He was a brilliant man and a very fine lawyer."

It served Long's purposes, however, to play the buffoon. By parodying the New Deal, he drew national attention away from Roosevelt and toward himself and softened the impression that he was a Louisiana autocrat. Instead of appearing as a would-be dictator, Huey created a picture of a lovable, amiable, harmless soul, an affable country philosopher. At one point he even stirred up a national controversy between dunkers and crumblers of cornpone and got Emily Post to render the verdict: "When in Rome, do as the Romans do."

If Long had been nothing more than a jester, though, he would only have been a seven-day wonder. He got as far as he did because his achievements in Louisiana commanded attention, especially from people disenchanted with the New Deal. Unlike many other demagogues, Huey was an innovator and a lawgiver. He was even called "the first Southerner since Calhoun to have an original idea." With a vivid sense of the iconography of politics, Long dismantled the structure of the old regime to make way for a new era in Louisiana. He built a modern skyscraper capitol that symbolized the new commonwealth he was creating on the ruins of the old. (Mark Twain had said of the old gingerbread capitol: "That comes from too much Walter Scott.") He also tore down the antiquated Governor's mansion and built a new Executive Mansion in Baton Rouge on the model of the White House, in order, it was explained, so that he would be "used to it when he got there."

But these actions were only symbolic. Long did a great deal more. He sponsored the state's first income tax law, eliminated the poll tax, revamped the barbarous state institutions for the insane, considerably expanded public health facilities, and initiated the greatest road-building program of any state in the Union. When he took office, Louisiana had less than three hundred miles of concrete roads, only three bridges; seven years later, there were more than thirty-seven hundred miles of paved, though narrow, highways and forty bridges. He distributed free textbooks to students and taxed the oil companies to pay for them. (Huey insisted: "What the good Lord put into the ground for the people of Loozyanna ain't a-goin' to come out unless something is paid on it. When these fellows suck an oil well dry, we want a new schoolhouse somewhere.") He instituted night schools to cope with the state's illiteracy, and by the time he left for Washington in 1932, one hundred thousand men and women had been taught to read, write, and cipher.

Long made significant contributions, too, to the development of Louisiana State University. He had once said, "Our kind don't need college." But as governor, he expanded considerably upon the work begun by his predecessor. He built LSU a first-rate medical school as well as a School of Art and Music ("there's eighty-seven grand pianos in that building," Huey boasted; "if you want to count 'em you'll find Huey's right"). By cutting tuition, he brought about a dramatic increase in enrollment. Long, the essayist Harold McSween has written, "stroked [LSU] as if he had been coddling a newborn pet elephant. During the last seven years of his life, during fiscal stringency in all other American states, Huey force-fed LSU with increasing appropriations while other universities were retrenching." McSween adds:

> When Huey became governor, LSU was understaffed and under-built: an Italian Renaissance village on a former sugar plantation large enough to have accommodated Renaissance Padua. With a few more than 1500 full-time students and a faculty of 168 members, it ranked 89th in enrollment among American universities and held a "C" rating from the Association of State Universities. Never had it awarded a doctorate. By the time of Huey's death LSU's enrollment was approaching 6,000, its faculty 400, including that of a new medical school that he inaugurated as if overnight. LSU's graduate school . . . had begun an ambitious doctoral regimen. The LSU Press had appeared. Its "C" rating, notwithstanding Huey's occasional indiscretions in impinging on academic freedom, . . . had improved to "A." LSU had become the thirteenth largest American university, the ninth largest state university.

The distinguished literary critics Robert Penn Warren and Cleanth Brooks joined the faculty; *The Southern Review* was launched; and in 1934 in Baton Rouge the Southern Historical Association was founded and *The Journal of Southern History* begun.

A generation later Robert Penn Warren, writing of his experiences as an assistant professor at LSU in the age of the Kingfish, recalled classrooms at "Huey Long's university":

> Among the students there sometimes appeared . . . that awkward boy from the depth of the "Cajun" country or from some scrabble-farm in North Louisiana, with burning ambition and frightening energy and a thirst for learning; and his presence there, you reminded yourself, with whatever complication of irony seemed necessary at the moment, was due to Huey, and to Huey alone. For the "better element" had done next to nothing in fifty years to get the boy out of the grim despair of his ignorance.

With so much going on, it was not always easy to recognize that Long's programs had shortcomings too, especially when contrasted to FDR's emerging Welfare State. Unlike other reform governors, Huey left no shelf of social legislation. Louisiana under Long had no public welfare department, no unemployment compensation, no minimum wage law. The legislature he dominated would not appropriate funds for pensions for the aged or for mothers, and it opposed limiting the hours worked by women and children. "Picking cotton is fun for kids anyway," Huey said. He appointed a head of the prison system who fostered brutal policies including an increase in flogging. In 1932 Louisiana spent $30,561 on school libraries for whites, $818 on libraries for blacks; $1,521,604 to transport white pupils, $2,550 for blacks. Long did nothing to establish the right of collective bargaining, and when a union delegation protested the low wages on public works projects, he responded, "The prevailing wage is as low as we can get men to take it." Despite his dictatorial hold on Louisiana, he never tried to carry out Share the Wealth in the one place he could put it into practice. In fact, the state income tax let the rich off easy. Moreover, his regime was shamelessly corrupt. "Politics in Louisiana," Huey claimed, "is as clean as an angel's ghost," but, in fact, he even invited Frank Costello, the New York mobster, to run the slot machines in the state.

The historian Anthony J. Badger, in an astute assessment, has asserted: "The New Deal directly and tangibly benefited the underprivileged in Louisiana far more than did the Long machine. Long's reforms in the state had done almost nothing for the poorest sections of the community—the able-bodied unemployed, unemployables, and the rural poor. The New Deal, for all its many limitations, revolutionised provision for these groups." Though critical of FDR's treatment of Huey, Badger points out that at its height Huey's road construction projects engaged only 22,000 men, in contrast to more than 80,000 employed in Louisiana by the Civil Works Administration. The Long regime provided no relief at all for the jobless before 1933, whereas the Federal Emergency Relief Agency alone sustained 12 percent of the population of the state, and New Deal agencies lent or gave money to nearly half the tenant farmers of Louisiana, who got not a penny from the Kingfish. "There is no doubt," Badger concludes, "that the benefits of New Deal liberalism were both more generous and spread more widely than those of Long's business progressivism."

Nonetheless, Long's reign, though not only deficient but also undemocratic, also brought unprecedented change to Louisiana. At election time, the Kingfish could declare:

> They tell you that you've got to tear up "Longism" in this state. All right, my friends—get you a bomb or some dynamite and blow up that new state Capitol. Then go out and tear up the concrete roads I've built. Get your spades and your shovels and scrape the gravel off them roads we graveled and let a rain come in on 'em. That'll put 'em back like they was before I come. Tear down all the new buildings I've built at the university. And when your child starts to school tomorrow morning snatch the free textbooks out of his hands. Then, my friends, you'll be rid of Longism in this state—and not before.

With that record of performance in Louisiana, Long was able to mount an effective attack on the New Deal. He questioned whether Roosevelt was concerned with the welfare of the poor (after all, FDR had never known the hardships of Winn Parish), and he denied that the Administration had found the road to recovery. Long's assault came at a particularly embarrassing time: when, after the upturn of the First Hundred Days of 1933, the economy had come to a standstill. At precisely that point—in February 1934—Huey made his bid for national power by establishing a political organization with an arresting slogan: "Share Our Wealth."

Although the details of Long's program shifted from time to time, the main features remained constant. Huey proposed to liquidate all fortunes above a certain sum; from the fund the government would accumulate, every family would get enough to purchase a home, a car, and a radio, as well as an annual income. His plan also envisaged old-age pensions, scholarships for college, and some notions that bordered on the grandiose—a "war on disease" led by the Mayo brothers, a thousand new colleges staffed by one hundred thousand professors, and public works spending that would put surplus farmers to work on projects such as laying out golf courses. Though it was far from clear how he proposed to do so, Huey would redistribute not only cash but also real property and securities. "No, sir, money is not all of it by a jugful," he explained. "We are going to redistribute in kind so the poor devil who needs a house can get one from some rich bird who has too many houses; so the man who needs a bedstead can get one from the man who has more than he will ever need."

In vain did critics point out that the economic assumptions behind Huey's proposal were riddled with error. There were simply too many poor people and not enough millionaires for his numbers to come close to adding up, and, though he claimed to be a foe of the federal bureaucracy, he would have needed a *Gestapo* to carry out his redistribution scheme. Long himself acknowledged privately that his Share-Our-Wealth plan would not work, but confided, "When they figure that out, I'll have something new for them." But in a period when FDR was involved in such complicated operations as gold buying, code authorities, and deficit finance, Share Our Wealth had the appeal of a specificity of promise Roosevelt could not match.

His national organizer, Gerald L. K. Smith, a fifth-generation minister of the Disciples of Christ, knew just how to translate these specifics into popular idiom. A stump speaker of unrivaled power, who, it has been said, was a combination of Savonarola and Elmer Gantry, Smith urged his followers to "pull down these huge piles of gold until there shall be a real job, not a little old sow-belly, black-eyed pea job but a real spending money, beefsteak and gravy, Chevrolet, Ford in the garage, new suit, Thomas Jefferson, Jesus Christ, red, white and blue job for every man."

Share Our Wealth quickly took off, and in 1934 Long, who three years earlier had not even been a sectional leader, was winning national and even international notice. The French journal *L'Europe Nouvelle* published an article on "Huey Long contre Roosevelt," and H. G. Wells sailed across the Atlantic to interview the Senator. After talking to the Kingfish, Wells reported that he was "like a Winston Churchill who has never been at Harrow. He abounds in promise." For a while, it even seemed that Long might eclipse the President.

Roosevelt viewed these developments with grave concern, both because he understood that Long intended nothing less than to drive him from power and also because he feared what Long portended for the republic. "If I could," Roosevelt said from his wheelchair, "the way I'd handle Huey Long would be physically. He's a physical coward." In February 1935 Colonel Edward House warned the President, "Many people believe he can do to your administration what Theodore Roosevelt did to the Taft administration in '12," and that same month, after lunching with the President at the White House, the U. S. ambassador to Germany, William Dodd, who had been horrified by what he had witnessed in Berlin, recorded in his diary what Roosevelt had said to him:

> Long plans to be a candidate of the Hitler type for the presidency in 1936. He thinks he will have a hundred votes in the Democratic convention. Then he will set up as an independent with Southern and mid-western Progressives, Senator X___ and others. Thus he hopes to defeat the Democratic party and put in a reactionary Republican. That would bring the country to such a state by 1940 that Long thinks he would be made dictator. . . . Thus it is an ominous situation.

The Roosevelt administration responded to Long's challenge in a variety of ways. The President even toyed with the drastic notion of sending U.S. troops to restore republican government to the people of Louisiana, but he settled instead for encouraging the Treasury to look into troublesome rumors of tax evasion there, an employment of the Internal Revenue Office for political ends that historians have condemned as an abuse of the powers of his office. Early in 1934, shortly after FDR's friend and Hudson Valley neighbor, Henry Morgenthau, Jr., was confirmed as Secretary of the Treasury, thirty-two Treasury agents were installed at the Monteleone Hotel in New Orleans to investigate the finances of the Long crowd. In the fall of 1934 a grand jury indicted a number of Long's followers, including such important associates as Seymour Weiss and Abe Shushan, for income tax evasion, and by April 1935 one of Huey's men in the legislature had been sentenced to eighteen months in prison after being charged with failure to pay taxes on kickbacks he had received from highway contractors.

The President also stepped up his use of patronage against Long. That action meant not only denying federal jobs to Huey's supporters—at a time of mass unemployment when such positions were especially desirable—but also deliberately giving the posts to his enemies to enable them to build an effective rival organization. He did so even though most of Long's opponents were conservative opportunists. Early in February 1935 Roosevelt underscored his determination by scolding Cabinet officers and other key officials for awarding patronage to opponents of the Administration. Some people, he said, should be fired on principle. "In a delicate situation like Louisiana we may have to ask your advice," Secretary Wallace interposed. "You won't have to do that," the President replied forcefully. "Don't put anybody in and don't keep anybody that is working for Huey Long or his crowd! That is a hundred percent!" "That goes for everybody!" Vice President Garner chimed in. "Everybody and every agency," the President reiterated. "Anybody working for Huey Long is not working for us." Infuriated at these tactics, Long warned a New Deal official, "I'll be giving you . . . and that fucker in the White House unshirted hell every day from now on."

Roosevelt and his appointees hit out at Long, too, by denying Louisiana a share of New Deal spending. In March 1935 Secretary Morgenthau recorded in his diary: "The Vice-President said at Cabinet to-day: 'Don't give those people in New Orleans $1.00. Let them starve to death. If they get rid of Huey Long we will give them some money—otherwise we will not.' The President agreed with the Vice-President." The following month, when Long attempted to supervise the distribution of federal funds in Louisiana, he met his match in Public Works Administrator Harold Ickes, who announced that "no public works money is going to build up any Share-the-Wealth political machine." Huey answered: "We are doing the United States government a compliment when we let them do business with us." To which Ickes replied: "The emperor of Louisiana has halitosis of the intellect." (The President told his Secretary of the Interior that his riposte was "the best thing that has been said about Huey Long.") As rough a political foe as the Kingfish, Ickes withdrew a substantial amount of federal money that had been destined for Louisiana.

It has often been suggested that the most important response to Long came in the New Deal legislation of the Second Hundred Days of 1935.

Some writers believe that Roosevelt advanced reforms that year with the deliberate purpose of "stealing Huey's thunder." Two acts in particular are said to show Long's influence. The first was FDR's allocation of fifty million dollars to the National Youth Administration, an agency that, by giving part-time employment to students, offset the appeal of Long's plank for free college education. In June 1935 the President took another step that seemed more manifestly a response to Long: his "soak the rich" tax message, asking Congress for a revenue law based on the idea of redistributing the wealth. When FDR's message was being read to the Senate, the Kingfish, a big grin on his face, sauntered the floor of the chamber, jabbing his thumb at his chest. At the end of the reading, he cried "Amen." "For the time being," wrote the *Los Angeles Times*, "he has silenced Huey and taken him into camp. However hard it comes, the Kingfish must perforce applaud."

Yet it is by no means clear either that Roosevelt's ventures in the Second Hundred Days were undertaken as a rejoinder to Long or that they significantly diminished Huey's strength. Though it is often said that Roosevelt, like other shrewd statesmen, destroyed the appeal of men such as Long by sponsoring reforms that ended the discontent on which these men fed, that conclusion suffers from too rationalistic a conception of political behavior. Long won allegiance not simply by advocating specific programs but because he appealed to a whole constellation of loyalties and resentments that FDR could not, or would not, embody.

With each passing month, Long found it harder to restrain his assaults on Roosevelt. In mid-March 1933, even when noisily opposing measures that had originated in the White House, he was careful to combine these attacks with praise for "our great President" who had kept the faith. When some months later he openly criticized FDR, crowds in Louisiana booed him, compelling him to tone down his words while claiming credit for "my friend Roosevelt's" nomination in Chicago. In private he was less discreet. In December 1934 the mayor of New Orleans informed Morgenthau that Long had told his political lieutenants: "I have something on that SOB cripple in the White House that will keep him from doing anything against me. I know that he tours around in a boat with a degenerate and that if I ever spring that he can't touch me." (It was not at all clear to whom he was alluding.)

In 1935 Long abandoned all caution. In one speech, he declared: "Hoover is a hoot owl. Roosevelt is a scrootch owl. A hoot owl bangs into the roost and knocks the hen clean off and catches her while she's falling. But a scrootch owl slips into the roost and scrootches up to the hen and talks softly to her. And the hen just falls in love with him and the next thing you know, there ain't no hen." In July he told a New Orleans crowd: "I'm as big as President Roosevelt. Why, he's copying my share-the-wealth speeches now that I was writing when I was fourteen years old. So he's just now getting as smart as I was when I was in knee breeches." FDR, he said, was a "liar and a faker." He defied "them" to "indict me for that."

Long's conspicuous unwillingness to serve in the Army in World War I did not deter him, in the course of a speech on behalf of bonuses for veterans which Roosevelt opposed, from spinning out a fantasy of interrogating the President:

"How much money did you get for your services? Of course, sir, we know that you gave your services to the country during the World War as a matter of patriotism only; but how much did you get?"

". . . $10,000 for that year's work."

"How many cannon did you face, sir?"

"None."

"How many nights did you sleep on the ground, sir?"

"None."

"How many nights did you hear the rain on the tents? How many days and nights did you hear the crack of German rifles and endure the smell of poison gas? How many times did you see the flames of the burning fires of hell and destruction and carnage searing the lives and the souls of men?"

"None."

"And yet you got $10,000, Mr. Roosevelt, for the patriotic services which you gave to the country in the scourge of that war."

The vast following Long had acquired posed a serious threat to Roosevelt in itself, and if the Kingfish could align the supporters of the "Radio Priest" Father Coughlin, the old-age pension advocate Dr. Francis Townsend, and the farm leader Milo Reno behind him, he would be more potent still. Although for a moment he was silenced by FDR's tax message, within a short time he found occasion to quarrel with the President again and challenge his national leadership. That was a confrontation no one took lightly.

The Share-Our-Wealth clubs provided Long not merely with backing for his scheme but with a countrywide political organization, or at least mailing list, that might shape the outcome of the 1936 election, and Share Our Wealth was sweeping the country like a prairie fire. Estimates of membership totals have been placed at as high as eight million, with very considerable strength on the Pacific Coast to which Long had not yet gone. Raymond Moley, Roosevelt's former adviser, has written that the Administration came to feel that Long "could make himself political master of the whole, vast Lower Mississippi Valley—perhaps even of great hunks of the West. Who knew where Huey . . . would end?" A confidential poll conducted for the Democratic party in 1935 showed Long strength in all sections—from urban as well as rural America—and found that Huey, by pulling some 12 percent of the vote, would cost FDR large states such as New York, Illinois, Michigan, and Ohio in the next election. Party leaders were alarmed by the prospect that Long might split the Democrats in 1936, and even more by the fear that there appeared to be no limits to the power the Kingfish might ultimately have.

Maybe the Democrats worried too much. The subsequent fiasco of the Union party in 1936, a third party that attempted to unite the Long, Coughlin, and Townsend followers, demonstrated what Roosevelt had earlier foreseen. "There is no question that it is all a dangerous situation," he had confided to Colonel House in 1935, "but when it comes to Showdown these fellows cannot all lie in the same bed and will fight among themselves with almost absolute certainty." Moreover, many of Long's followers, however inconsistently, continued to admire FDR and showed no signs that they would be willing to abandon him in 1936. A Georgia women's club even proclaimed, "God Save the President . . . and His Instrument, Huey Long."

Yet in 1935 Huey was still only forty-two, and Roosevelt had a long way to go to get the country out of the Depression. Many wondered if the fates might be not with FDR but with the Kingfish. By 1935 Long's ambitions were boundless; so, many believed, were his prospects. And there was no mistaking his intent. "I can take him," Huey boasted. "He's a phony. I can out-promise him and he knows it. People will believe me and they won't believe him. His mother's watching him and she won't let him go too far. . . . He's living on inherited income." In a bid to be regarded altogether seriously as a presidential contender, Long began to dress less gaudily, and he hit the bottle less often. "I'll tell you here and now," he informed newspapermen late in the summer of 1935, "that Franklin Roosevelt will not be the next President of the United States. If the Democrats nominate Roosevelt and the Republicans nominate Hoover, Huey Long will be your next President."

"As God is my judge," Gerald L. K. Smith cried in 1935, "the only way they will keep Huey Long from the White House is to kill him." At least as early as 1934, Long's opponents were talking openly of violence as the one hope of ridding the state of the Senator and his cronies. The mayor of Shreveport announced, "If it is necessary to teach them decency at the end of a hempen rope, I for one am willing to swing the rope." In the spring of 1935, one of the few remaining Long opponents at Baton Rouge warned: "I am not gifted with second sight. . . . But I can see blood on the polished floor of this Capitol. For if you ride this thing through, you will travel with the white horse of death." Only a few months later the prophecy was confirmed—apparently not as the result of a conspiracy, as is sometimes charged, but as the act of a lone individual, unconnected with any organization.

It took place on the night of September 8, 1935, when the Louisiana legislature was meeting in special session to adopt a series of recommendations, some of which stunned even Huey's disciples. One, a redistricting measure, aimed to terminate the career of a Long opponent, Judge Benjamin Pavy. Another portended a constitutional crisis with the national government by providing for the imprisonment of federal officials, a bill the *Washington Post* characterized as "the broadest and boldest defiance of federal authority since the Civil War." Huey wandered around the legislative chamber that evening in his usual manner, as though he owned it, and then walked out into the corridor of the state capitol. At 9:30 P.M., a white-clad, bespectacled figure stepped out of the shadows from behind a pillar, approached Huey, and fired a small Belgian automatic pistol. Long's bodyguards and Capitol policemen emptied their guns into the assassin, whose bullet-ridden body was subsequently identified as that of Judge Pavy's son-in-law, Carl Austin Weiss. At twenty-nine one of the most highly regarded surgeons in the state, Dr. Weiss, who had seen the Dollfuss tyranny as a medical student in Vienna, had resented Long's vendetta against his family. He may possibly, too, have heard a rumor that Long was planning to revive an old canard that the Pavys, and hence Weiss's son, had Negro blood. Mortally wounded in the abdomen, Huey reeled down the stairs and into a car in a parking lot. Two days later he died.

The assassination of Long ended the only potentially serious political threat to FDR in the 1930s. The Share-Our-Wealth movement quickly disintegrated. Gerald L. K. Smith tried to seize control of the organization, but Long's henchmen in Louisiana would have none of him. They had no interest in sharing the wealth, no thirst for national power, merely a desire for plunder. As a Louisiana governor later explained: "I swore to uphold the Constitutions of Louisiana and the United States, but I didn't take any vow of poverty." At the 1936 Democratic convention, Long's lieutenants waved FDR banners and paraded the aisles for the great and good Franklin Delano Roosevelt.

When word got out that the President was planning to address the centennial fair in Texas, the Louisiana legislature did something absolutely extraordinary—it moved en masse to the next state in order to applaud him, the only time in the history of the country that a legislature has ever met in another state. The joint session of the legislature, convened in the Cotton Bowl, expressed gratitude that "Divine Providence . . . interceded and the people chose Franklin D. Roosevelt to lead and move the nation." The LSU band, the Kingfish's favorite, then serenaded the President. As the historian Betty Field has written, "How Huey's bones must have rattled!"

Roosevelt's critics charged that this happy denouement was the direct result of a deal the President had struck with the Louisiana machine. When the opponents of the Long organization went down to defeat in 1936, Roosevelt, with no viable alternative, did make an accommodation with Huey's heirs. That same year the tax prosecutions were dropped, and an anti–New Deal columnist raised an outcry about "the Second Louisiana Purchase." In fact, there is no evidence that Roosevelt influenced that decision. Nor did the Long crowd escape unscathed. Three years later another round of prosecutions resulted in the governor of Louisiana, the president of LSU, and other Long henchmen being sentenced to the penitentiary.

The Administration greeted Long's death with ill-concealed relief. A few weeks afterward, the Democratic national chairman, Jim Farley, remarked: "I always laughed Huey off, but I did not feel that way about him. He was good for that many votes," and then he went on to list a number of states that FDR would have lost if the Louisiana Senator had run for president. In his lengthy memoir and biography, Rexford Tugwell has reflected: "When he was gone it seemed that a beneficent peace had fallen on the land. Father Coughlin, Reno, Townsend, et al., were after all pygmies compared with Huey. He had been a major phenomenon."

Tugwell, one of the original members of the Brain Trust, has captured better than anyone Roosevelt's own response to the death of Long, his most troublesome rival. "I think he had really given Franklin concern for a bit," Tugwell writes. "It was not a happy circumstance that one of the most effective demagogues the country had ever known should be attacking with spectacular effect every move and every measure devised to meet the situation. It did get on Franklin's nerves. He must have regarded Huey's removal as something of a providential occurrence—one more sign that he himself moved under a star."

FOUR

The Election of 1936

[I wrote the first version of this essay, at the request of the editors, for Volume III of the four-volume *History of American Presidential Elections, 1789–1968*, edited by Arthur M. Schlesinger, Jr., and Fred L. Israel (New York: Chelsea House, 1971). My approach was influenced by what I learned as a member of the Government Department at Smith College in 1949–51 and as a Fellow at the Center for Advanced Study in the Behavioral Sciences at Stanford in 1961–62, where I had long conversations on the patterns of election returns with Warren Miller of the Survey Research Center at Ann Arbor. Subsequently, I spent a summer in Michigan as a Fellow at that Center. During these years also, starting in November 1964, I served as presidential elections analyst for NBC, first for Chet Huntley and David Brinkley and then for John Chancellor. In revising my original essay, I have incorporated additional research in recently opened papers such as those of Stanley High at the Roosevelt Library; have benefited from the work of scholars such as John Allswang, Kristi Anderson, and James Sundquist that was published since my essay appeared; and have scrutinized the controversy among political scientists about whether the realignment of the 1930s was, or was not, the consequence of "conversion."]

I

The historian who writes about the campaign of 1936 has one big advantage over the people who lived at the time—he knows how it all turned out. So decisive were the election totals that it seems, in retrospect, that everyone must always have recognized that the campaign would end in a landslide. But at the beginning of 1936, the outcome seemed very much in question. The January poll of the American Institute of Public Opinion asserted that if Roosevelt held five states listed as borderline Democrat, he would win, but by only twenty-five electoral votes. Much more alarming to the Democrats were the findings of the prestigious *Literary Digest* poll, that "*Great* and *Sure* Barometer" that had come within 1 percent of calling FDR's popular majority in 1932. When in the fall of 1935, the *Digest* asked what people thought of the New Deal, 63 percent of the straw ballots were negative; FDR's policies found approval in only twelve states, almost all in the South. "Roosevelt will not run as strongly in the coming election as he did before," confided Key Pittman, a loyal Senate Democrat. "The New England States will be solidly Republican." The Democratic National Committee's statisticians virtually wrote off New York and Illinois and saw only an outside chance for victory in Ohio, Indiana, and Minnesota. When the *Literary Digest* launched its presidential poll that summer, it stated, "Not since Hughes battled Wilson in 1916 have the lines been so sharply drawn, the outcome so in doubt."

To be sure, the Democrats had won resounding victories in 1932 and in the 1934 midterm elections, but they had enjoyed short-lived intervals of success before, under Cleveland and Wilson, only to have the country return to Republicanism. The nationally syndicated columnist Paul Mallon wrote in July 1935 that for three-quarters of a century, it had been understood "that this is a Republican country; that the Republicans alone can bring prosperity; that the voters merely chastise them occasionally, but always restore them to favor after a brief, unsatisfactory experience with the Democrats." The 1936 election would demonstrate whether Roosevelt's four-year tenure was only another such interregnum or whether his election in 1932 marked the beginning of a significant realignment.

The 1936 election would also give the country its first opportunity in a national contest to indicate whether Big Government was to be a permanent feature of American society. In little more than two years, the New Deal had established such novel agencies as the Agricultural Adjustment Administration (AAA), which dispensed bounties to farmers; the Works Progress Administration (WPA), which operated a multi-billion dollar relief operation for the unemployed; and the Public Works Administration (PWA), which constructed highways, schools, and bridges. Conservatives deplored this proliferation of alphabet agencies and expressed their displeasure at such episodes as the devaluation of the dollar and the slaughter of little pigs to raise farm prices. Democratic campaigners, though, found that they made the greatest headway by emphasizing "the politics of the deed"—the many benefits that the national government was distributing directly to the people. Mayor Daniel Shields of Johnstown, Pennsylvania, a Republican for thirty years, concluded that the WPA had saved his city and added, "Johnstown should vote solid for President Roosevelt."

Because of the New Deal, the parties divided on issues in 1936 as they had at no previous time in this century. As late as 1931 one Congressman had remarked, "The aisles don't mean anything except a good place to walk in and walk out." By 1936 the aisles that demarcated the two parties in Congress separated two divergent sets of assumptions about the role of government, even though neither party was an ideological monolith. The Democratic party, the historic defender of states' rights, had become the instrument of the Welfare State, while the Republican party, the traditional advocate of a strong national union, now preferred a weak central government and laissez-faire. When in the spring of 1936 the Gallup poll asked respondents whether they favored an amendment to ban child labor, Democrats answered "Yes" almost 3–1, while a majority of Republicans replied "No." The ensuing campaign centered on a range of questions markedly different from those that had seemed significant as recently as 1932. A Little Rock newspaper commented, "Such matters as tax and tariff laws have given way to universally human things, the living problems and opportunities of the average man and the average family."

The President believed that he would win the greatest response by exploiting the class antagonisms of the Great Depression. When he took office in March 1933, he had attempted to forge an all-class alliance in which business would have a central role. Well before the 1936 campaign, however, he had come to question the feasibility of government cooperation with business since so many corporation leaders opposed his policies. In the spring and summer of 1935 a new circle of advisers, some of whom were protégés of Justice Louis Brandeis, encouraged him to declare war on Big Business. Thomas G. Corcoran was quoted as saying: "Fighting with a businessman is like fighting with a Polack. You can give no quarter." In early May 1936, aboard the yacht *Potomac*, Roosevelt told Raymond Moley, the leader of the 1932 "Brain Trust," that businessmen as a class were stupid and that they had no sense of moral indignation about the sins of other businessmen. Newspaper publishers were just as bad. The President thought that nothing would help him more than to have newspapers, bankers, and business aligned against him, for their attacks would only win him more votes.

To take advantage of the class cleavages in 1936, Roosevelt directed the Democratic National Committee to concentrate its fire not on the

Republicans, but on such symbols of wealth as the American Liberty League, associated by the public with the du Ponts of Delaware and J. Howard Pew, Jr., the Sun Oil Company tycoon. The President, for his part, missed few opportunities to point out that the rich and well-born detested him, and he seemed to take a puckish pleasure in the fact. At Harvard's tercentenary celebration in 1936, where undergraduates booed him, he noted that at the 200th anniversary celebration a century before "many of the alumni of Harvard were sorely troubled by the state of the Nation. Andrew Jackson was President. On the 250th anniversary of the founding of Harvard College, alumni were again sorely troubled. Grover Cleveland was President." He paused. "Now, on the 300th anniversary, *I* am President."

The 1936 campaign would range over a wide variety of issues, but the significance of the election would lie in these questions: whether the Democrats could make good their claim to be the nation's new majority party; whether the country would put its stamp of approval on Big Government; and whether class would prove the most important determinant of how the electorate made its choices on November 3.

II

The devastating 1934 elections left the Republicans with almost no one of national stature as a potential presidential candidate in 1936. So closely was Herbert Hoover linked to the disaster of the Depression that few party leaders seriously considered renominating him, although he retained the support of a number of his old associates. Nor did it seem wise to choose a man from the East, if the party hoped to win the allegiance of the mid-western farmer. Even the Old Guard agreed that the Republican nominee must come from west of the Alleghenies, a vast region that had gone solidly to the Democrats in 1932. Eastern industrialists looked for a candidate who combined the ancient Republican virtues with a mild reputation for liberalism. Some thought they had such a man in Frank Lowden, the former Illinois governor who had been a front-runner in 1920. The septuagenarian "Sage of Sinnissippi" made clear, however, that he did not wish to run and privately deplored the dearth of outstanding possibilities, a situation he blamed on the direct primary. Others admired the bombast of Arthur Vandenberg, but the Michigan Senator was shrewd enough to prefer to wait until 1940 when Roosevelt, because of the two-term tradition, would presumably not be a candidate.

A poll of party leaders by the former executive director of the Republican National Committee, taken in September 1935, showed Senator William E. Borah of Idaho the leading contender with 367 votes, over one hundred more than his nearest rival. The "Lion of Idaho" had been a national figure for three decades; in Europe no Senator was so well known. He had a reputation, rather inflated, for progressivism, and many farmers admired his stand on currency issues. But Borah, at seventy, was too old, and his views on inflation made him unacceptable to the Old Guard. Few took his showing in the poll seriously, for he had displayed strength in other election years without winning the nomination. Even when he captured the Wisconsin primary and ran strongly in downstate Illinois, he failed to impress. James A. Farley, the Democratic national chairman, remarked to Roosevelt: "I have always felt personally that Borah was a quarter-mile runner. He generally broke well at the barrier with those who always ran, but by the time they reached the head of the stretch, he was well back in the field, and never heard from after that."

The same poll reported Borah's closest rival to be the Chicago publisher Frank Knox. Chairman of the Credentials Committee at the Bull Moose convention in 1912 and Leonard Wood's floor manager in 1920, he could claim to speak for the Theodore Roosevelt tradition. He had, in fact, been a Rough Rider in the Spanish-American War and was fond of aping Colonel Roosevelt's mannerisms. Knox, too, was a colonel, a commission he had won in World War I, in which he had enlisted as a private and seen service overseas. He had once worked with Vandenberg on the *Grand Rapids Herald*, had published newspapers in three states, had managed the Hearst chain for three years, and, as publisher of the *Chicago Daily News*, operated a journal known for its distinguished staff of foreign correspondents. He had the advantage, too, of coming from a big state. But Knox had never held public office, and he was opposed in his own state by the most powerful Republican newspaper, the *Chicago Tribune*. Moreover, he offended many by his spread-eagle nationalism, and, for all his claims to the T. R. legacy, he was an ardent conservative. Knox, said one writer, "stands for everything that Mencken and [Sinclair] Lewis kidded the country about in the last decade."

Since neither Borah nor Knox engendered much enthusiasm, party potentates began to turn their attention to the forty-eight-year-old governor of Kansas, Alfred Mossman Landon, better known as Alf, a nickname he had acquired in the Kansas oil fields. Landon had once said that the party was not "so hard up as to name a man from Kansas," a state with few

electoral votes and usually safely Republican, but he had exceptional qual-
ifications. One of only seven GOP governors in the country, Landon was
the sole Republican chief executive elected in 1932 who gained reelection
in the Democratic tide of 1934. Expected to run well in the farm belt, he
had the kind of personality that Main Street would find attractive: the
pleasant manners and easy charm of a man who spent his summer
evenings in a rocker on the front porch of a white frame house. James
MacGregor Burns has written, "Middle class by every test and in every
dimension, he had the shrewd, guileless face, the rimless glasses, and the
slightly graying hair that made him indistinguishable from a million other
middle-aged Americans."

Landon stood at the crossroads of the party. As a successful independent
oil operator, he would appeal to businessmen. An advocate of retrench-
ment, a balanced budget, and the gold standard, he was more orthodox on
fiscal and monetary matters than many eastern conservatives. On the
other hand, he had been allied with the progressive wing of the Republican
party in Kansas since the Teddy Roosevelt era. A Bull Moose county chairman in 1912, he had served as private secretary to the progressive governor, Henry Allen, in 1922; had voted for Robert M. La Follette, Sr. for
president in 1924; and had backed the campaign of William Allen White,
the nationally known Emporia editor, against the Ku Klux Klan. As governor, Landon had chaired a meeting in Topeka at which the Socialist
leader, Norman Thomas, spoke, and he had refused to sanction a proposed
investigation of alleged "Red" activities in the university. Under his leadership, Kansas had abolished the poll tax, strengthened utility regulation,
and injected new life into the "blue sky" laws banning the marketing of
fraudulent securities. Governor Landon had pledged help to Roosevelt in
the war against the Depression and had endorsed New Deal projects in
words that were to be quoted against him during the campaign. Indeed, as
the historian Roger Biles has written, "The Republican's campaign never
seemed to engage the masses, . . . in large part because of his own ambiva-
lence toward Roosevelt's policies." But he was wary of strong central government and sought "the middle of the road between a government by
plutocracy and a government by bureaucracy." He summed up his position in November 1935 when he wrote, "I think four more years of the
same policies that we have had will wreck our parliamentary government,
and four years of the old policies will do the job also."

Governor Landon's campaign received its greatest impetus from newspaper editors and publishers. The *Kansas City Star* and other regional pub-

lications got Landon off to a good start in his contest with Knox, whose own bid rested on the fact that he was a Midwestern publisher. But Landon did not capture national attention until the Hearst chain took him up, much as the Luce empire would promote Wendell Willkie in 1940. In July 1935 William Randolph Hearst assigned Damon Runyon and Adela Rogers St. John to write articles on Landon for two Hearst magazines, *Cosmopolitan* and *Good Housekeeping*; Runyon's "Horse and Buggy Governor" created a national stir. In December Hearst, accompanied by his longtime companion, the actress Marion Davies, led an entourage that included Paul Block, head of another newspaper chain, and Cissy Patterson, publisher of the *Washington Herald*, to Topeka to look Landon over. "I think he is marvelous!" Hearst said on leaving the Governor's office. "I thought of Lincoln," confided Mrs. Patterson.

The publicists promoted Landon as a "liberal Coolidge," a wonder-worker who had proven in Kansas that one could be humane without being a spendthrift. New Dealers might scoff that Landon's reputation rested in good part on the achievements of his Democratic predecessor and on the millions the federal government had poured into Kansas. But Landon's campaign manager, John D. M. Hamilton, a forty-four-year-old Topeka lawyer who had risen through the ranks in Republican politics, found that Eastern financiers placed a high value on the Governor's role as budget-balancer. On the other hand, William Allen White, who stumped the country for his fellow Kansan, fretted that the Governor was being oversold as a conservative. Landon, White told the New York Republican Club, was "about as much like Coolidge as the Wild Man of Borneo is like Billy Sunday."

With the publicity barrage that Hearst provided, Landon moved rapidly into first position among the contenders, a vantage point he was careful to protect. He decided to stay out of the primary contests in the thirteen states that chose delegates in that fashion. Confident of victory, he did not want to jeopardize his chances by antagonizing party leaders who were favorite sons. Nor did he have the money for expensive primary campaigns. If he raised funds from men of wealth, the Democrats would claim he was the rich man's favorite. In more than one state, however, Landon was entered in primaries against his wishes. In California his slate was defeated by an uninstructed ticket which some thought represented a stop-Landon maneuver, but in New Jersey he won a smashing 4–1 victory over Borah.

By the time the Republican National Convention opened on June 9 in Cleveland's civic auditorium, Landon had the nomination all but cinched.

The only threat came on the second day when Hoover received a thunderous ovation in response to his call for a "crusade for liberty." For a moment, it seemed that the delegates might be so carried away as to nominate him for a third time. But Borah refused to join Knox and Vandenberg in a stop-Landon movement, and Hoover hesitated to announce himself as a candidate. By the next morning, all of Landon's opponents had withdrawn. In seconding Landon's nomination, Vandenberg announced, "I belong to but one bloc and it has but one slogan—'stop Roosevelt.' " That night the delegates chose Landon on the first ballot, 984 to 19 for Borah (18 from Wisconsin, 1 from West Virginia), although the Idaho Senator had pulled out of the race. Subsequently, the delegates made the nomination unanimous.

As early as the summer of 1935 Hearst had said that "Landon and Knox would make a very appealing ticket," but it took the Republicans a while to reach the same conclusion. The Landon circle, curiously, had not settled on a vice-presidential nominee. Some, including Hamilton, favored a coalition ticket with an anti–New Deal Democrat like Lewis Douglas, who had resigned as Roosevelt's budget director, but that notion encountered too many objections. Governor Styles Bridges of New Hampshire was eliminated because "Landon-Bridges falling down" would offer irresistible possibilities to Democratic sloganeers. Even on the night Landon was nominated, he and his aides remained undecided. Not until dawn did they agree on Vandenberg, only to have the Michigan Senator turn them down. They then resolved to get "off the rocks with Landon and Knox."

In a year in which the GOP was burdened by the accusation that it was the tool of Big Business, the Republican ticket, as Donald McCoy has noted, "was headed by two old Bull Moosers, and its national committee was loaded with Main Street rather than Wall Street figures." Landon and Knox, who knew one another only slightly, tried to make up for their distance by affecting T. R. lingo such as "bully" in their correspondence. "WE ARE AT ARMAGEDDON," Knox wired Landon after he had been nominated. He added in an odd phrase, "CONDITIONS CALL FOR A DISPLAY OF THE SAME GREAT QUALITIES WHICH ENDEARED US BOTH TO THEODORE ROOSEVELT."

Governor Landon found platform-making unexpectedly difficult. In anticipation of his nomination, he had designated the Cincinnati civic reformer Charles P. Taft to coordinate the drafting of planks to be submitted to the Convention. But to the dismay of the Landon forces, the Resolutions Committee turned out to be controlled by party conservatives. William Allen White, the governor's representative on the committee, had to fight for days to restore Landon's ideas to the platform draft. Borah exploited the plight of the Landon group by inserting his own notions on isolationism, anti-monopoly, and currency. White got most of the Landon proposals reinstated, but, wearied by the struggle, did not see to it that the Governor's convictions on labor, monetary matters, and civil service were included.

Landon decided to shun a floor fight in favor of a more effective way of winning his points. After the Resolutions Committee had completed its work (and all his rivals had withdrawn), Landon sent a telegram that he asked Hamilton to read to the convention. On the night of June 11 Hamilton recited the wire in which Landon explained that he wanted the delegates to have his interpretation of several planks before they voted on the nomination of a presidential candidate. He announced that he favored "a Constitutional amendment permitting the states to adopt such legislation as may be necessary to adequately protect women and children in the matter of maximum hours, minimum wages, and working conditions." He interpreted the plank demanding "a sound currency to be preserved at all hazards" to mean "a currency expressed in terms of gold and convertible into gold," but stipulated that it should not "be made effective until and unless it can be done without penalizing our domestic economy and without injury to our producers of agricultural products and other raw materials." He also advocated applying the civil service merit system to "the entire post office department," as well as to all other administrative posts below the rank of assistant secretary. The delegates responded without enthusiasm to Hamilton's reading, but since they went on to nominate Landon, the telegram gained quasi-official status as a gloss on the platform.

From its opening sentence warning that America was in peril, the Republican platform left the impression that the country was on the verge of collapse, but the substance was somewhat more moderate than the tone, and some were surprised by how much of the New Deal the party was willing to accept. It approved national regulation of utilities and of the marketing of securities, supplementary payments to the aged, soil conservation, "a national land-use program," and, "as an emergency measure," federal subsidies to farmers. Although it did not go nearly as far as the Democratic platform and still generally viewed government as a menace, the Republican platform marked a considerable change from the party's position four years earlier. When the GOP was accused of stealing the 1932 Democratic platform, Republicans replied, "Why not? The Demo-

crats have no more use for it. Moreover it is in perfectly good condition—
it was never used."

The Republicans entered the campaign in a feisty mood. In an era when
Sally Rand excited attention at the Chicago world's fair by her daring fan
dance, the keynote speaker at the Republican convention, Senator Frederick
Steiwer of Oregon, cried, to the tune of "Three Blind Mice":

> Three long years . . .
> Full of grief and tears
> Roosevelt gave us to understand
> If we would lend a helping hand
> He'd lead us all to the promised land
> For three long years! . . .
> When we got to the promised land
> We found it nothing but shifting sand,
> And he left us stripped like Sally Rand
> For three long years!

III

In winning the Republican nomination, Landon became the first of a
series of GOP candidates who would confront a fundamental question of
strategy: whether to take sharp issue with a popular Democratic incum-
bent or become a "me too" candidate. If Landon veered in a conservative
direction, he risked the displeasure of an electorate that appeared to
approve much of the New Deal. But if he sanctioned most of the
Administration's actions, he would blur his own identity and leave voters
with no reason to prefer him to Roosevelt. If he combined the two
approaches, he would appear vacillating and unsure of himself.

At the beginning of his campaign, Landon emphasized his progressive
proclivities. At Chautauqua he braved the wrath of Hearst by saying, "In
Kansas we insist that no teacher should be required to take any oath not
required of all citizens," and before a convention of the American Legion,
he denounced racial and religious bigotry. Landon also deliberately sought
to dissociate himself from the Old Guard and from ostentatious wealth.
Hoover was treated so coolly that he took little part in the campaign, and
Paul Block was told he could not attach his private railroad car to the campaign train. Since Landon believed he could win only by carrying the
Midwest, he tried to out-promise the New Dealers in order to attract farm

votes. In Des Moines in late September, he pledged drought relief, seed loans, conservation, aid to the tenant farmer, and perhaps even crop insurance, a program that appeared to be more costly and far-reaching than the AAA. For a budget-balancer, this was strange doctrine. Moreover, his concern for the midwestern farm vote led him to take unexpected stands. At Minneapolis, he compromised his belief in a low tariff by charging that reciprocal trade had "sold the American farmer down the river."

Democrats seized the opportunity to point to the inconsistency between Landon's image as a Kansas Coolidge and his pledges of government largesse. "You cannot be an old-guard Republican in the east and a New Deal Republican in the west," Roosevelt said. "You cannot repeal taxes before one audience and promise to spend more of the taxpayers' money before another audience." Secretary of the Interior Harold Ickes charged that Landon was a "changeling candidate," a foe of government power who had once been a state Socialist in favor of publicly owned telephone and natural gas distribution systems. When Landon countered that he had consistently supported government ownership "as a gun behind the door" to secure fair utility rates, Ickes rejoined, "I wonder how many other concealed weapons he carries about. The utility interests had better frisk him before they go any further."

The Republicans left an impression of floundering and divided counsels, mostly because of a split between Landon and his running mate. While Landon, at least in the opening days of his campaign, was trying to distinguish his position from that of the Old Guard, Colonel Knox was making extravagant charges. "The New Deal candidate," Knox insisted, "has been leading us toward Moscow." The contrast between such speeches and Landon's early remarks led *Time* to write: "The Republican gospel of salvation being preached by Alf Landon on one hand and that being preached by John Hamilton and Frank Knox on the other seemed about as dissonant and confusing to voters as the competing Christianities of a Boston Unitarian and a hard-shell Southern Baptist would be to Hottentot bushmen."

Knox's speeches probably did less damage to the Republican cause than the activities of John Hamilton who, in a year when class feeling ran high, left the unfortunate impression that he preferred the milieu of Long Island estates to Main Street. "If John Hamilton is a progressive," wrote William Allen White, "Wally Simpson is a nun." To Landon's dismay, Hamilton surrounded him with conservative advisers. "Why don't you ever bring workingmen to see me?" Landon asked his manager. "All I ever see are stuffed-shirt businessmen and bankers." A month after the election, White wrote a Kansas progressive: "You are dead right that the great damage was done to Landon when he selected his ultra-conservative advisors. Hamilton was awful. . . . He loved the rich and was proud to associate with them and his association with them advertised their control of the party. The stink of money was over the whole campaign." More startling was the judgment Hoover offered in a letter to White: "When the Republican Party starts out to mix populism, oil, Hearst, munitions and the Liberty League, it is bound to come to grief. You used the exact phrase that I did to some of the gentlemen in charge—that is, that if the money was taken from Du Pont, Pew and Company they would 'sell the Party down the river.' And I am not sure that it has not been sold."

Hamilton may not have "sold" the Republican party, but he did see to it that the campaign did not suffer from lack of funds. He tapped the bank accounts not only of GOP industrialists but also of the Liberty League's "angels." Huge sums were funneled into the party. The Republicans and their allies subsequently reported $14,198,203 in expenditures to the Democratic forces' $9,228,407. Nevertheless, Hamilton and his associates dissipated much of this advantage in allocating funds. Too often the Republicans left the impression that the campaign was a struggle of the few against the many. The Republican National Committee employed twenty-four workers in its industrial division, headed by the salt tycoon Sterling Morton, but only three on its labor staff. The GOP distributed literature estimated at from 125 million to 170 million pieces, but some of the flyers expressed open contempt for the poor. Handbills accused the Administration of providing "Free lunch to hoboes, Relief Clients, Underprivileged Transients, and others who won't work, and those who have missed the Social Values of the More Abundant Life" and of having supplied a "Large quantity of PWA picks, spades, shovels, rakes, etc. etc. which have been used only to lean on."

The Republicans broke new ground in using "spot announcements" on radio for the first time, but here also Hamilton erred by identifying the party too closely with Madison Avenue. To sell Landon to the American public, the GOP hired Hill Blackett, senior partner of the leading agency in radio advertising, with such choice accounts as General Mills and Procter and Gamble. *Variety* commented: "Political parties are being reduced to merchandise which can be exchanged for votes in accordance with a well-conceived marketing plan, taking stock of income levels, race, local problems, exactly as does a commercial sponsor. This differs no whit from the tactics employed by Lifebuoy, Chase and Sanborn, or any other of a thousand consumer commodities."

Even when the Republicans did make a strong bid for the vote of the disadvantaged, it did not turn out well. To appeal to black voters, the party financed a national tour by Jesse Owens, the hero of the 1936 Olympics, and distributed three-minute movies to race theaters (Mamie Smith and the Beale Street Boys sang the GOP theme song, "Oh, Susannah"). Landon, who had a good record on civil rights issues, came out in favor of an anti-lynching law and denounced "the attempt of the New Deal to use relief rolls as modern reservations on which the great colored race is to be confined forever as a ward of the federal government." But this effort to hold blacks in the Republican column made little headway. The NAACP protested that the Governor's proposal to shift relief administration to the states would increase discrimination, and the *Baltimore Afro-American* reminded black voters: "ABRAHAM LINCOLN IS NOT A CANDIDATE IN THE PRESENT CAMPAIGN."

Much of the responsibility for turning the campaign in a conservative direction lay not with Hamilton but with Landon. As early as September it had become clear that there were sharp limits to the Governor's progressivism and, in particular, that he advocated a diminished role for the national government. On September 26 in Milwaukee he denounced the Social Security Act as "unjust, unworkable, stupidly drafted and wastefully financed." In Detroit in mid-October Landon began to drum home a new question: whether Roosevelt "intends to change the form of our government—whether labor, agriculture, and business are to be directed and managed by government." Thereafter his addresses became increasingly shrill. The policies of the New Deal, he argued in Baltimore, would lead to the guillotine.

At a rally in Madison Square Garden Landon raised a series of inquiries about FDR's intentions. To each, he gave the same reply, and soon the crowd was joining him in the refrain, "The answer is: no one can be sure." The most important question, Landon asserted, was "whether our American form of government is to be preserved." He charged that Roosevelt had carried out nine unconstitutional acts, had urged Congress to pass laws of doubtful validity, and had belittled both the Supreme Court and the Constitution. "What are the intentions of the President with respect to the Constitution?" he asked. "Does he believe changes are required? If so, will an amendment be submitted to the people, or will he attempt to get around the Constitution by tampering with the Supreme Court? The answer is: no one can be sure." He pointed out that forty-eight hours later Roosevelt would be standing at the same spot in Madison Square Garden, just two days before Election Day. Landon flung a challenge: "Tell us where you stand, Mr. President. Tell us not in generalities, but clearly so that no one can mistake your meaning. And tell us why you have evaded the issue until the eve of the election." (Years later, Landon said that he had heard from Paul Block that Roosevelt might attempt to pack the Court, and he had raised this challenge in anticipation that the President would evade it and hence could not claim he had a mandate to reform the judiciary.)

Landon's criticism of Big Government, however inadvisable at a time when millions depended on bounty from Washington, had the advantage of coinciding with the views of the older America that gave the Kansas governor his strongest backing. "Oh, Susannah" appealed to nostalgia for a simpler day, and in distributing forty-two million sunflower buttons, the Republicans emphasized their candidate's rural background. At a time when the Irish Catholic Jim Farley was rounding up polyglot ethnic support for Roosevelt, the Yankee Protestant John Hamilton's organization was making the most headway with old-stock, rural Americans. "There is one thing quite noticeable of all our crowds," observed one of Landon's lieutenants. "They have that clean upstanding appearance." Landon himself said that he felt during the campaign "like the country boy going to take a job in Toronto for the first time."

The GOP hoped that the nation would find Landon's unpretentious small-town manner a pleasant relief from the cosmopolitan Roosevelt with his public-relations grin, his Groton accent, and his polished style. A Republican inserted in the *Congressional Record* in 1936 a bit of doggerel that had already become a staple of business throwaways. It read in part:

> I'm tired, oh, so tired, of the whole New Deal,
> Of the juggler's smile and the barker's spiel,
> Of the mushy speech and the loud bassoon,
> And tiredest of all of our leader's croon.

A Republican Congressman from Missouri, who criticized Roosevelt for fishing from cruisers and yachts, noted approvingly that, "being so plain and simple," Alf used "a cane pole and a can of worms." Landon, too, believed the contrast to FDR would prove advantageous, for "the American people have always been fearful, in the end, of a *great* man."

The Republicans did not apologize for the fact that Landon was a poor speaker—they boasted of it. In Minneapolis he was introduced as a man who was not a "radio crooner." "Do urge Governor Landon not to try to improve his delivery," the ex–Bull Mooser Amos Pinchot advised a party official. When a New York financier wrote Landon that he was worried about the candidate's performance on the radio, the Governor replied: "But we agreed a long time ago, I think, that Mr. Roosevelt would be defeated by his direct antithesis. In other words, I don't want to get too much out of character."

Yet Landon's personality and his attributes as a speaker could hardly be expected to attract the kind of national following that the magnetic Roosevelt was winning. H. L. Mencken wrote that the Governor "is an honest fellow, and would make an excellent President, but he simply lacks the power to inflame the boobs." Moreover, the Republican candidate never learned how to impress metropolitan audiences with his capacity for leadership or how to turn a phrase that would capture headlines. In fact, his most memorable statement was a sentence that has become hallowed in the annals of campaign trivia: "Wherever I have gone in this country, I have found Americans." Landon seemed to many only a fair-to-middling hinterland politician who lacked FDR's preparation for dealing with the chancelleries of Berlin, Rome, and Tokyo. According to one apocryphal tale, when Hearst visited Landon in 1935, he asked the Governor what he thought of the international situation. Landon stared at the floor and, after pondering the question for a full five minutes, answered: "Well, Mr. Hearst, I'll tell you. I don't think International ought to be getting all of that business. I think it ought to be divided up with Deering, the Moline people and some of the independents in the plow business."

As Landon's campaign foundered, the Republicans resorted to desperate devices. They eagerly embraced a scheme advanced by Detroit businessmen to exploit the imminence of January 1, 1937, when the payroll tax provision of the Social Security Act would take effect. By concealing the requirement that employers also had to contribute to the pension fund and by raising doubts about what would happen to the money, they hoped to arouse indignation at the Administration over deductions from the workers' wages. In the last two weeks of the campaign, factory placards announced: "YOU'RE SENTENCED TO A WEEKLY PAY REDUCTION FOR ALL

YOUR WORKING LIFE. YOU'LL HAVE TO SERVE THE SENTENCE UNLESS YOU HELP REVERSE IT NOVEMBER 3." A message inserted in pay envelopes read:

> Effective January, 1937, we are compelled by a Roosevelt "New Deal" law to make a 1 percent deduction from your wages and turn it over to the government. Finally, this may go as high as 4 percent. You might get this money back . . . but only if Congress decides to make the appropriation for this purpose. There is NO guarantee. Decide before November 3—election day—whether or not you wish to take these chances.

On the final weekend of the presidential contest, the Republicans carried this roorback to excessive lengths. Landon said: "Imagine the field opened for federal snooping. Are these twenty-six million going to be finger-printed? Are their photographs going to be kept on file in a Washington office? Or are they going to have identification tags put around their necks?" John Hamilton had no doubt that every worker in the Social Security system would be required to wear a metal dog tag, "such as the one I hold in my hand." The Hearst press made its customary contribution to the clarification of public issues by showing a picture of a man wearing such a tag above the caption "YOU." Since the Social Security Act was probably the most popular New Deal measure, the scheme, although momentarily effective, appears to have backfired by Election Day. It had the enormous disadvantage for the Republicans of once again identifying their cause with that of the factory owners. After the election Representative Hamilton Fish told fellow Republicans that this last-minute operation probably "drove millions of the wage earners out of our party in the big industrial centers." In a campaign in which the Welfare State and class alignments were crucial, the GOP had stumbled on an issue that put them on the wrong side of both questions.

IV

Landon's best hope for victory lay in the possibility that a sizeable number of votes would be diverted from Roosevelt by the emergence of a powerful third party. In 1935 Democrats feared most of all an alliance of the flamboyant Louisiana Senator, Huey Pierce Long, with the demagogic "Radio Priest," the Reverend Charles E. Coughlin of Royal Oak,

Michigan, and Dr. Francis Townsend, the head of an old-age pension organization. When Long was murdered in September 1935, the Reverend Gerald L. K. Smith, a rabble-rousing Shreveport minister, laid claim to the leadership of Long's Share-Our-Wealth society. Each of these movements, as the historian David Bennett has noted, offered panaceas based upon "the manipulation of money," and each promised to heal psychic wounds that New Deal potions did not reach. While Share Our Wealth had its greatest following in the Deep South, Coughlin's National Union for Social Justice mustered most of its adherents from Irish and German Catholics in the working class districts of northeastern and midwestern cities, and Townsend's Old Age Revolving Pensions, Limited found its largest support in the Far West. The potential of this combination appeared to be enormous.

By the fall of 1935 Townsendism had become the strongest of the three movements. One magazine called it "easily the outstanding political sensation of the year." In December Edwin Witte, one of the authors of the Social Security Act, wrote, "The battle against the Townsend Plan has been lost, I think, in pretty nearly every state west of the Mississippi, and the entire Middle-Western area is likewise badly infected." A poll of editors taken by the *Portland Oregonian* indicated that the Townsendites could decide the outcome of Congressional races almost everywhere in Washington, California, Oregon, Idaho, Nevada, and Colorado. "Fear of the Townsend opposition," observed the columnist Frank Kent, "smears the whole Western political picture."

Even before the 1936 campaign began, the Democrats had taken steps to blunt each of these three threats, with mixed success. The Roosevelt administration patched up differences with Long's heirs, while, in turn, the Governor of Louisiana made it clear that Gerald L. K. Smith was *persona non grata* in his state and Louisiana politicians liquidated the Share-Our-Wealth organization. In Congress Democrats joined with Republicans to air internal division in Dr. Townsend's organization and block the Frazier-Lemke bill to refinance farm mortgages with issues of paper money, a measure Father Coughlin supported, but they did so at a cost. The Congressional probe threw Dr. Townsend into the arms of Gerald L. K. Smith, and the rejection of the Frazier-Lemke measure precipitated the creation of the third party Democrats had hoped to forestall.

The details of the founding of the new party remain obscure, but in the five weeks that followed the defeat of the Frazier-Lemke bill, Father Coughlin appears to have been the prime mover. Early in June his lieutenants negotiated with the Gerald Smith and Townsend forces, for by then Smith had won a reluctant Townsend to an uneasy pledge of alliance. "Dr. Townsend and I," he declared, "stood under the historic arch at Valley Forge and vowed to take over the government." In his organ, *Social Justice*, Coughlin wrote: "The activities of the National Union will increase tremendously immediately following June 16th or 17th. Approximately at that time I shall lay down a plan for action which will thrill you and inspire you beyond anything that I have ever said or accomplished in the past." But on June 16 Smith beat Coughlin to a headline by publicizing the new coalition.

On June 19 Representative William Lemke of North Dakota, co-sponsor of the Frazier-Lemke legislation, announced he was running for president on a "Union party" ticket. Thomas O'Brien, a Boston Irish Catholic lawyer who had worked his way through Harvard College and Harvard Law School as a railway brakeman and had served as counsel to unions and as district attorney, would be his running mate. That night Coughlin, who had probably handpicked both men, stated that Lemke was "eligible for indorsation" by the National Union for Social Justice. The ticket, Coughlin cried, was "Lemke and Yale, Agriculture and Republican! O'Brien and Harvard, Labor and Democrat! East and West! Protestant and Catholic!" In this informal manner, without benefit of a national nominating convention but with benefit of clergy, the new party was born.

Despite the Union party's origins, its platform did not specifically adopt either the Townsend Plan or sharing the wealth, and it omitted half the principles of the National Union for Social Justice, including labor's right to organize, nationalization of key resources, and control of private property for the public good. The platform did reflect Coughlin's cheap money, antifinancier outlook in recommending a central bank under Congressional control, limits on net income and inheritance, and conscription of wealth as well as men in the event of war. A strange amalgam of progressive and conservative elements, it embraced old-age security, antimonopoly, and public works planks, but also called for the protection of private property from confiscation by unnecessary taxation.

So little did most Americans know about "Liberty Bill" Lemke that even some of his rural followers thought his first name was Frazier. To eastern city-dwellers, he seemed an odd sort. Nearly completely bald, his head was dotted with yellow freckles, and his face was pitted by smallpox scars. One eye was glass, the other "always screwed up a little as if he were on the verge of imparting secret information." His baggy suit looked as though it had just been handed to him by the warden, and his blue work shirt, bright-colored galluses, and farmer's cap all revealed his rural origins. H. L. Mencken wrote a friend: "Lemke is not a human being at all, but a werewolf. I had several long gabbles with him in Cleveland. Get him on his favorite project—to dig 250,000 lakes out in the cow country—and you will howl. With his glass eye, his bald head, and his large yellow freckles, he is the most astonishing looking candidate that I have ever seen."

Yet Lemke had a more cosmopolitan background and more modern ideas than his appearance suggested. He had attended the University of North Dakota, Georgetown University, and Yale Law School. Westbrook Pegler pointed out that he had gone "around more colleges than an old-time tramp tackle and . . . is positively no hick." The first presidential candidate to use a plane extensively, he traveled thirty thousand miles by air.

Lemke's ideas, however, revealed his Populist and Nonpartisan League background. He derived his money notions from his hero Charles Lindbergh (father of the aviator) and from W. H. "Coin" Harvey, with whom he corresponded regularly. Representative of a district in which two-thirds of the farms had been foreclosed during the Depression, Lemke wanted a "just" price for the farmer and a "just" wage for the worker, but he was as critical as any Tory of the eastern New Dealers with their social-service emphases. He denounced Secretary of Agriculture Henry A. Wallace as "the greatest vandal in history" and Roosevelt "as the bewildered Kerensky of a provisional government."

The Union party ticket worried the Democrats because Lemke would draw chiefly from the President. An American Institute of Public Opinion poll reported that of those who favored Lemke, 70 percent had voted for Roosevelt in 1932, only 9 percent for Hoover. (To be sure, many of these FDR voters who were defecting to Lemke might have backed Landon, or stayed away from the polls, had there been no Union party candidate.) Lemke did not conceive of himself as merely a gadfly but thought he could capture enough states to throw the election into the House of Representatives where he and his allies would have enhanced bargaining power. In a close election, even his own state of North Dakota might spell the difference. Coughlin told reporters that Lemke needed only 6 percent of the electoral vote to transfer the final decision to the House.

Some thought Lemke would have little trouble polling well over 6 percent, because of the enthusiasm his sponsors elicited. With varying degrees of implausibility, Townsend claimed to have ten million followers; Smith put his Share-Our-Wealth legions at six million; and on the eve of the

National Union for Social Justice convention in August, Coughlin told reporters that if he did not deliver nine million votes to Lemke he would stop broadcasting. The convention at Cleveland's Municipal Stadium left no doubt that the Radio Priest's supporters gave him unquestioning fealty. Throughout the proceedings, Coughlin was called simply "Father": "Father says," "Father thinks," "Father told us." In her speech nominating him as president of the National Union, Helen Elizabeth Martin of the Bronx told delegates that "for those of us who haven't a material father— whose father is in the Great Beyond—he can be our father, and we won't need to feel lonesome." A Maryland delegate proposed: "Resolved, that we give thanks to the mother of the Reverend Charles E. Coughlin for bearing him." The devotion of Dr. Townsend's admirers at the national convention of his organization in Cleveland a month earlier seemed no less impressive. The *New York Times* observed that they "would follow him anywhere—into Old Guard Republicanism, socialism or a movement to set up a Stuart monarchy in Kansas."

Ostensibly, the Union party repudiated both major parties, but in fact it aimed almost all its fire at Roosevelt. Coughlin based his campaign not on praise for Lemke but on abuse of the President. In one speech he devoted two minutes to endorsing Lemke, five minutes to criticizing Landon, and an hour to denouncing the Roosevelt administration. He asserted at one and the same time that the New Deal was "bent on communistic revolution" and that it had surrendered to "international bankers." He ridiculed one of the AAA's officials, Mordecai Ezekiel, as "the modern Margaret Sanger of the pigs." Gerald L. K. Smith, who seemed to share little of the redistributionist outlook of Huey Long despite his claim to leadership of Share Our Wealth, said the choice between the President and Lemke was one between "the Russian primer or the Holy Bible," and insisted, "We are going to keep and re-establish the old Holy Bible, Red-White-and-Blue, Honest-to-God, Go-to-Meetin', bread-and-butter, wood splittin' America." By mid-October, Townsend, who called the President a "political savage," was asking his supporters to vote for Landon in any state where Lemke was not on the ballot.

In part because they sensed the conservative predisposition of the Union party, despite its antibanker idiom, most progressives and radicals rejected the Lemke ticket. The Socialist leader Norman Thomas dismissed the new party as a union of "two and a half rival messiahs . . . plus some neopopulists." Neither farm nor labor groups gave Coughlin the backing he had counted on. The National Farm Holiday Association dropped Lemke, while *Labor*, the organ of the railway unions, brushed off O'Brien as a "Boston attorney." Many liberals abhorred Coughlin's growingly pronounced anti-Semitism, as well as Smith's anti-democratic ambitions and his promise "to drive that cripple out of the White House."

As support for the Union party dwindled, Coughlin became increasingly more violent in his rhetoric and behavior. At the Townsendite convention in mid-July, he ripped off his coat and clerical collar and denounced the President as a "great betrayer and liar." In August he ranted, "As I was instrumental in removing Herbert Hoover from the White House, so help me God, I will be instrumental in taking a Communist from the chair once occupied by Washington." On September 25 he called Roosevelt "anti-God" and proposed using bullets "when an upstart dictator in the United States succeeds in making this a one party form of government and when the ballot is useless." If they were to achieve their aims, Coughlin told his followers, they would have to "ride rough-shod over the press of this country." When in the last week in October Coughlin called Roosevelt a "scab-President," even his indulgent bishop felt he had gone too far and required him to apologize. By then, Coughlin had been reprimanded by the Vatican publication, *L'Osservatore Romano*; the Pope was rumored to have taken steps to silence him; and Catholic clergymen in the United States had made common cause against the obstreperous priest.

In the summer of 1936 the Reverend Maurice Sheehy, Assistant to the Rector of the Catholic University of America, informed the President that a meeting of four bishops, three monsignori, and two priests in New York had agreed on a plan to answer Coughlin's attacks. Roosevelt, he said, should ignore the Michigan priest and let the President's friends within the Church deal with him, advice the White House readily accepted. Two of the bishops worked with Father Sheehy to secure statements from other prelates denying that Roosevelt was a Communist, and Sheehy also supplied Democratic propaganda to the Catholic press. In September the extremely influential Cardinal Mundelein of Chicago announced his support of the Administration. On October 8 the Reverend John A. Ryan, the best-known clerical advocate of social reform, delivered an important address over a national radio network on "Roosevelt Safeguards America." He denounced Coughlin's "ugly, cowardly, and flagrant calumnies" and said those who made such allegations were breaking the Eighth Commandment. "The charge of communism directed at President Roosevelt,"

Monsignor Ryan declared, "is the silliest, falsest, most cruel and most unjust accusation ever made against a President in all the years of American history."

Coughlin's and Smith's performances not only provoked such censure and cost Lemke popular support, but also deepened divisions within the Union party. When Smith declared that he planned to "seize the government of the United States," Townsend and Lemke rebuked him. At best, the leaders of the movement had not been mutual admirers. Coughlin had once called the Townsend Plan "economic insanity," and Townsend said that the Radio Priest's sixteen-point program had "fourteen points too many." Moreover, as *The Nation* pointed out: "The grand conclave of Messrs. Townsend, Smith, Coughlin, and Lemke at Cleveland violated every tradition of demagoguery. Obviously, there is nothing so damaging to a panacea as another panacea on the same platform. For a demagogue to admit even in a whisper that another demagogue has any of the truth is to demoralize the whole Utopian market." Well before Election Day, the inherent disharmony of the leaders and of their followings had become manifest, and it was clear that Lemke was going to fall far short of the millions of votes he had been promised.

V

The New Deal reforms antagonized so many of the country's leading Democrats that Republicans anticipated a large-scale defection from Roosevelt in 1936. As early as September 1933 Newton D. Baker, who had been Wilson's Secretary of War and a leading contender for the presidential nomination in 1932, had written John W. Davis, the Democratic presidential nominee in 1924: "In domestic matters just how much opportunity for personal initiative is to be left seems hard to guess. I never felt so regimented and disciplined in my life." In June 1935 William Pattangall, Maine's chief justice, resigned from the bench to join with Bainbridge Colby, who had been Secretary of State under Wilson, and other Democrats in a "Hartford Convention" to form an alliance against FDR. At Macon, Georgia in January 1936, a convention of dissident Democrats coalesced behind Eugene Talmadge, the governor of Georgia. On every seat lay a copy of the *Georgia Woman's World* featuring a photograph of Mrs. Roosevelt escorted by two black men and including a denunciation of the President for allowing "negroes to come to the White House banquets and sleep in the White House beds" and of the anti-lynching bill for encouraging "permissive ravishment."

None of FDR's critics, however, captured so much attention as Alfred E. Smith, who had run unsuccessfully for the presidency in 1928 on the same Democratic ticket on which FDR won election as governor of New York. Long before 1936 Smith and Roosevelt had come to a parting of the ways, but it was unclear whether Smith would carry his disapproval of the New Deal to the point of bolting his party. On January 25, 1936, clad in white tie and tails that seemed a far cry from the brown derby that had once been his trademark, Smith told a banquet of two thousand, including a dozen du Ponts, that Roosevelt and his lieutenants were headed in a Socialist direction. "It is all right with me if they want to disguise themselves as Norman Thomas or Karl Marx or Lenin, or any of the rest of that bunch," he cried, "but what I won't stand for is allowing them to march under the banner of Jefferson, Jackson and Cleveland." In November, Smith warned, he and other disaffected Democrats would probably "take a walk."

Smith made his address under the auspices of the American Liberty League, an organization founded in 1934 by a group of industrialists and anti-Administration Democrats such as John J. Raskob, a high du Pont official who had been displaced as the Democratic party's national chairman. The Liberty League claimed to be an association of liberty-loving Americans of all classes, but it was patently an alliance of the well-to-do. It never succeeded in setting up a labor or farm division, and most of its support came from men of wealth who found it difficult to dissemble their class bias. A Chicago attorney who headed the Illinois division of the Liberty League stated, "The New Deal is nothing more or less than an effort sponsored by inexperienced sentimentalists and demagogues to take away from the thrifty what the thrifty or their ancestors have accumulated, or may accumulate, and give it to others who have not earned it."

When the Liberty League was set up, Frank Knox hoped that it would "eventuate in the formation of an independent democratic group like the Palmer-Buckner ticket in 1896 of Gold Democrats," but instead of running an independent slate, the "Jeffersonian Democrats" campaigned for Landon and Knox. In addition to Colby, their leaders included Joseph T. Ely, former governor of Massachusetts; James Reed, who had been United States Senator from Missouri; Henry Breckinridge, onetime Assistant Secretary of War; and Richard Cleveland, Grover's son. In October at Carnegie Hall, Al Smith accused the New Dealers of having stolen the Democratic party from its rightful owners. The Administration would accept support from anybody, he protested: "even a communist with wire whiskers and a torch in his hands is welcome so long as he signs on the dotted line." He wound up his address by saying: "I am an American before I am a Democrat. I firmly believe that the remedy for all the ills that we are suffering from today is the election of Alfred M. Landon."

This recommendation may have hurt Landon more than it helped him, for it was charged that Smith had betrayed his party and deserted his class. In November the *New Republic* published Slater Brown's "Empedocles on the Empire State":

> But enough of talk.
> Hand me a stovepipe hat, I'll take a walk.
> I'll step off this here parapet and fall
> Not back into Oliver Street but into Wall
> Where du Pont's acolytes from ten to three
> Do homage to the Goddess Liberty.
> Where members of his League in suppliance kneel
> Before the post of motors, oil or steel.
> Telling their beads and wondering if 'twas wrong
> To play Steel short or Studebaker long.

By dividing the country on class lines in the midst of the Depression, the right-wing Democrats gave Roosevelt an added advantage. The Liberty League, in particular, proved an embarrassment to the Republicans, because it was transparently an upper-class front. The Democratic party chairman, James A. Farley, said that it "ought to be called the American Cellophane League" because "first, it's a du Pont product and second, you can see right through it." Another critic jeered that the Liberty Leaguers apparently thought the American Revolution "was fought to make Long Island safe for polo players." The political efforts of the Democratic dissidents failed miserably. In primaries in New Jersey, Pennsylvania, Maryland, and Massachusetts, Roosevelt overwhelmed Breckinridge and Talmadge by margins that ran as high as 18–1. Nor did they succeed in rallying most of the conservative Democrats to Landon. Anti-FDR Senators such as Carter Glass, Harry Byrd, and Millard Tydings refused to bolt, and in the end even the regimented Newton Baker stayed with his party.

VI

Since Roosevelt had no serious opposition for renomination to a second term, he could concentrate his pre-convention activities on the party platform. Although he did not plan to go to Philadelphia until the main business of the convention had been completed, he gave close attention to drafting the platform, a task in which he was assisted by his trusted associate from Albany days, Samuel Rosenman. The President instructed Rosenman to keep the document short and to base it on the sentence of the Declaration of Independence stating self-evident truths.

"It is no secret," Rosenman has written, "that the first draft of a platform on which a President is to run for reelection is generally prepared at the White House and not at the convention." At the White House on the Sunday evening before the opening of the Democratic convention gathered Roosevelt, Senator Robert F. Wagner, who would be chairman of the Resolutions Committee, and several aides, including Rosenman, Assistant Attorney General John Dickinson, Ambassador William C. Bullitt, and Stanley High, a former Republican who had been recruited by the President as a speech writer and had proven to be a gifted phrase-maker. A little after midnight, the group broke up after assigning Rosenman the task of piecing together a draft. "I must say that I considered myself wholly inadequate to the task," Rosenman recalled. "I had hardly made a practice of reading party platforms, let alone writing them." Rosenman and High worked through the night, and in the morning Roosevelt found a typed draft on his breakfast tray.

In the President's bedroom his lieutenants put the final touches on the document. Donald Richberg, former NRA Administrator, added a plank on the Supreme Court; Bullitt a foreign affairs section; and Harry Hopkins, who headed the WPA, a peroration. A freshly typed draft had just been finished for Wagner to take to Philadelphia, when Robert M. La Follette, Jr., phoned. "I think you ought to know that the peroration which Harry gave you and which I understand the President is using was given to Harry by me, and it is practically the same peroration which my father used back in 1924 when he ran for President on the Progressive ticket," the Wisconsin Senator cautioned. Roosevelt ordered a new peroration written while Wagner waited. When that assignment had been completed, Wagner departed for the convention, manuscript in hand.

At Philadelphia, Senator Wagner steered the draft through his committee and won the approval of the delegates. Although some changes were made, the platform closely followed the lines laid down at the White House, especially in approving New Deal doctrines of government responsibility. It stated: "We hold this truth to be self-evident—that government in a modern civilization has certain inescapable obligations to its citizens, among which are: (1) Protection of the family and the home; (2) Establishment of a democracy of opportunity for all the people; (3) Aid to those overtaken by disaster." The platform also reflected Roosevelt's determination to exploit class antagonisms. The original draft promised to "rid our land of kidnappers, bandits, and malefactors of great wealth," and even after being modified at Philadelphia the plank grouped criminals and financiers in the same paragraph.

When the President came to Philadelphia on June 27 to accept the nomination, he found more than one hundred thousand people gathered at rain-soaked Franklin Field. His speech wove together, not altogether successfully, two separate threads—a conciliatory approach offered by Moley and Corcoran and a militant emphasis suggested by Rosenman and High. The President plucked from each such phrases as "rendezvous with destiny" contributed by Corcoran and "economic royalist" coined by High. As a hundred spotlights played on him, Roosevelt told the cheering throng:

> Governments can err, Presidents do make mistakes, but the immortal Dante tells us that divine justice weighs the sins of the cold-blooded and the sins of the warm-hearted in different scales.
>
> Better the occasional faults of a Government that lives in a spirit of charity than the consistent omissions of a Government frozen in the ice of its own indifference.
>
> There is a mysterious cycle in human events. To some generations much is given. Of other generations much is expected. This generation of Americans has a rendezvous with destiny.

The most controversial passages of his speech came when he sounded the class theme by hitting out at "economic royalists" who took "other people's money " (a phrase borrowed from Louis Brandeis) to impose a "new industrial dictatorship." "These economic royalists complain that we seek to overthrow the institutions of America," he said. "What they really complain of is that we seek to take away their power." The stadium crowd, noted the newspaperman Marquis Childs, cheered ecstatically "as though the roar out of the warm, sticky night came from a single throat."

The President took advantage of his enormous popularity and the strength of urban elements in the New Deal to put through a reform that had once been denied him. Backed by Northern delegations dominated by their big city components, the Administration assaulted the century-old rule requiring a two-thirds vote to nominate a Democratic presidential candidate. The Roosevelt forces chose the chairman of the convention's Rules Committee, Senator Bennett Champ Clark of Missouri, to lead the fight because they knew he would carry out his assignment with a special ardor. Clark had seen the Baltimore convention of 1912 deny his father, who had held a majority of the votes for several ballots, the Democratic nomination and hence, in a year when the Republicans were divided, the presidency. Advocates of repeal claimed that the change would make the Democrats a more national party and would facilitate their ability to expand in the North. Southern opponents insisted that abolition of the rule would punish the South, which had been loyal to the party, by turning over control to populous northern states that often went Republican. Conservatives chimed in that abrogation would make it easier for a president to dictate his own nomination or that of someone acceptable to him because he would now require only a simple majority.

In 1932 Roosevelt had been balked in a premature attempt to wipe out the two-thirds rule, but in 1936 the champions of change overwhelmed the opposition. The convention tried to mollify the South by giving increased representation at future conventions to states that the Democrats carried. But Southern conservatives soon recognized that the change in the convention rules symbolized a significant loss in their section's relative power. Less than two years later, Senator Josiah Bailey of North Carolina would write of his party: "Since the abolition of the Two-Thirds Rule, there is grave danger that it will fall into the hands of very objectionable men whose politics are entirely distasteful to the Southern Democracy. They get elected by the negro vote in New York, Pennsylvania, Boston, Chicago, and the cities of the Middle West. They are common fellows of the baser sort."

VII

Roosevelt had not been content to rest on the organization that had put him in office in 1932 but instead had created a broadly based coalition centered on the masses in the great cities. His leadership of this urban coalition was a new role for him, since he had long felt more comfortable with rural and small-town audiences. As late as 1932 he had confided: "Al Smith knows these city people better. He can move them. I can't." Moreover, in 1932 many of the urban machines had opposed his nomination. Frank Hague, the Jersey City boss, had called him "the weakest candidate before the people." But in 1936 Hague backed him enthusiastically, and Roosevelt, who had little of the patrician reformer's distaste for machines, praised Hague and cooperated with bosses like Ed Kelly in Chicago. In other cities, the Great Depression had encouraged the rise of a different kind of urban leader, typified by Pittsburgh's David Lawrence and Detroit's Frank Murphy, who worked closely with unions and established "Little New Deals" in their states. As a consequence of the Democratic success in 1932 and 1934, Farley could count on the assistance not only of these municipal organizations but also of thirty-seven state administrations with their armies of officeholders and beneficiaries.

The Democratic party's urban coalition drew strength from the gratitude of ethnic groups for New Deal welfare measures and for "recognition" in dispensing patronage. The President's many Catholic and Jewish advisers made him an attractive figure to ethnic minorities, and Catholic ward politicians felt they had a friend at court in Jim Farley. While Harding, Coolidge, and Hoover had named eight Catholics to federal judgeships, Roosevelt in his years in the White House appointed fifty-one, including the first Italo-American ever to attain this honor. Catholic theologians praised New Deal measures for fulfilling the social teaching of papal encyclicals, and at the Democratic convention in Philadelphia a scarlet-robed Roman Catholic bishop gave the convocation. To win the backing of various nationality and religious groups, the President suggested calling home ambassadors to send them on campaign tours of cities with large populations from the countries to which they were assigned abroad. In the 1936 campaign Roosevelt received the support of groups such as the Lithuanian Roman Catholic Alliance of America, the Slovak Catholic Sokol of New Jersey, the Croatian Catholic Union of America, and the National Alliance of Bohemian Czech Catholics of America.

At the same time that he wooed Catholics and Jews, the President—an Episcopalian—did not neglect his fellow Protestants, who were thought to be predominantly Republican. Farley recalls a conversation with Roosevelt about setting up one of the auxiliary committees of the campaign:

"In the Committee of Twelve," . . . [the President said,] "I would like to have five clergymen. I think we should have a Catholic priest, a Baptist minister, a Presbyterian minister, an Episcopalian minister, and a rabbi."

"What about the Methodists?" I asked.

"Well, we could leave out the Jews," he laughed. "No, there are more of them than there are Episcopalians. Take the Jews and leave out the Episcopalians."

Before his death in April, Louis Howe, FDR's closest political associate, had suggested creating an organization to win the allegiance of clergymen, social workers, and people of good will to the President. Roosevelt and Farley approved the idea, and the Good Neighbor League was set up with the social worker Lillian Wald and the philanthropist George Foster Peabody as co-chairs. Although the League included a labor leader and a rabbi, it directed its main appeal to middle-class Protestants who were attracted by the social ideals of the New Deal but had an ancestral distrust of the party of Rum, Romanism, and Rebellion. Many who admired Roosevelt were uneasy about a range of Democratic policies from repeal of the prohibition amendment to the expansion of the government payroll attributed to Farley. To reassure Protestants, the Democratic National Committee named Stanley High, who had once served as editor of the *Christian Herald*, as organizer of the League, an appointment that served to counter allegations that the President relied exclusively on Jewish and Catholic advisers. Directors of the Good Neighbor League included the suffragist Carrie Chapman Catt and a Methodist bishop, the Reverend Edgar Blake. Endorsement by such prominent representatives of moral causes helped persuade voters who might otherwise have spurned the Democrats.

The Democratic party appeared to face an even more formidable task in wooing black voters. Ever since the Civil War era, African Americans who were able to go to the polls had been wedded to the Republican party, the home of the Great Emancipator, Abraham Lincoln. Despite the impact of the Great Depression and the lily-white policies pursued by the Hoover administration, African Americans had voted solidly for Hoover in 1932. In Cincinnati's predominantly black Ward Sixteen, Hoover had received almost three-quarters of the ballots, and in Chicago he had run more strongly in African-American wards than he had in 1928. After Roosevelt took office, many black leaders, already suspicious of the Democrats as the party of the white ruling class in the South, expressed their displeasure at the acquiescence by the New Deal in the patterns of racial segregation. The young political scientist Ralph Bunche protested that "the New Deal only serves to crystallize those abuses and oppressions which the exploited Negro citizenry of America have long suffered under laissez-faire capitalism."

But many African Americans found the Roosevelt administration exceptionally responsive. Although blacks were discriminated against in many New Deal projects, they also received relief substantially greater than their proportion of the population. Furthermore, Roosevelt named an unusually large number of blacks to important government posts. By 1936 dozens of advisers held places in the President's "Black Cabinet." Eleanor Roosevelt and Secretary of the Interior Ickes, a former president of the Chicago NAACP, played especially conspicuous roles in the battle against racial discrimination. As early as 1934 in states like Pennsylvania, African-American voters began a massive swing to the Democratic party. That same year, Chicago sent to Congress Arthur W. Mitchell, the first black ever to be nominated for a Congressional seat by the Democrats.

In 1936 the Roosevelt administration made a bold bid for the African-American vote, even at the risk of alienating southern whites. Twelve states, including the border states of Kentucky and West Virginia, sent ten black delegates and twenty-two alternates to the Philadelphia convention, an unprecedented showing in a party that had permitted no black to attend in any formal capacity before 1924. The convention was the first to seat a black woman as a regular delegate and the first to provide for a black press conference and to seat blacks in the regular press box. As an African-American minister gave the invocation at one session—another "first"— Senator "Cotton Ed" Smith stormed out crying, "My God, he's black as melted midnight." (Carter Glass refused to join the walkout. "God knows I stand in need of prayer," the Virginia Senator said. "I wish every Negro in the country would pray for me.") When Congressman Mitchell became the first black ever to address a Democratic convention, Smith stalked out for good and went home to South Carolina. "I cannot and will not be a party to the recognition of the Fourteenth and Fifteenth Amendments," he explained. Throughout the ensuing campaign, northern Democrats courted the African-American voter, with growing evidence of success. Blacks who once would not have turned out to see any Democrat lined the streets of New York for Roosevelt.

Since much of FDR's following among urban ethnic groups came from factory workers, labor unions in 1936 had a unique opportunity to contribute to the President's reelection. Four years earlier, organized labor had been of little help to Roosevelt, because in the big industries few employees were unionized. But labor had a new political significance in 1936, chiefly as a result of the emergence in the intervening years of the Committee for Industrial Organization (subsequently to be known as the Congress of Industrial Organizations) under the militant leadership of John L. Lewis of the United Mine Workers. A lifelong Republican, Lewis had voted for Hoover in 1932, while his CIO collaborators, Sidney Hillman of the Amalgamated Clothing Workers and David Dubinsky of the International Ladies' Garment Workers Union, had backed the Socialists that year. Since then, though, they had come to value how a Democratic administration benefited industrial labor, and they were dismayed that Roosevelt planned to entrust the labor campaign once again to the conservative foe of the CIO, Daniel Tobin of the AFL Teamsters. Lewis and Hillman moved swiftly to take matters in their own hands.

With the cooperation of Major George Berry of the AFL International Printing Pressmen's Union, the CIO leaders set up Labor's Non-Partisan League. "Non-Partisan" suggested to some that unions, while seeking to reelect Roosevelt, did not identify with the Democratic party; to others that the organization bridged the AFL and CIO without taking sides in their dispute. The League carried out an ambitious operation to mobilize the low-income vote in the large industrial states. It held 109 rallies in the city of Chicago, sent seventy speakers through Ohio to talk to union meetings, and beamed a national radio broadcast to workers daily in the final month of the campaign. In Pennsylvania thirty-five thousand union officials engaged in the drive to get working-class families to the polls.

The League also provided a big chunk of the bankroll for FDR's campaign. When Lewis, who aimed to buy his way into national decision-making, decided to make a huge contribution, he arrived at the White House with a photographer prepared to record the event for the maximum publicity effect. But after the United Mine Workers' chief magnanimously offered Roosevelt a draft for $250,000, the President answered: "No, John, I don't want your check, much as I appreciate the thought. Just keep it and I'll call on you, if and when any small need arises." As André Maurois later wrote, "Lewis then grasped that the campaign was going to be very much more expensive." During the following weeks, nearly half a million dollars left the union treasury, without attracting much notice in the newspapers. In all, labor made available to the Democrats $770,218, including loans of $85,000; $469,000 came from the Mine Workers. These figures contrasted markedly with the $7,500 which represented the total union contribution to La Follette in 1924 and with the $95,000 which was the grand sum given by the national AFL to presidential campaigns in the preceding thirty years.

While labor advanced these munificent amounts, the proportion of donations from businessmen to the party tailed off sharply. To be sure, Roosevelt did get large checks from individuals such as Sidney Weinberg of Goldman, Sachs, the New Orleans financier Rudolph Hecht, and the oil mogul Sid Richardson. But in contrast to 1932 when bankers and brokers gave 24 percent of all contributions of $1,000 or more to the Democrats, in 1936 they chipped in less than 4 percent. As one political scientist observed, it was a "new chapter" in the history of the labor movement "when an organization of miners is the largest contributor to a major political party."

Labor's Non-Partisan League proved especially effective in New York City where Dubinsky, as well as Emil Rieve of the Hosiery Workers, resigned from the Socialist party to take part in the campaign to reelect Roosevelt. Hillman told the executive board of the Amalgamated Clothing Workers:

In my judgment, up to a few years ago we had no labor movement in this country. Even in our so-called radical organizations we paid lip service to the need for organization, but what did we actually do toward making a real labor movement? That, I am sure, would have been impossible without the NRA. . . .

Now . . . are we supposed to let the chance go by and wait until the Socialist Party comes into power? There is no labor party—let us not fool ourselves about that. And since there is no labor party, are we just to sit down and admit that we cannot do anything? . . . You talk labor party. But can you have a labor party without an economic labor movement? I do not mean to criticize the Socialist movement, but it is composed of intellectuals. . . . I say to you that the defeat of Roosevelt and the introduction of a real Fascist administration such as we will have is going to make the work of building a labor movement impossible.

As veteran Socialists in the garment unions followed Hillman and Dubinsky into the Roosevelt coalition, Norman Thomas protested, "This is to repeat the mistake of the German Social Democrats who voted for Hindenburg because they did not want Hitler."

In New York, Labor's Non-Partisan League took advantage of defections from the Socialists to create a new statewide third party, the

American Labor Party, organized around three needle trades unions: the men's clothing workers headed by Hillman, the ladies' garment union under Dubinsky, and the millinery workers led by Max Zaritsky. The ALP also found a home for right-wing Socialists, mobilized by the labor lawyer Louis Waldman. They had been purged from the Socialist party in May but had taken with them such important publications as the *New Leader* and Abe Cahan's *Jewish Daily Forward*, as well as institutions like the Rand School of Social Science and Camp Tamiment. In August, organized as the Social Democratic Federation, they voted to affiliate with the ALP. "Ironically," the historian David Shannon has pointed out, the anti-Stalinist Socialists, who "had thought the majority Socialists too close to communism, now had avowed Communist comrades in their new American Labor Party." The ALP not only enlisted Social Democrats for Roosevelt, but also made it possible for independents who disapproved of Tammany Hall to vote for FDR without pulling down the Democratic levers.

Although in previous campaigns union labor had divided its support, in 1936 Roosevelt achieved a near-monopoly of backing from union leaders. William Green, the head of the AFL, did not give the President an outright endorsement, but he did say, "I estimate that 90 percent of labor, organized and unorganized, is for Mr. Roosevelt's re-election. . . . Such unanimous action by labor has never been taken in any campaign heretofore so far as I know." "Big Bill" Hutcheson of the Carpenters, who had traded punches with Lewis in a symbolic fight between the craft unionists and the industrial unionists, headed the labor division of the Republican National Committee, but large segments of his own union deserted him to boost FDR. "The labor leaders are all tied up with this administration," Landon wrote glumly. The President, in turn, as the historian Robert S. McElvaine has written, though "never before noted as a great friend of organized labor, proudly displayed a union card given to him in New York at the beginning of October."

Labor's Non-Partisan League put an emphasis on New Deal ideology that was matched by only one branch of the Democratic National Committee: the Women's Division. In 1934 the energetic head of the division, Mary W. Dewson, had urged Democratic women to appoint twenty-two of their number in each county to serve as an information corps on the work of New Deal agencies. By 1936 there were fifteen thousand of these "reporters" prepared to tout the virtues of the New Deal in a campaign year. At Molly Dewson's request, Farley agreed to expand the news bulletin of the National Democratic Women's Club in Washington into a monthly magazine, the *Democratic Digest*, which included in each issue a syllabus of the activities of a New Deal agency. The Women's Division also sponsored regional conferences and institutes featuring explorations of significant government policies.

In the 1936 campaign Molly Dewson's indefatigable work between elections made a considerable contribution to energizing the Democratic bid for votes. At the Philadelphia convention the party accredited 219 women delegates (compared to sixty at the Republican convention) and 302 female alternates. Democratic women shared the limelight when eight of them made seconding speeches for the FDR's nomination, and each state was empowered to name a woman alternate to the Resolutions Committee. At the convention Dewson unveiled one of her creations, the "rainbow fliers"—a set of brightly colored leaflets each devoted to a particular field of the New Deal. They proved so popular that during the campaign the Democrats distributed eighty-three million, more than four-fifths of all the party's literature.

The record of the New Deal enabled the President to seek votes less as the Democratic nominee than as the leader of a liberal movement that cut across party lines. As FDR's biographer Patrick Maney has pointed out:

> To the dismay of Democratic chieftains like James Farley, the mobilization of labor and other groups often proceeded outside regular party channels and thus reduced the control of party managers over the campaign organization. Roosevelt added further to their discomfiture by minimizing the importance of party affiliation. During the entire campaign, he rarely mentioned the Democratic party by name, and in a few states he supported liberal Republicans or independents against their Democratic opponents.

The Administration worked with Progressives in Wisconsin and Farmer-Laborites in Minnesota, as well as with the American Labor Party in New York, and the President snubbed the Democratic Senatorial nominee in Nebraska to commend George Norris, who ran as an Independent. After Roosevelt's nomination, Bob La Follette and the veteran labor attorney Frank Walsh put together a coalition of independent progressives to form yet another of FDR's auxiliary organizations. On September 11, 1936 a Progressive Conference of liberals of all parties, including such luminaries as Mayor Fiorello La Guardia of New York, announced for the President, and many of the independent progressives sought to persuade non-Democrats to vote for him.

Roosevelt, seeking the broadest possible following, was annoyed when in late May in a speech to Michigan Democrats Farley referred to Landon as "the governor of a typical prairie state." The President sent a memo scolding him:

I thought we had decided any reference to Landon or any other Republican candidate was inadvisable.

Now that the water is over the dam, a somewhat facetious reference to Frank Knox by you might soften the effect of the Landon reference. Another good rule which should be passed down the line to all who are concerned with speech material is that no section of the country should be spoken of as "typical" but only with some laudatory adjective. If the sentence had read "One of those splendid prairie States," no one could have picked us up on it, but the word "typical" coming from any New Yorker is meat for the opposition.

Republicans took advantage of Farley's blunder. When Landon came to Los Angeles, the California national committeeman, Earl Warren, introduced him by saying, "We glory in this opportunity to welcome to California this Governor of a typical prairie state."

Throughout the year, Roosevelt made a special effort to court Republicans, especially those of a progressive persuasion. He was careful never to suggest that Republican voters were his opponents, and he featured in his campaign former GOP notables, such as Secretary Ickes. For their part, Republican Senators James Couzens of Michigan and Peter Norbeck of South Dakota backed FDR, while other GOP Senators— William E. Borah, Hiram W. Johnson, Gerald P. Nye, and the Minority Leader, Charles L. McNary—took no part in the presidential campaign. Senator Arthur Capper, a Republican from Landon's home state, pointedly reminded Kansas voters that they could split their tickets. As a consequence of these defections, Landon was stripped of the support of much of the liberal wing of his party. In sum, Landon faced a virtually impossible task in trying to overcome the formidable coalition arrayed against him—urban machines, nationality groups, the Good Neighbor League, Socialist defectors, the Women's Division, independent progressives,

Republican moderates, and assorted New Deal beneficiaries, as well as one large predetermined bloc, the Solid South.

VIII

A master of timing, Roosevelt refused to launch his campaign until the attention centering on the Republican National Convention and the new GOP nominee had begun to wane. In July, while Democratic politicians chafed, he went cruising. He did not go on the stump until August and even then confined himself, save for a talk on peace in Chautauqua, to a "nonpolitical" inspection of flooded regions. Yet everyone understood that the tour had partisan implications. When he told Farley that "of course, there won't be anything political about the inspection trips," the President gave him a broad wink, threw back his head, and laughed.

In keeping with the "inspection" scenario, Roosevelt snapped up a suggestion that he meet with governors of the Dust Bowl states, and in late August and early September the presidential train carried him through the Dakotas, Wisconsin, and Iowa. Wherever he went, the rains came. (They also fell on Alf Landon during his tour; in this election, the Lord was nonpartisan.) At Des Moines the President conferred with midwestern governors, including his rival, the governor of Kansas. Not since 1912, when Woodrow Wilson encountered William Howard Taft at Boston's Copley Plaza Hotel, had two major party presidential candidates come together during a campaign. Their exchange was cordial. In fact, Senator Capper remarked, "Harmony dripped so steadily from every rafter that I fully expected one of the candidates to withdraw."

Roosevelt did not open his formal campaign until September 29, when he spoke to the New York State Democratic Convention in Syracuse. He began by dealing directly with the charge that he had succumbed to Communist influence, an allegation that had particularly disturbed many Catholics. Republicans had voiced this accusation frequently, and on September 19 in a front-page editorial the Hearst chain claimed that Moscow had ordered American Communists to back FDR. "Naturally the Communists flock to him," Hearst said. "'Every bird knows its own nest.'" To the President's discomfiture, the Communists, who once had denounced him as a "social fascist," were now in a United Front phase. While they sought to poll the largest possible vote for Earl Browder and his black running mate, James Ford, they focused their criticism on

Landon rather than Roosevelt. At Syracuse the President told his fellow Democrats, "I have not sought, I do not seek, I repudiate the support of any advocate of Communism or any other alien 'ism' which would by fair means or foul change our American democracy."

Not content with this defensive stance, Roosevelt brandished the main weapon in his arsenal: identifying his opponents with the privileged few. He told the crowd:

> In the summer of 1933, a nice old gentleman wearing a silk hat fell off the end of a pier. He was unable to swim. A friend ran down the pier, dived overboard and pulled him out; but the silk hat floated off with the tide. After the old gentleman had been revived he was effusive in his thanks. He praised his friend for saving his life. Today, three years later, the old gentleman is berating his friend because the silk hat was lost.

(Hoover later commented, "I have some inside information about that incident. The old gentleman was surreptitiously pushed off the dock in order that the hero could gain the plaudits of the crowd as a life saver.")

The President varied this appeal to class differences with boasts of the gains his administration had secured, but he was sometimes hard put to square the actions he had taken with his campaign pledges in 1932. Especially embarrassing was his address at the home of the Pittsburgh Pirates in which he had denounced Hoover as a profligate spender and promised to slash the federal budget. Rosenman recalled:

> Just before the start of the campaign of 1936, he said to me: "I'm going to make the first major campaign speech in Pittsburgh at the ball park in exactly the same spot I made that 1932 Pittsburgh speech; and in the speech I want to explain my 1932 statement. See whether you can prepare a draft giving a good and convincing explanation of it. . . ."
>
> That evening I went in to see the President in his study and said that as long as he insisted on referring to the speech, I had found the only kind of explanation that could be made. He turned to me rather hopefully and, I think, with a little surprise, and said, "Fine, what sort of an explanation would you make?"

I replied, "Mr. President, the only thing you can say about that 1932 speech is to deny categorically that you ever made it."

Instead, Roosevelt decided to make no direct mention of his 1932 address but to expound on why the budget had not been balanced. When he came to Forbes Field on October 1, he said: "The only way to keep the Government out of the red is to keep the people out of the red. And so we had to balance the budget of the American people before we could balance the budget of the national Government." Some folks in 1933 had urged him to let Nature take its course, but the President recalled, "I rejected that advice because Nature was in an angry mood." He declared:

> To balance our budget in 1933 or 1934 or 1935 would have been a crime against the American people. To do so we should either have had to make a capital levy that would have been confiscatory, or we would have had to set our face against human suffering with callous indifference. When Americans suffered, we refused to pass by on the other side. Humanity came first.

Having gotten past the impediment presented by his 1932 talk, Roosevelt offered himself in his more congenial role of prosperity-maker. In so doing he employed an analogy appropriate to a ballpark speech:

> Compare the scoreboard which you have in Pittsburgh now with the scoreboard which you had when I stood here at second base in this field four years ago. At that time, as I drove through these great valleys, I could see mile after mile of this greatest mill and factory area in the world, a dead panorama of silent black structures and smokeless stacks. I saw idleness and hunger instead of the whirl of machinery. Today as I came north from West Virginia, I saw mines operating, I found bustle and life, and hiss of steam, the ring of steel on steel—the roaring song of industry.

(A week later in Chicago, Landon replied: "If the administration wants a baseball analogy—if they want the score—it is easy to give. It is written across this country: Twenty-five billion dollars spent. Thirteen billion dollars added to the public debt. Eleven million unemployed left on base.")

FDR's critics had claimed that his failure to balance the budget would have disastrous consequences, and the President himself was uneasy about the mounting deficits, but in 1936 the economy began to surge—at a propitious time for the Democrats. Since March 1935, a "Roosevelt boom" had sent prices soaring on the stock market. In 1936 Allied Chemical climbed almost 69 points, Paramount Pictures preferred, 94 ½. The gross national product was half again as high as it had been in 1933, and farmers' net income had risen some $3.5 billion since the President took office. With eight million jobless, the country still had a long way to go to achieve full employment. But as one report noted, "Even to the casual observer the signs of returning prosperity were unmistakable: crowded resorts, highways congested with weekend trippers, fewer empty theater seats, the rising popularity of night clubs, and record crowds at baseball and football games."

The President perceived that, for all the good will New Deal legislation had won, his strongest card in bidding for reelection would be hard evidence that the country was "in the money" again. He instructed Secretary of Agriculture Wallace: "Henry, through July, August, September, October and up to the fifth of November, I want cotton to sell at twelve cents. I do not care how you do it. That is your problem. It can't go below twelve cents. Is that clear?" When the WPA planned to dismiss relief workers on October 1, Roosevelt scolded Secretary of the Treasury Henry Morgenthau, Jr., "You tell Corrington Gill that I don't give a goddam where he gets the money from but not one person is to be laid off on the first of October."

Roosevelt made the most of the contrast between America in 1936 and in 1932. From the rear platform of a train in Colorado Springs on October 12, he said: "You know, there has been a good deal of difference in tourists. In 1932, when I came out through here, there were a lot of tourists—but they were riding in box cars. This year there are more of them—and they are riding in Pullmans." As the economic indices continued to climb, the President moved farther ahead of his Republican rival. "I knew the case was hopeless as early as June," Landon told a reporter twenty years later. "Shortly after I was nominated in June, I sent for Mr. Benjamin Anderson of the Chase National Bank and Colonel Ayres of the Cleveland Trust Co. I asked them what business conditions would be like from June to November. They advised me each month would be better than the succeeding month. I realized then the campaign was pretty hopeless."

However often he dwelt on his success as prosperity-maker, though, never abandoned his role as champion of the underdog. At Madison Square Garden on the eve of the election, the President, angered by the Republican charge that workers might not receive their Social Security benefits, let out all the stops in an unrestrained attack on his opponents as the minions of avaricious interests. He told an explosively cheering, chanting crowd:

> Tonight I call the roll—the roll of honor of those who stood with us in 1932 and still stand with us today.
> Written on it are the names of millions who never had a chance—men at starvation wages, women in sweatshops, children at looms.

Having identified himself with the cause of the sweatshop laborer, he pinned the blame for the worker's misfortunes on the capture of the Republican party and the national government by wealth and greed. As the crowd roared its approval, Roosevelt said:

> For twelve years this Nation was afflicted with hear-nothing, see-nothing, do-nothing Government. The Nation looked to Government but the Government looked away. Nine mocking years with the golden calf and three long years of the scourge! Nine crazy years at the ticker and three long years in the breadlines! Nine mad years of mirage and three long years of despair! Powerful influences strive today to restore that kind of government with its doctrine that that Government is best which is most indifferent. . . .
> They had begun to consider the Government of the United States as a mere appendage to their own affairs. We know now that Government by organized money is just as dangerous as Government by organized mob.
> Never before in all our history have these forces been so united against one candidate as they stand today. They are unanimous in their hate for me—and I welcome their hatred. I should like to have it said of my first Administration that in it the forces of selfishness and of lust for power met their match. I should like to have it said of my second Administration that in it these forces met their master.

The President wound up his speech by responding to Landon's challenge:

This is our answer to those who, silent about their own plans, ask us to state our objectives.

Of course we will continue to seek to improve working conditions for the workers of America. . . . Of course we will continue to work for cheaper electricity in the homes and on the farms of America. . . . Of course we will continue our efforts for young men and women . . . for the crippled, for the blind, for the mothers, our insurance for the unemployed, our security for the aged. . . .

For these things, too, and for a multitude of things like them, we have only just begun to fight.

IX

As Roosevelt barnstormed the country, crowd response startled veterans of previous campaigns. In 1932 the country had voted less for FDR than against Hoover. "Mr. Roosevelt was no great popular idol during the presidential campaign of 1932," wrote the White House correspondent Ernest K. Lindley. "Vast crowds came out to look at him eagerly, hopefully. They liked him but went away still skeptical." In the intervening years, however, many Americans had come to view the President as one who was intimately concerned with their welfare. In 1936 at Bridgeport, Connecticut, he rode past signs saying, "Thank God for Roosevelt," and in the Denver freight yards a message scrawled in chalk on the side of a boxcar read, "Roosevelt Is My Friend."

Ambassador Breckinridge Long, who had ridden on the campaign train in 1932, found an "astonishing contrast" when he accompanied the President four years later. He noted in his diary:

Four years ago . . . the people were quiet and undemonstrative. There was a glumness and semblance of sullenness about their faces and their demeanor. They were awe-struck and in a terrible quandary. . . .

This year the crowds were larger than they were then and they were very enthusiastic. They passed any bounds for enthusiasm— really wild enthusiasm—that I have ever seen in any political gathering. . . .

[In] Detroit . . . the President spoke from the steps of the city hall, which opens onto a sort of circular space into which streets lead from five or six different directions. The whole space was a seething mass of people, standing packed closely together, and up each street as far as one could see in the dim electric light . . . the crowd was just as thick. It was boisterous in its enthusiasm, and it was almost impossible for the cars following the President to keep in line with him because of the seething people [who] swarmed around his car as it started away. In addition, the streets were lined all the way from Hamtramck through the city to the railroad station. . . .

Even at small stops, where there was no possibility of the train to stop and where it would go whizzing by at forty, fifty, and sixty miles an hour and all the way from seven o'clock in the morning till midnight, there would be assembled anywhere from ten to two or three hundred people. Every crossroad would have its collection.

Newspapermen observed the same phenomenon. Marquis Childs wrote of the President's reception in Jersey City: "From the moment that the procession of cars rolled out of the Holland Tunnel the thunder of bombs assaulted the ear, and the whole city under a cloudless blue sky seemed one mass of flag-waving humanity." Chicago, he reported, gave Roosevelt an even more impressive welcome:

In the early evening the President rode for five miles in an open car through streets so crowded that only a narrow lane was left. In spite of protests of the Secret Service, people had been allowed to swarm off the curbs and it was all that the motorcycle police could do to force a way through for the presidential cavalcade.

This was King Crowd. They were out to have a large time and they had it. Every kind of band—bagpipers, piano, accordions, jazz, fife-and-drum, bugle corps—lined the narrow lane of humanity through which the presidential party passed. As the parade turned off Michigan Boulevard into West Madison Street the mass of people became denser and noisier. They shrieked from rooftops; they sang and danced; they leaned from tenement windows and left windows to wave and shout. And all the time a rain of torn paper fluttered down, like gray snow in the half-lighted streets.

Senator Joseph Guffey of Pennsylvania said that "only ecstatic frenzy" could characterize the reception Roosevelt received in Pittsburgh, where crowds lined the street five and six deep. In the wealthy districts, houses were all dark, but servants stood in front of mansions in small knots and cheered. Earlier in the day, a campaign aide had phoned Stanley High from Pittsburgh: "It's been pouring rain here all day. But the president just reached the city and the sun has broken through." High noted in his diary: "More R. luck. As Eddie Roddan said—probably have a rainbow before he's through."

Despite the evidence of FDR's popularity, Republicans persisted in the belief that FDR was a one-termer, or at least that the GOP had a good chance of returning to power. In May Landon told a Republican Congressman: "I have seen a recent poll of a farm journal which gave several things of tremendous interest. One fact is that in Missouri I am personally within 48 votes of Roosevelt's vote. . . . In Nebraska I now exceed Roosevelt's own strength by 60." He had an edge in Indiana too, he found. Two months later, a prominent Republican recorded in his diary that a Tammany man "told us today that New York state was . . . absolutely safely Republican . . . actually said that he thought the City might well go against Roosevelt in November," and in September the country's best-known public relations counsel, Albert Lasker, wrote the columnist Frank R. Kent: "I am glad to get your judgment on Maine. I am even more heartened as a result of Michigan, but beyond that I have some very confidential figures of a very important poll that has been made with every check possible, I feel, to get down into every strata. This poll, which is on an enormous scale, indicates Democratic defeat by landslide proportions."

Conservative publicists reinforced the Republicans' sanguine expectations. The *Boston Evening Transcript* headlined one David Lawrence column, "Landon to win in Pennsylvania by 250,000," and another, "New York for Landon." A writer for the diehard Republican *New York Sun* chimed in, "California swings to Landon with rest of West Coast." No GOP organ was more widely read or elicited more trust from its subscribers than the *New York Herald Tribune*. In reporting confidently on "a new type of presidential forecast," the *Trib* stated: "Landon To Win 33 States, New Forecast Shows."

A surprising number of political experts anticipated a close election and even a Landon victory. On September 18 Arthur Krock wrote in the *New York Times* that "the Republican party will poll a far larger popular and electoral vote than in 1932. . . . Roosevelt's big majorities are over." Two weeks before the election, Archibald Crossley, head of the Crossley Political Poll, lunched in New York's financial district with thirteen other prognosticators. Their consensus: a narrow Landon win. The *Cleveland News* calculated that a capitulation of more than three thousand straw ballots taken by newspapers and magazines showed a Landon triumph with 307 electoral votes.

But the biggest splash was made by the final reckoning of the *Literary Digest* poll, which had called every election correctly since 1920. In 1932 Jim Farley had called the *Digest* survey "a poll fairly and evenly conducted," words that the magazine threw back at him now. In mid-October a count of nearly two million ballots gave Landon 1,004,086, Roosevelt, 728,088, with more than two-thirds of the electoral votes in Landon's column. "Even should Mr. Roosevelt gain in the remaining weeks before November 3," the editors declared, "he will have to do SOME gaining to upset the indicated outcome." In its very last summary, the *Literary Digest* forecast an electoral margin of 370–161 for Landon. Roosevelt led in no states outside the South and border regions save New Mexico and Utah; he trailed in Rhode Island by almost 3–1, in Massachusetts by $3^1/_2$–1.

On the other hand, the Gallup and Crossley polls, the *Fortune* survey, a group of more than twelve thousand editors canvassed by *Liberty*, a confidential survey of Washington correspondents, and the professional oddsmakers all predicted that Roosevelt would win, and handily. As early as March, Bernard Baruch had complained that he could not find Republicans willing to wager even in Palm Beach, and in late September a British embassy official in Washington informed Foreign Secretary Anthony Eden:

> Newspaper polls still give the Democrats a handsome lead and the betting on Wall Street is 8 to 5 in favour of Mr. Roosevelt. The "Baltimore Sun," which is against him, has been carrying out an exhaustive poll of Maryland which is considered a doubtful State and the result gives a forecast of nearly 2 to 1 for Mr. Roosevelt. The Republicans are nervous of losing the negro vote, which has usually been a safe asset for them, but which is likely to be influenced by the Government's relief measures.

Private polls prepared by the Nielsen Corporation for the Republicans showed the President with so substantial a lead that many GOP leaders were skeptical of the *Literary Digest's* findings.

But it was left to Jim Farley to make the prediction that would become the most famous in the history of political prognostication. On November 2 the Democratic chairman wrote Roosevelt that he had studied the memoranda he had received. "After looking them all over carefully and discounting everything that has been given in these reports," Farley said, "I am still definitely of the opinion that you will carry every state but two—Maine and Vermont."

Landon had few illusions about his prospects as the campaign wound down. The economic indicators were running against him, and the crowds were too cool. Workers in Shopton, Iowa, the location of the Santa Fe railroad shops, had to be all but dragged from a porch railing to be photographed with him. In Maine he was told that a meeting he addressed was one of the warmest ever held in that state. "It may have been warm for Maine," Landon responded, "but it was damn cold for Kansas." When, despite his chill reception, the Republicans carried Maine in its then-traditional early election in September, Landon voiced the old cry, "As Maine goes, so goes the nation," and for a moment hope flickered. But before the campaign had ended, Landon knew he was beaten. At lunch on October 28 two former Republican Senators, after telling Landon he would not win New Jersey, asked him if he thought he would carry the country. "No chance," the Governor replied. On election night when a photographer asked the Republican candidate to pose beside a large "Landon Victory Cake," he said to his wife, "Come on, Mother, and get your picture took. It will be the last chance."

X

When the first returns reached Hyde Park, the President leaned back, blew a smoke ring, and said, "Wow!" New Haven, Connecticut, a bellwether city, had gone to FDR by 15,000—the earliest indication of the power of his urban coalition. Through the night, to the accompaniment of Tommy Corcoran's accordion, the wire services chattered the glad evidence of a landslide. The President's 27,751,841 votes (to Landon's 16,679,491) set a new mark. His proportion of the popular vote (60.8 percent) was the greatest in recorded history (adequate data do not exist before 1824). In fourteen states no Democratic presidential candidate had ever matched Roosevelt's 1936 percentage. Nor had anyone ever equaled FDR's more than eleven million plurality. Even more impressive was the tally in electoral votes, 523–8, the greatest electoral triumph since James Monroe won in 1820 at a time of party breakdown. Just as Jim Farley had foreseen, every state but Maine and Vermont fell into the Democratic column. "I knew I should have gone to Maine and Vermont," the President said, "but Jim wouldn't let me."

Except for Maine and Vermont, FDR's victory combination bracketed the country. The Democrats made their traditionally strong showing in the South, which after a deviation in 1928 had become "Solid" again in 1932. Roosevelt received 76 percent of the two-party vote in that section, and in South Carolina, long the banner Democratic state, he rolled up a stunning 98.57 percent. The President did next best in the Far West with 68 percent of the two-party vote; he carried California and Washington by 2–1. He polled roughly that average in the West Central states with 61 percent, the Middle Atlantic states with 60 percent, and the East Central states with 59 percent. Only in New England, with 54 percent, did Roosevelt run several points below that average. Farley should never have made his prediction about Maine and Vermont, Molly Dewson said. With enough work, they could have carried Vermont.

Yet in no election in the history of the two-party system had section made so little difference. Even in the Northeast, a Democratic presidential candidate carried Delaware and Connecticut for the first time since 1912 and Pennsylvania for the first time since 1856, when a Pennsylvanian, James Buchanan, had run. The chief sectional impact of the election was to reduce the influence of the South in the Democratic party. While the former Confederate states contributed twenty-six of the thirty-seven Senate seats held by the Democrats in 1918, they had twenty-six of seventy-five in 1936. In 1920 almost every Democratic Congressman came from the South (107 of 131); by 1936 Southerners were a decided minority with 116 of 333. The most influential voices in party councils now came from the Northern cities, which commanded big blocs of electoral votes. In 1936 the Democrats recognized for the first time that there were greater rewards from appeals to northern blacks than to southern whites. The South, irritated by this turn of events, would remain "Solid" for only two more elections.

Landon had suffered the most crushing electoral defeat of any major party candidate in history, and his popular percentage (36.5) was the smallest for any Republican nominee since Taft's in 1912 when Theodore Roosevelt's "Bull Moose" challenge divided the party. In only four states did Landon get as much as 45 percent of the vote. The GOP was left with only eighty-eight seats in the House of Representatives (compared to 333 for the Democrats, with thirteen to minor parties, one vacant) and just six-teen in the Senate (compared to seventy-five for the Democrats, with four to minor parties, one vacant). The Republican *Portland* (Maine) *Press-Herald* called the 1936 election "a death blow perhaps to the Republican Party," and other periodicals speculated about whether the GOP would not, like its predecessor, the Whig party, disappear from the political scene. "If the outcome of this election hasn't taught you Republicans not to meddle in politics," jeered one writer, "I don't know what will."

It had long been said that "As Maine goes, so goes the nation," but after the 1936 results became known, a new maxim circulated: "As Maine goes, so goes Vermont." A bridge over the Salmon Falls River dividing New Hampshire from Maine was adorned with the sign, "You Are Now Leaving the United States," and Democrats regaled one another with gibes about the failure of the GOP to take more than two states. Harold Ickes proposed establishing Vermont as a national park to "foster and protect that rapidly disappearing specimen, the homo Republicanus," and Alben Barkley suggested that "Maine and Vermont should be given to the Duke of Windsor as a wedding present."

Yet Landon did not do quite so badly as first impressions implied. Roosevelt's enormous margin in the Electoral College exaggerated the dimensions of his victory, for Landon's 36.5 percent of the popular vote earned him only 1.5 percent of the electoral vote. Since Landon's defeat in 1936 seemed much more devastating than Hoover's in 1932, it was often overlooked, too, that Landon drew nearly a million more votes than Hoover had. Although Landon carried only 459 counties to Roosevelt's 2,636, that was still eighty-seven more than Hoover had won. If Landon polled the smallest percentage ever received by a Republican presidential candidate in a predominantly two-party race, he got a higher proportion than either Cox or Davis had on the Democratic line in the 1920s. Even FDR's percentage of the popular vote was not so exceptional as many thought; it roughly approximated Harding's in 1920.

Landon also gained back some of the GOP's following in the country-side. While the President received 59 percent of the two-party vote of farmers, only slightly under his overall national average, Landon did reasonably well with corn and wheat growers and even better with dairymen. The Governor, however, found his greatest support in that traditional Republican stronghold, the market town. Roosevelt received 61 percent of the farm vote in Iowa but only 48 percent of the town vote. In a tier of states from South Dakota to Oklahoma, and including Iowa, Missouri, and New Mexico, Landon improved on Hoover's performance in 1932, as he also did in five Southern and border states.

Lemke received 892,390 votes (2 percent) and no electoral votes. He polled his largest state total in Ohio (132,212), but recorded the best percentage (13.4) in his own state of North Dakota, still not outstanding. He held the balance of power in no state save New Hampshire, where a shift of the whole bloc of 4,819 Lemke voters would have put the state in Landon's column. It was a disappointing showing, far below Coughlin's expectation. On the other hand, Lemke would have done appreciably better if he had not failed to qualify for a line on the ballot in fourteen states, including New York, where Coughlin had a large following; California, the seat of Townsend strength; and Louisiana, the stronghold of Share Our Wealth. In some other states, he could not use the name "Union party"; in Ohio and Pennsylvania, he ran as the candidate of the Royal Oak party. Lemke drew some comfort from the fact that he had won reelection to Congress on the Republican ticket. In Massachusetts O'Brien, as a candidate for the U. S. Senate, took enough votes from James Michael Curley to permit Henry Cabot Lodge, Jr. to win a narrow victory.

Samuel Lubell has contended that Lemke's vote was the product not of economic protest but of foreign policy concerns, especially Irish-American Anglophobia and German-American fear that Roosevelt would lead the country into another war against the Reich. He pointed out that of the thirty-nine counties outside of North Dakota where Lemke got more than 10 percent of the vote, twenty-eight were predominantly German, and that in the four cities where Lemke polled over 5 percent—St. Paul, Dubuque, Boston, and Cincinnati—his support appears to have come from German and Irish voters. Lubell, though, does not explain why this minority was so disposed when the vast majority of German and Irish voters backed the major parties. Moreover, there may be more compelling explanations of even this limited ethnic pattern. Lemke was of German descent, O'Brien an Irish-American, and Coughlin had a considerable following in both groups. Furthermore, foreign policy issues did not figure prominently in the campaign, and the image of Roosevelt as an interventionist had not crystallized by 1936.

When international concerns did become paramount in FDR's second term, the Union party remnant, which lasted only until the spring of 1939, failed to capitalize on them. In its declining years, the party was captured in some areas by anti-Semites, to the dismay of Lemke who agreed to serve as a sponsor of the American Jewish Congress—an ironic denouement to Coughlin's efforts. The National Union for Social Justice also failed to survive Lemke's defeat. On the day after the election, Father Coughlin said: "The National Union may be compared to Joe Louis in his recent fight against Max Schmeling. Our aim now is a trip to the showers, and a new training camp for our comeback, if and when it is required." But three days later he conceded his Union was "thoroughly discredited," and he disbanded it.

The two major parties dominated the election with 97.3 percent of the popular returns and all the electoral votes. (The minor parties' 2.7 percent does not include the American Labor party totals which were recorded for Roosevelt.) The biggest portion of the minor party tally was accounted for by the Union party, which made its appearance in only this one presidential election. Each of the minor parties which had taken part in previous contests—the Socialist, Communist, Prohibitionist, and the Socialist Labor parties—suffered a decline in 1936 from its total four years earlier. One unwelcome newcomer, the Christian party, headed by William Dudley Pelley, founder of the quasi-fascist Silver Shirt Legion of America, got less than 1,600 votes.

The Socialist Norman Thomas and his running mate George Nelson of the Farmers Union polled 188,497 votes (0.4 percent), a precipitous drop from the 884,781 (2.2 percent) Thomas had won on the Socialist line in 1932. The party had not received so few votes since 1900 when its proportion was much higher. In 1928 the wife of the Socialist candidate opposing FDR for the governorship had warned her husband, "Roosevelt is the most formidable opponent that the Socialist Party will ever have in the United States," and the 1936 results showed her prescience. In some states the drop-off all but wiped out the party as an effective force; Thomas's total in Iowa plunged from 20,467 to 1,373, in Illinois from 67,258 to 7,530.

Thomas had been unable to hold his ranks against the appeal of the New Deal. Although he retained the support of John Dewey and Reinhold Niebuhr, most intellectuals backed FDR. A. Philip Randolph, the able leader of the Brotherhood of Sleeping Car Porters, directed the Labor League for Thomas and Nelson, but no large unions backed the ticket. Two Socialists, Jerry Voorhis of California and Andrew J. Biemiller of Wisconsin, left the Socialist party for the Democrats; they would subsequently represent their new party in Congress. Thomas himself had no doubt of the cause of his grief. From 1931 to 1934, he later said, "it looked as if we were going to go places. . . . What cut the ground out pretty completely from under us was . . . Roosevelt in a word. You don't need anything more."

The 1936 election confirmed the status of the Democrats as the country's new majority party. It established that Roosevelt's election in 1932 had not been an erratic event but rather signaled the beginning of a new political era. Even a scholar who has emphasized incremental rather than seismic change has acknowledged that "the 1930s has been the only realignment" in the twentieth century. "The New Deal realignment was one of the great formative experiences of the 'post-party period,'" wrote Gerald Gamm in 1989. "It gave renewed, if temporary, vigor to political parties and helped create fierce party attachments which have corroded only slowly. Not since has the party system been so suddenly and thoroughly transformed." The Republicans, long known as the party of the full dinner pail, were fated to be thought of as the party of economic breakdown, while the Democrats, who had been in power during the panics of 1837, 1857, and 1893, and the recession of 1913, came to be regarded as, if not the party of good times, at least the shield of "one third of a nation." For the next half century, the Republicans were to win only two Congressional elections, in large part because of the legacy of the Great Depression and the New Deal. In the 1950s a Chicago Democrat said: "Franklin Roosevelt was the greatest precinct captain we ever had. He elected everybody—governors, senators, sheriffs, aldermen."

Though the 1936 contest bears many of the marks of the political scientist V. O. Key's definition of a "critical election"—intense involvement, profound readjustments of power, the formation of new and durable electoral groups—it should be categorized rather as the capstone of a "critical period," another of Key's conceptions. The big reshuffling had come four years earlier when Franklin D. Roosevelt became the first Democratic presidential candidate to win with a majority of the popular vote since Pierce in 1852. Yet it was by no means clear during FDR's first term that this transformation would endure. The Survey Research Center analysts have commented:

> The nationwide shift toward the Democratic Party during the 1930s was not fully accomplished in a single election. Although Mr. Roosevelt's margin of victory in 1932 was large . . . , it was not until 1936 that the Democratic wave reached its peak. The long-entrenched Republican sympathies of the electorate may not have given way easily in the early years of the Depression. Had not Mr.

Roosevelt and his New Deal won the confidence of many of these people during his first administration—or even his second—there might have been a return to earlier party lines similar to that which occurred in 1920. From this point of view we may do well to speak of a realigning electoral era rather than a realigning election.

In like manner, James Sundquist has emphasized that "the realignment of the 1930's was powered by a historic ideological dispute" that left "an activist Democratic party confronting a conservative Republican party," while Everett Carll Ladd, Jr. and Charles D. Hadley have stressed that "party coalitions have attained majority status in the American experience when . . . they represented a public philosophy" widely accepted as "positive, forward-looking, progressive, and that the Democrats achieved that status as a result not just of the Great Depression but of the espousal of governmental nationalism by the Roosevelt administration."

The Democratic vote in 1936 contrasted vividly with the returns in the 1920s, the apogee of the age of Republican supremacy. Roosevelt tripled the Democratic presidential total in 1920, while Landon received roughly the same figure that Harding had polled sixteen years earlier. Some states showed a staggering change; Michigan, which gave the Democratic presidential candidate only 152,000 votes in 1924, chalked up 1,017,000 for FDR in 1936. In one article, Key, drawing on the New England experience, suggested that this realignment took place in 1928. But in the nation as a whole the salient change did not occur until the onset of the Depression. Pennsylvania, the "Verdun of Toryism," returned Democratic majorities in no more than four of its sixty-seven counties in the 1920s; in 1936 Roosevelt captured forty-one. In California the Republicans boasted 78 percent of the registered voters as late as 1930. In the next six years, however, the totals for Democratic registrants rose 313 percent, while GOP adherents dropped off 24 percent. By 1936 the Democrats had 60 percent of California's registration, a ratio that persisted into the 1960s.

Scholars differ boisterously about what brought about the realignment. The most natural assumption is that Democrats must have become the majority party because Republican voters switched to the Democratic faith. For a long time, though, most students of the subject—writers such as Kristi Anderson, Howard Allen, Erik Austin, David Prindle, and John R. Petrocik—believed that "conversion" was less important in accounting for the change than "mobilization" by the Democrats of first-time voters, both young people coming of age in the Great Depression and older

Americans who had not seen enough difference between the parties to induce them to go to the polls. More recently, however, analysts such as Robert Erikson and Kent Tedin have placed greater emphasis on the conversion hypothesis, as have Ladd and Hadley. The debate is far from resolved, and the most reasonable conclusion at present, as the historian Bernard Sternsher has written, is that "both mobilization and conversion played significant roles in the 1930s realignment."

A great deal of evidence demonstrates abandonment by voters of their old allegiances. Some conservative Democrats crossed over to the GOP—such as the Minneapolis man who said, "I was born and raised a Democrat, but if this President is a Democrat, I do not know a speckled cow from a grasshopper"—and FDR's onetime Assistant Secretary of Commerce wrote a conservative Michigan Congressman a few days before the election, "Although I have been a life-long Democrat and was President Roosevelt's pre-convention manager in Missouri in 1932, I am going to vote not only for Landon and Knox but the straight Republican state ticket in Missouri next month."

On the other hand, an even larger number of Republicans migrated to the party of the New Deal. In Sedgwick County (Wichita) in Alf Landon's Kansas, 1,237 registrants switched party affiliations in the four months beginning March 1: seventy from Democrat to Republican, 1,167 from Republican to Democrat. "Like most descendants of Civil War Veterans I was born a Republican," declared the social worker Grace Abbott. Not once had she voted in a Democratic primary. But, she went on, "I have learned that the most important thing for children is security in their own homes and because greater progress has been made toward this ideal during the past three years than the previous thirty years I am ready to vote for President Roosevelt and to ask others to vote for him."

Yet "conversion" falls well short of accounting for all of the returns. Of the increased turnout of nearly six million over 1932, the Democrats secured almost five million. That first-time voters made a disproportionate contribution to the Democratic margin is suggested by the fact that FDR's share of the two-party vote fluctuated with age, from 68 percent of the twenty-one to twenty-four-year-old bracket to 55 percent of those fifty-five and over. The hospitality of the Roosevelt coalition to all ethnic groups and the public assistance extended by the New Deal without discrimination persuaded a generation of Mexican-Americans who had thought of themselves as citizens of Mexico temporarily away (*Mexicanos de afuera*) to abandon the dream of repatriation and take an active part instead in the American political process. From 1934 to 1936 applications for naturalization nearly doubled over the previous three-year period as benefits derived from the New Deal reverberated through the south-western *barrios*. The historian Rodolfo Acuña has stated that "most Chicanos have been nurtured to believe in the Virgin of Guadalupe, the Sacred Heart, and the party of Franklin D. Roosevelt," and a social worker in Los Angeles has said that "Franklin D. Roosevelt's name was the spark that started thousands of Spanish-speaking persons to the polls."

In this new era of Democratic supremacy, whether primarily the result of conversion or mobilization, social stratification was the hallmark. At the second game of the World Series between the Yankees and the Giants, men in the expensive boxes adjacent to the President all wore conspicuous sun-flowers, Landon's symbol, but when the bleacher crowd spotted Roosevelt they broke out in wild applause. Gallup found that in 1936 FDR, who got 62.5 percent of the two-party vote nationally, received 42 percent of the upper income share, 60 percent of middle income, and 76 percent of lower income. His proportion of the labor vote varied inversely with skill—61 percent from white collar employees, 67 percent from skilled artisans, 74 percent from semi-skilled workers, and 81 percent from unskilled laborers. He won 84 percent of the ballots cast for the major par-ties by relief recipients and 80 percent of the labor union vote. (In New York the President polled 275,000 votes on the American Labor party line.) The historian Paul Kleppner calculated that Roosevelt had run 4.9 percent ahead of his Republican rival among the highest income voters in 1932, but fell 29.1 points behind his GOP opponent in that category in 1936, at the same time that he was mobilizing an "extraordinary number of lower income voters . . . turning out at unusually high rates . . . as if they perceived that the alternatives differed in ways that were relevant to their lives." After the election a furniture worker from Paris, Texas wrote the President, "Now that we have had a land Slide and done just what was best for our country . . . I will Say . . . you are the one & only President that ever helped a Working Class of People."

When the *Literary Digest* folded shortly after the 1936 election, most commentators attributed its demise to the impact of class politics. The *Digest* had been right in every election up until 1936, but woefully mis-taken that year, it was argued, because the magazine's sample failed to allow for the influence of class, which was pivotal in 1936 as it had not been as recently as 1932. This analysis may be correct, but certain demur-rers should be noted, quite apart from the fact that the *Digest* was already in difficulty. Although data are inadequate, there were discernible class influences on partisan alignment well before the Depression, and some studies have revealed a sharp class cleavage in the 1932 election. Furthermore, class differences in 1936 were obscured by the fact that Roosevelt received so large a share of the vote that he ran quite well among the moderately well-to-do. Yet there can be little doubt that a sizeable number of lower-income voters—reliefers, blacks, industrial unionists, New Deal beneficiaries, erstwhile Socialists—switched over to the Democrats in 1936, while still others cast their first votes for FDR. Four years later, after examining the 1940 election returns, the political writer Samuel Lubell concluded, "The New Deal appears to have accomplished what the Socialists, the I.W.W. and the Communists never could approach. It has drawn a class line across the face of American politics."

The 1936 outcome led many to dismiss editorials as reflecting the class bias of publishers and to discount the influence of the press on public opinion. In 1932 Roosevelt had enjoyed the support of both Hearst and Colonel Robert R. McCormick of the *Chicago Tribune*, but each soon became a bitter foe, and in 1936 even such normally Democratic newspapers as the *St. Louis Post-Dispatch* backed Landon. Many publishers shared the hostility of other businessmen toward the President, and they had been especially aggrieved when the National Recovery Administration insisted that they meet wages and hours standards. Although FDR held his own among small circulation newspapers, he had the backing of only one-fifth of the large dailies in 1936, and the behavior of some journals toward Roosevelt—that "traitor to his class"—lost all sense of proportion. When immoral practices were exposed in Wisconsin, the *Chicago Tribune* headlined its story: ROOSEVELT AREA IN WISCONSIN IS HOTBED OF VICE. As the majorities for the President mounted on Election Night, a crowd in Chicago burned a truckload of the *Tribune*. Subsequently, when a Chicagoan was asked what he thought of the campaign that his city's three largest dailies were waging against syphilis, he replied, "I hate to see it." His questioner, startled, asked, "Why?" "Because," the man answered, "I hate to see syphilis win."

The transit of lower-income groups to the Democrats took place largely in the great cities. The President rolled up margins of better than 2–1 in Baltimore, Cleveland, and Detroit, 3–1 in San Francisco and New York City (which gave him a lavish 1,367,000 plurality), and 4–1 in Milwaukee. Southern cities—Atlanta, Birmingham, New Orleans, Houston—handed him still bigger majorities. In some metropolises the change in urban allegiance had come with the "Al Smith Revolution" in 1928. Roosevelt, in fact, actually got fewer votes in predominantly Catholic Boston and Lowell in 1936 than Smith had in 1928. More characteristic, however, was Los Angeles where Smith polled only 28.7 percent in 1928 while Roosevelt received 57.3 percent in 1932 and 67.0 in 1936. In Philadelphia Roosevelt in 1932 had built Smith's 39.5 percent up only to 42.9 percent; the big leap came in 1936 when FDR amassed 60.5 percent. Flint, which had given Smith a mere 19 percent in 1928, voted 72 percent Roosevelt in 1936; San Diego jumped from 32 percent to 65 percent in the same period.

The most dramatic change came in Pittsburgh. Democratic registration in that steel town, which had been an incredibly low 3 percent in 1929, had reached 18.5 percent by September 1933, but that still accounted for less than one-fifth of registered voters. In April 1936, however, the Democratic boss, Dave Lawrence, announced that for the first time since the Civil War Pittsburgh had more Democrats registered than Republicans, and in November Roosevelt carried every ward in the smoky city. In the Jones and Laughlin ward, at a time when the steel company was carrying a challenge to the constitutionality of the Wagner Act to the Supreme Court, the President rolled up 5,870 votes to only 925 for Landon, while neighboring Homestead, nursing bitter memories of the violent suppression of the 1892 steel strike, went 4–1 for Roosevelt.

FDR's impressive showing in metropolitan areas concealed a divergence between core city and suburb. In 1936 Landon polled only 24 percent of the New York City vote but 54 percent of the nearby suburbs, 30 percent of the Cleveland vote but 54 percent of the suburbs, 33 percent of Chicago's vote but 50 percent of the suburbs. These differences reflected the influence less of locality than of socioeconomic status.

Roosevelt's success in the cities derived in large part from his attention to ethnic groups, especially the newer immigrants. "Our people did not know anything about the government until the depression," said a Slovak worker in Chicago who had grown up in Back of the Yards. His father had never been in a polling booth. Indeed, "in my neighborhood, I don't remember anyone voting." But with the coming of the New Deal, political consciousness quickened and the people he knew registered and voted to make sure that FERA or CCC or WPA programs were sustained. Congressman John Dingell told the President that in Hamtramck, Michigan, "where the population is almost one hundred percent Polish you received almost one hundred percent of the vote." One historian has

gone so far as to say that the New Deal was "a social revolution complet-
ing the overthrow of the Protestant Republic."

Jews, who admired FDR's liberal programs and his association with
"Brain Trust" intellectuals, gave the President enthusiastic support,
although not to the degree that they would when he became an outspoken
foe of Hitler. In Paterson, New Jersey's predominantly Jewish Fourth
Ward, Landon came away with just 30 percent. This marked a major shift.
In Jewish neighborhoods in Chicago in 1920, the Democratic candidate
had received only 15 percent of the vote, a miserable showing. But in 1932
Jews switched decisively to Roosevelt, and in the 1930s the Democratic
governors of the country's two most populous states, New York and
Illinois, were both Jews. In 1936 the Jewish community of Lawndale in
Chicago's West Side gave the President a 24,000 to 700 advantage; it was,
he said, "the best Democratic ward in the country." That same year, the
predominantly Jewish ward in Boston in which the journalist Theodore
White was raised gave the President better than 85 percent of its ballots.
"Far away, remote, there was FDR," White later recalled, "who, thank
God, believed in jobs for people. As I grew older, it also turned out that he
was against Hitler, and we enshrined him in our hearts." By the end of the
decade, Roosevelt and the Democrats were getting close to 90 percent of
votes cast by Jews, even among the wealthy, for Jews were the only group
whose voting revealed no class cleavage. In 1936 upper-middle-class
Jewish precincts in Boston went 93 percent for FDR, and four years later
Lubell found that in Jewish neighborhoods in Brooklyn Roosevelt carried
even "apartment houses with doormen."

Estimates of Roosevelt's share of Catholic ballots varied from better
than 70 percent to 81 percent. As early as August, Monsignor Ryan
reported that "everybody in California is for Roosevelt, especially the
nuns." Another cleric reckoned that of the 106 American bishops, 103 had
voted for the President. Immediately after the election, Monsignor R. F.
Keegan, Secretary to Cardinal Hayes, wrote Roosevelt, "You are an answer
to prayer—the prayer of all of us close to the man in the street, the factory,
on the farm, and for whom any other result would have been the worst
calamity that could have befallen America." In 1940 a priest in an automobile worker precinct in Detroit told a reporter, "If I ever attacked
Roosevelt from the pulpit, it would be the end of me here."

While the President scored heavily with non-Protestant nationality
groups, he received only a bare majority of the Protestant vote. John H.

Fenton has noted "the fears of some native white Hoosiers that the party of Franklin Roosevelt was an advance agent for a plundering horde of foreigners led by the pope." In much of the nation, Landon ran particularly well among native-born rural voters of Anglo-Saxon descent. Perhaps more noteworthy, however, may be the degree to which the President cut into that native-born vote, long regarded as the Republicans' special domain. GOP ballots in largely old-stock Multnomah County, Oregon (Portland) declined from nearly 76,000 in 1928 to under 42,000 in 1936. In winning so large a share of working-class ballots, Roosevelt united groups that had hitherto been divided by race and nationality. The 1936 election, Norman Graebner has written, marked the first time since the Civil War that native laborers voted Democratic.

Of all the changes in 1936, none demonstrated so historic a shift of allegiance as that of the African-American voter. Blacks in northern states, Gallup reported, gave the President 76 percent of their major party ballots. The Democrats made deep inroads into the Republican grip on black districts in the northern cities. Roosevelt, who had received only 21 percent of the black vote in Chicago in 1932, won 49 percent in 1936, almost breaking even. In Cincinnati's Ward Sixteen, FDR, who had polled less than 29 percent in 1932, improved to better than 65 percent in 1936, a higher proportion than he received in the city as a whole.

The change came not because of the President's record on civil rights, though it was somewhat of an improvement on that of his predecessors, but out of gratitude for programs that by 1935 put 3.5 million African Americans on relief rolls. "The key to black electoral behavior lay in economics rather than race," the historian Nancy Weiss has concluded. "Folks where I come from," cried a young black man in the Illinois Federal Writers' Project, Richard Wright, "they're all singing:

> Roosevelt! You're my man!
> When the time come
> I ain't got a cent,
> You buy my groceries
> And pay my rent.
> Mr. Roosevelt, you're my man."

Even in the South, black ballots helped to swell his totals. "Every Negro I have registered so far has said he would vote for President Roosevelt," revealed a registrar in Columbia, South Carolina. "They say Roosevelt saved them from starvation, gave them aid when they were in distress."

XI

Roosevelt's reelection in 1936 represented not only a personal triumph, but also a victory for his ideas. William Allen White observed: "The water of liberalism has been dammed up for forty years by the two major parties. The dam is out. Landon went down the creek in the torrent." To be sure, many ballots must have been cast for FDR by voters who admired his personality and cared not a hoot about his principles, especially since the President had given so few specifics about his plans for his second term. Henry Breckinridge wrote sourly, "The people have spoken and in the fullness of time Roosevelt will tell us what they have said." It is true, too, that the President profited from improving economic conditions. But no such considerations should cloud the fact that the election was widely seen as a ratification of the Welfare State. As the historian John Braeman has written, "Although the Democratic gains in 1932 may be interpreted primarily as a protest vote against the 'ins' because of hard times, the continued Democratic upsurge four years later can be regarded only as an affirmative endorsement of New Deal policies and programs." The voters had been offered an opportunity to reject the party that had identified itself with the growth of the central government and had instead given that party a thumping endorsement. In authenticating the position of the Democrats as the nation's majority party and demonstrating the decisive influence of class in American politics, the voters on November 3, 1936 made unmistakably clear that Big Government was here to stay.

FIVE

Roosevelt, Norris, and the "Seven Little TVAs"

[During high school and college, and for some years afterward, I found the Tennessee Valley Authority far more captivating than any other feature of the New Deal. The problem that bedeviled my generation, and was the subject of a conference I participated in as an undergraduate at Cornell, was how to augment the influence of the State at a time when the market system had broken down while avoiding the excesses of governmental power all too manifest in contemporary regimes such as Hitler's Germany and Stalin's USSR. The TVA appeared to have the answer—a public corporation endowed with all the authority it needed to embark on an ambitious experiment in hydroelectric power development and watershed planning, yet centered not in Washington but in the valley and responsive to the people of the region. It seemed a brilliant resolution of the dilemma of modern governance. My dissertation sponsor at Columbia, Henry Steele Commager, called the TVA "a philosophical and historical as well as a political and social laboratory, . . . the proving ground . . . of a dynamic democracy," and a feature writer in the *New York Times Magazine* in the spring of 1938 even asserted, "Upon the degree of success or failure shown by the TVA depends to a large extent the course of American history."

The Tennessee Valley Authority offered an American version of Sweden's "Middle Way." The TVA official would engage in government planning, but unlike the Soviet commissar would do so not to crush private initiative but to promote it, and, in fidelity to the regionalist premises of Howard Odum and Rupert Vance, would decentralize power and respect the idiosyncrasies of locality. TVA promised that, in contrast to the messiness of an acquisitive society, there would be harmony achieved by the application of reason. That in turn meant decisions would be made by those who held letters patent on reason—the new generation of the university-trained eager for its place in the sun. The experiment would be carried out not by grubby businessmen but by our crowd.

This conception of "grassroots" democracy generated enormous excitement. No agency at the time or since has commanded the same kind of allegiance. No one has ever felt toward the Home Owners' Loan Corporation or the Securities and Exchange Commission what the magical rubric "TVA" elicited. Sir Denis Brogan, author of the volume on the New Deal in the Chronicles of America series, occasioned no surprise when, in a very short treatment, he devoted an entire chapter to "The Dazzling TVA." For a long while, I carried around with me a well-thumbed copy of David Lilienthal's *TVA: Democracy on the March*, a paean at once practical and mystical that, better than any other book, provided a text for the liberal creed.

The ineluctable appeal of the TVA to me, though, derived from more than its attractiveness as a new mode of polity. To a boy raised in a New York City apartment, "Tupelo" and "Pickwick Landing" intimated words to a melody as "the Bronx," "Flatbush," and "Hoboken" did not, and "Tennessee" sounded less like the name of a river or a state than a whisper in the wind. The images of stark white concrete dams, deep blue lakes, foaming spillways, and taut transmission lines suggested a Charles Sheeler painting come to life. "The unity, the humanity, and the grandeur of the TVA concept . . . are so compelling as to make a kind of lyricism inevitable in the writing of those who understand what the TVA has been trying to do," observed the political scientist C. Herman Pritchett. "R. L. Duffus has spoken of the 'obvious poetry' of the TVA."

In later years I adopted a less rhapsodic attitude toward the TVA. Too much of the history of the agency in the post-Roosevelt era is encapsulated in the titles of magazine articles such as "The Strip Mine Scandals" and "TVA Ravages the Land." It became the country's worst emitter of sulfur dioxide, opposed black-lung and mine safety laws, took an uncritical view of nuclear power, displaced the Cherokees, and warred against pollution legislation. Well before then, Philip Selznick and other scholars had caused me to recognize that, even in the 1930s, "grassroots democracy" often meant deferring to entrenched interests in the region, especially powerful white landowners. These second thoughts were reinforced by my experience in serving as a consultant for Ross Spears's film, *The Electric Valley*, and in reading searching accounts by Nancy Grant and by Michael J. McDonald and John Muldowny. Still, for all the shortcomings of the TVA, the historian Thomas McCraw, who, though critical of much that it had done or failed to do, concluded, "The unified development of the Tennessee River was a spectacular achievement, unmatched for any other stream in the world."

The accomplishments of the Tennessee Valley Authority led me to ask, at a time when my conception of it was largely uncritical, why the TVA approach could not be replicated in other regions. "The Tennessee Valley Authority is but a great laboratory for the nation," Arthur E. Morgan, the chairman of the TVA, wrote in the spring of 1934. "What can be done there can be done for the rest of America." That inquiry resulted in my article, "Roosevelt, Norris and the 'Seven Little TVA's.'" I sent drafts of the essay to some of the leading actors in the drama and got back pages of thoughtful single-spaced letters from Harold Ickes, Ben Cohen, Paul Appleby of the Department of Agriculture, Marguerite Owen of the TVA, and Judson King, the public power lobbyist. As I reread that correspondence now, I do not know whether to be more impressed by the generosity of these busy people or by the temerity of a young instructor in imposing upon them. In addition, I received an extraordinarily helpful memo from E. B. Nixon of the staff of the Franklin D. Roosevelt Library that both facilitated and supplemented my research at Hyde Park. The final version appeared in *The Journal of Politics* 14 (August 1952): 418–41. I have emended it considerably, not only to take advantage of new sources, but more particularly to give broader context to the flow of events.]

I

In his message to Congress in the spring of 1933 urging enactment of the Tennessee Valley Authority bill, President Roosevelt observed: "If we are successful here we can march on, step by step, in a like development of other great natural territorial units within our borders." In the next few years glowing reports of the success of the TVA moved regional leaders to urge the President to "march on, step by step" to extend the TVA idea to the other big river valleys of the nation. On February 5, 1937 "the father of the TVA," Senator George W. Norris of Nebraska, who FDR had called "the very perfect gentle knight of American progressive ideals," capped the agitation by proposing "enough TVAs to cover the entire country," and on March 31, on leaving the White House after a conference with Roosevelt, Norris informed the press that he had discussed a national power and flood control plan with the President and that he would draft legislation for regional authorities modeled on the TVA.[1]

During the following month Roosevelt told newsmen he was scrutinizing various proposals for regional authorities, and on May 1 the

Washington Post reported that he was expected to back the Norris plan to blanket the nation with TVAs. On returning to Washington on May 14 from a trip to the Gulf of Mexico, he presented Administration legislators with a "must" calendar that included a national power program. "I think the President, probably within a few days—probably next week—will send to Congress his views for the establishment of additional TVAs in this country," Speaker William Bankhead announced. Throughout the spring of 1937 newspaper dispatches left little reason to conclude anything but that Roosevelt and Norris were one in attempting to extend the TVA pattern and that the Norris proposal had FDR's enthusiastic support. Hence, when on June 3 Norris finally introduced his bill in the Senate, his action appeared to be the culmination of several weeks of united efforts by the Nebraska senator and the Roosevelt administration to divide the nation among seven regional authorities.[2]

On the very same day, however, Representative Joseph Mansfield of Texas, the powerful chairman of the House Rivers and Harbors Committee, dropped a very different measure into the hopper in the House—to create agencies with planning functions only, although the President was also authorized to establish regional bodies to generate and market hydroelectric power. This legislation contrasted markedly with Norris's measure for a series of regional planning authorities that could also serve as operating agencies, with capabilities like those of the TVA. Unlike Mansfield, Norris envisioned authorities that would submit annual plans to the President to be forwarded to Congress; if Congress approved, these same authorities could administer these plans. They would do so in a variety of fields—hydroelectric power, reforestation, soil conservation, flood control, and still other aspects of river valley development.

Mansfield's maneuver caught Washington by surprise, but it was not nearly so startling as the President's response. Instead of repudiating the Mansfield measure and heartily endorsing the Norris bill, Roosevelt, in an address to Congress that day, was restrained to the point of ambiguity. He not only failed to demand a network of TVAs, but actually appeared to reflect Mansfield's approach.

What had happened during the spring of 1937 that resulted in the introduction of two different types of legislation? What forces produced the Mansfield bill? Why was FDR's message so restrained, and why was it so vague? What was the President's role in the campaign for regional authorities? Most important, who killed the "seven little TVAs?"

II

In the early years, Roosevelt had taken a firm stand against pressure for more valley authorities. On March 5, 1935 the acting director of the Bureau of the Budget, Daniel Bell, sent him a memo asking whether the more than twenty bills pending in the current session of Congress proposing regional authorities were in accord with his fiscal program, and the President replied that no new authorities were to be established that year. Five weeks later Roosevelt wrote Congressman William Citron of Connecticut, sponsor of legislation for a Connecticut Valley Authority:

> Before I can really consider going along with any further Regional Authorities, such as a Connecticut Valley Authority, it seems to me that there should be a fairly unanimous sentiment in the area affected. Do you think that the Governors of Vermont, New Hampshire, Massachusetts, and Connecticut would support the idea of an Authority? Each of these states would be affected in more ways than one.

Nearly a year later, in March 1936, in response to a letter from the president of the White and Black Rivers Flood Control Association asking for a TVA in Arkansas, Roosevelt once more affirmed that until the program of the Tennessee Valley Authority was completed, no other regional authorities should be started.[3]

By the end of 1936, however, Roosevelt recognized that he would have to discard temporizing in favor of a comprehensive national energy policy because a number of controversial issues were coming to a head. The Administration needed to decide whether to try to work out an agreement with the private utilities or to push for a bold public power program, whether the Tennessee Valley Authority was to be an isolated yardstick experiment or whether it was to set the pattern for national resources development. The one reality Roosevelt especially could not ignore was that power from Bonneville dam in the Columbia River basin would be coming on line in 1937, and a bill had to be drafted to provide for its distribution. As the *Electrical World*, with a clash of metaphors, put it, the President had succeeded heretofore in "taking the boiling pot off the fire and placing it on the back of the stove to simmer. . . . Now, the Administration finds itself, however unwillingly, in the middle of the ring and some decision must be made."[4]

To give coherence to his multifarious activities in the field, Roosevelt announced on January 18, 1937 the establishment of an Informal Committee on Power Policy, headed by Secretary of the Interior Harold Ickes, with FDR's uncle Frederic A. Delano (Vice-Chairman of the National Resources Committee), Morris L. Cooke (Administrator of the Rural Electrification Administration), Frank R. McNinch (Chairman of the Federal Power Commission), and Robert E. Healy (Securities and Exchange Commissioner) as the other members.[5] He gave the committee two weeks to recommend legislation on Bonneville and also handed it the task of formulating a federal power program.

Eight days later the President, at a meeting at the White House, told the committee of a plan he had been discussing moments before with Senator Norris "by which," Ickes noted in his diary, "the country would be divided roughly into eight great districts. Some agency would be set up for each district along the lines of TVA." The eight districts included one for the Territories. Roosevelt wanted the committee to draft appropriate legislation, to which he would call attention in a special message to Congress.[6]

While the committee took up this new assignment, the movement to create more valley authorities gained momentum. Not only was Senator Norris advocating a network of regional TVAs, but in addition Senator Alben Barkley of Kentucky and Senator Robert Bulkley of Ohio filed a more modest proposal to set up regional flood control authorities, with regional boards that could recommend, but not execute, plans for multi-purpose dams.[7] On February 12 the President noted that he had received the Bonneville report three days before from his Informal Committee on Power Policy and that it "would tie in very nicely with any subsequent legislation in relation to the regional power districts."[8] In sum, it appeared at this juncture that Norris's aspiration for a country-wide network of valley authorities had an excellent prospect of being achieved.

III

The committee had hardly begun its labors on regional planning legislation, however, when it became acutely aware that any bill it framed would have to run the gauntlet of several rival government agencies, each of them jealous of prerogatives, each of them committed to a particular administrative theory, each of them beholden to clients, each of them sensitive to how its behavior was monitored by lawmakers on Capitol Hill, and each of them capable of intense animosity. In addition, the committee recognized that it was being eyed warily by Washington lobbyists and special interests in the regions.

The experience of Senator James Pope suggested the kind of difficulty the committee was going to encounter. In 1935 he had introduced legislation to create a Columbia Valley Authority only to meet stout resistance from corporations (especially utilities), government agencies protective of their turf, and champions of states' rights resentful of any intrusion by Washington. Even in Pope's home state of Idaho, "the articulate regional reaction was overwhelmingly hostile," the political scientist Charles McKinley has noted. "A special committee of the Idaho State Chamber of Commerce, which included representatives of the leading wool-growers' association, the principal reclamation projects of the Boise Valley, the state mining association, the state bankers association, and the Master of the state grange, voiced determined opposition."[9]

In the summer of 1935 the Pacific Northwest Regional Planning Commission sought to ameliorate the controversy by conducting a study under the auspices of the National Resources Committee, an agency that the President, who wanted to "put the physical development of the country on a planned basis," had established by executive order. The Commission dealt a blow to the valley authority approach in that region by expressing dismay at the thought of combining electric energy generation and distribution with "ameliorative and philanthropic tasks" of the sort the TVA was supposed to be undertaking, though it had no hesitancy about supporting public power development. The National Resources Committee, with one conspicuous abstention, passed on the recommendations to the President with its approval. The lone holdout was the Secretary of War, who would not countenance any proposal that stripped the Corps of Engineers of the right to transmit and market power. In taking this stand, he could depend on the strong backing of businessmen in the region, who had a chummy relationship with the Corps and who were disturbed by the possibility that the report's advocacy of a new administrative agency would jeopardize the utilities and might ultimately lead to a valley authority in the Columbia basin. This alliance between the Corps and the business community had an influential agent in Washington in Charles McNary of Oregon, who permitted the lobbyist of the Portland Chamber of Commerce to set up a desk in his office in the United States Senate.[10]

The Secretary of War's recalcitrance aroused the ire of Ickes, who, quite apart from the fact that he was always spoiling for a fight, came in conflict with the War Department in each of his three roles—as Secretary of the Interior, as Public Works Administrator, and as chairman of the Informal Committee on Power Policy. Ickes first learned of the bias of the Corps of Engineers when early in the First Hundred Days of 1933 the President, at the urging of Senator Norris, asked him to look into a rumor of collusion between the Corps and the Alabama Power Company, an allegation that turned out to be well-founded. That experience instilled a distrust he never got over. Nearly two decades later he was still fuming:

> It is to be doubted whether any Federal agency in the history of this country has so wantonly wasted money on worthless projects as has the Corps of Army Engineers. It is beyond human imagination. . . . No more lawless or irresponsible Federal group . . . has ever attempted to operate in the United States, either outside of or within the law. . . . Nothing could be worse for the country than this wilful and expensive Corps of Army Engineers closely banded together in a self-serving clique in defiance of their superior officers and in contempt of the public welfare. The United States has had enough of "mutiny *for* the bounty."[11]

All through the spring of 1937 Ickes railed at the War Department. In particular, he sought, at first with poor results, to persuade Roosevelt to vest control of generating, transmitting, and marketing power at Bonneville in Interior rather than the War Department. "I do not trust the Army engineers on power," he noted in his diary. Early in May Ickes had a heated set-to with Secretary of War Harry Woodring over "a most extraordinary request for funds by the Army engineers for flood-control projects, especially in the Ohio and Mississippi Valleys." He found Woodring "very dogmatic and arbitrary," "very lordly," "contemptuous," and "sarcastic," in sum a "midget General MacArthur" who "struts about with inflated chest more sure of himself and more disagreeable and dictatorial than any man I have met in the Government."[12]

Roosevelt, recognizing how intense was the hostility of business groups and legislators such as McNary in the Pacific Northwest to anything approaching a valley authority and how potent was the sentiment for states' rights, chose to compromise on a "temporary" solution that would not delay disposal of Bonneville power, but it was a compromise, McKinley has written, that was "a distinct victory over the private-utility and chamber-of-commerce views on power policy" and "also a setback to the ambitions of the Corps of Engineers," as well as those of the Bureau of Reclamation. The statute, while leaving the Corps with the assignment of generating power, provided for an administrator chosen by and responsible to the Secretary of the Interior and stipulated, contrary to what the Corps wanted, that when energy was marketed, public distribution agencies and consumers should be favored. It also did not foreclose the possibility of a Columbia Valley Authority in the future. "Had it not been for the active, though delayed, intervention of the president, buttressed by the studies and recommendations of the National Resources Committee and its regional agency," McKinley has concluded, "the legislation would have lacked many features of a regional program." Still, the Columbia River saga suggested that if the committee decided to embrace "the little TVAs" solution, it would not have easy going.[13]

The fate of valley authority legislation also got caught up in another feud of cabinet officials, this one carried on by the pugnacious Ickes and Secretary of Agriculture Henry Wallace, a squabble that, as the historian T. H. Watkins has said, became unusually nasty "even by the standards of the often feral world of Washington bureaucracy." The controversy centered on Ickes's determination to detach the Forest Service from Agriculture and incorporate it in Interior—or, even better, in a renamed and expanded Department of Conservation. Ickes professed that he wanted to do so in order to redeem the honor of his department, which had been blemished by scandals, notably Teapot Dome, in the past, and because it was logical to have all conservation agencies in a single department, a point of view for which Roosevelt had considerable sympathy, though never enough to give Ickes his wish. Others, however, saw this ambition as motivated by nothing but gross empire-building. After hearing Ickes express his craving for the Forest Service, the TVA director David Lilienthal wrote in his diary: "Good God! No issue of fundamental policy whatever—just a man mad for power." Ickes's maneuvering encountered stiff resistance. The notion of creating a Department of Conservation, scoffed the Chief Forester, Ferdinand Silcox, "would be a little like setting up a Department of Prosperity."

In May 1936, Ickes wrote the President:

Here is a bill which I never would have introduced except with your consent. In flagrant violation of your orders, the Department of Agriculture has opposed it by hook and crook from the beginning.

The Forest Service particularly stirs up opposition and then Henry
Wallace tells you that there exists the opposition which he and assistants have stirred up. . . .
I feel this matter very keenly. I am willing to take my licking in a
fair fight, but this has not been a fair fight. Is the Department of
Agriculture to have its way in all matters? Isn't it time that we really
did something real about conservation?[14]

One of Wallace's principal aides, Paul Appleby, has perceived this dispute to be not a petty ruckus over jurisdictional rights but a genuine difference about administrative theory:

The quarrel between Ickes and Wallace was a perfectly sincere quarrel based quite simply on two different preoccupations—both functional. Ickes saw land in terms of "conservation" as a base value
around which to organize; Wallace saw "resource use" as the base
value. . . . Agriculture would have said that the problem was to make
land *users* take sufficient account of conservation needs; Ickes would
have said that conservation came first and use second. The President
was emotionally on Ickes' side; he saw some trees being cut in a
national forest and thought that exploitation; the foresters pointed
out that trees have a life span and inevitably die, that the right kind
of cutting made a total of much more trees and more lumber, too.[15]

More than a difference over theory motivated Wallace, however. In the
tedious wrangle between the two men, Ickes has traditionally been singled
out for blame, for his cupidity and bad temper are all too evident. At one
point in the bickering over the Forest Service, Wallace handed James F.
Byrnes a four-page communication he had received from Ickes that the
South Carolina senator called "as insulting as any letter I ever read." When
Wallace asked him what to do about it, Byrnes replied, "The only suggestion I can make is that you either tear up the letter and pretend you never
saw it or, when you next see Ickes, punch him and hope you will be separated before harm is done to either; you certainly cannot win a name-call-
ing contest with Ickes." But Wallace was no less chauvinistic about his
bailiwick, and he cast covetous eyes on certain bureaus in Interior, especially the Grazing Service. In grappling with Ickes he knew that he could
bank upon what the historian Richard Polenberg has called "the virtually

incestuous relationship between conservationists and the Forest Service," but his support was not limited to groups such as the Izaak Walton League. He also drew considerable political strength from lumbermen and stockmen who feared not that a Department of Conservation under Ickes would despoil the forests but that it would deny them access by acquiring the lands for national parks.[16]

Early in 1937 Ickes gained a significant advantage in this contest of wills. In March 1936 Roosevelt had appointed a Committee on Administrative Management headed by Louis Brownlow, director of the Public Administration Clearing House in Chicago, to recommend to him how to get better control of the executive branch, and at the beginning of 1937 it reported. The Brownlow Committee, among its many conclusions, called for a permanent central planning agency (a National Resources Board) and a new Public Works Department, set a schedule of priorities for projects in ninety-four river basins, and, most pertinent of all for the Wallace-Ickes imbroglio, advocated renaming the Department of the Interior the Department of Conservation.[17] This name change proposal was, in itself, altogether innocuous, but Wallace found it alarming, for it implied that Ickes, who was slated to head this department with its omnibus designation, was going to have his way with the Forest Service. When two years earlier newspapers interpreted Ickes's campaign for a Department of Conservation as a maneuver to grab the Forest Service, Ickes himself had conceded in his diary, "They are not far wrong at that."[18]

The very thought of that possibility enraged Wallace. Ickes recorded in his diary his version of an encounter with Secretary Wallace on January 8:

At this point, Henry turned on me savagely. Apparently he thought that what I meant was that I was going to try to build up a conservation department at the expense of Agriculture. I had meant nothing of the sort, although it had never been a secret that I am in favor of such a department. Before I realized what was happening I found myself under a very bitter attack. . . . At this I began to get hot under the collar. . . . Until the end I did my very best to avoid a discussion that plainly was becoming hotter and hotter, but evidently Henry had a lot on his chest that he was determined to blow off. . . . Altogether it was a heated and unpleasant session. Perhaps I said some things that I should not have said.

Afterward, one of his aides told Ickes that "Wallace appeared to be entirely oblivious of the presence of others; that his eyes were blazing and his chin thrust in my direction. It was plain . . . that he had reached the boiling point and that he could not overlook the opportunity . . . to make an onslaught."[19]

IV

All of these contesting actors and interests came into play in the disputation about the Norris proposal, with Secretary Wallace stepping forward as the leader of the fight against creating any more regional corporations like TVA. He may have felt particularly aggrieved because, as Ickes recorded in his diary after his meeting with Roosevelt in January about the regions, "It is the President's idea to have all these areas . . . head up through the new Department of Conservation." On February 17 Wallace wrote Ickes that he warmly seconded FDR's proposal for regional planning agencies but that he understood the President had in mind agencies with advisory rather than administrative functions. His support of the proposition, Wallace warned, was

> in sharpest contrast to any plan that would contemplate the establishment of over-all regional agencies with definite administrative powers, and, in turn, responsible to a single executive department. Against this, I should have to advise with the utmost vigor. Any such proposal would violate basic principles of sound organization, would demoralize the executive departments, and would deny to the President the over-all help to which he is entitled. Administrative confusion, personal jealousies, and bitterness would be rampant both in the field and in Washington. I earnestly hope that no such action will be recommended by your committee; I feel so strongly about the matter that if such a recommendation were made I should have to ask for an opportunity to present my views to the President before he reached a final decision.[20]

The committee, despite Wallace's threat, gave its approval to a draft bill prepared by Benjamin V. Cohen, its general counsel, creating a series of regional agencies that each year would submit plans to the Department of Conservation. That department, presumably headed by Ickes, would forward the plans to Congress at its discretion, and Congress would then assign the operation of any projects either to the regular departments or to the new regional planning agencies. Thus the regional agencies, though not as autonomous as the Tennessee Valley Authority, might, like TVA, have both planning and administrative powers, and Cohen's draft, in this sense, provided for "eight little TVAs."

On March 17 Wallace once again protested to Ickes:

> While I believe that the regional planning agencies should stick to planning, and should not be given administrative duties as well, nevertheless, if the President has definitely decided that these regional planning agencies are the appropriate authorities to administer the power, navigation, flood control, and reclamation projects, then I believe the President's purposes can be accomplished without needlessly interfering with effective administration of many existing programs.

It would be bad enough, Wallace continued, for the regional authorities to administer navigation, flood control, reclamation, and power projects, but they certainly should not intervene in fields such as soil conservation and forestry, now in the domain of the Department of Agriculture. Wallace further urged the committee to consult with the War Department as well before it permitted duplication of the flood control and navigation work of the Army Engineers. In short, if Mr. Ickes and the public power crowd were so obsessed by the idea of regional authorities, then the authorities should cut into the jurisdiction of the Department of the Interior and the Federal Power Commission and leave the other agencies alone.[21]

The National Resources Committee resisted no less strenuously the idea of cobwebbing the country with TVAs. Charles W. Eliot, 2d, Executive Officer of the Committee, prepared a report on the draft bill, about which he wrote Delano on March 25, "I feel so strongly and so perturbed." He took his rejoinder to Boston on March 27 for a conference with Delano, who agreed that Eliot's statement represented his own views, which he instructed a fellow member of the NRC, Charles Merriam, the prominent political scientist, to present to Ickes. In his report Eliot objected, first, that the draft bill ran counter to the recommendations of the Brownlow committee on government reorganization, for it mixed up functions the committee had divided among the proposed Conservation

Department, Public Works Department, and National Resources Board. He also observed that the draft bill provided for three-member agency boards on the TVA model, instead of the single administrators favored by the Brownlow committee and decided on for Bonneville. Second, Eliot asserted, the draft bill was not consistent with the counsel of the National Resources Committee. It ignored the report, *Public Works Planning*, which proposed a Public Works Department with a six-year program, revised annually. In addition, it flew in the face of the report, *Regional Factors in National Planning and Development*, in that it divided the country into regions with demarcated boundaries instead of relying on regional centers, and in that the boundaries of the regions would cut across state lines. Third, Eliot found the scheme badly timed. No action of this sort should be considered, he maintained, until the executive branch of the government had been reorganized, with the creation of a Public Works Department and a National Resources Board.[22]

The President saw the need to be responsive to these objections. He assured the National Resources Committee at a White House gathering that he wanted the bill to conform to its recommendations and those of the Brownlow committee, even turning his copy of Cohen's draft over to Brownlow for corrections. The Informal Committee on Power Policy also got marching orders. On April 6, as Ickes was concluding a meeting with Roosevelt, Louis Brownlow walked in. Ickes recorded in his diary: "I started to leave but the President told me to stay because I was interested. The talk was on the reorganization plan and on the Conservation District bill that Ben Cohen had drafted. The President wants some radical changes in this bill and I asked Brownlow to take it up direct with Ben Cohen." That same day, when a reporter asked the President about "several schemes up on the Hill to create authorities of various sorts," he replied: "I am trying to boil them down and see if we can't get them in somewhat orderly shape, which they are not in now." Under instructions from Roosevelt, the Informal Committee adopted a number of revisions of the draft bill, including reducing the number of authorities from eight to seven by striking out the provision for the Territories.[23]

On April 27 Roosevelt gave copies of his proposed message to Congress on regional authorities to his son, James, who was on his White House staff, and his press secretary, Stephen Early, asking them "to send them to Congress just as soon as Charlie West or Ben Cohen tell you the bill is ready for introduction by Senator Norris and Representative Whittington." At this point Roosevelt still thought of his message as a recommendation of "the bill" to be sponsored by Senator Norris, and April 27 was the very day of a White House conference with Norris, Cohen, and J. D. Ross of the Securities and Exchange Commission to discuss the proposed legislation.[24]

It was the day, too, that Ickes set down in his diary his own dissatisfaction with what had been happening. After meeting, at Ickes's direction, with Brownlow, Ben Cohen, he noted, had altered the original draft. Ickes continued:

Then it had been turned over, at the President's instance, to Senator Norris who doesn't like some of the provisions of the bill as set up by Cohen. Apparently he wants to duplicate the TVA setup throughout the country. This would mean seven independent authorities, and it seems to me that it runs directly counter to the President's plan to reorganize the executive branch of the Government.[25]

This surprising entry is significant for two reasons. First, it signals that Ickes had not been aware that Norris sought TVAs, although, since this was evident all along, one has to wonder where Ickes's attention was focused. Second, it reveals that Ickes had no more appetite than Wallace for more TVAs.

There is no indication, however, that Ickes imparted this intelligence to Wallace, and on May 8 Wallace radioed the President urging him to hold up approval of any program until he had a chance to see him, and Roosevelt radioed back: "Will make no endorsement of any flood control or conservation measure until we can meet."[26] Three days later Wallace wrote the President that he and Secretary of War Harry Woodring firmly opposed establishment of any more TVAs and that their disagreement with Ickes over federal policy had reached the point where it was no longer sensible for them to continue to confer. Their difficulties even extended to their relationship with the National Resources Committee. That situation, Wallace stated bluntly, "would be very greatly strengthened if you could move the Committee from the Interior Building, put it in an independent location and then have the Chairman report direct to you and not through a Member of the Cabinet."

"You are fully informed," Wallace said ingratiatingly, "of how much I sympathize with you in your endeavors to bring about an effective program of national and regional planning," which, the Secretary agreed, should embrace flood control, conservation, and power development. "In your public life for many years you have driven straight toward the objective of an integrated program in these fields and I want to do what I can to help you attain your objective." Toward that end, "I would like to write you as frankly as though I were speaking to you face to face."

Wallace continued:

Two months ago I received from the National Power Policy Committee a proposed draft of a bill and on March 17 I sent to Secretary Ickes a strong objection to the procedure and machinery outlined in the bill. Last Saturday when I learned that most of the provisions of the tentative draft prepared by the National Power Policy Committee had been incorporated in the Norris Bill, I thought the matter sufficiently urgent to send you the wire. While I have talked very little with Secretary Woodring about the matter, I am confident that he will join me in proposing an alternative method of achieving national power development, flood control, conservation and related objectives. I believe this alternative will appeal to you as workable, sound, and attractive. I think you will like it.

"The first essential is that overall planning should not be permitted to get mixed up with administration," the Secretary of Agriculture went on, for it would be fatal for the same agency to plan and execute. "Further, if the regional authorities, encompassing the entire area of the United States, were empowered to administer the projects they plan, then there would eventually be a complete regional duplication of identical national programs." He continued:

For example, all the bills to establish regional authorities include soil conservation as one of the basic functions. Soil conservation is mainly the adoption by farmers of improved farm techniques. These practices must be in accord not only with the farm's physical requirements, but also with the *farmer's* economic requirements. As you know, farm income is the largest single factor in the difference between soil exploitation and soil conservation. If soil conservation were managed by seven or eight regional authorities, as contemplated in most of the bills on this subject, it is almost inconceivable that all eight plans would fit harmoniously into a national farm program that would yield an adequate farm income and that would, at the same time, induce soil conservation practices.

Wallace proposed instead the creation of regional planning agencies, with most of their members drawn from federal agencies, whose only function would be to draft plans for their regions and report them to a National Planning Agency, which would be part of the presidential staff, and whose members should be drawn largely from the departments concerned. Once approved by the president, the plans would be carried out by the regular departments. "Under no circumstances" should the National Planning Agency or the regional planning agencies have the authority to execute. Power development, Wallace added, was a separate problem, and it might be necessary to have regional power administrators. "I think Harry Woodring and I will be sufficiently in accord by the time you return that we can present a common recommendation to you," he concluded.[27]

To oblige Wallace, Cohen once again modified the Norris proposal, but his effort failed to assuage the Department of Agriculture, even though the revision provided that the regional authorities should submit plans directly to the president instead of to the Department of Conservation. On May 17 Wallace's aide Milton Eisenhower prepared a memo on the latest draft, contending that although concessions had been made, the basic faults remained and that in some respects the measure was worse than previous drafts, "mainly because it is more adroit."[28]

On the following day Wallace spelled out his objections to the most recent version. First, he reiterated, it intermingled planning and administration, duplicating both National Resources Committee and departmental planning "without being clear-cut in either field." Second, the bill "still insists upon setting up seven Departments of Agriculture, seven Departments of the Interior, seven Corps of Engineers—duplicating regionally what the Departments do nationally." Third, "it places the operating of dams in the hands of authorities interested primarily in power, rather than turning power, which results from flood-control and navigation operations, over to an administrator for disposition," a murky sentence that may imply disapproval of the public power bloc.[29] Wallace and Woodring then went to the White House and told the President why they so vehemently rejected the Norris bill. After hearing them out, he instructed them to go ahead and write the kind of legislation they would prefer and to let him see it.

On May 24 Wallace and Woodring sent a draft of a new measure to the President. It provided for a national planning commission and a series of regional agencies whose functions were wholly limited to planning. Administration and planning were sharply divorced throughout, with the regular departments and agencies executing the programs. Liaison representatives would coordinate activities, both in Washington and in the regions. ("You will note that in providing for this liaison between the departments and the commission we have followed the suggestions you made to us at the Monday conference," Wallace and Woodring remarked shrewdly.) Finally, to market electric power, the proposal established regional administrators who would be responsible to the Federal Power Commission, with the FPC reviewing rates recommended in the regions.[30]

Wallace and Woodring realized that their draft constituted a complete departure from Norris's intention for TVAs, and they hit upon a clever plan to gain their ends without forcing Roosevelt into a rupture with Norris:

While we have used the Norris bill as a framework we feel reasonably certain, after discussing with Mr. Cohen what it is that Senator Norris desires, that the Senator will not accept this draft. If you believe that our draft has merit and deserves consideration by Congress, but at the same time wish to avoid endorsing a specific measure, then we suggest: (1) That by changing three or four sentences in your Message to Congress it can be made to apply equally well to both bills; if we may have a copy of the proposed message we can within an hour or two submit changes for your consideration, and (2) that we discuss informally with Judge Whittington his willingness to introduce this draft in the House at the time Senator Norris introduces his bill in the Senate.[31]

On May 26 Roosevelt instructed Wallace and Ickes that "in order not to complicate legislative procedure of getting the thing started that you let the bills that Senator Norris and Congressman Rayburn are going to introduce go ahead and be referred to the committees. Then take up your suggestions with the committees and have them considered as amendments to these bills in committee rather than in separate bills."[32] Originally, Roosevelt had spoken of one bill that Norris and Whittington would handle; presumably, Whittington was to introduce the Norris bill in the House. But the reference by Wallace and Woodring to Whittington in their letter to Roosevelt suggests that Whittington, not particularly friendly toward valley authority legislation, was reluctant to sponsor a Norris-type bill and might be induced to lend his name to the kind of measure Wallace and Woodring favored. FDR's allusion to the "bills" Norris and Congressman Sam Rayburn of Texas were to introduce seems to have meant, when placed in the context of the rest of the letter, that Norris and Rayburn were to introduce the same bill, with Rayburn having the assignment originally held by Whittington. The President was telling the Department of Agriculture not to sponsor an entirely separate measure that would indicate a sharp cleavage within the Administration on resources policy. On the other hand, he apparently was willing to give Wallace a free hand in spiking the Norris bill in committee. Hence, he did not make Norris's heart's desire an Administration project the cabinet was expected to support.

Confronted by the animus of the Department of Agriculture, the Corps of Engineers, and the National Resources Committee, and with the knowledge that the Norris bill had little or no hope of surviving Congressman Mansfield's Rivers and Harbors Committee, the President sought to salvage as much as he could. He directed Cohen to prepare alternative legislation based on the Department of Agriculture's modification of the Norris proposal and to have Mansfield introduce this second measure in the House. Cohen later explained, "We thought that if Senator Norris was able to get his bill through the Senate he might get some sort of compromise in conference."[33]

During the same period that the President was plotting legislative strategy, he was putting the final touches on his message to Congress. It had been prepared as early as April 27, but a number of significant changes were made in the final document. Where "regional authorities" appeared, the words "or agencies" were added, and throughout the rest of the message "regional bodies" was inserted, so that neither the Norris bill for "regional authorities" nor the Mansfield bill for "regional planning agencies" would be favored. In addition, to avoid comment on the omission of any specific reference to power, the ambiguous sentence was added: "And provision should be made for the effective administration of hydro-electric projects which have or may be undertaken as a part of a multiple purpose watershed development."[34] The sapling that Wallace and Woodring had planted in suggesting "that by changing three or four sentences in your

Message to Congress it can be made to apply equally well to both bills" had taken root.

In sum, Roosevelt had decided to take no stand at all. When the Budget Bureau informed Wallace and other cabinet officials later in the month that they could make any statement not inconsistent with FDR's message of June 3, the Administration was, in effect, sanctioning a fight to the finish. After months of careful study, the President had instructed Cohen to draft two conflicting bills and then had sent a special message to Congress, also written by Cohen, calculatedly so worded to allow either of two widely divergent interpretations to be put on it.[35]

V

Thus far, it might appear that Roosevelt was as enthusiastic as Senator Norris for establishing a series of valley authorities and that he was frustrated from creating "seven TVAs" only by a league of bureaucrats and Congressional potentates, but to make such an assumption would be to misstate FDR's position. To be sure, there is some evidence of the President's interest in transplanting the TVA approach. On February 25 he wrote the TVA board: "As I have known for several weeks that Mr. Blandford has been working on a tentative report on administrative organization of the TVA, I have asked him to show me what he now has. I do this because whatever final report he makes will have a direct bearing on the form of set-up proposed for other regional Authorities in other parts of the country." Roosevelt's desire that John Blandford, General Manager of TVA, get back to him immediately and his reference to "other regional Authorities" might indicate that at least at this early stage the President was considering additional valley authorities on the TVA pattern. Again in his speech at the Democratic Victory Dinner in Washington on March 4, he asked how, with courts issuing injunctions, the Administration could "confidently complete the Tennessee valley project or extend the idea to the Ohio and other valleys."[36]

Actually, at no time during the controversy did Roosevelt view a septet of TVAs as the *sine qua non* of resources development. It was not that he opposed more TVAs, but that he regarded the issue of what type of agency would administer projects as only a secondary consideration; the main question was how to establish a unified system of planning. The persistence of departmental autonomy, with each department acting independently of every other and badgering Congress to adopt its current wish list, created disorder. Congress had little way of knowing how Department of Agriculture projects tied in with those of the Department of the Interior or other agencies, little way of telling which proposal should have the highest priority, and, more particularly, how all the demands should be weighed with regard to capital budgeting. As a result, there was no "Administration" program, and Congress was at the mercy of special interests manipulating government agencies and aligned with entrenched Congressional committee chairmen. Particularly flagrant offenders were the cronies of the Corps of Engineers in the Rivers and Harbors Congress, mostly composed of members of the House hungry for pork barrel projects for their districts.[37]

The President much preferred the recommendation of the Brownlow committee for a central planning agency that would survey all of the departmental proposals and establish an order of priority, sending an A list to Congress of the most worthy projects that could be adopted within the budget and a B list of less impressive propositions that Congress might substitute, if it wished, for those in group A, and still stay within the budget. At a press conference late in January, Roosevelt observed, in discussing floods in the Ohio Valley, that every time a river overran its banks, a great many groups rushed to Washington, each with a separate panacea. He continued:

> I have come to the conclusion that we have to pursue all of these things simultaneously. They all tie in a general picture; and, for the first time, we have in the last three or four years been developing a synchronized program to tie in the entire field of flood prevention and soil erosion. That is one reason why I hope, in the Reorganization bill, we can have a central planning authority, which will be responsible for a plan which will cover all of the watersheds that go into the Mississippi. And then all the work that is being carried on will have some relationship to the work that is being carried on at some other point.[38]

Roosevelt regarded this one feature as quintessential: creation of a central planning agency to establish priorities. He also believed, though, that the success of the TVA demonstrated the wisdom of decentralization. "National planning," he stated, "should start at the bottom, or in other words, the problems of townships, counties, and States should be coordinated through large geographical regions, and come to the Capital of the Nation for final coordination." When he met with the National Resources Committee on February 20, he outlined an arrangement for eight authorities that would submit reports to a central planning board which would in turn make an A and a B list of projects to send to Congress.[39]

Only as a third and rather minor consideration did Roosevelt concern himself about who carried out the plans after Congress approved them. He had small patience with nice distinctions between planning and execution, or between geographical and functional forms. The TVA had been a success, and he saw no reason why an agency could not both plan and administer; at the same time, he did not envisage that the regional agencies would actually do much administering, save in the Columbia Valley. Hence, he did not regard his proposal, as Norris did, as one for "little TVAs." In this connection, his message to Congress is revealing, because the most important paragraphs were drafted in April before there was any question of a Mansfield bill. The President declared:

> Apart from the Tennessee Valley Authority, the Columbia Valley Authority, and the Mississippi River Commission, the work of these regional bodies, at least in their early years, would consist chiefly in developing integrated plans to conserve and safeguard the prudent use of waters, water power, soils, forests, and other resources of the areas entrusted to their charge. . . . Projects authorized to be undertaken by the Congress could then be carried out in whole or in part by those departments of the Government best equipped for the purpose, or if desirable in any particular case by one of the regional bodies.

The entire message is characterized by the tentative nature of FDR's thinking on regional agencies:

> Neither the exact scope nor the most appropriate administrative mechanism for regional husbandry can at the start be projected upon any single blueprint. But it is important that we set up without delay some regional machinery to acquaint us with our problem.[40]

Roosevelt set forth his ideas most clearly at a press conference on February 9:

Q: Mr. President, has anyone introduced an Arkansas Valley Authority bill?

The President: Oh, I think there have been bills last session and this for two or three dozen authorities. I will tell you what we are talking about at the present time in regard to natural resources and public works. After looking at a dozen different schemes and examining into these individual bills for authorities like a Potomac River Authority, an Ohio River Authority, et cetera, we have come around to this point of view: I told this to the Senators this morning, that in the interest of orderly planning it seems best to set up perhaps eight regions. . . .

Each of these regional authorities or administrations or whatever Congress wanted to call them would have the task every year of submitting a list of projects for flood or drought or soil erosion or navigable channels or reforestation within their region, listing them in the order of preference.

After all the regional reports were in—oh, say July or August—we would add up the figures of their recommendations and, based on the condition of the Treasury—in other words, a careful check-up by the Budget as part of the Budget Message—determine how much the President could recommend to the Congress for the Nation as a whole in his budget. Thereupon, under the reorganization plan the third agency under the President, the National Planning Agency, would get hold of these eight regional agencies and say to them. "The President can only approve so many dollars to go into this budget; therefore, will you all cut (of course it would be every year a cut) your recommendations down to fit into the total budget figure that is possible, and give us a list for each region of the things that would fit into the budget sum, then put down at the same time a B list of projects that you approve, that you have recommended, that are all ready to shoot on the following fiscal year."

The President thereupon submits both lists to Congress the first list being within the budget, and the second list being what might be called alternative projects, leaving it to Congress to determine whether they want to go along with the original recommendations or lift anything out and put something else in—wholly a matter of Congressional discretion. . . .

Q: These would be regional divisions, not corporate authorities?

The President: They would be regional divisions. In working it out, possibly in some cases the regional divisions would also have administrative duties—as, for instance, in the case of the T.V.A.—but in most instances they would be planning authorities.[41]

Much of the misunderstanding between Roosevelt and Norris, and Norris's ultimate disappointment at FDR's unwillingness to go down the line for his proposal, stemmed from a failure to comprehend the President's mind-set. The Norris bill, as it was framed, permitted both Norris's expectation of "seven little TVAs" and Roosevelt's desire for regional planning agencies that might or might not have administrative powers. If Congress chose, it could, under Cohen's original draft of the Norris bill, turn the planning agencies into valley authorities, but it might just as readily decide to restrict the agencies to planning. Norris believed that the power to establish authorities was all-important; the President, on the other hand, regarded this provision as incidental to the main purpose of coordination in order to establish priorities. Hence, Roosevelt was willing to yield to Wallace's and Woodring's demands for a second bill that preserved the features the President thought essential, while Norris remained committed to valley authorities.

VI

Lacking aggressive Administration support, the Norris bill faced doom before it ever got started. At a press conference on June 4 Roosevelt, when asked how the planning bills were related to the St. Lawrence seaway project and Passamaquoddy, replied disingenuously:

It depends entirely how they set up these planning commissions. . . . You see of all these agencies that are proposed, there would only be three—really only two—that would have any administrative functions at all. One would be the TVA in that area and the other would be the Columbia Basin when the Bonneville Dam goes through. Another is the existing agency of the Mississippi Valley Commission.

Q: Are you referring to the House Bill as distinct from the Norris Bill when you say that?

The President: To tell the honest truth, I have not read either so I cannot answer the question.[42]

After hearings before the friendly Senate Committee on Agriculture, a subcommittee reported the Norris bill favorably early in August, but only after two striking concessions to Secretary Wallace. The committee amended the bill to provide that activities primarily concerned with soil conservation, forest conservation, economic development of arid and swampy lands, protection of wild game, and prevention of siltation of navigable rivers would be entrusted not to an authority but to existing departments or agencies. A second amendment gave the authorities power to "recommend" coordination of the work of existing departments, but not to "effect" it.[43]

The House counterpart to the Norris measure, a bill sponsored by Mississippi Congressman John Rankin, got much rougher treatment in the House Committee on Rivers and Harbors headed by Mansfield. Committee members entertained and encouraged the most farfetched attacks on the Norris-Rankin proposal, and even insulted advocates of the measure. One witness declared that the stream pollution provisions of the Norris bill would provide "a powerful and compulsive weapon . . . in the hands of some Federal department which might want to compel an Ohio industry to sign a contract with an irresponsible and communistic labor organization." Another witness observed:

> The act further provides that no person can be appointed to the position of one of these little czars unless he professes a belief in the feasibility and wisdom of the act. In other words, he has got to be a full-fledged little Fascist before he can get one of these jobs, because no one who believes in democratic principles ever could so stultify himself as to profess a belief in the feasibility and wisdom of the act.[44]

Even more alarming to advocates of the Norris proposal was the conduct of Chairman Mansfield, who seemed hostile to the TVA and even to his own bill. Early in the hearings, Mansfield said to one witness: "I know that Pittsburgh would not favor the provisions of my bill as to pollution; I do not favor it, either." On July 22 Mansfield foreshadowed the ultimate fate of the measure when he asked a witness: "What would be your view if a bill should be reported out that would just simply provide for investigation and planning and reports to Congress for such action as Congress hereafter might want to take?"[45]

When the House committee voted to adjourn on August 5 until the following January, there appeared to be scant hope for enactment of the Mansfield alternative and almost none for the Norris-Rankin measure, but that fall prospects for regional planning legislation revived when rumors circulated that Roosevelt would bring Congress back in November. At a press conference in Hyde Park on October 6, a reporter asked what would be taken up at that special session, if the President decided to summon it. He replied:

If I were writing the story I would mention the principal things such as the crop bill, wages and hours, reorganization, regional planning, and, by the way, on regional planning, of course it is easy to say "the little TVA's," but of course they are not. . . . They are not at all TVA's. In other words, the TVA, under the law, is given complete charge over a whole region, a whole watershed, and, if a dam is to be built, the TVA builds it. When an electric transmission line is to be run, the TVA runs it. When there is soil erosion work to be done, the TVA does it, and the TVA is doing quite a lot of that replanting. When it is a question of building certain communities, you will notice that the TVA is doing it. In other words, it is a complete administrative agency for that region.

Now, the bill which Senator Norris has is an entirely different thing. It does not create any board or Commission with administrative authority. It is merely a planning agency and, as the bill is drawn, it is nothing more than a planning agency.[46]

This was, of course, an altogether misleading précis of the Norris proposal.

When, in his fireside chat of October 12, Roosevelt made the dramatic announcement that he was calling Congress back on November 15, he listed as one of the reasons for the special session the need to create "seven planning regions, in which local people will originate and co-ordinate recommendations . . . in particular regions." In his address to the emergency session on November 15, the President again urged creation of regional agencies of the type envisaged in the Mansfield bill as one point in a five-point program recommended to Congress. Throughout the session, Administration leaders stressed that Roosevelt was advocating advisory planning bodies, not regional TVAs. Following a visit to the White House on November 22, Speaker Bankhead said that expectations for passage of a planning bill were now much higher because "many [had] thought that the plan was for seven TVAs." That was "not in contemplation at this time," save in the Columbia Valley.[47] Opponents of the President, though, pointed out not only that he had misrepresented the Norris proposal at his conference on October 6, but also that the Mansfield bill was not as trifling as Roosevelt made it out to be, since it authorized him to establish by executive order regional power authorities that would actually operate hydroelectric facilities.

Many commentators interpreted FDR's declaration that he did not propose to establish TVAs but merely planning agencies as a retreat to appease the private utilities. The columnists Joseph Alsop and Robert Kintner wrote that the President's moderate advisers wanted concessions to restore business confidence and encourage spending by the power companies. Utilities spokesmen, in turn, claimed that the expansion they could undertake would provide "a vast, untapped reservoir of jobs, outrivaling the programs of P.W.A. and W.P.A." The *Washington Herald* reported that Roosevelt had met with Mansfield, Whittington, and Congressman William J. Driver of Arkansas, president of the National Rivers and Harbors Congress, and told them he did not want any "little TVAs" but would work for the enactment of flood control and navigation legislation, rather than the expansion of the federal power program.[48] The explanation of a "retreat" gained added weight from the announcement that the President would meet with Wendell Willkie and other utility executives to discuss modification of the "death sentence" provisions of the Holding Company Act and the curbing of federal transmission lines.[49] A wire from McAlister Coleman of the National Utility Consumers Committee to Senator Norris expressed a popular attitude: "Hope you will continue your magnificent fight for electric light consumers by pressing your advocacy of the 7 T.V.A. bill. You may be assured consumers are behind you despite retreat of administration. From coast to coast we have received protests against the surrender of the administration to the power trust."[50]

Senator Norris had been stricken at the hearings in Washington in June and, after treatment at the Naval Hospital for a "gastrointestinal upset," was forced to retire from public life for several weeks, but he had returned to Washington in the fall fully determined to continue the battle for his proposal. He was encouraged by such statements as that of the *Sacramento Bee* which saw his bill as a crusade "to restore to the people those God given rights which were pilfered from them and destroyed under the now discredited doctrine of laissez faire." Whatever understanding he may have reached with Roosevelt in the spring, Norris appeared to be stunned by FDR's statements that fall. When reporters asked Norris about them, he replied: "Maybe the President has changed his mind, but I thought they were to be TVAs."[51]

On November 22 the *Washington Post* reported that a "thorough revision of the Administration regional planning bill as an overture to private utilities and encouragement to business has been agreed to by Democratic leaders in Congress and by the White House." This capitulation, declared the *Post*, was the result of statements by utilities that four billion dollars of investment in expansion and modernization had been held up by uncertainty on federal policies.[52] In short, not only would the Norris bill be scrapped but also the Mansfield bill would be gutted by removing the possibility of additional power development by regional authorities. All that would be left of the original proposal would be an insipid planning provision.

Despite the wide acceptance of the theory that Roosevelt's actions represented deliberate appeasement of the utilities, there is no clear evidence that the Administration's behavior constituted a "retreat." In the first place, the President had at no time flatly advocated "seven little TVAs," either in his original message or in any other public statement, although he appeared willing to leave the matter ambiguous enough to permit such a development if political conditions proved favorable. The decision to delete the power feature from the Mansfield bill, if Roosevelt made such a decision, was unquestionably a downsizing, but it may have resulted from the failure of the legislation to gain any considerable political support rather than from a desire to placate the utilities. Certainly the utilities gained nothing from their talks with the President about modifying the "death sentence." By the end of November Senator Norris was able to reaffirm his faith in the Administration, although somewhat unconvincingly:

> I am satisfied although I couldn't prove it—that the President has made no concessions or change in administration policy toward utilities.
>
> The government's policy of establishing a yardstick and regional planning can go side by side with the program to encourage expansion of private utilities. In fact, the private utilities have profited in areas of government operation such as TVA.[53]

Norris could not have been pleased, though, by the subsequent behavior of the Administration. On December 10 Congresswoman Nan

Honeyman of Oregon phoned the White House to divulge that "hearings on the Regional Planning Bill before the Rivers and Harbors Committee are not going at all satisfactorily." She "wanted to know how much interested you were and whether you had any suggestions as to what they could do," Roosevelt was told. Apparently he was not very interested, because no Administration pressure was brought to bear. On December 15 Delano informed Jimmy Roosevelt that "our [National Resources] Committee has purposely avoided discussion of [regional authorities], but I am of the opinion that regional planning will come much more rapidly if it is allowed to come rather naturally and as regions of common interest arise." As for the Norris and Mansfield measures, "it seems to be a wiser policy for us not to take an active part in urging either one of these bills, but this does not mean that we are opposing them either actively or clandestinely."[54] Things had reached such a sorry pass that the President's principal adviser on natural resources had to assure the White House that he was not covertly undermining Administration legislation only two months after the President had called a special session of Congress in part to enact this very legislation.

By mid-December the Administration, which failed to get a single major bill through the special session, appeared to be in full flight on the question of regional planning. The House Rivers and Harbors Committee let it be known that it was going to strike all references to hydroelectric development from the legislation, except in the Columbia Valley where Bonneville was already in operation. Mansfield explained that the committee had already decided to jettison the power provisions of his bill, even though hearings were still in progress. He added that a new measure would be drafted providing for a national planning board to coordinate the work of the Corps of Engineers, the Department of Agriculture, and the Reclamation Bureau, each of which would remain supreme in its own field.[55]

On March 2, 1938 Cohen sent the President a copy of the bill that the House Rivers and Harbors Committee was about to report out as a substitute for the Mansfield measure, "a pretty weak, mealy-mouthed sort of a bill which does little more than set up a National Resources Board with more limited powers than those provided by the Byrnes Reorganization Bill." He added:

My guess is that the present National Resources Board and the Brownlow Committee would much prefer the set-up in the Byrnes Reorganization bill to that provided in the Mansfield substitute. On the other hand, it might be desirable to let the Mansfield bill be reported out so that if Senator Norris gets his bill through the Senate something could be worked out in conference. But Senator Norris does not seem optimistic as to the chances of getting his bill through the Senate this session. . . . Senator Norris seems to think it would be just as well if the Mansfield bill were kept in the House Committee for the present.

I spoke to Sam Rayburn who said he would suggest to Judge Mansfield that he hold the bill in committee for a few days, and Judge Mansfield has agreed to hold the bill until Friday.[56]

The end of the struggle came swiftly. On March 8 Roosevelt informed Cohen that he thought it "probably better strategy to have Judge Mansfield get his bill reported out in a few days. It gives us something to work on." When, though, two weeks later, Chairman Mansfield announced the unanimous agreement of twenty Democrats and seven Republicans to report out the "mealy-mouthed" substitute, he left little to "work on."[57] Moreover, Norris's bill, buried by the Mansfield committee in the House, never saw the light of day in the Senate either. These developments proved to be the death blows for the proposal to make the Tennessee Valley Authority the model for national resources development. Though Representative Rankin made sporadic attempts to revive the measure, and in 1940 Senator Homer T. Bone introduced a bill for a Columbia Valley Authority drafted by Ben Cohen, the plan to create "seven little TVAS" never got serious consideration again.[58]

VII

Who, then, killed the seven little TVAs? According to more than one theory of history, the answer ought to be self-evident. The executioners must have been the forces of capital, especially the private utilities, headquartered in Wall Street but with tentacles reaching out into regions in the hinterland. After all, it had been these very elements that had dragged the Tennessee Valley Authority through the courts and had done everything they could to destroy it. Granted, all of the leading players in the drama appeared to be federal officials, but they should always be understood to be merely the agents of omnipotent external interests.

These assumptions, though, simply do not accord with the facts. The death of the seven little TVAs was brought about not by financial titans manipulating the strings in a Grand Guignol puppet show but by a few well-placed individuals within the government who were largely motivated by the territorial imperative. As early as 1934 when Roosevelt sought to set up an independent planning board, a cabinet official only tangentially involved in planning issues, Secretary of Labor Frances Perkins, circulated a remonstrance supported by Ickes, Wallace, and Relief Administrator Harry Hopkins, and the President was compelled to back down.[59] In 1937 Woodring, Wallace, and Ickes were even more determined not to let any new agency or agencies encroach on their prerogatives.

In short, the course of events is much more congruent with state-centered theory, even though this approach sometimes exaggerates the "autonomy" of bureaucrats. With regard to the denouement of the seven little TVAs, the theoretician Eric Nordlinger was close to the mark when he wrote:

The preferences of the state are at least as important as those of civil society in accounting for what the democratic state does and does not do; the democratic state is not only frequently autonomous insofar as it regularly acts upon its preferences, but also markedly autonomous in doing so even when its preferences diverge from the demands of the most powerful groups in civil society.[60]

Cabinet officials, notably Woodring, undoubtedly reflected the ambitions of particular pressure groups, but they appear to have been primarily impelled by bureaucratic jousting.

The hostility of Woodring to planning legislation occasions no surprise. As Ickes later wrote sneeringly:

The Army Engineers are doubtless brave soldiers, when they work at their trade, but to a surprising and disproportionate degree, they have gradually accepted and adapted themselves to the safer and less rigorous field of flood control. They have taken on, over the years, always with the taxpayer standing by with open purse, such warlike and dangerous undertakings as the regulation and development of domestic and industrial water supplies, the creation and supervision of navigation facilities, the irrigation of farm lands, and the development of hydroelectric power. They have even been reaching out greedily for the function of land drainage. Every little drop of water that falls is a potential flood to the ubiquitous Army Engineers and they therefore assume it to be their duty to control its destiny from the cradle to the grave.[61]

Woodring in this area regarded himself as responsible not to the President but to Congress, and he had no tolerance for Roosevelt's effort to introduce planning upstarts into his sovereign realm.

Wallace's leadership role in balking valley authority legislation may startle those who think of him as the champion of the people against the interests, a reputation writ large in the 1940s, but his attitude becomes comprehensible when placed in the context of the relationship of his department to the Tennessee Valley Authority. Wallace felt keenly the determination of the TVA to monopolize functions in its large region that the line departments carried on everywhere else in America. It even banned agencies such as the Soil Conservation Service from its domain; the TVA refused to permit the SCS to organize soil conservation districts in the valley. With that pain of displacement still searing, Wallace found the thought of requiring the bureaus of the Department of Agriculture to be answerable to planning agencies covering the entire country insufferable.

More than a decade later, Paul Appleby summed up what he understood to have been Wallace's attitude at the time:

> He could not have failed . . . to be impressed with the basic confusion involved in the valley authority. In its simplest form, this might be expressed as a "lack of agricultural knowledge" demonstrated by an agency not equally agricultural; again, it might be in recognizing that the Department of Agriculture had largely to act as if the Tennessee Valley had seceded from the United States; all Department programs had to be treated as if the TVA area wasn't there, and special arrangements made for that area. If all the country had been similarly organized, a revolution in the government as it had previously existed would have been required.

At the heart of the question, Appleby emphasized, was "the conflict between functional and geographical structure." He continued:

In Agriculture we New Dealers recognized the TVA as a New Deal program, and were generally for it, willing to make the exceptions required by its existence. More, we recognized positive values in it; it represented a drive for areal integration of federal activities which the functional form had not provided and with which we were struggling by setting up departmental and interdepartmental committees . . . in a number of important areas. But of course to go completely to the areal form would have posed exactly the same problem in reverse—an inability to relate and integrate the regional programs.[62]

The remonstrance by Wallace and Woodring may make it appear that Ickes was the sole paladin of valley authority legislation, but he was no more willing than they to welcome intruders. As the Washington representative of the Tennessee Valley Authority later pointed out, Ickes favored the creation of new TVAs only "provided those new regional agencies and TVA itself should be made subordinate to the Department of the Interior." Indeed, he wanted not less power but more. In addition to having designs on the Forest Service, he favored, as he later acknowledged, "transferring the civil activities of the Corps to the Department of the Interior where they belong." And he conducted himself in a manner that made him a poor advocate for regional planning, for he alienated almost everyone of the same rank with whom he came in contact. Jim Farley, who served in the cabinet with him, later said:

Ickes I thought—I don't want to be profane and won't be. But I met two terrible men in my lifetime, and he was on top of the list. Impossible person. Thought everybody else was dishonest except Ickes. . . . I sat alongside of him for six months without talking to him. Because he would tap my wires and he denied that he tapped them. And I accused him of tapping my wires and those of the President Mr. Roosevelt. And he denied it but I put it right down his throat and insisted that he did.[63]

Does that mean, then, that Ickes and Wallace, two of the most ardent New Dealers, disapproved of the TVA, the showpiece of the New Deal? Not exactly, though it does suggest that historians need to take care not to assume that the convenient term "New Deal" conveys a monolith. FDR's lieutenants sometimes wearied of hearing the hallelujahs that the Tennessee Valley Authority kept evoking. In 1944 Ickes said in his sardonic fashion that answers to problems of resources development could not be found "merely by lighting a candle and intoning, 'TVA, TVA, TVA.'"[64] Nonetheless, Ickes and Wallace recognized that the experiment in the valley earned credit for their common effort, and they took a measure of pride in it. One TVA, however, was enough—perhaps more than an enough. Seven they found truly menacing.

It is understandable that they felt concern, for whatever the proposed seven TVAs were, "little" they were not, though the press succeeded in fastening that label on them. Among them were the TVA itself with an expanded grant; an Atlantic Seaboard Authority, "for the drainage basins of the rivers flowing into the Atlantic Ocean and the Gulf of Mexico, from the east, below the Suwanee River"; a Great Lakes–Ohio Valley Authority, "for the drainage basins of the rivers flowing into any of the Great Lakes and of the Ohio River, except the drainage basins of the Tennessee and Cumberland Rivers, and of the rivers flowing into the Mississippi River above Cairo, Ill., from the east"; a Missouri Valley Authority, "for the drainage basins of the Missouri River and the Red River of the North, and of the rivers flowing into the Mississippi River above Cairo, Ill., from the west"; an Arkansas Valley Authority, "for the drainage basins of the Arkansas, Red, and Rio Grande rivers flowing into the Gulf of Mexico west of the Mississippi River"; and a Southwestern Authority, "for the drainage basins of the Colorado River and of the rivers flowing into the Pacific Ocean south of the California-Oregon line, and for the Great Basin."[65] If all of these new institutions were to be action agencies, the regular department would have little left to do in the sphere of water resources.

The mulish resistance of Woodring, Ickes, and Wallace, as well as of the National Resources Committee, to creating anything approaching TVAs in a region pretty much defined the parameters of FDR's field of operation. "The President," it has been charged, "blew hot and cold on regional planning," and "the manner in which Norris and the 'little TVAs' bill were abandoned, after unduly raising the hopes of public-power supporters," it has been said, "did not bring credit upon the administration." Roosevelt's opportunities, though, were sharply circumscribed. Ben Cohen later reflected:

President Roosevelt was very much interested in integrated valley-basin development as exemplified in TVA. He wished to see the idea extended to other river basins. . . . It was natural that at the start we thought of this legislation as extending the TVA idea and that we should model the first drafts which became the Norris bill on TVA legislation. . . .

While some opposition was expected at the start from the War Department (Army Engineers) as well as private interests it was only after the first drafts were drawn that I became aware of the intensity of the opposition of the old-line departments, Agriculture and the Reclamation Division in Interior, the National Planning Resources Board and the Brownlow Committee to certain aspects of the TVA form of legislation.[66]

Given these circumstances, Roosevelt had little choice but to strike the best deal he could. Judson King recalled subsequently:

His political method . . . was to let the conflicting factions advance their proposals or introduce their bills and then at the end of the conflict attempt to force the decision he desired. That was exactly what happened in respect to the TVA Act of 1933. It was comparatively easy in the first flush of his power and with the Nation in despair for him to succeed, but four years later it was a different story and the opposition to more TVAs inside and outside his official family had grown menacing and he had to tack back and forth, fight on and bide his time.

Years later Paul Appleby reflected:

Roosevelt would never have expressed himself about a legislative proposal in terms that deprived him of alternative positions and lines of retreat and modification. What he would have given was general word of encouragement and approbation, and his words usually would be exaggerated by the interested listener, and made more specific than their author made them. . . . A general inclination to defer to "Uncle George" would enter into the picture, along with a general understanding of Norris' inability to deliver in precisely his own terms.

Cohen adds:

The President probably would have been happy if either bill had passed or with a compromise between them. The President was much more conscious than Senator Norris of the necessity, and probably of the political and administrative wisdom, of trying to meet some of the opposition within the administration.[67]

Cohen, in the best position of anyone to know what transpired, has explained:

The president's primary interest was integrated river-basin develop-ment and he naturally wished to see the divergent viewpoints within the government reconciled as much as possible consistent with his general objective. And he knew as I knew that if we did not obtain some measure of agreement within the administration, these differ-ences would be exploited by hostile private interests and the pro-posed legislation would in all probability fail to secure the necessary Congressional support.
   So we worked hard to draft a revised bill which would promote integrated river-basin development which would have some regard for the desire of the old-line departments to preserve their own nation-wide activities and some regard for the desire of the reorga-nizers to keep planning and administration separate. The . . . Mansfield bill was the result.[68]

Cohen's allusion to "hostile private interests" indicates that a wholly state-centered explanation of the demise of the seven little TVAs will not suffice. Roosevelt and his aides, quite apart from the consideration that each of them absorbed certain societal values, were always aware that any legislation they submitted would have to win Congressional approval and that the lawmakers in turn were responsive to local and national interests. Congress revealed its own sentiments on planning when both houses of Congress approved, with no opposition, a joint resolution which autho-rized the Corps of Engineers to bypass the President by reporting directly to Congress and gave it jurisdiction over flood control, power, "and all works necessary for . . . effective soil and water conservation." In August Roosevelt, fighting a rear guard action, vetoed the resolution. Congress took this step fully aware that the Corps of Engineers had forged strong links to the rivers and harbors bloc and that it cozied up to the utilities.[69]

In forming its attitudes toward planning, Congress may well have been reflecting less subservience to Big Business than a jealous regard for local rights. Western legislators felt this especially keenly. Every member of Congress from thirteen Western states opposed even the mild Mansfield bill. The Wyoming Democrat Joseph O'Mahoney, who had a fierce distrust of concentrated power whether exercised by the trusts or by the federal government, sought "to guarantee to the states affected a substantial degree of self-government" by amending the planning legislation to stipulate "that each state shall be entitled to a member of its own selection on every regional committee in which it has an interest." To be sure, as the quarrels over Bonneville and the Forest Service revealed, the invocation of states' rights could mask the avarice of timber barons and stockmen, but a powerful sentiment for locality pervaded all classes. "Westerners," the historian John Braeman has written, "looked to Washington for assistance in the fulfillment of their entrepreneurial ambitions. What they opposed were restrictions upon their freedom to exploit the resulting opportunities. . . . Westerners voted for Roosevelt to keep the federal spigot open, but also voted for Republicans or conservative Democrats for Congress and state offices to make sure that no strings were attached threatening local autonomy."[70]

Though the historian, then, in assessing responsibility for the demise of the seven little TVAs, needs to bear in mind these external influences, state-centered explanations remain the most convincing. "The world of the state, in the late 1930s and 1940s at least, *was* in many ways a rarefied and self-referential place, in which ideas reverberated among political and intellectual elites and to which the larger public had only limited access," the historian Alan Brinkley has written in a sophisticated discussion of the subject. "There are . . . moments when the character of public issues makes for a more contained public world, when the clamor of popular protest and the power of social movements does not effectively penetrate policy deliberations in significant ways. The later years of the New Deal . . . were, it seems to me, such a time." Given the confluence of state-centered perspectives in 1937—the animus of the cabinet secretaries, the distaste of the National Resources Committee for balkanizing the nation with region-wide action agencies, and the unwillingness, and inability, of the President to commit himself to a particular administrative mode—Senator Norris's dream of seven little TVAs never had a chance.[71]

SIX

Hurricane Politics

[I drafted the article on the "seven little TVAs" in the course of writing my Ph.D. dissertation, another enterprise resulting from my fascination with the Tennessee Valley Authority, though I got to that subject by a circuitous route. For a time I abandoned pursuit of the Ph.D. to engage in liberal politics, with the ideal of the TVA never far from my mind, and in 1949, while Massachusetts state director of Americans for Democratic Action, I began to explore whether valley authorities were feasible in New England. In examining that question, I played a small part, in collaboration with Myres MacDougall of the Yale Law School faculty, in getting valley authority legislation introduced in Congress; prepared speech material on water resources policy for Governor Paul Dever; and testified at hearings on the matter in the State House on Beacon Hill. I also published two articles: "Lights Out Along the Merrimack," *The Progressive* 13 (July 1949): 21–22, and "Power War in New England," *The Survey* 75 (September 1949): 461–64.

This interest also framed the topic of my doctoral dissertation. When I returned to the graduate program at Columbia, I did so only after striking an agreement with Henry Steele Commager that I could write on why there was no TVA on the Connecticut, a river I had become especially fond of while teaching at Smith College. The result was *Flood Control Politics: The Connecticut River Valley Problem, 1927–1950* (Harvard University Press, 1953). From that book, I have excerpted chapter 7, little changed from its original form.

This chapter is pertinent not only to the history of water resources development in the 1930s, but also to an understanding of why and how the New Deal came to an end. In seeking to answer that question historians have, understandably, focused their attention on macropolitical explanations, especially the resentment engendered in 1937 by FDR's "Court-packing" plan, sitdown strikes, and the recession. But in many parts of the country the New Deal also lost momentum because of local controversies, and certainly that was true in the Connecticut Valley states.

In 1936 the Connecticut River jumped its banks, broke through dikes, turned streets in the capital city of Hartford into canals on which rowboats plied, left 77,000 homeless, and took twenty-four lives. Afterward, a cry for effective flood control, guaranteeing that such a catastrophe would never be repeated, resounded through the valley. Congress responded with the Omnibus Flood Control Act of 1936, which required the states to contribute to the cost of reservoirs and authorized them to engage in interstate compacts to determine how to allocate those costs. For many months, despite alarm at the possibility of another devastating flood, efforts to reach agreement on a compact foundered because upriver states, especially Vermont, had no desire to see their arable valleys lost to reservoirs merely to benefit their downstream neighbors. Not until July 1937 was agreement reached, and that accord stipulated that hydroelectric power rights were reserved to the states and that the federal government could develop power only with the consent of the states.

That proviso triggered a new round of controversy. One Connecticut Congressman, noting the prominence of utility interests in the deliberations, characterized the resolution as "an attempted steal by the power people," and the Federal Power Commission denounced it as "a radical departure from the established policy of the federal government." In the office of FDR's son, Jimmy Roosevelt, two Democratic legislators, Senator Fred Brown of New Hampshire and Representative Joseph Casey of Massachusetts, drafted a new resolution giving advance consent to a Connecticut River compact if it acknowledged that power rights belonged to the national government, which President Roosevelt insisted upon. Congress took no action on either resolution, but in 1938 it modified the 1936 act by authorizing the federal government to absorb all costs of reservoir construction. That provision torpedoed the compact approach and permitted the federal government to go into Vermont and New Hampshire to build dams without the consent of the states, a solution favored by New Deal Congressmen in New England, including William Citron, the sponsor of a bill to create a Connecticut Valley Authority. It is at this point that chapter 7 begins.]

I

The morning of September 21, 1938 was an uneasy one in New England. Four days of rain had turned northern streams into torrents, breaking small dams and washing away roads and bridges; by September 20 the storm had already claimed ten lives. A locomotive and four freight cars had been derailed by a landslide in East Deerfield, killing two men, and another man had plunged to his death as an automobile ran off a causeway into the Charles River. Charles Street, cutting between Boston Common and the Public Gardens, lay under a foot of water. The Connecticut River had risen two feet in three days and was still rising at over an inch an hour. The 1936 flood had been the worst in at least three centuries, but now, only two years later, New England appeared to be in for one just as bad.

It was not the fear of people along the river banks, nor even the mounting anxiety over Nazi Germany's demand for Czech territory, that accounted for the disquiet. There was something strange about the day itself, oppressively warm for late September, about the very air, hot and moist and salty, and the decreasing atmospheric pressure left a queer feeling in one's ears. On the southern shore, Portuguese fishermen refused to go out in their boats, because there had been two coppery sunrises in succession. Vermonters wondered at the smell of sea in the air. Through the morning, the anxiety grew as the barometer continued to drop and a high wind started to blow. By 1 P.M., the gusts had reached gale force and carried a salt spray. At 2 P.M., the rain began to fall once more, only with a purposeful ferocity that the earlier storm had lacked. A man in a boat off the southern coast saw what appeared to be a thick gray fog racing in from the sea; suddenly, terror-struck, he realized it was not fog but a mass of wind-lashed, green-black water riding toward shore. A few minutes before, at 2:30, New Englanders, who had turned on their radios to catch British Foreign Secretary Anthony Eden's speech about the crisis in Europe, heard instead awesome news of a very different sort: a tropical hurricane had struck New England.

To be sure, it was not the first they had heard of the hurricane. If they read their newspapers with care, they had seen for some days past small dispatches of a tempest headed for the Florida coast. But these accounts related that the storm had veered to sea, and if the subject was given any thought at all, it was only to provide an occasion to say how fortunate New England was to be free of such a menace, and to wonder why anyone would live in hurricane country. The West Indian storm moved north off Cape Hatteras at forty-five miles an hour, and its curve indicated clearly that it would spend its force at sea. When the hurricane moved oceanward, however, it struck a North Atlantic high, which was exceptionally close to

shore. To the west was another high, leaving a narrow low-pressure chan-
nel of sultry air straight up through New England. Headed north through
this funnel, the hurricane, with no chance to expand and thus dissipate,
was advancing toward eastern Long Island and New England with full
force at the almost unheard-of speed of sixty miles an hour.

The center of the storm struck the New England coast a little west
of New Haven and moved northward along the western rim of the
Connecticut River Valley through Vermont, crossing the Canadian border
around midnight. The fiercest segment was on its eastern edge where
cyclonic winds of more than 110 miles an hour hit the Rhode Island shore.
In Boston, winds reached at least 186 miles an hour. The greatest single
disaster occurred at Watch Hill, Rhode Island, where a host of people
looking at the storm from the hillside recoiled in horror as mountainous
waves descended on them. More than fifty bodies were taken from the sea
near Westerly. Hour after hour, people huddled in cottages along the
shore, a nightmare world of blackness, as horizontal sheets of salt rain
seeped into houses and the shrill, squealing wind battered walls. A huge
tidal wave swept the Shore Line New York–Boston express from a causeway, leaving two rail cars dangling in the water and the engine's nose
pressed against a sixty-foot trawler deposited on the tracks. Passengers had
to leap out to fight their way to land. The sea clawed small cottages from
the coast and tossed boats into trees. In Essex Harbor, near the mouth of
the Connecticut River, all but five or six of two hundred boats were
destroyed in an hour, while 350 craft in Boston harbor were battered into
driftwood.

Winds of 125 miles an hour thrust up V-shaped Narragansett Bay, the
storm waves hemmed in as they approached Providence Harbor, so that
they were driven higher and higher, lashing the waters from the bay into
narrow Providence River. In an instant, the main square of Rhode Island's
capital was flooded ten feet deep and water poured into second-story windows. Trolleys were dislodged from their tracks, and scores of shoppers had
to swim to safety. In the heart of Providence, a woman driving along what
had moments before been a dry street was drowned in her car before she
could move. So powerful were the waves that huge coal barges were lifted
out of the water and dropped into downtown. In a few minutes, the one
sensation in the city was of a terrible, persistent noise, the awful din of
short-circuited alarm-bells and ambulance sirens.

Nearly half a century later, Jan Myrdal, son of the Swedish social scientists Alva and Gunnar Myrdal, could still call to mind his experience, as an

eleven-year-old newly arrived in New York, trying to ease his loneliness by listening to the wireless:

On the radio, the announcer now said the hurricane had struck a town on Buzzards Bay, Massachusetts, so hard that a man almost drowned in the center of the town square. When the storm struck, he went to get a little girl who had been left in a car in the square. As he went to rescue her, he was able to walk all the way to the car without getting wet. But carrying her back, a flood of water struck the town. He had to wade through water that rose to his chin, and he almost drowned. They were both saved, however, by neighbors, who threw a fire rescue line from the window of the mayor's office. He was able to haul himself and the girl up onto the steps of the city hall. According to the radio, they were all still up on the roof of the city hall waiting to be rescued.

In New London, Connecticut on Long Island Sound, the winds blew the barkentine *Marcelas* ashore, upsetting its galley stove, which set fire to buildings along the wharf. Firefighters were helpless, their engines blocked by fallen trees across the exits of the firehouse. By nightfall, an entire block had burned down, and the inferno was still raging. New London officials called it the worst disaster since the city was torched by Benedict Arnold.

The sheer force of the hurricane surpassed belief. Seismographs in Sitka, Alaska recorded the shocks of the pounding of waves on the New England coast. A large yacht starting out for sea with engines at full power was blown all the way back to its pier. The storm deposited ocean salt on the windows of houses in Montpelier, Vermont and salt spray turned pine needles brown forty miles inland in Connecticut.

Once again, the Connecticut Valley felt the impact of a major flood. The river inundated the east side of Hartford, and lamp post bulbs glowed "like floating Japanese lanterns" in Bushnell Park in front of the State-house. For a time, it appeared that a greater catastrophe than that of 1936 menaced the city, but the "Battle of Colt's Dike" held the ramparts. Heroic efforts created a two-mile barricade of sandbags that the pounding river failed to crack. At Northampton, CCC boys from the camp at Mount Tom saved the key dike.

The "big wind" blew down and damaged two hundred and fifty million trees, two and a half billion board feet of timber. Twenty percent of
the sugar maples of Vermont, some over a century old, were felled—a
heavy loss, for it takes almost fifty years to grow a producing sugar bush.
Of three thousand sugar maples in one section of central Vermont, only
one hundred were left standing. In Stonington, Connecticut the tree warden had marked one dying tree to be cut down; after the storm, it was the
only one on an entire block that remained. Fifteen hundred specimen trees
in the Arnold Arboretum were killed. On a dozen New England campuses,
the great oaks were toppled.

The property damage was the greatest of any disaster in American history, worse than the San Francisco earthquake or the Chicago fire. The
storm took a particularly heavy toll of New England crops at a time when
the economy was already reeling from the recession of 1938. Four million
apples were blown to the ground. Carloads of onions were immersed in
the Connecticut River to mix with the strange cargo of tapioca swept
downstream from a plant in Orange, Massachusetts. The failure of electric
power cut off incubators, killing thousands of unborn chicks. In the
tobacco country of western New England, the gale blew through slits in
the sheds, ruining the drying leaves, while other sheds caught fire from
charcoal braziers used to dry the tobacco.

The storm savagely recast the New England shoreline, scouring out new
channels, heaving oyster beds, piling debris on carefully tended seaside
gardens. Bailey's Beach at Society's summer capital of Newport was
destroyed, and the Ocean Drive was rent in a dozen places by the angry
surf. Three sisters in Connecticut were planning to sell a fifty-acre seashore
tract, their only property in the world, in a few days; after the hurricane,
only two acres were left.

Ancient landmarks vanished in the wake of the storm, doubtless nothing so ancient as the dinosaur tracks near Holyoke, many of which were
lost when the fierce rain dislodged slabs of rock. The War of 1812 frigate
Old Ironsides was torn from its moorings in Boston Navy Yard but survived
the rigors of the blast. The three-century-old Sentinel Pine at The Flume,
New Hampshire, was blown down, and the big wind felled trees at
Dartmouth College that had been planted by Daniel Webster. Scores of
the lovely old elms of New Haven and many of the historic trees of Boston
Common went down before the fury of the wind. "The face of New
England," concluded one writer, "had been changed forever."[1]

The hurricane took 488 lives. In Easthampton, a newsboy making his rounds was electrocuted by a wire snapped off by the wind. In Worcester, a man was blown through a window to his death. Three girls were killed by a falling chimney at Northfield Seminary. The Republican candidate for Secretary of State in Connecticut was drowned in the waters of Long Island Sound. One wave engulfed ten women gathered for a church social in a cottage. When the storm subsided, the bodies of seven children were found in a bus on an island in Narragansett Bay. A woman in Connecticut parked her car under a tree to wait out the storm; the tree fell, crushing the car—when police removed her, they found she had been reading *Gone with the Wind.*

For a time, it appeared that the universe had assumed some strange new form, changing all the familiar patterns of life. Pelagic birds such as the gannet and rare seabirds such as Leach's petrel found themselves perched in trees in Vermont alongside yellow-billed arrivals from the tropics. Telegrams went from Boston to New York via London, and milk from Vermont farms reached Boston by way of Montreal. New Englanders heard the alien accents of men from Nebraska and Arkansas rushed in to untangle the maze of telephone wires, while gay-shirted Mexicans repaired railroad tracks in Connecticut. Ducks got a new lease on life in Lake Champlain on the eve of the hunting season, as the storm washed away hunters' blinds.

Years later, the mere mention of the word "hurricane" was enough to start most New Englanders off on a long reminiscence of their adventures in the storm. No single act of nature had ever provided so universal an experience for them. Everyone had a tale to tell; a favorite was that of the burglars who failed to crack a safe because the hurricane cut off the power for their electric detonator. In Providence, they told of the man, knee-deep in water, who calmly tried on hat after hat floating out of a haberdashery until he found the right fit. In New Hampshire, each October, the ghost of Ocean-born Mary comes to visit her eighteenth-century home on a hilltop near Concord, riding in a phantom stagecoach. This year she came early, the night of the storm, "her ghostly skirts whipped by the wind," to save her dwelling from the wrath of the gale. A sandwich man allegedly walked through Boston Common with the sign: "For twenty-five cents I'll listen to your story of the hurricane."

The very next morning New England housewives were busy scrubbing leaf juice from the white paint on their walls, but the memory of the hurricane was not so easily erased. No act of man could have halted it, but people who had seen their homes inundated by the rising Connecticut just two years before, and who had since heard so much confusing talk about flood control, wanted to know why the river had not been checked in all that time, why the dams had not been constructed, why the dikes had not been built. There was bound to be a political reckoning.[2]

II

From the very first, New England Congressmen had recognized that their opposition to interstate compacts left them politically vulnerable unless the Administration was able to produce a workable flood control program. As early as the spring of 1936, Congressman William Citron had charged the power companies with launching a campaign to defeat him at the polls, noting that he, Congressman Herman Kopplemann, and Senator Francis T. Maloney, all Connecticut Democrats, were listed in the annual reports of the Hartford Electric Light Company and the Connecticut Power Company as supporters of "destructive" legislation, each having voted for the Wheeler-Rayburn bill to curb holding companies.[3] Samuel Ferguson, president of the Hartford Electric Light Company, admitted that his report had included the data, but added: "We considered it proper information for our stockholders. I presume the shoe pinches. However, I know of no 'campaign' against the congressmen."[4] At the hearings on the Brown-Casey bill in the summer of 1937, Kopplemann explained:

> In opposing the compact I realize I am putting myself on the spot—that I am laying myself open to the charge of holding up flood control. . . . The public quickly gets the picture when they tell them they won't have flood control. They remember all too well the suffering they underwent during two successive years. They tremble lest there be a recurrence next year. The power question does not grip them emotionally. Power does not leave them wet and cold. Floods do. Power does not cover their homes and their belongings with disease-infested slime. Floodwaters do. Power does not creep into their places of business, wreck their machinery, ruin their merchandise—floodwaters do.[5]

That fall, another Connecticut Democrat, Congressman Alfred N. Phillips, declared: "I heard a high official in the State of Connecticut say that it was regarded as a fact, practically, in our State, that our colleague, Congressman Casey, would not be returned to Congress because he opposed these compacts, and the same thing about our colleague, Mr. Kopplemann."[6]

In May, when the flood control bill of 1938 came before Congress, Representative John McCormack of Massachusetts had written President Roosevelt:

> I consider this to be a matter of vital importance to New England and, if I may speak from a Party angle, without being misunderstood, to the Democratic Party in New England. I am inclined to feel that we are likely to be put on the defensive unless some provision is inserted into the pending bill which will enable the projects in New England, authorized by the 1936 act, to be constructed. This would be particularly so if any people, living in any part of New England which is in the flood area, should be visited by another flood between now and next November.[7]

When the hurricane struck New England in September and the Connecticut River towns were once more flooded, the Republicans and their supporters lost no time in capitalizing on the disaster. In a long, seething editorial called "Ol' Man River Mocks Mr. Kopplemann," the *Hartford Courant* remonstrated:

> As Congressman Kopplemann and Congressman Citron view the turbulent waters of the Connecticut, witness the inconvenience and suffering to which thousands of persons have been put and note the damage that is being done to property over a large area, they may perhaps begin to suspect that their unreasonable, not to say demagogic, opposition to the Flood Control Compact . . . will now receive the full force of the public condemnation it deserves. . . . The opinion seems to be general that they have rendered this entire community a great disservice for which they can make no possible atonement. . . . Let Mr. Kopplemann tell it today to the suffering East Side, to the people rendered homeless, to the small merchants whose business has been paralyzed and whose stocks have been damaged, how sincerely devoted he is to the alleviation of human distress and what abiding faith he has in the objectives and promises of the New Deal.[8]

Republican candidates in Connecticut made the hurricane the main issue of the 1938 campaign. William J. Miller of Wethersfield, running for Congress against Kopplemann, told an East Side Hartford meeting: "The New Deal fiddles while we get flooded."[9] Dr. James L. McConaughty, president of Wesleyan College and Republican nominee for lieutenant-governor, asserted:

Some of the flood damage might have been avoided and all of our fears of the flood lessened if a few stubborn, blind Democratic Congressmen had been willing to put the welfare of the citizens of their State above a will-o'-the-wisp about which they could make political speeches. I have yet to find a thoughtful person in any party in the State, including all my newspaper editor friends, Democratic as well as Republican, who believes that Congressmen Citron and Kopplemann were justified in the selfish attitude which they took.[10]

The White House was deluged with desperate pleas for help from Democratic leaders in Connecticut, New Hampshire, and Massachusetts. Representative Citron told the President he must act quickly, or "some of your friends may be defeated because of the attacks of the power group."[11] Kopplemann observed, "If the timing of this flood is any criterion, God and nature must be on the side of the Republicans this year!"[12] Owen Johnson, Democratic candidate for Congress against Allen Treadway in western Massachusetts, explained:

The State Compacts people and the Republican leaders are trying desperately to save their faces over their obstructionist program over the last two years by these partisan tactics. The whole election will turn on this issue. My own prospects for election were excellent before this crisis and they should be doubled if I can be of immediate service along the lines which every community is demanding.[13]

On September 30, in letters to Kopplemann and Democratic Senator Fred Brown of New Hampshire, Roosevelt declared that the charge that the compacts would have averted the floods was "wholly untrue." Even if the compacts had been ratified, "it would have been physically impossible to have completed any reservoir this summer," he pointed out. "The mentality of those guilty of such implications and suggestions for purely partisan reasons is not very different from the words of those in international affairs who seek, in very similar ways, to play with human lives. . . . You and I do not get angry with such people, we have for them only the utmost pity."[14] On the same day, he told Clyde Seavey of the Federal Power Commission to do something about helping out Citron, Kopplemann, and a third Democratic Congressman, William J. Fitzgerald, in Connecticut, and on the following day, the President's press secretary, Steve Early, ordered Seavey, Harry Hopkins, and General Julian L. Schley of the Corps of Engineers to meet to work out a program of emergency flood control aid.[15]

III

Hopkins, Seavey, and a general representing Schley found that they could scrape together eleven million dollars for flood control projects in New England from War Department, WPA, and PWA funds, and recommended immediate construction by the Army Engineers of reservoirs at Knightville and Birch Hill, Massachusetts, Union Village, Vermont, and Surry Mountain, New Hampshire, as well as local protective works in the Connecticut Valley. On October 4 the President wired Hopkins to go ahead with construction.[16]

FDR's announcement delighted Administration supporters and the nervous Congressmen, but it got a sour response elsewhere. Republican Governor Francis P. Murphy of New Hampshire declared: "I will go to law if necessary and I hope the situation will not reach a point where I will have to call out the national guard."[17] The Republican governor of Vermont, George D. Aiken, said that the September hurricane had demonstrated that the most effective flood control for the downstream cities could be obtained by placing reservoirs on small streams in Massachusetts and Connecticut and by constructing dikes, and he hoped that the plan would be revised accordingly and "on a nonpolitical basis." New Hampshire's Republican Congressman, Charles W. Tobey, condemned the President's action as "an attempt to buy the election in New Hampshire." He declared: "New Hampshire will say pour in your millions. We'll take your money but we will vote as free men, so help us God." Yet another New Hampshire Republican, Senator Styles Bridges, thought it "very peculiar that President Roosevelt waited for a great disaster and the

arrival of an election campaign before taking any positive action to contribute to New England flood control." Even Senator Brown, while grateful for the money, announced he would seek to dissuade the Corps of
Engineers from erecting a dam in the Merrimack Valley.[18]

The last-minute decision to get started on flood control in New
England failed to save the day. The elections in November proved disastrous for the New Deal generally and for the foes of the compacts and the
advocates of a federal power program in New England in particular.
Kopplemann, Citron, Fitzgerald, and Phillips all went down to defeat in
Connecticut, as did Senator Brown in New Hampshire. Of the outspoken
opponents of the compacts, only one Congressman survived.

Advocates of a federal program of multipurpose development of New
England's rivers denied that flood control had anything to do with the
Democratic losses in their region. They pointed out that the Democratic
party had suffered a major setback nationally, and that the Republican tide
had swept away Democrats such as Governor Wilbur Cross of Connecticut,
who supported the compacts, as well as the Democratic governor and both
of the Democratic Congressmen from Rhode Island, who were not
involved in the flood control controversy at all.[19] Their protests carried little weight. The Republicans replied that it was passing strange that the
Democrats lost only four of their six seats in Connecticut, and that the four
opponents of the compacts were defeated while the two supporters of the
compacts won. Moreover, both in New Hampshire, where Tobey unseated
Brown, and in the Hartford district, where Kopplemann lost, the 1938
flood was probably the leading issue of the campaign.

The outcome of the 1938 elections fundamentally altered the situation
Roosevelt and the New Dealers confronted. At the very moment when the
Army Engineers were invading Vermont and New Hampshire to take
lands without the consent of the states, opponents of the 1938 flood control law had been fortified in their conviction that it was a hasty, intem-
perate statute enacted in the closing hours of the session by a Congress that
had been repudiated by the American electorate. The Administration now
faced the task of executing an unpopular law just when a change in political fortunes had placed their Republican foes in control of both the executive and legislative branches of every one of the six New England states,
men for the most part convinced that the movement to repeal the 1938
law was a righteous crusade that had just won the overwhelming endorsement of a long suffering, resentful people. In sum, at a moment when

Roosevelt was grappling with the large questions of economic policy raised by the stubbornly persistent recession and with the mounting menace of Hitler in Europe and the Japanese in Asia, the chance circumstance of an untimely hurricane had, in conjunction with other events, severely eroded the President's authority.

SEVEN

The Great Depression and the New Deal

[During most of the thirty years I taught at Columbia University, John A. Garraty was my esteemed colleague. Sometime in the late 1960s, he came to me with an idea. He proposed to interview twenty-nine American historians, of whom I would be one, about their fields and then put these exchanges together in a book. When completed, the volume would embrace the whole of American history—from the seventeenth century with scholars such as Bernard Bailyn to the more recent period with those such as Arthur Schlesinger, Jr. Each of us received a suggested set of questions ahead of time to permit us to reflect, but Garraty sometimes interposed new ones as the colloquy progressed. Over several hours in the afternoon and evening at the Garratys' town house on Manhattan's Upper West Side, he and I engaged in questions and answers about the Roosevelt era, while Gail Garraty quietly sketched my portrait. The result was a transcript of scores of pages, which Professor Garraty then edited down to a manageable length; I was given an opportunity, in turn, to edit this revised version. Hence, though the "conversation" that was printed captured much of the spontaneity of a chat, it also reflected afterthought. The set of twenty-nine interviews, accompanied by Gail Garraty's drawings, was published as John A. Garraty, *Interpreting American History: Conversations with Historians* (New York: Macmillan, 1970). Professor Garraty subsequently deposited the entire transcript of the tapes in the Columbia Oral History Collection, where it is available to researchers. I have made only minor emendations in the interview as it originally appeared, mostly to excise materials that I have used elsewhere in this volume.]

John A. Garraty: Professor Leuchtenburg, why did you call your history of the 1920s *The Perils of Prosperity*? Did you mean to suggest by the word "perils" not so much that the decade of the 1920s was an unsavory or dangerous period, but rather that the policies of those years caused the Depression?

William E. Leuchtenburg: I think the latter was implicit in the title, and to that extent I think the title unfortunate. I tried to look at the 1920s as an entity and to assume that the people of the time ought to be respected for their own opinions and actions. The period should not be seen simply as a foreshadowing.

J.A.G.:   But surely the economic policies of the 1920s were related to the Great Depression. To what extent can the Depression be blamed on the presidents of the decade?

W.E.L.:   Insofar as one accepts the theory that underconsumption explains the Depression, and I do, then one can say that the presidents of the 1920s are to blame for operating a single-interest government—that is, a government responsive mainly to large corporations. This led, among other unfortunate consequences, to the failure to maintain adequate purchasing power of workers and farmers, which left the economy with inadequate underpinnings.

J.A.G.:   How significant was this in causing the collapse?

W.E.L.:   That question is tougher to reply to than one might assume because the economic literature on the causes of the Depression is very unsatisfactory. In writing on the New Deal, I read through every volume of every economic journal of the 1930s. The question, which to a historian seems "commonsensical," has not attracted the attention of many economists.

J.A.G.:   Well, to be more specific, if Coolidge had signed the McNary-Haugen bill providing subsidies for farmers, or if the Muscle Shoals project, which has some connection with the TVA approach of the New Deal, had been adopted, is it likely that the impact of the Depression might have been moderated?

W.E.L.:   I would not think so. Muscle Shoals could have had no more than a modest effect, and the McNary-Haugen scheme seems to me to have been a mistake, since it was a move toward economic nationalism at a time when the United States was already headed too much in that direction. The problem is not simply that conservative policies were followed by the presidents, but that the reformers themselves were not speaking adequately to a great many of the issues.

J.A.G.:   Why were the effects of the Depression as profound as they were, and why did it last as long as it did?

W.E.L.: The Depression was a watershed in American history; no explanation of the 1930s or subsequent years is satisfactory if it does not recognize what an enormous blow the Depression was, what a tremendous sense people had that an era was ending. A big reason it lasted so long was simply lack of knowledge about the functioning of the economy and of useful statistical indicators. In addition, much of the accepted theory was wrong-headed. Then there were long-range developments. One was the slowdown in population increase, which cut down the national market and slowed the pace of growth. Furthermore, no new industries emerged to take the role that radio and automobiles had played earlier, and that plastics, electronics, and others were to hold later, in stimulating the economy. There were also fissures in the structure of the economy, such as the collapse of the banking system, that did enormous damage.

This was a worldwide depression; international repercussions bounced back and forth like a ball in a squash court. The blows to the U.S. economy buffeted other countries, and the collapse of the Kreditanstalt in Austria in 1931 had deleterious effects in the United States, and so on all through the 1930s.

There are also other answers to your question. The heavy burden of debt (farm mortgage indebtedness, home mortgage indebtedness) weighed heavily on the economy. And lastly, there were the various errors of policy of both Hoover and Franklin Roosevelt.

J.A.G.: With reference to the lack of sophisticated economic and social statistics and of economic knowledge generally, is it possible to defend the conservative argument of the 1920s and early 1930s that government intervention in the economy was dangerous? Perhaps laissez-faire was the only viable policy, given the absence of intelligent understanding of the economy.

W.E.L.: Not so. Still, at a minimum, one should say that, whatever excuses one makes for Franklin Roosevelt for failing to undertake various experiments (for example, for failing to pursue deficit financing more vigorously), one also ought, in all fairness, make for Hoover. Both Hoover and Roosevelt did have experiences that they might have made use of—in particular, World War I when active government intervention in the economy and increased spending resulted in national prosperity. Numbers of people were asking why, if we could spend so recklessly in World War I, we could not spend in the same way in this new war against the Depression. This argument did not persuade Hoover at all. Roosevelt was somewhat affected by it, but not enough.

J.A.G.: Would you comment on President Hoover's attempts to deal with the problems of the Depression?

W.E.L.: Almost every historian now recognizes that the image of Hoover as a "do-nothing" president is inaccurate. In comparison to presidents in previous depressions, particularly Cleveland in the 1890s, Hoover broke many precedents and showed considerable willingness to have the government intervene. He stepped up public works spending, asked businessmen to maintain wage rates, and encouraged the Federal Reserve to pursue an easy credit policy. Various subsidiaries of the Federal Farm Board purchased wheat and cotton. Within his own administration, Hoover defied the fatalism of Secretary of the Treasury Andrew Mellon and the bankers who were urging him to pursue a deflationary policy. In international affairs, he provided one of the few imaginative initiatives of that period in the moratorium on debts and reparations.

Yet, with all that, I think that historians have overcompensated in their current view of Hoover. Perhaps, because most of them are liberal Democrats, they feel a need to lean over backwards. Whatever can be said of the wisdom of Hoover's efforts in the first two years of the Depression, his policies clearly were not working by 1931. In essence, Hoover was pursuing programs that were not very different from those advocated by Mellon. He makes a great deal in his *Memoirs* about his disagreement with Mellon, but, in truth, he was fixated on budget balancing at a time of underutilization of resources and on the gold standard. Moreover, he was committed to voluntarism, particularly with respect to not aiding destitute farmers and jobless workers.

Consider his farm policy. Despite government intervention, cotton prices fell more than a third. Huge surpluses piled up, and the head of Hoover's Federal Farm Board advised planters to plow under every third row. But Hoover rejected this approach. The surpluses mounted, rural income fell, and the farmer became more and more desperate. Hoover's policies had become bankrupt, yet he had nothing to offer except more of the same.

The failure of his relief policies was even more striking. He placed his main reliance not on federal action, but on local community resources. But how could a city like Toledo, where 80 percent of the working force was unemployed, possibly meet the needs of the jobless through its own resources? This truth was recognized by many of the national welfare leaders who had started out sharing Hoover's views. A man like Allen Burns, for example, head of the Community Chest, originally opposed federal action, but by 1931 he had come around to favoring it. In 1932 there was a relief crisis in the country. Philadelphia had suspended aid. New York City had a big backlog of emergency cases. In Chicago they were sending husbands and wives to separate relief shelters. Yet Hoover continued to issue statements saying that the generosity of the public was adequately caring for the needy.

J.A.G.:   Can you suggest any explanation for his extreme rigidity? Hoover was an intelligent man and not completely without imagination. How did he justify his insistence on private relief in the face of the fact that 80 percent of the work force in Toledo was unemployed?

W.E.L.:   That is the big puzzle about Hoover. He came to office with a reputation as a great humanitarian; he had experience with massive relief spending in Belgium and, as head of the War Food Administration, with government intervention in the economy. He supported labor unions and had favored public works spending and counter-cyclical actions in a time of depression as early as 1921. Yet in office he became the most extreme kind of advocate of laissez-faire.

J.A.G.:   Do you think that his rigidity can be explained by the unreasonableness and partisan character of some of the critics of his handling of the Depression?

W.E.L.:   That probably had something to do with it. If you assume that there was a general fear of not maintaining a balanced budget and of going off the gold standard, it must have seemed to him grossly unfair to rail at him for not doing what every "sensible" person knew should not be done.

One other point ought to be made, though. There is a "Hoover theory" claiming that the country was coming out of the Depression in the summer of 1932 and that recovery would have been achieved had it not been for the election of Roosevelt, which created an anxiety that produced the bank crisis three months later and that subsequently eventuated in the faulty policies of the New Deal. I am not at all persuaded. Some economic indices did go up in the summer of 1932, but indices had gone up earlier in the Depression only to come down again. By autumn, the economy had slumped once more. Moreover, I find it very hard to believe that a country that had just overwhelmingly elected Franklin Roosevelt was terrified by his assuming office. The bank crisis occurred because there was something seriously wrong with the banking structure. Even in Wall Street many believed that the United States ought to go off gold, and when Roosevelt did go off gold in the spring of 1933, the House of Morgan hailed him.

J.A.C.:   At the time of his nomination for the presidency in 1932, many liberals considered Franklin Roosevelt too conservative and something of a lightweight. What led them to these opinions?

W.E.L.:   One has to recognize that the kinds of issues which seem to us to have been important, particularly those centering on unemployment, were not those that many writers and politicians considered central. There were three big questions that seemed significant with respect to FDR's record as Governor of New York. One was municipal corruption, the second was Prohibition, and the third was the League of Nations. On all three, he took positions that made him seem a vacillator. On municipal corruption, he faced the delicate question of what to do about Mayor Jimmy Walker of New York, a member of his own party, who was under investigation. Reformers charged him with temporizing. On Prohibition, he took a stand that satisfied neither the wets nor the drys, once more leaving the impression that he was not a forceful character. And on the League of Nations question, Roosevelt, although he had run for vice president in 1920 as a Wilsonian Democrat, bowed to William Randolph Hearst in January 1932 and indicated that he did not favor America's participation. Once more, he gave the impression of being weak.

Then, in the campaign itself, he failed to strike a clear enough note. Raymond Moley, an early member of the group of advisers who made up FDR's Brain Trust, tells of his horror at confronting Roosevelt with two different versions of a tariff speech, and of Roosevelt's saying, "Weave them together." Then there was that classic address at Forbes Field in which he accused Hoover of heading the greatest spending administration in all our history. His ability to make a speech of that sort, at the same time that he was saying he favored unemployment relief, once again left people with the impression that he was, in the phrase of a book at the time, "a gay reformer," without very much substance to him.

J.A.C.: Did Roosevelt really fashion the great coalition which produced his sweeping victories of 1932 through 1944?

W.E.L.: He did not do so in 1932. Arthur Krock of the *New York Times* wrote after the election that the country was voting a national grouch, and this seems to me very likely true. It was a vote against Hoover rather than one for Roosevelt. By 1936, however, the coalition had emerged full-blown. We do not know enough yet about how it was put together to say how much of it resulted from conscious effort on Roosevelt's part. He certainly was a political animal, and he knew that there were political benefits to be gained from "recognition." He was fashioning what was less a Democratic party than a New Deal party, grounded in class and ethnicity and built around what one writer called "the politics of the deed." Roosevelt could point to a series of specific benefits that had gone to particular individuals as a result of the New Deal.

J.A.C.: What of the argument, advanced by Samuel Lubell and others, that especially in the cities the swing of popular support from the Republicans to the Democrats had really occurred before 1932?

W.E.L.: There was some party realignment in the 1920s, especially a gravitation to the Democrats in predominantly Catholic cities. But we must remember that in 1928 Al Smith was badly beaten, while in 1936 Roosevelt scored one of the greatest victories in the history of the two-party system. This shift in the 1930s seems to me of vastly greater importance. Roosevelt ran much better than Smith had in cities such as Los Angeles, and there were many new groups, notably blacks, he won to the Democratic party for the first time.

J.A.C.: Much has been made of Roosevelt's apparent lack of an organized plan for coping with economic problems in 1933 and of the confusion and contradictions in many of his early actions. Is this criticism entirely fair?

W.E.L.: Certainly there were contradictions, particularly in the early years of the New Deal, and conflicts among Roosevelt's advisers—with an orthodox man such as Lewis Douglas, the Budget Director, opposing the policies advocated by Rexford Tugwell, who was a national planner—and between New Nationalists and the Brandeisian wing of the party represented by people such as Felix Frankfurter. Secretary of State Cordell Hull pursued a policy of expanding international trade at the same time that Roosevelt was scuttling the London Economic Conference. The Administration advocated supporting purchasing power and expanding productivity at the same time that it practiced restrictionism, symbolized by the famous episode of the slaughter of the little pigs in an effort to raise the price of pork.

Yet despite all of this, there was more cohesion to the policies of Roosevelt than critics allow. The basic idea he started with was that there was imbalance in the economy created by the overexpansion of the 1920s and by the fact that a single interest—business—controlled too large a percentage of national resources. He tried to achieve a new balance by increasing purchasing power, particularly that of farmers. He was more concerned about farmers than workers, in part because of the vast extent of the rural depression. He thought that although some gains might be made in international trade, recovery was essentially going to have to be a domestic operation, achieved by building up the home market, chiefly by augmenting the farmers' purchasing power. In addition, the New Dealers were led both by the experience of the World War I mobilization and by that of trade associations in the 1920s to seek recovery through greater cooperation between government and business. Although they were not out-and-out greenbackers, they favored some kind of inflation—actually, the decision to go off gold was all but inevitable. And the policies Roosevelt followed in his first term worked out reasonably well. By 1937 the country had about gotten back to 1929 levels of output, although not of employment. No doubt, other policies would have worked better, but that judgment comes from hindsight.

J.A.G.:   Historians frequently speak of a first New Deal and a second New Deal. Would you discuss the differences between these two New Deals?

W.E.L.:   The terms "first New Deal" and "second New Deal" are not terms that I find helpful, in part because they mean different things to different historians. There are at least three divergent sets of meanings historians have given to the term "the two New Deals." The first was popularized by Basil Rauch in his history of the New Deal published in 1944. He saw a shift in policies from right to left. The 1933 New Deal, essentially conservative in his view, was characterized by excessive business influence in the NRA and by solicitude for large farmers in the AAA. The aim of the first New Deal, he wrote, was recovery rather than reform. He perceived movement to a second New Deal starting in 1934 and maturing with the "Second Hundred

Days" of 1935, as the result of attacks on Roosevelt from the right (the Liberty League and United States Chamber of Commerce) and from the left (men such as Huey Long). As a consequence, Congress, he says, in 1935 enacted progressive measures such as the Social Security Act, the Holding Company Act, and the Wagner National Labor Relations Act.

The trouble with that scenario, though it is not wholly wrong, is that during the "conservative" first New Deal, advanced legislation such as the TVA Act was passed, and during the "liberal" second New Deal, emphases of the first New Deal persisted. Rauch's interpretation, which has been widely accepted, exaggerates the differences between the two periods, I believe. Roosevelt was making plans for the Social Security bill of 1935, for example, very early; it was held up in part only because some of the reformers wanted to refine the details.

A second conception of two New Deals was advanced by Eric Goldman in *Rendezvous with Destiny* (1952). He presented the first New Deal as essentially New Nationalist, the second New Deal as fundamentally New Freedom with Wilson's main counselor, Louis Brandeis, as the *éminence grise.* This conception, too, contains a certain amount of truth, but, again, there are problems. For one thing, during the so-called "New Nationalist" phase in 1933, Brandeisian legislation like the Securities Act was passed. Moreover, in the "New Freedom" period of 1935, measures that are hard to call Brandeisian, such as the Wagner Act, were adopted.

Finally, there is the version of the two New Deals developed first by Rexford Tugwell and given its fullest expression by Arthur M. Schlesinger, Jr., in his volumes on *The Age of Roosevelt.* Like Rauch, both writers saw two New Deals, but, reversing Rauch, they charted movement from the left to the right. The critical aspect of their first New Deal of 1933 was a commitment to national planning and a holistic view of the economy. They go on to say that, though the second New Deal of 1935 and later was much more antibusiness in its rhetoric, it was more capitalistic in substance. Here again, I dissent. Tugwell did indeed believe in national planning, but it is hard to find anybody else in 1933 who did. And how can measures such as the Wagner Act or the new agencies such as the Farm Security Administration or the National Planning Board be represented as marking a shift to the right?

J.A.C.:   Were such raucous radical critics of the New Deal as Senator Huey Long, the "Radio Priest" Father Coughlin, and the Townsendites really, in your opinion, reformers?

W.E.L.:   It is hard to classify Long. At the time, many considered him a fascist, and the comic pose he struck was thought to be simply a disguise. On the other hand, one can make a case for Long as a reformer, even a radical, for he did get a great deal done in Louisiana. Yet he was hostile to the CIO, tolerated child labor, and, particularly with regard to urban reform, was anything but forward-looking. It is probably too extreme to call him a fascist, nor was he a racist demagogue. But his manipulation of the Louisiana legislature and his use of police suggest a lust for power and a contempt for parliamentary institutions. Long himself, when asked whether he ought to be categorized as being on the left or the right, said, "Hell, I'm *sui generis*," and let it go at that. And that may be where the historian has to leave it.

Long certainly must be taken a good deal more seriously than Father Coughlin or Dr. Townsend. Most of Coughlin's emphasis revolved around the money question. One critic said that what he knew about economics, if turned to salt, would not physic a chickadee. Townsend was a one-idea man, concerned only with the old-age pension movement. He shared the values of much of his following— elderly Republican WASP elements on the decline—so that although he helped in the push for social security legislation, he did not contribute anything more. And by 1937 he was so strongly opposed to Roosevelt's Supreme Court–packing plan that he even neglected his old-age pension scheme.

J.A.C.:   Well, are there any threads binding these extremist critics together? Did they at any stage cooperate with one another?

W.E.L.:   By 1935 Long, Coughlin, and Townsend were moving toward a kind of political alliance. After Long was assassinated in September 1935, one of his followers, Gerald L. K. Smith, joined in a very loose federation with Coughlin and some of the Townsend forces in the Union party, which ran William Lemke for president in 1936. Other threads link the movements. They found their following often among the dispossessed who were not reached by New Deal programs. They spoke for a politics of revenge. All were distrustful of Eastern intellectuals and the liberal establishment, and all three heaped ridicule on the New Dealers. They were also captivated by the idea of a self-generating economics, which reminds one a lot of the chain-letter craze of the 1930s. And yet despite these common themes, there was a world of difference between the Brooklyn and South Boston constituency of Coughlin, the Deep South followers of Long, and the old folks of the West who backed Townsend. Moreover, the leaders diverged widely in their outlooks and had no capacity for sharing power. In 1936 the Union party quickly broke up in a series of squabbles among the different leaders.

J.A.G.: Would it be accurate to call them neo-Populists?

W.E.L.: Yes, indeed. Long came from a Populist stronghold in Louisiana, and he clearly was in the Populist tradition. Lemke corresponded regularly with "Coin" Harvey. As for the Coughlinites, Herman Kahn, the director of the Roosevelt Library, once said, "Scratch a Midwesterner and you find a funny money man." I think Townsend is a little harder to put in the Populist category, and, of course, these men had centers of strength, such as the Irish Catholic neighborhoods of Brooklyn, that were far removed from the old Populist heartland.

J.A.G.: How did the attacks of these men influence Roosevelt's behavior?

W.E.L.: He regarded them as rival political operators and sought to put them out of business or to lessen their appeal. Within Louisiana, he deliberately distributed patronage to Long's opponents, cut off public works funds, and sent a whole army of agents from the Internal Revenue Bureau into New Orleans to look into well-founded suspicions of wrongdoing by men in Long's organization. When the Union party was organized in 1936, and when Coughlin was becoming more and more vitriolic in his denunciations of Roosevelt, the President worked closely with members of the Catholic hierarchy to undercut him.

The most interesting question to historians is whether Roosevelt, in the phrase of the day, was "stealing Huey's thunder"—that is to say, did Roosevelt change his program to undercut these rivals? In particular, it has been suggested that the Wealth Tax Act of 1935 was a response to Long's Share-Our-Wealth program, that the National Youth Administration was a reply to Huey's proposal to give students a free college education and free textbooks, and that the Social Security Act was a consequence of the Townsend Plan. There seems little reason to doubt that Long and Townsend influenced these developments, but the Wealth Tax bill had been advocated for some time, and the Social Security bill was in the works well before the Townsend Plan had developed any considerable strength.

One often hears it said that Roosevelt destroyed the allure of these men by putting through social reforms that undercut the discontent on which they fed. There is something to this, but it ought to be noted that Townsend was much stronger *after* the passage of the Social Security Act. These men appealed to emotions that no mere statute could wipe out.

J.A.G.: In recent years, historians have pointed out that the New Deal did relatively little for underprivileged groups: blacks, the poor, sharecroppers in the South. If this was so, how can the overwhelming support that these groups gave Roosevelt in the 1936 election be explained?

W.E.L.: I don't agree that the New Deal did little for these groups. The historians you refer to may be confusing the question of whether the New Deal permanently changed the economic system with the question of what the government's response was to the particular crisis that these groups faced in the 1930s. In sharp contrast to the performance in the Hoover period, there was an enormous outpouring of federal relief funds. In some counties the majority of the population was on relief. By the end of 1934 more than twenty million Americans were receiving public assistance. This seemed to a great many people far more impressive than any inadequacies in the program.

The federal government was visible in the 1930s as it had not been before. When I entered Cornell as a freshman in 1939, with very little money and knowing that I would have to work my way through college, the first indication I had of a federal presence was the ease with which I was able to get an NYA job, cleaning out test tubes in a laboratory. My children in Dobbs Ferry go to a high school that was built by the WPA. This kind of experience was multiplied all around the country. The people who faced the foreclosure of farm mortgages and who were bailed out by the national government felt an allegiance to Roosevelt and the Democratic party, despite the shortcomings of the New Deal.

The attitudes of blacks are particularly interesting, because in some respects the New Deal was not merely inadequate but even injurious to their interests. The NRA often discriminated against black workers; the AAA drove numbers of black sharecroppers and tenant farmers off the land; the TVA operated segregated facilities; the CCC refrained from setting up camps in some Southern communities in order to appease white Southerners. How, then, does one account for the fact that blacks executed a historic change in their political allegiance in the 1930s, one that persists to this day? Simply because the discrimination they suffered at the hands of the New Deal was no different from what they had been suffering all along. What was *new* were the benefits they received from the New Deal—such things as relief programs and low-cost housing projects. Some three hundred thousand black illiterates were taught to read and write under the New Deal, and federal funds went to black schools. True, Roosevelt refused to fight for civil rights legislation, but I know no reason to suppose that his political judgment was wrong; he would not have gotten the legislation, and he would have jeopardized other reforms, some of which did benefit blacks. Finally, there was a political aspect to the appeal of the New Deal to blacks. They understood that, especially after the repeal of the two-thirds rule, Democratic party leaders valued them more than they did the white South.

One last point that might be made is that quite apart from any specific program, many workingmen, poor farmers, and others who felt themselves to have been neglected in the past regarded Roosevelt as their friend. They sensed that his was a humane administration, that the President cared about what happened to them. Roosevelt, said one worker, was the first man who had ever been in the White House who would understand that his boss was a son of a bitch. Probably without being able to explain exactly why, a lot of Americans had that sense in the 1930s.

J.A.C.: Why did Roosevelt try to pack the Supreme Court in 1937?

W.E.L.: Many historians argue that Roosevelt made a bad mistake in trying to pack the Court because he never needed to do so, especially given the switch by the Court that took place between 1936 and 1937. It was once thought that when the Supreme Court handed down its decision upholding a Washington minimum wage law in the spring of 1937, essentially reversing its ruling against a New York minimum wage law of 1936, FDR's plan was responsible for the shift. It was then discovered that the Washington decision had been reached *prior* to Roosevelt's announcement of the Court-packing plan. Hence, it was said, since the Court had already changed its mind, Roosevelt, if he had just waited, would have gotten all that he wanted. A second line of argument was developed by Justice Felix Frankfurter in an article in the *University of Pennsylvania Law Review.* He contended that the Court never did switch, that the only reason that Justice Owen

Roberts voted in the negative in the New York case was because of a technical matter concerning the way the case was presented by the state of New York.

I do not find either argument persuasive. There is no doubt at all, if you take the range of opinions from 1935 through 1937 (the Court's attitude toward the commerce clause in the *Schechter* and *Carter* cases contrasted with its view in *Jones and Laughlin*, or the *Rail Pension* and *Butler* decisions contrasted with the *Social Security* rulings), that what political scientists have called a "Constitutional Revolution" took place.

Considering the realities that Roosevelt faced, I think it is understandable that he concluded that he had to do something about the Court. After all, it had held that not even a state could enact minimum wage legislation. It had gone out of its way in *Carter* to deny that as large an enterprise as coal mining was a proper subject for Congressional action under the commerce clause. The Court was about to rule on the Wagner Act and the Social Security Act, and there was every reason to believe that it would hold both of these laws unconstitutional. In November 1936 Roosevelt had been elected by an unprecedented landslide, but what could he do with his victory? If the Court persisted in the line it had been following, most of the major New Deal measures would be declared unconstitutional and so, too, would the social legislation the President planned to recommend in his second term.

J.A.G.:   What about the old adage, "The Supreme Court follows the election returns"? Isn't it likely that the Court would have changed its tune of its own accord after the 1936 election?

W.E.L.:   I doubt that we shall ever have a satisfactory answer to that question, but I suppose some kind of response would have been made. Here too, however, the historian has information that the President did not have. One of the things I was struck by in going through Justice Van Devanter's papers is that he and men like him seriously thought a Republican victory possible in 1936. Many of the Justices may have believed that they were tribunes of the people, defending popular rights against an arbitrary ruler, and the Roosevelt landslide could well have brought them up short. Yet despite the landslide, Van Devanter did not alter his attitude, nor did any other of the conservative judges, the so-called "Four Horsemen." All four voted, for example, to strike down the Washington minimum wage law.

An argument can be made that Roosevelt would have been wiser to have waited to see how the Supreme Court would respond to his victory, but, given the performance of the Court as recently as the previous June, he had no reason to expect a basic shift in attitude. Even after Roosevelt introduced his Court-packing plan and the Court upheld the Washington minimum wage law in March, almost everyone expected that he was going to lose some of the Wagner Act cases in April. Roosevelt thought that he had to capitalize on his election victory at the outset, or he would lose the momentum. Moreover, if he waited until the Court handed down an adverse decision in the Wagner Act cases, he would appear to be arbitrarily attempting, by a political solution, to subvert the will of the judiciary.

But having said this, I must add that Roosevelt undoubtedly believed after the election that the world was his oyster and that a few Justices were not going to stand in his way. His behavior revealed some vindictiveness. The tone of his message suggests a desire to chastise the Court.

J.A.G.: Well then, why actually did the Court change its attitude?

W.E.L.: I would say it did so largely in response to the Court-packing plan. It was beating a strategic retreat. Chief Justice Hughes in particular was a very adroit politician and also a man with a sense of the need to preserve the integrity of the Court as an institution; he acted in part in a self-protective way. The fact that the Court had a different line of precedents which it could follow made it relatively easy for it to change.

J.A.G.: If the Court had not changed its position while the reform bill was being discussed, would the bill have passed?

W.E.L.: It might not have passed in the form that it did, but I think that Roosevelt would have gotten at least two additional Justices. Particularly if the Court had struck down the Social Security Act, the pressure for change would have been so great that some kind of Court-packing plan would undoubtedly have gone through.

J.A.G.: Is it therefore correct to say that in the Court fight Roosevelt "lost the battle but won the war"?

W.E.L.: Roosevelt himself advanced that claim, and if you believe, as I do, that a Constitutional Revolution occurred in 1937, there is a lot to support his argument. Within two-and-one-half years, he was able to appoint five new Justices. After 1937 every piece of New Deal legislation was upheld.

On the other hand, Roosevelt lost the war in that the Court fight greatly damaged his standing with Congress and within the Democratic party. It was probably the most important single event in the creation of the conservative coalition that brought the New Deal to a virtual standstill by the summer of 1938.

J.A.G.:   In the last analysis, why did the New Deal fail to restore real prosperity?

W.E.L.:   One has to start by saying that by the time Roosevelt took office so much damage had been done to the economy that a massive effort was required to straighten things out. Business confidence had been shattered; the banking system was in a state of collapse; the debt structure was extremely burdensome; the loss of purchasing power was so great, the reluctance to invest so considerable, that rapid recovery was unlikely.

One must add, though, that some of the measures Roosevelt pushed either did not contribute to recovery or actually worked in the wrong direction. The National Industrial Recovery Act probably accounted for a certain amount of re-employment, but on the whole the Administration invested more energy in it than it got out of it in economic improvement. Much the same could be said about gold buying. It did not do as much harm as its critics charged, but it represented a loss of valuable time. Probably the greatest mistake of the first term was the failure to do enough about public works and housing. The real impetus to recovery was to come from rapid, large-scale spending. This is what some of the Progressives like young Bob La Follette of Wisconsin had been pushing in the Hoover years. But throughout the New Deal, as Keynes pointed out in his letter to Roosevelt in 1938, the biggest single failure of policy came in this area.

Housing was particularly significant. One of the most important causes of the economic breakdown was the sharp decline in construction in the 1920s. Building continued to fall off in the 1930s. This was an area where the administration might well have done a great deal more than it did. To use Roosevelt's famous phrase, at least "one third of the nation" was ill-housed. A large-scale housing program of the sort that Britain and other countries undertook was practicable. Furthermore, not only had residential housing declined, but construction of other kinds was also down drastically. If the construction problem had been attacked in the 1930s, all kinds of beneficial results would have followed. Yet it must be repeated that, for all the weaknesses of the New Deal, by 1937 the 1929 levels of production had been reached.

Then came the precipitous recession of 1937–38, the sharpest decline in our history. There are numbers of explanations for this recession, but the biggest one is that Roosevelt, for all of his willingness to spend in an emergency, continued to believe in balancing the budget. By 1937 he had the budget in balance, only to precipitate the recession, because the improvement that had come in his first term had largely been the result of deficit spending at a time of less than full employment. His predicament in the recession revealed that, despite all his reforms, Roosevelt had failed to move the government into the center of economic decision-making, while, at the same time, business groups were reluctant to take the initiative. They suffered a loss of confidence because of the Depression and were also unsettled by the New Deal reforms. (One of the dilemmas faced by a reform government in a capitalist system is that it sometimes is confronted with a choice between either not initiating changes that ought to be undertaken, or going ahead with those reforms with the knowledge that they may cause hardship by impairing business's will to invest, thus prolonging a depression.) In 1938 Roosevelt abandoned budget-balancing and accepted the idea of accelerated government spending. An upturn followed once he had made that change, but not until World War II was full employment achieved.

J.A.G.:   Did Roosevelt ever really learn much about modern economics and its relationship to public policy? More specifically, to what extent did his advisers try to convert him to the new Keynesian economics?

W.E.L.:   It has often been implied that Roosevelt was something of a dunce with respect to economics, but he was a lot better informed about economic matters than one has any right to expect of an American politician, who has his own special skills. He got a rather good undergraduate education in economics at Harvard, and he had a certain amount of business experience in the 1920s. His grasp of detail was truly extraordinary; numbers of people have commented on his ability to recite economic data with remarkable precision. So he was far from being an ignoramus on economics.

The question of Keynes's influence is a more difficult one. Roosevelt appears to have disliked Keynes because of his attack on Woodrow Wilson's handling of the Versailles Conference in *The Economic Consequences of the Peace*. Keynes came to the United States in 1934, and there are conflicting views of what FDR's response was. Roosevelt wrote Felix Frankfurter that he had seen Keynes and thought him a splendid fellow. At the same time, he told Secretary of Labor Frances Perkins that all he had gotten from Keynes was a "rigmarole of figures." The weight of evidence suggests that the Perkins version is the right one. Roosevelt was not much impressed by Keynes, nor Keynes by Roosevelt. There was, however, a group of people around Roosevelt who, by the second term, had read Keynes's *General Theory*. They never to my knowledge, though, attempted to educate Roosevelt in the same way that Walter Heller gave Jack Kennedy training in the New Economics when he became President. By 1938 Roosevelt was moving more or less in a Keynesian direction, but while he may have grasped the idea that *spending* could be a good thing, he probably never grasped the counterintuitive conception that *deficits* were a good thing.

On this whole question, timing is of the greatest importance. Some of the doctrines that we think of as Keynesian were not what Keynes was arguing for in 1933, and if Roosevelt had followed the ideas of the most accepted professional economists when he took office, he would have done the wrong thing. The *General Theory* did not appear until 1936, which meant there was little time, even in FDR's second term, for a new administration to absorb a complex theory, especially one that seemed to fly in the face of common sense. So on the whole I am more impressed by how responsive Roosevelt was to Keynesian doctrine than by his failure to go along with it all the way. It took the experience of World War II to persuade most people. The war proved that massive spending under the right conditions produced full employment.

J.A.G.:   Was Roosevelt as bad an administrator as his critics have often charged?

W.E.L.:   From the point of view of the public administration theory that prevailed when he was in the White House, he was a very bad administrator. He did not follow organization charts and permitted all kinds of conflicts among his subordinates. He found it hard to fire people, and he frequently left men with the impression that he agreed with them when he did not.

But historians give Roosevelt higher marks as an administrator. Having a low opinion of organization charts, they point out that the new agencies he set up gave vigor and a spirit of innovation to the government that would not have been achieved under the old-line departments, and that the setting of administrators against one another brought choices between alternative policies out into the open. The airing of clashing views helped Roosevelt to decide difficult questions. But probably the greatest thing to be said in FDR's favor is that he was able to attract first-rate people to Washington. That is the highest tribute one can pay to an administrator.

J.A.G.:   How closely did Roosevelt follow the complexities of New Deal programs? Was he the leader or merely the cheerleader of the New Deal?

W.E.L.:   He scrutinized some programs more intently than others, but at the high policy level, he followed most programs remarkably closely. To be sure, some things were dearer to his heart than others. He could never get very interested in urban housing, but anything that had to do with conservation or the movement back to the land captured his attention. He liked to think of himself as a Georgia farmer, and he watched a whole range of agricultural questions from that perspective. He was terribly interested in anything that he had been involved with as Governor of New York—for example, public power. In short, so far as any president can keep on top of the proliferating federal bureaucracy, Roosevelt did a pretty good job.

J.A.G.:   Well, looking back on the New Deal from the perspective of today, what impact did Roosevelt make on the office of the President?

W.E.L.:   This question is less easy to answer than one might suppose. Roosevelt was an activist chief executive, who set a precedent for those who would follow him; the degree to which Lyndon Johnson thought of FDR as a model for some of his actions is one indication of this influence. If you compare Roosevelt in the White House with Coolidge, you immediately realize how the conception of the office expanded. Yet to try to spell out what he innovated is difficult. Probably what first comes to mind is FDR's pathbreaking performance as chief legislator, but, in fact, Theodore Roosevelt and Woodrow Wilson had both done a great deal along the same lines. In part because of Roosevelt's long period in office and the wealth of legislation enacted in his time, however, he carried on a much larger operation than any predecessor. Under him, the presidency was so much bigger in degree that it became bigger in kind.

Roosevelt also employed different instruments. I have in mind particularly the radio, his introduction of the fireside chat. But he also made better use of press conferences. Presidents had talked to newspaper people before, but there was a marked difference between the formal press conferences of Hoover and the free-swinging sessions that FDR carried on. He knew reporters by their first names; he obviously liked them and they liked him.

He expanded the office, too, by becoming, to use Sidney Hyman's phrase, chief economic engineer (something no President had ever been), and this development led subsequently to the Employment Act in 1946 and the Council of Economic Advisers.

Probably the main change he made in the presidency was his creation of the Executive Office of the President in 1939. He moved the Bureau of the Budget under his control at that time. A number of other agencies—the Council of Economic Advisers and the National Security Agency, among others—were added in the Truman-Eisenhower period. Many political scientists believe that this change has enabled presidents to impose some order on their administrations.

J.A.G.:   How has the New Deal experience permanently changed American life and American society?

W.E.L.:   There has been a tendency recently in writing about the New Deal to minimize the changes that were wrought, in part because so many social evils still exist. If the New Deal changed so much, how does it happen that things are still so bad? I recognize the limitations of the New Deal, including those in some areas where it might have brought change. Yet I do think of the New Deal and the Great Depression as a watershed, the most important episode in American history since the Civil War.

First of all, there was a vast expansion of the role of the federal government. Before 1933 the national government had made little impact on the lives of ordinary Americans. After the New Deal, it was inserting itself in a wide range of ways into the affairs of every citizen.

J.A.G.:   But was it the New Deal that caused this great expansion of government activity? Had not the expansion been taking place steadily for decades?

W.E.L.:   Yes, of course. But if you compare the status of the national government in 1932 with that in 1939, you will see that an enormous change has taken place. The expansion under Hoover, who was regarded in 1928 as a great social engineer, a man in touch with the latest developments in the social sciences, was trivial by comparison, and if Hoover had been re-elected, we would not have had the kinds of changes that came about under the New Deal. A development related to this expansion of government was the change from voluntarism to coercion. Instead of trying to persuade businessmen to be nicer to workers, the New Deal provided penalties to make them go along with unionization. And this growth of governmental power is validated by the Constitutional Revolution of 1937.

Another big change that took place as a consequence of the Great Depression and the New Deal was in American politics. For a period of some eighty years, the Republican party had been, with certain exceptions, the majority party in the United States, whereas since 1932 the Republicans have only rarely succeeded in capturing control of the House.

The outlook of the parties and the content of politics were also altered. The Democratic party as recently as the candidacy of John W. Davis in 1924 had been the party of small government; under FDR, it became the party of big government.

Still another permanent effect of the New Deal was to make poverty a national concern. Granted, there were areas in which the New Deal did not achieve effective social change, and there certainly was a hiatus in the Eisenhower period during which the country seemed indifferent to poverty. But Roosevelt's message, pointing out that one-third of the nation was ill-housed, ill-clad, and ill-nourished, put poverty on the national agenda. Critics point out that the New Deal never did all it should have done in housing, and I share that view. Still, there had been no national public housing projects in peacetime until the 1930s. In addition, the activities of the FHA in supporting private home building were an innovation of great importance. And with respect to the welfare of the most impoverished, the sweatshop and child labor were virtually erased in the New Deal years.

One of the most important changes of the 1930s was in the status of industrial labor. True, Roosevelt was often indifferent and even hostile to industrial unions at the beginning, but even in 1933 he helped establish an atmosphere conducive to unionism, and the NLRB subsequently did a lot more. In 1933 most factory workers were not unionized. Men in the mills worked without vacations; they were subject to the whims of foremen; they had no job security. In the coal fields, workers endured the tyranny of the company town and the company store; they were harassed by private police. Under the Roosevelt administration, a redistribution of power between labor and capital of the greatest significance took place. Writers of the New Left would say that practically nothing changed in the 1930s, but few steel workers or auto workers, having lived through the decade, would agree.

Roosevelt always had a deep interest in the conservation movement, and the Tennessee Valley Authority stands forth as one of the very big achievements of these years. Grand Coulee and Bonneville transformed much of the Pacific Northwest, and think of what the Rural Electrification Administration meant to farmers. But probably most important—what distinguishes New Deal efforts from the conservation movement of the Progressive era—were developments in soil conservation: the creation of the Soil Erosion Service and the Soil Conservation Service. Here were gains that permanently changed the landscape of the United States.

Yet another New Deal development was the greatly increased role of intellectuals in government. They had appeared briefly on the state level in Wisconsin in the Progressive era and in Washington during World War I, but not until the Brain Trust did the intimate association of the university campus and the government develop. A new administrative class arose, with a particular sense of values and ambitions and a unique power base that had not existed prior to the New Deal. Along with this came a series of new government activities, such as the Federal Art Project, the Federal Theatre, and the Federal Writers' Project.

If one examines the experience of the American farmer between 1932 and 1939, one is struck by the enormously increased involvement of the national government. Though the Department of Agriculture had been very active since the late nineteenth century, it had never been so intimately concerned with the everyday life or the economic welfare of the farmer. Under the New Deal this changes dramatically. (By the way, the developments I have been describing should not necessarily all be thought of as good. Whether the subsidy program has been a success, whether public housing projects are well conceived, whether intellectuals ought to be so involved in government are all debatable questions. But if the issue is whether the 1930s changed anything, the answer is self-evident.)

I ought also to mention some more subtle changes in American life unrelated to particular pieces of legislation. One was the recognition of ethnic diversity. For example, nowadays one frequently sees blacks as actors in commercials on television. There has been far too much self-congratulation on the part of white liberals because of this development. What is much more to the point is the shocking degree to which blacks in the past were not permitted to be a visible part of the national culture. The New Deal began the process of change, although painfully inadequately. Similarly, to a remarkable degree, American society prior to the Depression was a WASP society, but during the Roosevelt administration the names of Jews, of Catholics, of members of Italian and Slavic ethnic groups became prominent. Large numbers of groups were brought into government to a degree that had not been true in the past.

I think, too, that the nature of American liberalism changed markedly in the 1930s. Aside from the great proliferation of the functions of the federal government, there was a shift of another sort. It suddenly occurred to liberals that they could buy reforms. Expenditures by the national government could achieve all kinds of social changes. They turned away from Poor Richard's values of thrift; they rejected the orthodoxies of the old economics. The long tradition of emphasis on limits on the power of government was broken. There was a sense of a boundless range of activities which the State could undertake. This is one of the big differences, I think, between the Hoover era and the Roosevelt era. Related to this was the end of fatalism about the business cycle. No longer did people believe that they had to wait out a depression, that somehow a depression was the judgment of a wrathful God. The New Deal created countercyclical tools. Later administrations have not always been willing to use them, but they have been there.

J.A.G.:   What are the chief unanswered questions about the period that you think historians should investigate?

W.E.L.:   The largest single question is, "How much social change actually took place?"

This is related to the debate about continuity and discontinuity. Does one see the New Deal as an outgrowth of the 1920s and the Progressive era, or as a significant departure from the past?

The answer to that question shapes not only our perception of the New Deal, but also our interpretation of subsequent history. How much welfare has been accorded under the Welfare State? Has social security in fact been achieved? It is often said that the Fair Labor Standards Act of 1938 was inadequate, and certainly it was. And yet admirers of the New Deal might reply, "In America you begin by establishing the principle and then you make it better. The minimum wage has been raised steadily over the years. If it is still too low, is this a fault of the New Deal or of subsequent generations?"

Historians should also look at what the range of actual possibilities was for Roosevelt instead of imposing on his period our latter-day expectations. We also need to scrutinize his intentions. It has frequently been said that the Supreme Court fight and other developments cut short reform, but it is not altogether clear what Roosevelt would have advocated had he not encountered these setbacks.

And despite all the writing on the New Deal, it is remarkable how many of the big stories have yet to be told. We have no adequate accounts of most of the important New Deal agencies. There is no book that puts together the whole history of the NRA, for example, or of the TVA, or of the AAA. One of the most glaring deficiencies in our scholarship involves the story of the movement of financial control from Wall Street to Washington. How exactly did the Securities and Exchange Commission affect the operation of Wall Street?

We have given much more attention to the New Deal than we have to the Great Depression. A lot of the social history of the Depression has yet to be written. And the Depression in America ought to be looked at as an aspect of the worldwide depression.

J.A.G.: What is your opinion of the New Left interpretation of the New Deal era?

W.E.L.: There has not really been very much of it; no book sums up a New Left interpretation of the New Deal. Although the implications of the New Left approach are being heard more and more at history conventions and in articles in scholarly journals, the most sustained effort has been the essay by Barton Bernstein in *Towards a New Past*. Actually, there is no basic distinction between the New Left and the Old Left in interpreting the New Deal. All of us who were raised in the Roosevelt era and lived through the intellectual arguments of the 1940s grappled with the Marxist critique of the New Deal. The attacks of Marxist critics were quite sharp; for instance, Stolberg and Vinton commented that there was nothing that the New Deal had done in agriculture that an earthquake could not have done better. No New Left critic has damned the New Deal with more abandon than the old Marxists.

The main contribution of the New Left has been its emphasis on participatory democracy. This, too, is something that has interested me since I wrote on the works council movement in Germany and England in Franz Neumann's seminar. It seems to me rather curious that given this interest the New Left historians have not chosen to look at the various evidences of participatory democracy in the 1930s: the production control associations and the "grass-roots democracy" of the TVA and the soil conservation and grazing districts. If they did, they would discover that experiences with participatory democracy in the 1930s, like those with the modern poverty program, often did not turn out very well.

There is something rather ironical about the approach of the New Left writers. Their main targets are the "consensus" historians who, they say, homogenized American history, yet their own commentary homogenizes American history to a far greater degree by making it appear that nothing really ever happened. Since socialism was not attained, they seem to suggest, no other development mattered. In short, they are interested less in what happened in the 1930s than in what did not happen—the triumph of socialism.

I took part in a panel on the Left and the New Deal with Arthur M. Schlesinger, Jr., and Irving Howe a couple of years ago. One of the members of the audience was FDR's former adviser, Ben Cohen. He got up and chided all three of us gently, saying that we were talking about the ardent New Dealers and forgetting that this was also the administration of conservatives such as Cordell Hull and the banker Jesse Jones.

No adequate history of the 1930s can overlook the fact not merely that Roosevelt had to contend with the Jesse Joneses, but also that the great majority of ordinary people rejected radical solutions to the problems of the day. New Left historians accuse their predecessors of being elitists who deny the virtues of participatory democracy, but they do not know what to make of the fact that the mass of citizens in the 1930s did not support radical movements and were enthusiastic about FDR. They are left with the rather lame (and incidentally elitist) explanation that the masses simply did not know what was good for them and were swept away by Rooseveltian rhetoric.

J.A.G.:   What are the half-dozen or so books that you would recommend to persons interested in the subject we have been discussing? In each case would you indicate briefly what the particular contribution of the volume is?

W.E.L.: The most important study, of course, is Arthur M. Schlesinger, Jr.'s *The Age of Roosevelt* (1957–60), a three-volume synthesis by a historian who is sympathetic to the New Deal. Probably the best critique from a conservative viewpoint is still Raymond Moley's *After Seven Years* (1939). The major biography is Frank Freidel's, also in three volumes (1952–56), which carries through the 1932 election. The most discerning memoir is Frances Perkins's *The Roosevelt I Knew* (1956). James MacGregor Burns's *Roosevelt: The Lion and the Fox* (1956) is a lively political biography which claims that FDR missed an opportunity for party realignment. Rexford G. Tugwell's *The Democratic Roosevelt* (1957) examines the period from the viewpoint of a social planner. Especially good on economic aspects are John M. Blum's *From the Morgenthau Diaries* (3 volumes, 1959–1969) and Ellis Hawley's *The New Deal and the Problem of Monopoly* (1966). There is no adequate history of the Depression, a monumental assignment, but Irving Bernstein's *The Lean Years* (1960) and *Turbulent Years* (1969) are indispensable on labor, and J. Kenneth Galbraith, *The Great Crash, 1929* (1955), written with characteristic wit and grace, is a delight. A small list of titles, however, does not begin to suggest the great number of first-rate monographs now available on the New Deal.

Epilogue

If I were asked that Question today, I would call attention to a number of more recent contributions of great value, most of them more impressed by the shortcomings of the New Deal than its accomplishments. The late Frank Freidel, whose presence is so sorely missed, completed a fourth volume of his opus on FDR as well as a one-volume synthesis of his subject's life. Geoffrey S. Ward, *A First Class Temperament* (1989), an elegant rendering of "the emergence of Franklin D. Roosevelt," carries down to 1928, five years before his protagonist entered the White House, while Doris Kearns Goodwin's *No Ordinary Times* (1994) pursues the fascinating adventures of Eleanor and Franklin to the very end. Robert S. McElvaine, *The Great Depression: America, 1929–1941* (1984) embraces, in an engaging manner, the history of popular culture as well as political and economic developments. By adopting topical approaches, Anthony J. Badger,

The New Deal: The Depression Years, 1933–1940 (1989) offers an incisive evaluation, and Roger Biles, *A New Deal for the American People* (1991) presents a fresh outlook. Jordan Schwarz's absorbing *The New Dealers* (1993) illuminates areas that other historians have neglected, as does Alan Brinkley's *The End of Reform: New Deal Liberalism in Recession and War* (1995), an important analysis that pushes beyond the period on which most historians have concentrated. William R. Brock, *Welfare, Democracy, and the New Deal* (1988) is a fair-minded appraisal by a distinguished British scholar. Patrick Maney's *The Roosevelt Presence: A Biography of Franklin Delano Roosevelt* (1992), which like Kenneth Davis's ambitious trilogy, is often disapproving of FDR, takes advantage of the two decades of monographic literature published since I spoke to Garraty.

EIGHT

The Achievement of the New Deal

[In 1971–72 I held the Harmsworth chair at Oxford, where the curriculum in American history is rigidly prescribed. For a long while, it consisted only of the history of the colonial era and the period of slavery and secession. Twentieth-century America was recognized only belatedly with the inception of a course, "Industrial America and the Rise of Governmental Power, 1865–1916," which A. E. Campbell of Keble College (and later of Birmingham) and I taught in the Michaelmas term. But as late as 1971 there was no acknowledgment of any U.S. history from 1917 on. Then in the Hilary term early in 1972 Herbert Nicholas, the Rhodes Professor, and I introduced the New Deal as a "Special Subject."

That development provided me with the topic for the "Inaugural Lecture," a requirement for any new chair holder, that I delivered in May 1972. (Curiously, though it was my "inaugural" lecture, it was the very last lecture I gave at Oxford.) Inaugural Lectures are splendid affairs. The speaker, adorned in cap and gown, marches down the aisle in the company of the Vice Chancellor, the highest ranking academic officer in the University (the titular post of Chancellor was held that year by former Prime Minister Harold Macmillan), and a beadle bearing a mace. When the procession reaches the front of the hall, the speaker walks to the lectern and doffs his cap. He (and it was almost always a "he") stands there alone, and is not, in any way, introduced. After a fleeting moment, he nods deferentially to the Vice Chancellor, who has taken his seat, for permission to speak. When on that spring day in 1972 the scarcely noticeable signal of assent came, I began my remarks.

This Inaugural Address has never been published before, but it provided the basis for a talk I gave as the wind-up speech at a conference at the University of New Hampshire on March 19, 1983 that was published in Harvard Sitkoff, ed., *Fifty Years Later: The New Deal Evaluated* (New York: Alfred A. Knopf, 1985). I have buttressed the argument made in the

Inaugural Address and in the Sitkoff volume with new material, but I have taken care not to intrude latter-day items that would, in the context of a 1972 address, be anachronistic.]

I

In the late spring of 1937 the Warden of New College disembarked in New York where he was to receive an honorary degree from Columbia University. On that occasion he declared, "I need hardly say that all my fellow countrymen are much interested in and attracted by the commanding figure of your President. We admire the courage with which he has conquered his physical disabilities, his power of making big and momentous decisions, his frank eloquence, and the charm of his character." Though the British people would differ in assessing Roosevelt's policies, there would be "a large measure of support" for the proposition "that the economic developments in recent years have necessitated many sharp departures from traditional policy and far reaching changes in social organisation."

The Warden's comments on Roosevelt and the New Deal represented but one instance of an appreciation of the American Experiment that has characterized much of British response from the Hundred Days of 1933 to the present, and that frequently has been missing from recent American commentary. In a dispatch to the *New York Times* in the fall of 1933 the foreign correspondent "Augur" reported from London:

> Few people in England understand President Roosevelt's plans for economic recovery. Fewer still approve of them. Yet the American President is popular with the English. They admire him for the quality, which their own leaders today do not possess—he is a man of courage. . . . This suffices to create for the President a following which any British Minister would give a fortune to acquire.

That same year George Bernard Shaw said:

> Possibly America may save human society yet by solving the great political problems which have baffled and destroyed all previous attempts at permanent civilization. I have hopes, because America has got this irrepressible social instinct, this wonderful surging thing inside itself, that you do not find in the same reckless profusion elsewhere.

While the New Deal was only in its second year, Winston Churchill wrote of the presidency: "It is certain that Franklin Roosevelt will rank among the greatest of men who have occupied that proud position." Mr. Churchill, never fond of the drys, was impressed by FDR's achievement in freeing the United States from the evil of Prohibition. Beyond that, he admired Roosevelt's "generous sympathy for the underdog, his intense desire for a nearer approach to social justice, . . . and the vigour of his administrative measures of relief and credit expansion. . . . He has known how to gain the confidence and the loyalty of the most numerous and the most ebullient of civilized communities, and all the world watches his valiant effort to solve their problems with an anxiety which is only the shadow of high hope." Roosevelt, Churchill concluded, "is an explorer who has embarked . . . upon a quest which might conceivably be as important as the discovery of the New World." More than a decade later, H. G. Nicholas, writing in *Fortnightly* in May 1945, observed:

When Franklin Roosevelt died on April 12 he concluded a longer period of continuous office than any President of the United States or any British Minister since the Reform Bill. During these twelve crowded years, by political speech and ceremonial proclamation, by executive action and legislative direction, in his three roles of party leader, chief executive and titular head of state, he exercised a cumulative influence on the American public mind which for duration and intensity can hardly be paralleled in the history of modern democracies.

The widespread British approbation owed something to the fact that FDR seemed accessible in a way that a Huey Long or an Al Smith were not. As a member of the landed gentry, he could be readily situated. Even before Roosevelt took office, a Boston Brahmin wrote Sir Charles Hobhouse with regard to country life in England:

We have, I think, slowly in the making, the same institution so far as it is possible, without the principal ingredients, primogeniture and entail, in America. Franklin Roosevelt who, if nominated, will almost certainly be our next President, is one of the many New York families having estates on the Hudson River and one of the group which has established country life in America most nearly akin to yours here.

In his remarks in New York, the Warden of New College, H. A. L. Fisher, thought it would be generally agreed in Great Britain "that it is fortunate that this inevitable challenge should come to the existing order, not as it might possibly have come, from a violent uncultured demagogue playing down to the lowest passions of the mob, but from a man belonging to one of your famous families, educated in one of your famous universities, and representing with single personal distinction the best traditions of American culture."

The appraisal owed much, also, to international concerns—to enthusiasm less for the New Deal than for Roosevelt's foreign policy, especially after the outbreak of war in 1939. Yet, in truth, it is difficult to separate domestic from foreign aspects, for the Roosevelt administration seemed from the very beginning to be offering an alternative answer from that of the fascist powers, to be affirming that it was possible to enhance the power of the State without denying democratic liberties.

To be sure, Roosevelt and the New Deal did not lack critics in Britain. Socialists such as Harold Laski and John Strachey were committed to the view that substantial progress could not be achieved within the capitalist system. Orthodox economists such as Lionel Robbins deplored the return to the mercantilism of Colbert, while Lord Keynes was exasperated with the inability of the President to understand his teachings. In 1934 Keynes went to America where he was awarded an honorary degree by Columbia. (It appears that any Englishman who set foot on Manhattan Island in the 1930s ran the danger of being hauled off the streets by a representative of my university and presented with an honorary degree.) After a conversation with Roosevelt, Keynes confided to Secretary Perkins that he had "supposed the President was more literate, economically speaking."

Yet unlike many historians in America today, most of the British critics did not deny the magnitude of what the New Dealers were attempting or of what they were achieving. In 1933, in an open letter to the President, Keynes declared:

You have made yourself the trustee for those in every country who seek to mend the evils of our condition by reasoned experiment within the framework of the existing social system. If you fail, ratio-

nal change will be gravely prejudiced throughout the world, leaving
orthodoxy and revolution to fight it out. But, if you succeed, new
and bolder methods will be tried elsewhere, and we may date the first
chapter of a new economic era from your accession to office.

Other observers, including those on the left, shared this perception. The
New Deal, wrote Laski in 1934, "compared with . . . the unimaginative
activity of the British government . . . is an exhilarating experiment." At
the end of the decade, Strachey, who devoted more than 100 of the 350
pages of his *Programme for Progress* to the New Deal, acknowledged that
Roosevelt's had been the "one and only . . . attempt to apply an expan-
sionist policy." Isaiah Berlin conceded that there were features of the New
Deal that might be open to objection, but he insisted:

What the Germans thought Hitler to be, Hitler, in fact, largely was,
and what free men in Europe and America and in Asia and in Africa
and in Australia, and wherever else the rudiments of political
thought stirred at all, what all these felt Roosevelt to be, he in fact
was. He was the greatest leader of democracy, the greatest champion
of social progress in the twentieth century.

II

In the United States in the 1960s a very different assessment of the New
Deal took hold. Whereas during the Great Depression the main argument
centered on how revolutionary the changes wrought by the New Deal
were, in the 1960s there was growing agreement that the New Deal altered
virtually nothing, that it never became "much more than a spirited evasion
of the overriding issues of the twentieth century."

Much of the criticism simply reiterated familiar strictures. Most historians had long since recognized that New Deal policies were often inconsistent; that Roosevelt failed to grasp countercyclical fiscal theory; that full
recovery did not come until armaments orders fueled the economy; that
the President never sponsored civil rights legislation; that he was credited
with certain reforms that he, in fact, opposed; and that a number of New
Deal programs—notably those in housing and aid for the marginal
farmer—were inadequately financed. One of the foremost Roosevelt biographers, James MacGregor Burns, had blamed him for not daring to make

fundamental changes, especially by failing to transform the Democratic party into a thoroughly liberal organization—for being too much the fox, too little the lion.

But during the sixties American historians not only dressed up this disapprobation as though it was a new revelation, but also carried their disappointment with contemporary liberalism to the point of arguing either that the New Deal was so negligible that it constituted a meaningless episode or that it was actually pernicious. These estimates derived in large part from disaffection with the Welfare State, which Herbert Marcuse in *One-Dimensional Man* characterized as "a state of unfreedom," and which, as one critic noted, some considered "the ultimate form of repressive super-ego." The New Deal was now perceived to be elitist, since it had neglected to consult the poor about what legislation they wanted, or to encourage the participation of ghetto-dwellers in decision-making. Furthermore, historians contended, it redounded to the benefit of those who already had advantages—wealthier staple farmers, organized workers, business corporations, the "deserving poor"—while displacing sharecroppers, neglecting the unorganized, and sanctioning racial segregation. An "antirevolutionary response to a situation that had revolutionary potentialities," the New Deal, it was said, missed opportunities to nationalize the banks and radically restructure the social order. Even "providing assistance to the needy and . . . rescuing them from starvation" served conservative ends, historians complained, for these efforts "sapped organized radicalism of its waning strength and of its potential constituency among the unorganized discontented." The Roosevelt administration, these writers contend, failed to achieve more than it did not as a result of the strength of conservative opposition but because of the intellectual deficiencies of the New Dealers and because Roosevelt deliberately sought to save "large-scale corporate capitalism." In sum, the historian Paul Conkin has concluded, "The story of the New Deal is a sad story, the ever recurring story of what might have been."

In *Towards a New Past* the most prominent New Left historian of the subject, Barton J. Bernstein, summed up this point of view:

> The liberal reforms of the New Deal did not transform the American system; they conserved and protected American corporate capitalism, occasionally by absorbing parts of threatening programs. There was no significant redistribution of power in American society, only limited recognition of other organized groups. . . . The

New Deal failed to solve the problem of depression, it failed to raise the impoverished, it failed to redistribute income, it failed to extend equality and generally countenanced racial discrimination and segregation.

Although the characterization of Bernstein as "New Left" suggests that he represents a deviant persuasion, the "New Left" attitude has actually become the new orthodoxy in America. This emphasis has so permeated writing on the New Deal that an instructor who wishes to assign the latest monographs has a wide choice among studies that document the errors of the New Deal but very little of recent vintage that explores its achievements. A former Harmsworth Professor told me that his students at Harvard take it to be axiomatic that the New Deal amounted to very little. In short, at precisely the point when Oxford has granted diplomatic recognition to the New Deal by incorporating it in the syllabus as a Special Subject, American scholars seem bent on consigning it to the dustbin of history.

III

The advent of the New Deal as a Special Subject provides the occasion for a modest proposal—that we reintroduce some tension into the argument over the interpretation of the Roosevelt years. If historians are to develop a credible synthesis, it is important to regain a sense of the achievement of the New Deal. As it now stands, we have a dialectic that is all antithesis with no thesis. The so-called "debate" about the New Deal is not truly a debate, for even historians who dispute the New Left assertions agree that one can only take a melancholy view of the period. The single question asked is whether the failure of the New Deal was the fault of the Roosevelt administration or the result of the strength of conservative forces beyond the government's control, but the fact of failure is taken to be a first postulate. Such an assumption does less than justice to the accomplishments of the New Deal. As a first step toward a more balanced evaluation, one has to remind oneself not only of what the New Deal did not do, but also of what it did do—of what it was that earned the respect of British statesmen and scholars.

The New Deal, it should be noted at the outset, radically altered the character of the State in America. As late as Hoover's presidency, policymakers believed that government activity should be minimal; economic decisions should be determined in the market place, and the government should confine its function to that of neutral referee. Even organized labor and the National Conference of Social Workers opposed federal action on behalf of the unemployed. Under Roosevelt these shibboleths were sharply challenged, and the government intervened in a myriad of ways from energizing the economy to generating electric power to fostering unionization. As a South Carolina labor leader put it, "Franklin Delano Roosevelt is void of the laissez-faire personality."

Writers on both continents have understood this. In the United States the historian Daniel Fusfeld concluded:

The most important aspect of the social philosophy of the New Deal was the belief that society as a whole, functioning through government, must protect itself against the impersonal and amoral forces of supply and demand. It represented a great shift away from the philosophy that the self-adjusting market should be given free sway, and that people, resources and wealth ought to be treated essentially as commodities.

And in Great Britain Laski declared that FDR was the first statesman "to use the power of the state to subordinate the primary assumptions of that society to certain vital social purposes, . . . the first to attack not the secondary but the primary manifestations of the doctrine of laissez-faire."

The directing agency of this expanded government was the presidency, whose authority was greatly augmented in the 1930s. Rexford Tugwell has written of Roosevelt: "No monarch, . . . unless it may have been Elizabeth or her magnificent Tudor father, or maybe Alexander or Augustus Caesar, can have given quite that sense of serene presiding, of gathering up into himself, of really representing, a whole people." The President became, in Sidney Hyman's words, "the chief economic engineer," to whom Congress naturally turned for the setting of economic policy. Roosevelt modernized public relations by his use of the radio and the press conference, shifted the balance between the White House and Capitol Hill by assuming the role of Chief Legislator, and bypassed the traditional departments by creating emergency agencies. In 1939 he established the Executive Office of the President, giving the chief executive a central staff office for the first time. "The verdict of history," wrote Clinton Rossiter, "will surely be that he left the Presidency a more splendid instrument of democracy than he found it."

To staff the new agencies, the Administration recruited young attorneys fresh out of law school and social scientists from university campuses. The role of the Brain Trust in the 1932 campaign indicated FDR's enthusiasm for new ideas, and soon there were thousands of professors making their way to the capital. The left-wing critic Edmund Wilson wrote, "Everywhere in the streets and offices you run into old acquaintances: the editors and writers of the liberal press, the 'progressive' young instructors from the colleges, the intelligent foundation workers, the practical idealists of settlement houses."

Everybody wanted to know the professors, reported one magazine. "Office-seekers dog their footsteps. Hostesses vie to land them as guest of honor. Professors are the fad." "On a routine administration matter you go to a Cabinet member," observed a reporter, "but on matters of policy and the higher statesmanship you consult the professoriat." He added:

> All Washington is going to school to the professors. Debutantes hang on their exposition of the quantitative theory of money, the law of diminishing returns, and the intricacies of foreign exchange. Bookstores are selling their books like hot cakes. Their works are not available at the Library of Congress, the volumes having been withdrawn by the Senators and Congressmen.

This new corps of administrators made it possible for Roosevelt to carry out a major change in the role of the federal government. Although the New Deal always operated within a capitalist framework and the government deliberately sought to enhance profitmaking, the President and his lieutenants rejected the traditional view that government was the handmaiden of business. As a consequence, they adopted measures to discipline corporations, to require a sharing of authority with government and unions, and to hold businessmen accountable. In the fall of 1933 the novelist Sherwood Anderson wrote:

> I went to several code hearings. No one has quite got their significance. Here for the first time you see these men of business, little ones and big ones, . . . coming up on the platform to give an accounting. It does seem the death knell of the old idea that a man owning a factory office or store has a right to run it in his own way. There is at least an effort to relate it now to the whole thing, man's

relations with his fellow men etc. Of course it is crude and there will be no end of crookedness, objections, etc. but I do think an entire new principle in American life is being established.

IV

In a series of edicts and statutes, the Administration invaded the realm of the banker by establishing control over the nation's money supply. The government clamped an embargo on gold, took the United States off the gold standard, and nullified the requirement for the payment of gold in private contracts. In 1935 a resentful Supreme Court sustained this authority, although a dissenting Justice said that this was Nero at his worst. The Glass-Steagall Act stripped commercial banks of the privilege of engaging in investment banking and established federal insurance of bank deposits, an innovation that the leading monetary historians have called "the structural change most conducive to monetary stability since state bank notes were taxed out of existence immediately after the Civil War." The Banking Act of 1935 gave the United States what other industrial nations had long had, but America lacked—central banking.

The Reconstruction Finance Corporation, created under Hoover but given a very different direction under Roosevelt, became the largest bank in America and the biggest investor. At its head was the aggressive Houston financier Jesse Jones, a man, the historian James Olson has written, Roosevelt respected because Jones gave him credibility in the business world, though FDR's feelings toward the headstrong, conservative Texan "probably more resembled those of the mongoose for the cobra." Under Jones the RFC provided the omnibus Farm Credit Administration with more than a billion dollars to save millions of rural families from foreclosure, and the RFC spun off a number of important subsidiaries, including the Export-Import Bank, the Electric Home and Farm Authority, and the Commodity Credit Corporation that, by greatly enhancing the farmer's position in the market, made a significant contribution to raising crop prices and lifting rural income. Subsequently, it set up the Federal National Mortgage Association ("Fannie Mae") to gear up home construction. As Olson has written: "Its creditor relationship with thousands of banks, savings banks, building and loan associations, and railroads allowed the RFC to make industrial policy—control the flow of capital, determine dividend rates, hire and fire management, and limit corporate salaries."

This set of changes transformed the relationship between the government and the financial community from what it had been in the era of J. P. Morgan and Grover Cleveland. As Charles Beard observed, "Having lost their gold coins and bullion to the Federal Government and having filled their vaults with federal bonds and other paper, bankers have become in a large measure mere agents of the Government in Washington. No longer do these powerful interests stand, so to speak, 'outside the Government' and in a position to control or dictate to it." When America went off the gold standard, a French commentator observed:

No matter how uncertain the future seems to be, one point has been established: The United States took the measure of directing the dollar. It is the government that has taken hold of the wheel of the monetary command. Elsewhere it is held by the Central Bank which is mostly the agent of the great financial powers. In America now the state is master of its money. A capital event, practically a revolution.

A number of other enactments helped to transfer power from Wall Street to Washington. The Securities Act of 1933 established government supervision of the issue of new securities and made company directors civilly and criminally liable for misinformation on the statements they were required to file with each new issue, and the Securities and Exchange Act of 1934 initiated federal supervision of the stock exchanges and created a new agency to administer both laws: the Securities and Exchange Commission. In 1935 the Holding Company Act leveled some of the utility pyramids and added to the SEC's domain. When the securities legislation was enacted, "advanced reformers," the British historian Andrew Shonfield has noted, regarded it as "contemptibly cautious." He adds, "Yet thirty years after the SEC was set up, Western Europe is still groping for some means of matching the public supervision of the activities of private enterprise management which it secured in the United States. . . . There was no sign that any British Government of the early 1960s, whether of the Right or the Left, was prepared to contemplate any reform of company law as radical as this."

The most stubborn resistance to federal regulation came from the New York Stock Exchange under its haughty chieftain Richard Whitney, but the SEC would not be deterred. Its demand that the Big Board democratize its procedures got a great boost when Whitney was indicted on two counts of grand larceny and sentenced to five to ten years in Sing Sing penitentiary on each count. Even without that episode the Exchange could not have held out much longer and, with their leader disgraced, the recalcitrants lost their will. A reported colloquy between the counsel for the Stock Exchange and the chairman of the SEC, William O. Douglas, suggests the changed atmosphere:

Counsel: Have you read the last draft of our proposed statement?
Douglas: The SEC has read it and it is not satisfactory. The negotiations are off.
Counsel: Well, I suppose you'll go ahead with your own program?
Douglas: You're damned right I will.
Counsel: When you take over the Exchange, I hope you'll remember we've been in business 150 years. There may be some things you will like to ask us.
Douglas: There is one thing I'd like to ask.
Counsel: What is it?
Douglas: Where do you keep the paper and pencils?

Contemporaries remarked again and again upon the startling transformation. By the spring of 1934 one writer was already reporting:

News of a financial nature in Wall Street now is merely an echo of events which take place in Washington. . . . The pace of the ticker is determined now in Washington, not in company boardrooms or in brokerage offices. . . . In Wall Street it is no longer asked what some big trader is doing, what some important banker thinks, what opinion some eminent lawyer holds about some pressing question of the day. The query in Wall Street has become: "What's the news from Washington?"

Four years later, a financial commentator noted:

So far from having any inside dope on what is going on in Washington, Wall Street today lives in constant apprehension that new and unsuspected moves on the part of the government may suddenly alter the conditions under which it is operating. Not even the private adventures of the erstwhile Money Barons can escape the vigilant supervision of Washington.

That perception has been confirmed by historians. "Where, in economic life, people had previously looked upon business decisions as the ones that had shaped their destiny, now they would have regard for government decisions as well, or instead," John Kenneth Galbraith has observed. "Those of an Assistant Secretary of the Treasury on interest rates were now of more importance than those of any banker." William Manchester remarked that "in one stroke the President had shifted the news capital of the country from New York to Washington," and Robert Sobel has concluded that the 1934 law marked "the beginning of the end of Wall Street's domination of finance capitalism" and "represented the shift of economic power from the lower part of Manhattan, where it had been for over a century, to Washington."

To be sure, "federal securities regulation," as the historian Michael Parrish has commented, "did not . . . transform a nation of speculators into a nation of cautious, sober investors." The legislation, far from radical, and the SEC's prudent administration "only reduced opportunities for corporate theft and restricted the methods by which individuals, while inflicting pecuniary damage upon one another, could derange the entire economy." The legislation, as the historian Vincent Carosso has emphasized, was more effective at eliminating malpractices than in lessening the power of Wall Street over investment. Nonetheless, Parrish concludes, the New Dealers did "fashion political tools like the SEC that held the possibility of more orderly, enduring economic growth in the future. This was their lasting achievement."

The New Deal focused attention on Washington, too, by initiatives in fields that had been regarded as exclusively within the private realm, as in housing. By refinancing mortgages, the Home Owners' Loan Corporation, created in 1933, saved tens of thousands of homes from foreclosure. In 1934 the Federal Housing Administration began its program of insuring loans for the construction and renovation of private homes. The HOLC initiated the long-term, self-amortizing mortgage which, by sharply lowering required monthly payments, revolutionized the housing industry by making the prospect of financing a home much more attractive, and the FHA established standards for construction that even builders outside the FHA orbit found prospective buyers insisted upon. Over the next three decades the FHA insured nearly two million dwellings in multi-unit developments, made it possible for nearly eleven million families to own homes, and helped another twenty-two million make improvements. During that period the proportion of homeowners rose from 44 percent to 63 percent.

Before the age of Roosevelt, the national government had never engaged in public housing, save for the World War I emergency, but such agencies as the Public Works Administration now broke precedent. The Tennessee Valley Authority laid out the model town of Norris; the Federal Emergency Relief Administration experimented with subsistence homesteads; and the Resettlement Administration created greenbelt communities. No longer, noted one critic, did the United States have to "rely altogether on statistics, blue prints, photographs of architects' models and of European examples." When in 1937 the Wagner-Steagall Act created the U.S. Housing Authority, it assured federal housing a permanent place in American life.

These efforts have been roundly assailed—sometimes fairly, sometimes not. Commentators have charged that the subsistence homestead program was ill-conceived, and that FHA policies promoted suburban blight. A number of analysts have also pointed out that, in contrast to what European governments provided, American ventures were woefully small-scale. Others, though, have said that slum clearance should never have been undertaken, for it destroyed cohesive neighborhoods and housing projects warrened off the poor in soulless structures. Undeniably, the New Deal approach was flawed. Though the HOLC did not discriminate (in fact, most of its loans went to families in "definitely declining" or "hazardous" neighborhoods), it did institute a system of classification, called "redlining," that, when adopted by the FHA, unhappily resulted in very unfair treatment of ethnic minorities. But some of this criticism was inconsistent, conflated the experience of the post-Roosevelt era with that of the 1930s, sentimentalized the slums, and revealed ill-considered hostility toward suburbs and the bourgeoisie who live there.

In the context not of European but of American history, the New Deal performance was without precedent. More than one hundred thousand public housing units were built under the 1937 law, which paved the way for more ambitious, albeit still inadequate, legislation a decade later. "On one level public housing was a resounding success," writes the historian Kenneth Jackson, a penetrating critic of government policy. Within a generation New Deal initiatives provided shelter for two million people, and "if the quality and design of the projects frequently invited derision, they were nevertheless superior to the dilapidated structures they replaced."

V

The New Deal profoundly altered industrial relations by throwing the weight of government behind efforts to organize the workingman. At the outset of the Great Depression, the American labor movement was "an anachronism in the world," for only a tiny minority of factory workers were unionized, in steel less than 2 percent. Employers hired and fired and imposed punishments at will, used thugs as strikebreakers and private police, stockpiled industrial munitions, and ran company towns as feudal fiefs. In an astonishingly short period of time in the Roosevelt years, the situation was reordered. Under the umbrella of section 7(a) of the National Industrial Recovery Act of 1933 and of the far-reaching National Labor Relations Act (Wagner Act) of 1935, union organizers won millions of recruits in such open-shop strongholds as steel, automobiles, and textiles. From 1933 to 1941 union membership in manufacturing nearly quadrupled.

The National Labor Relations Act, the historian Robert Zieger has written, "was one of the seminal enactments in American history." Before then, he notes, "literally hundreds of workers had been killed and thousands injured in a long history of disputes stretching back into the nineteenth century"; afterward, "deaths and serious injuries in labor disputes became rare." He adds:

> The Wagner Act . . . promised that the government would guarantee a fair procedure for determining bargaining rights and for the disposition of unfair practices. While strikes and picket lines remained important, workers could turn to the National Labor Relations Board, operating under clearly specified rules and procedures to protect their rights. For their part, employers now had to contend with an agency armed with powers that made intimidation, delay, and union-breaking far more costly.

Some historians, curiously, have seen the Wagner Act as the creation of wily capitalists, but as Stanley Vittoz has observed, "the managers of the nation's leading industrial corporations, almost without exception, resisted . . . the adoption of the National Labor Relations Act" because it signaled "an unusually direct intrusion by the state into a traditionally autonomous sphere of employer discretion." In 1948 a U.S. Circuit Court of Appeals pointed out that "prior to the National Labor Relations Act no federal law prevented *employers* from discharging employees" for exercising the right to join a union or from refusing to bargain with representatives of the workers. Hence, "the NLRA created rights *against employers* which did not exist before."

It took a while for Roosevelt to grasp the significance of industrial unionism, and much of the credit for the change belongs to Senator Robert Wagner rather than to him, but one should not ignore the testimony of the unionists themselves. "We pinch ourselves occasionally to make sure we're not dreaming as the reports of new members come across our desk," wrote the editor of the journal of one of the railway brotherhoods. "For more than a year the stream of applications has been unbroken." In accounting for this spectacular increase, the head of the union declared: "We benefited from the wave of organization sentiment throughout the country which resulted from the influence of a pro-labor President. His conception . . . is the most progressive and constructive stand taken by a President in our history." More surprisingly, a leftist commentator acknowledged in 1937:

The difference that the attitude of high political authorities can make may be illustrated by the difference between 1922, when the Attorney General obtained a sweeping injunction from a federal judge against the railway shopmen, and 1937, when the President, first through his Secretary of Labor and then through the Governor of Michigan, threw his influence on the side of conference and agreement in the General Motors strike.

When sit-down strikers took over automobile plants in 1937, outraged citizens demanded that the President use force to oust them and restore the factories to their rightful owners, but he refused to do so. His decision was politically costly, but it made it possible for the workers to prevail. Roosevelt ruminated:

Well, it is illegal, but what law are they breaking? The law of trespass, and that is about the only law that could be invoked. And what do you do when a man trespasses on your property? Sure you order him off. You get the sheriff to order him off if he tries to pitch a tent in your field without your permission. If he comes on your place to steal, why, you have him for theft, of course. But shooting it out and killing a lot of people because they have violated the law of trespass somehow offends me. I just don't see that as an answer. The punishment doesn't fit the crime. There must be another way. Why can't these fellows in General Motors meet with a committee of workers? Talk it all out. They would get a settlement. It wouldn't be so terrible.

During the New Deal years, employees won wage rises, reductions in hours, greater job security, freedom from the tyranny of company guards, and protection against arbitrary punishment. Thanks to the NRA and the Guffey acts, coal miners achieved the outlawing of compulsory company houses and stores, along with the introduction of mandatory checkweighmen, grievance machinery, and a nationwide wage scale. Steel workers, who in the 1920s labored twelve-hour shifts seven days a week at the blast furnaces, would become so powerful that in the postwar era they would win not merely paid vacations but sabbatical leaves, and the open shop town, Muncie, Indiana—the Lynds' prototypical "Middletown"—would elect a UAW member as its mayor.

Many of the gains owed less to government intervention than to the tenacity of industrial unionists, but millions of workers had no doubt about the source of the difference in their lives. In 1940 a clothing worker from Cincinnati, reporting "I take a vacation every year," commented, "I thought a vacation was only for the rich before Roosevelt," and a clothing worker from Philadelphia, who testified that his work week had been shortened and he was making "a fine living," declared: "A miracle happened to me and my family. . . . Roosevelt . . . made possible our dream come true."

A British analyst, Vivian Vale of Southampton, has concluded: "From one of the most restrictive among industrially advanced nations, the labour code of the United States (insofar as it could be said to exist before 1933) was rapidly transformed into one of the most liberal," and these reforms, he adds, "were not the harvest of long-sustained agitation by trade unions, but were forced upon a partly sceptical labour movement by a government which led or carried it into maturity."

VI

Helen Lynd has observed that the history of the United States follows fifty years behind that of England, and a half century after the Welfare State had come to Western Europe the New Deal brought it to America. The NRA wiped out sweatshops, ended various forms of exploitation, and removed some 150,000 child laborers from factories. The Walsh-Healey Act of 1936 and the Fair Labor Standards Act of 1938 established the principle of a federally imposed minimal level of working conditions. In a message to Congress asking for the Fair Labor Standards Act legislation, the President said, "A self-supporting and self-respecting democracy can plead no justification for the existence of child labor, no economic reason for chiseling workers' wages or stretching workers' hours." Critics have pointed out that the FLSA left many uncovered, but within a year of its passage the law, for all its shortcomings, had already improved working conditions for more than four million employees. Isador Lubin, the well-respected head of the Bureau of Labor Statistics, called the statute "probably the most vital social legislation" in the history of the country.

Years later, when David E. Lilienthal, the director of the Tennessee Valley Authority, was being taken to the airport to fly to Roosevelt's funeral, the TVA driver said to him:

> I won't forget what he did for me. . . . I spent the best years of my life working at the Appalachian Mills . . . and they didn't even treat us like humans. If you didn't do like they said, they always told you there was someone else to take your job. I had my mother and my sister to take care of. Sixteen cents an hour was what we got; a fellow can't live on that, and you had to get production even to get that, this Bedaux system; some fellows only got twelve cents. If you asked to get off on a Sunday, the foreman would say, "All right you stay away Sunday, but when you come back Monday someone else will have your job." No, sir, I won't forget what he done for us.

Most important, the New Deal originated a new system of social rights to replace dependence on private charity. The Social Security Act of 1935 created America's first national system of old-age pensions, though one that was based on regressive taxation and left out too many at the bottom of the economic pyramid, and it initiated a federal-state program of unemployment insurance. It also authorized grants for the blind, for the incapacitated, and for dependent children, a feature that would have important long-range consequences. The Social Security Act has been criticized justly for its many inadequacies, but Roosevelt knew that if he could break ground by getting Congress to enact a law, improvements would follow. In signing the bill, Roosevelt said that it was but "a cornerstone in a structure which is being built but is by no means complete." Only four years after the Social Security law was adopted, a set of amendments extended old-age insurance benefits to wives and children and stepped up federal contributions for programs such as maternal health and child welfare. From 1935 to 1939 the number of blind persons receiving aid doubled. The less than 400,000 pensioners in 1935 had grown to well over two million a year in 1941 and government outlays over the period had multiplied more than eightfold, while the number of dependent children benefiting from ADC (286,000 in the first year) was by 1941 approaching one million.

The President himself affirmed the newly assumed attitudes in Washington when in his annual message to Congress in 1938 he declared:

> Government has a final responsibility for the well-being of its citizenship. If private co-operative endeavor fails to provide work for willing hands and relief for the unfortunate, those suffering hardship from no fault of their own have a right to call upon the Government for aid; and a government worthy of its name must make fitting response.

FDR's most important agent in creating the Welfare State, Harry Hopkins, expressed this thought with characteristic bluntness. In 1936 he said in Los Angeles:

> I am getting sick and tired of these people on the W.P.A. and local relief rolls being called chiselers and cheats. . . . These people . . . are just like the rest of us. They don't drink any more than the rest of us, they don't lie any more, they're no lazier than the rest of us—they're pretty much a cross section of the American people. . . . I have never believed that with our capitalistic system people have to be poor. I think it is an outrage that we should permit hundreds and hundreds of thousands of people to be ill clad, to live in miserable homes, not to have enough to eat; not to be able to send their children to school for the only reason that they are poor. I don't believe ever again in America are we going to permit the things to happen that have happened in the past to people. We are never going back . . . to the days of putting . . . old people in . . . alms houses, when a decent dignified pension at home will keep them there. We are coming to the day

when we are going to have decent houses for the poor, when there is genuine and real security for everybody. I have gone all over the moral hurdles that people are poor because they are bad. I don't believe it. A system of government on that basis is fallacious.

Nothing revealed this approach so well as the New Deal's response to the needs of the millions of unemployed. As one scholar wrote, "A system of local poor relief which had remained practically unchanged for a century and a half was superseded not only by new methods but by a new philosophy of governmental responsibility for people in need." Roosevelt had hardly taken office when he approved legislation making outright grants to the states for the first time ever to provide money for the jobless. In the ensuing years a series of agencies—Federal Emergency Relief Administration, the Civil Works Administration, the Works Progress Administration—gave jobs to the unemployed; provided shelter for more than 50,000 young transients ("the wild boys of the road"); and took care of nearly a quarter of a million homeless, while, though motivated more by a desire to aid farmers than the needy, the Federal Surplus Relief Corporation distributed sweet potatoes, apples, beans, canned mutton, peaches, flour, pork, cabbages, and other commodities, a program given different form later in the decade by the creation of a federal food stamp project. In 1932 under Hoover the federal government spent $208 million on relief; in 1935 under FDR more than $3 billion, and that sum was rising. Eventually the total would reach more than $11 billion. The director of the American Public Welfare Association concluded, "The decade of the 1930's might well have been known as the decade of destitution but for the humane leadership provided by the Roosevelt administration."

The Roosevelt government also gave special attention to the problems of young people. The National Youth Administration set up a program of apprenticeship training for 2.7 million jobless, nearly half of them young women, and of work-study grants that made it possible for another two million impecunious high school and college students to continue their studies, enabling a remarkable variety of students to get by. At the University of Michigan the NYA gave to an undergraduate who was an aspiring playwright the job of feeding laboratory mice. His name was Arthur Miller. Roosevelt put in charge of the NYA for the entire state of Texas a twenty-seven-year-old former Congressional assistant, Lyndon Johnson, who later remembered that one NYA job had gone to the son of a sharecropper who had come "without a dollar in his pocket" to work his way through the University of Texas, John Connally. And in North Carolina, where 38,000 were on the NYA rolls, the agency employed, at thirty-five cents an hour, a Duke University law student, Richard Nixon.

After the 1940 election, a journalist recorded the explanation of a ward leader who had been asked to account for why voters in Charlestown, Massachusetts "in the shadow of the Bunker Hill monument" had marked four out of every five ballots for FDR:

> Hundreds got pay raises under the wage-hour law; more hundreds of seasonal workers are having slack months cushioned by unemployment-insurance benefits. The NYA is helping from 300 to 500 youths; at the worst of the depression thousands held WPA jobs; of 1500 persons past sixty-five in the ward, more than 600 receive old-age assistance; another 600 cases are on direct relief and get aid for dependent children. Charlestown is a food-stamp area; the WPA improved its bathing beach; a new low-cost housing project will relieve some of the ward's congestion.

The Emergency Relief Appropriations Act of 1935 from which both the WPA and the NYA derived their funds constituted the single greatest outlay in peacetime by any government of any country in the history of the world. Even so, the New Deal work relief programs did not take care of most of the jobless, and they had other shortcomings. "We have never given adequate relief," Hopkins acknowledged. Yet the historian James T. Patterson has concluded that the New Deal, despite its grievous flaws, "responded with a level of public aid scarcely imaginable in 1929." The program, he observes, "marked a substantial advance in American treatment of the poor. During the 1930s some 46 million people, 35 percent of the population, received public aid or social insurance at one time or another. Public funds for these programs scarcely existed in 1929; in 1939 they amounted to . . . 27 percent of government expenditures at all levels."

VII

The projects of the relief agencies and of the Public Works Administration changed the face of the land. They built the San Francisco Zoo, the San Antonio Zoo, and the National Zoo at Rock Creek Park; raised a boardwalk at the birdwatchers' Mecca, Cape May, New Jersey; completed a skating rink in Minnesota's Otter Tail County; gave Denver and Los Angeles new water supply systems and Vermont's Grand Isle County in the Lake Champlain country its first high school. It channeled the Cape Cod Canal in Massachusetts and the All-American Canal in California's Imperial and Coachella valleys. At Brownsville, Texas, the government constructed "a port for ocean-going ships in the middle of a prairie," eighteen miles from the sea, and in Virginia a deepwater terminal making Richmond in the interior a harbor for vessels from the Atlantic. New Deal agencies in Mississippi planted flower beds in Greenville, mended the sea wall at Biloxi, and built close to 21,000 birdhouses. In the Vieux Carré in New Orleans, the government renovated the French Market, where, the PWA reported, "every day trucks arrive, laden with Florida cucumbers, Louisiana peppers, Texas broccoli, . . . red snapper and mackerel from the Gulf, shrimp from the bays, soft shell crabs from the bayous."

Few New Yorkers today realize the long reach of the New Deal. If they drive across the Triborough Bridge or through the Lincoln Tunnel, they are on thoroughfares the PWA financed. If they fly into La Guardia Airport, they are coming into a landing field laid out by the WPA. If they get caught in a traffic jam on the FDR Drive or the Belt Parkway, on the Grand Central Parkway or the Henry Hudson Parkway, they are using yet another artery built by the WPA. Even the animal cages in Central Park Zoo were reconstructed by WPA workers. Years later a man who had lived through the New Deal period said of the Children's Zoo in Central Park: "This was built during the Depression by WPA workers. It's an absolutely lovely place. I go to the Park often. And I cannot help remembering— look, this came out of the Depression. Because men were out of work, because they were given a way to earn money, good things were created."

Both of the New Deal public works agencies made their presence felt in the five boroughs. The PWA erected the Williamsburg Houses in Brooklyn, the Harlem River Houses in Manhattan, and the Boulevard Garden Apartments in Queens. The WPA built or renovated hundreds of school buildings, gave Orchard Beach a bathhouse, a mall, and a lagoon, landscaped Bryant Park and the campus of Hunter College, conducted examinations for venereal disease, filled teeth, operated pollen count stations, performed puppet shows for disturbed children, built dioramas for the Brooklyn Museum, put unemployed teachers back in the classroom to give instruction in everything from family law to Russian literature, ran street dances in Harlem and an open-air night club in Central Park, and, by combing neglected archives under the guidance of historians, turned up forgotten documents such as the marriage license issued Captain Kidd. The WPA for New York City alone employed more people than the entire War Department.

The federal government kept the Arkansas public school system from collapsing, financed 750 new school buses in North Carolina, and, across the breadth of the land, put up 39,000 new schools. Harold Ickes wrote of the PWA:

> School buildings erected as part of the program dot the map from the small town of Whitefield in northern New Hampshire to Honolulu, Hawaii, and from far northern villages in Alaska to the tropical Canal Zone. In size they range from a tiny country school of the Prairie Creek Common School District in Van Zandt County, Texas, costing $2,695, to the huge $2,250,000 Bayside High School of New York City.

The impact on education only begins to suggest the construction ventures of the New Deal. It built a skyscraper city hall in Kansas City, a new courthouse in Nashville, a public auditorium in Topeka, the United States Mint in San Francisco, and the United States Gold Depository at Fort Knox with a bombproof vault. It funded the Will Rogers Memorial at Fort Worth, where ten thousand at a time could gather for rodeos; came up with more than a million dollars for a new capital for the Navajo tribes; and reconstructed the Mall in Washington, D.C. It tunneled Chicago's very first subway and added to Boston's system with the Huntington Avenue subway. It was responsible for the Orange Bowl and the football stadiums at the University of Arkansas, LSU, and Ole Miss, as well as the University of Texas Library; financed the Medical Center in Jersey City and the Charity Hospital in New Orleans; and added three hundred beds to General Hospital in Boston. The morning after the state capitol in Oregon went up in flames, the governor got a call from the PWA assuring him that it would put up the money for a new building, and before long marble from Maine was at the site in Salem. In Oregon, too, at snow-capped Mount Hood in the Cascades, WPA workers constructed an alpine hideaway, Timberline Lodge, with every feature fashioned by hand: wrought iron gates; hewn logs of cedar and fir; a fieldstone fireplace; newel posts with carvings of badgers and coyotes; hooked rugs made from scraps of government discards; and stained glass murals.

New Deal agencies carried out projects to generate hydroelectric power and develop water resources on a colossal scale. Mammoth dams at Grand Coulee and Bonneville in the Columbia Valley reaching all the way upstream to the mouth of the Snake River had an enormous impact on the economy of the Pacific Northwest. The greatest concrete structure in the world, Grand Coulee backed up water into a lake 150 miles long. South Carolina got the ambitious Santee-Cooper project and Montana the biggest earth-fill dam in the world at Fort Peck. In the Rockies the government started the extraordinary Colorado–Big Thompson Project, which drilled a thirteen-mile tunnel under the Continental Divide to transfer water from west of the mountain peaks to the parched counties of the South Platte on the east, an enterprise entailing "10 reservoirs, 15 dams, 24 tunnels, . . . 11 canals, . . . 821 circuit miles of transmission lines, 43 power substations, and 23,000,000 cubic yards of embankment."

Far from being unique, La Guardia Airport turned out to be one of 325 landing fields on which the federal government worked. New Deal agencies were largely responsible for National Airport in Washington, Philadelphia Airport, Cleveland Airport, and the Chicago Municipal Airport. In the latter half of the 1930s the WPA constructed or improved nine out of every ten major airfields in the country.

The New Deal built and rebuilt enough miles of roadway to pave the continent from coast to coast more than two hundred times. You could hardly round a curve on a North Carolina highway in 1938, said an English visitor, without seeing a sign, "WPA—Men at Work," and toward the end of FDR's second term, a novelist wrote: "The sidewalks of Johnstown bear the initials of their makers. At night the initials fill the darkness: W.P.A. 1936. Street after street repeats: W.P.A. 1936." The government resurfaced U.S. 6 from Lincoln, Nebraska to Denver, Colorado; gouged out the Mobile Tunnel in Alabama; widened the Storm King Highway along the Hudson; and modernized U.S. 40 between Baltimore and the Delaware line, a road that once curved and dipped its way through narrow city streets.

New Deal engineers beribboned the nation with scenic highways: the inviting Natchez Trace following the old Indian trail in Mississippi, a lakeshore drive in Cleveland along the banks of Lake Erie and another in Chicago accompanying Lake Michigan, the George Washington Memorial Parkway skirting the Potomac, the Pennsylvania Turnpike breaching the Alleghenies, the four-hundred-mile-long Oregon Coastal Highway along a stretch of the Pacific where cars had previously vanished in quicksand, and in Virginia the Colonial Parkway linking historic Yorktown, where Cornwallis made his last stand, with the colonial capital of Williamsburg. The Overseas Highway, by leaping from key to key (with the blue waters of the Atlantic to the east, the Gulf of Mexico to the west), reunited Key West, which had been isolated by a devastating hurricane that had washed away its one railroad link, with the rest of America. (That enterprise took the lives of dozens of WPA workers, most of them World War I veterans who had been bonus marchers, when a tropical tempest swept across the keys.) In the Southern Appalachians the Skyline Drive and the Blue Ridge Parkway opened to the motorist stunning vistas of rhododendron and mountain laurel from the Shenandoah Valley to the Smokies. The government bridged the Susquehanna at Havre de Grace, Maryland and the Mississippi at Davenport, Iowa; constructed new bridges at Natchez, Mississippi and in Deer Isle, Maine; erected the Calvin Coolidge Bridge spanning the Connecticut River at Northampton, Massachusetts; and in Seattle built the Floating Bridge crossing Lake Washington on concrete pontoons.

VIII

Though much of federal relief was inevitably preoccupied with activities like road building, the government showed unusual sensitivity toward the needs of jobless white-collar workers. Afterwards, John Steinbeck recalled:

> When W.P.A. came, we were delighted, because it offered work. . . . I was given the project of taking a census of all the dogs on the Monterey Peninsula, their breeds, weight and characters. I did it very thoroughly and, since I knew my reports were not likely to get to the hands of the mighty, I wrote some pretty searching character studies of poodles and beagles and hounds. If such records were kept, somewhere in Washington, there will be a complete dog record of the Monterey Peninsula in the early Thirties.

Critics denounced such makework activities as "boondoggling," but a number of these endeavors proved highly worthwhile, notably those in aesthetic fields. The Federal Art Project, like the Public Works of Art Project before it, gave an opportunity to muralists eager for a chance to work in the style of Rivera, Orozco, and Siqueiros—with felicitous consequences in Reginald Marsh's splendid murals for the dome of the rotunda of the New York Custom House and Edward Laning's superb rendering of the immigrant experience at Ellis Island. It also fostered the careers of sculptors such as David Smith and any number of young easel painters: Jackson Pollock and Arshile Gorky, Stuart Davis and Yasuo Kunoyoshi, Jack Levine and Jacob Lawrence. Without that opportunity, Lawrence, looking back on his experience at the Harlem Art Center, later said, "I would never have become an artist. It was a turning point for me."

Out of that same project came gallery-workshops at community art centers across the country. They were eye-openers for high school art teachers who had spent their lives teaching painting without ever having seen an original work of art, but "the glory of the centers," one scholar has written, "lay in their children's classes." These centers, which started in a storefront in Raleigh, North Carolina, sprang up in places as remote from metropolitan showrooms as Big Stone Gap, Virginia and Casper, Wyoming, and ran the length of the Florida peninsula. In Arizona they numbered more than one hundred, and in New Mexico skills learned in WPA classes in Hispanic crafts were to provide the basis for a Chicano cultural revival movement in decades to come.

Graphic artists turned out over a quarter of a million designs, including sketches for the nickel and for postage stamps, and the magnificent *Index of American Design*, which reflected the enthusiasm for folk art of Constance Rourke and Holger Cahill, resulted in some twenty thousand plates illustrating pottery, glassware, furniture, and other crafts and rendering brilliantly objects such as iron toys, weather vanes, tavern signs, carousel horses, and ship figureheads. The compendium, declared one art critic, "showed that thousands of nameless Yankees had wrought superbly in wood and iron, silver and wool." The depiction of Pennsylvania Dutch pottery influenced the design of dishware, and the illustrations of Shaker chairs and tables inspired furniture makers.

A generation later, the sculptor Louise Nevelson summed up what the whole enterprise meant:

> When I came back from Germany where I studied with Hans Hofmann, . . . I got on the WPA. Now that gave me a certain kind of freedom and I think that our great artists like Rothko, de Kooning, Franz Kline, all these people that have promise today and are creative, had that moment of peace . . . to continue with their work. So, I feel that that was a great benefit, a great contribution to

our creative people and very important in the history of art. And not only in the visual arts but in the theater, and the folk arts, there wasn't a thing that they didn't touch on. . . . At that period, people in our country didn't have jobs and the head of government was able so intelligently to use mankind and manpower. I think it's a highlight of our American history.

The Federal Writers' Project provided support for scores of talented novelists and poets, editors and literary critics, people such as John Cheever and Vardis Fisher, Saul Bellow and Margaret Walker. Ralph Ellison's experience on the FWP later informed his classic, *The Invisible Man*. These writers turned out an exceptional set of state guides, with features such as Conrad Aiken's delineation of Deerfield, Massachusetts, a place "with the deepest poetic and historic significance to be found in America," a town so transfixed by its bloody early encounter of colonists and Indians that for more than two centuries life there had been only a "long reminiscence" about that "tragic and creative moment when one civilization is destroyed by another." Though the writers labored under some constraints, their comments could be unsparing. In remarking on a site where the Colonial Dames of America had placed a marker on the triumph of Civilization over Savagery, the authors of the Alabama guide observed: "Here, in 1802, was negotiated one of the series of treaties by which the United States absorbed the Choctaw lands at a price of one broken promise per square mile."

The Project also won acclaim for special volumes like *These Are Our Lives*, a graphic portfolio of life histories in North Carolina; *Panorama*, with Vincent McHugh's depiction of "the infinite pueblo of the Bronx"; and Josef Berger's *Cape Cod Pilot* with absorbing tales of buccaneers and of army officers who divided their time "between virgin forests abroad and the virgins at home." A gifted stylist, Berger, who used the pseudonym "Jeremiah Digges," transmuted what might have been mundane geographical data into vivid prose: "The town of Barnstable, like a mackerel seiner with a full trip of fish, carries the biggest part of her story below the water line."

Project workers transcribed chain gang blues songs, recovered folklore that would otherwise have been lost, and interviewed more than two thousand elderly former slaves, an invaluable archive later drawn upon in *Lay My Burden Down*. In Chicago WPA workers translated half a century of foreign language newspapers, a project requiring seventy-seven reels of microfilm, and in New England, a leading authority noted, the WPA gathered the "lore of Connecticut clockmakers and munitions workers, Rhode Island fishermen, and French-Canadian textile workers, Maine clam diggers, Vermont Welsh slate workers, and Italian granite workers." When the magazine *Story* conducted a contest for the best contribution by a Project employee, the prize was won by an unpublished twenty-nine-year-old who had been working on the essay on the Negro for the Illinois project. With the prize money for his tales, subsequently published as *Uncle Tom's Children*, Richard Wright gained the time to write his remarkable first novel, *Native Son*.

Scholars are in debt to the Historical Records Survey, which got independent status in 1936, for any number of contributions. It put together an *American Imprints Inventory* of early American broadsides and other publications; assembled all of the printed materials of the first fourteen American Congresses; and collected the maritime records of the port of Philadelphia over 171 years, the files of the Matador Land and Cattle Company in Texas, and the documents concerning North Carolina in the Spanish archives. It found the lost papers of a member of Lincoln's cabinet, unearthed the court proceedings in the Aaron Burr libel case, and turned up the journals of the Mormon Battalion's continental trek from Nauvoo, Illinois to Salt Lake City by way of San Diego.

Some thought it an ill omen that the Federal Theatre Project's first production was Shakespeare's *Comedy of Errors*, but the program not only gave employment to actors and stage technicians (including such "unknowns" as Joseph Cotten, John Huston, and Joseph Losey), but also offered many American communities such as Valley, Nebraska (pop. 1000) their first glimpse of live drama. Touring companies, reported Archibald MacLeish, "have gone into the back country behind Portland and Seattle; . . . have gone into the hay valleys in northern New England; . . . have worked through the high plains towns in Nebraska and the Dakotas; . . . [and] have penetrated the Black Ankle Belt of the Carolinas where no trouper has been seen time out of mind." The Federal Theatre produced plays by an extraordinary range of writers—Aristophanes, Plautus, Ben Jonson, Oliver Goldsmith, Lady Gregory, Sean O'Casey, Maxwell Anderson, and Clifford Odets, among others. It sponsored the first U. S. presentation of T. S. Eliot's *Murder in the Cathedral*, which, though it was regarded as a "difficult" play, drew forty thousand people in packed houses, and its Detroit unit staged the original professional production of Arthur Miller's first play. As co-director of the Harlem Federal Theatre Project, John

Houseman resolved to produce *Macbeth* with an all-black cast and, to direct the play, hired a nineteen-year-old phenom, that "monstrous boy" Orson Welles. On opening night the police had to rope off four city blocks as, according to *Fortune*, "the biggest crowd ever gathered on upper Seventh Avenue."

Not until Eugene O'Neill was called upon by the director of the Project, Hallie Flanagan, did America's foremost playwright fully grasp the dimensions of what the government was doing. "He was pleased by the pictures of marionettes in *The Emperor Jones*," and, she writes:

> I was able to report on either the performance or the plans for *Anna Christie* in Atlanta, San Diego, Denver, Hartford, and Detroit; *Beyond the Horizon* in San Francisco, Mt. Holyoke, and Warren, Mass.; *Days Without End* in Los Angeles and Denver; *Diff'rent* in Roslyn and New Jersey; *The First Man* in Salem; *The Straw* and *The Long Voyage Home* in Chicago; *Moon of the Caribbees* in New Orleans, New York and Philadelphia; the cycle of *In the Zone, Bound East for Cardiff,* and *The Long Voyage Home* in Philadelphia and New York; *Welded* in Portland, Oregon; *Where the Cross Is Made* in Manchester, New Hampshire; and on the productions of *Ah, Wilderness!* in Los Angeles, San Diego, Miami, New Orleans, Cincinnati, Seattle, Newark, Salem, Peoria, and in twenty other places on tour.

The Project did not limit itself to traditional theater. In Chicago audiences danced in the aisles at performances of an all-black swing version of Gilbert and Sullivan's *Mikado,* and its radio division started Studs Terkel on his career. In New York City George Bernard Shaw's *Androcles and the Lion* won raves in Harlem, and the Living Newspaper, "the one original form of drama developed in the United States" in the opinion of one critic, offered "an amalgam of motion-picture, epic theatre, commedia dell'arte, and American minstrel show techniques . . . within the framework of a question asked, usually by a puzzled little man who represents the public." The Dance Group gave an opportunity to Katherine Dunham, Doris Humphrey, and Charles Weidman. Marionette performers delighted hundreds of thousands of young people in schools, hospitals, and institutions for the deaf and dumb. In Oklahoma puppeteers brought smiles to the faces of children—in Maud and Kiowa, in Kingfisher and Idabel and

Broken Bow. The Federal Theatre trotted out vaudeville hoofers to regale wounded doughboys at veterans' hospitals and children at foundling asylums, and it staged Paul Green's historical pageant at North Carolina's Roanoke Island. It even had its own circus—with Burt Lancaster on the trapeze. Hallie Flanagan noted seeing "against the night sky . . . the colored balls of the jugglers make music in the air," and a commentator remarked upon "the sawdust circle, the mingled smell of animals, popcorn, the announcer with his high-hat, the sad white smile of the clowns."

The Federal Music Project, too, gave an innovative reading to its mandate. To be sure, the director of the Project, Nikolai Sokoloff, the distinguished conductor of the Cleveland Symphony, could be counted on not to neglect classical music. In fact, three orchestras—the Buffalo Philharmonic, the Oklahoma Symphony, and the Utah State Symphony—originated in the Project and carried on as permanent institutions. In New York City, hundreds of concert-goers milled around on sidewalks trying in vain to get into jam-packed halls where a newly created WPA orchestra was performing, and one night a week at Billy Rose's Casino de Paree, a Composers' Forum-Laboratory gave an opportunity to men of the stature of Aaron Copland, Howard Hanson, William Schuman, and Roy Harris to hear their compositions performed. One Milwaukee teenager, with the encouragement of a summer job on the WPA Music Project, went on to become first cellist for the Boston Symphony and head of Oberlin's chamber music department.

But the Federal Music Project also reached out in less traditional directions, including sponsoring fifty-five dance bands. It transcribed, as Jane De Hart Mathews has noted, "Creole ballads in Louisiana, bayou songs of the Mississippi delta, folk songs of the Appalachian hills, white and Negro spirituals of the Carolinas, Spanish songs of the Southwest, and liturgical music from the California missions." On a sound truck rumbling through the South, it recorded river chanteys in Mississippi, Acadian tunes in Louisiana, and black shouts and jubilees in North Carolina. In New Mexico it collected Hispanic folk songs in isolated villages where tunes that had disappeared in Spain and Mexico were still sung; gave impoverished school children the opportunity to play an instrument; sponsored guitar ensembles at fiestas; and even organized an orchestra among inmates in the state penitentiary. In Vicksburg, the Federal Music Project nurtured an all-blind orchestra.

This collectivity of projects had an inevitable influence on the aesthetic sensibility. As the historian William Stott has observed:

The WPA brought the American artist and the American public face to face for the first time. It created a mass audience for what had been privileged entertainment: art galleries in thousands of towns that had never seen one; Federal Theatre productions for half a million spectators each week; WPA concerts with several million in attendance, nationwide, on a warm summer night.

No longer was the painter or composer obliged to respond to "a coterie— monied, urban, and European in taste." Instead, "the WPA subsidized another audience into being." As a result, he notes, Aaron Copland "began writing 'music for the people, for as large an audience as possible,' music 'in the simplest possible terms,' music based on folk melodies, music one could whistle, because . . . 'an entire new public for music had grown up.'"

These developments in the United States excited enthusiastic, indeed extravagant, admiration in Europe. "To consider in a time of general distress starving artists as artists and not simply as paupers is unique to the Roosevelt administration," said W. H. Auden. Other commentators were positively hyperbolic. "The level of work is astonishingly high," the novelist Ford Madox Ford told reporters in the autumn of 1937. "Art in America is being given a chance and there has been nothing like it since the Reformation." "Nowhere in Europe is there anything to compare with it," agreed the Austrian composer Erich Wolfgang Korngold. "Of course we have state subsidized opera but no country in Europe has anything to equal this."

If the creation of America's first federal arts project was an unusual departure, no less surprising were the New Deal's ventures in documentary films. With Resettlement Administration funds, Pare Lorentz turned out *The Plow That Broke the Plains* in 1936 and the classic *The River* in 1937. He engaged cameramen such as Paul Strand, who had won acclaim for his movie on a fishermen's strike in Mexico; invited the young composer Virgil Thomson, who had just scored Gertrude Stein's *Four Saints in Three Acts*, to compose the background music; and employed Thomas Chalmers, who had sung at the Metropolitan Opera in the era of Caruso, to read the narration. Lorentz's films were eye-openers. Though the British government had been encouraging this kind of enterprise under the aegis of John Grierson, American government documentaries before the New Deal had been limited to short subjects on topics like the love life of the honeybee. *The River*, which won first prize in Venice at the International Exposition of Cinematographic Art in 1938, proved that there was an

audience in the United States for well-wrought documentaries, by drawing more than ten million people, while *The Plow That Broke the Plains*,
said one critic, made "the rape of millions of acres . . . more moving than
the downfall of a Hollywood blonde."

In these same years, still photographers, among them such talented
people as Walker Evans, Ben Shahn, and Marion Post-Wolcott, produced
270,000 photo-documents, including such classic frames as Dorothea
Lange's "Migrant Mother," a photo of a stranded pea-picker, desperate with want, who had been living on birds her hungry children had
killed, and Arthur Rothstein's riveting "Dust Storm, Cimarron County,
Oklahoma," while Mississippi's guidebook found space for the photographs of Eudora Welty. The dean of American photographers, Edward
Steichen, called the New Deal portfolio "the most remarkable [collection
of] human documents ever rendered in pictures."

IX

Both Lorentz's films and the work of documentary photographers suggest
the concern of the New Deal for the land. Franklin Roosevelt, as Rex
Tugwell has written, had a "proprietary interest in the nation's estate."
During his presidency, the government created the Everglades National
Park in a land of mangroves and roseate spoonbills, the Joshua Tree
National Monument above Palm Springs, remote Big Bend National Park
in the Rio Grande valley, Cape Hatteras National Seashore (America's first
national seashore), Isle Royal National Park in the vastness of Lake
Superior and Organ Pipe Cactus National Monument in the Arizona
desert; completed the Great Smoky Mountains National Park; and overcame private utility lobbyists to establish the Kings Canyon National Park
in the California wilderness John Muir had cherished. In the Pacific
Northwest, where a bitter quarrel raged over the exploitation of the
Olympic peninsula, the last refuge of the Olympic elk and the last stand
of Sitka spruce and Douglas fir, Roosevelt made a point of paying a visit.
Shocked at the ruthless cutting of virgin timber and moved by a sign children had posted at a school asking for his help (a placard he called "the
appealingest appeal that I have seen in all my travels"), he pledged that he
would create an Olympic National Park, and he was good to his word.

The multipurpose dams of the Tennessee Valley Authority drew admirers from all over the world. Though the TVA focused most of its attention
on generating electric power, it also terraced hillsides, created recreational

lakes, and employed sixty motor boats to spray shore lines to eliminate the scourge of malaria. While noting that the TVA fell well short of its aspirations as a regional planning agency, the political scientist Norman Wengert also praised it for "a magnificent piece of multi-purpose engineering"; stated that "its power activities reflect standards of public service that are unequalled"; lauded its fertilizer program as "a high-quality industrial pioneering enterprise"; and paid tribute to its contributions to local government and public health.

In like manner, the historian Thomas McCraw, though also critical of the Tennessee Valley Authority, concluded that it left a "grand legacy" that

lives on, in the flood control system, so well designed that the Tennessee River can be shut off like a kitchen tap; in the 650-mile inland waterway from Paducah to Knoxville, providing an avenue for inexpensive barge transportation; in the architectural grandeur of almost all TVA water projects . . . ; in the verdant valley that once ran dirty with washing topsoil; in the enhanced living standard made possible by regional electrification; and, perhaps above all, in the example that this kind of superior achievement could be accomplished in the public sector, not for profit but—as the plaques on all its projects say—"For the People of the United States of America."

Roosevelt's "tree army," the Civilian Conservation Corps, enrolled 25,000 World War I veterans in the spring of 1933 and another 25,000 woodsmen in addition to its main complement—a quarter of a million jobless young men. Before it was over the CCC had recruited more than three million volunteers, and even at the end of the decade more young men signed up with the CCC each year than entered college. There were CCC camps from Alaska to the Virgin Islands, with seventy-one for Native Americans. From hundreds of these camps, the historian George Blakey has written, "came legendary stories of the youthful armies marching across the American landscape like Johnny Appleseeds dressed in army surplus. In their wake rose new forests, brush dams, lookout towers, and windbreaks." The CCC planted nearly three billion trees, raised 85,000 miles of telephone lines, built a million miles of roads and forest trails, laid out picnic sites and camp grounds, and stocked nearly a billion fish. With the help of the WPA it developed a new park in Kentucky in honor of John James Audubon, and, on the outskirts of Madison, Wisconsin, restored a sixty-five-acre prairie in which dozens of wild species of plants flourished. It renovated the Jenny Lake campgrounds in the Grand Tetons, created thousands of acres of duck ponds in South Carolina marshlands, and preserved prehistoric ruins at the Bandolier National Monument in New Mexico. Often, the CCCers were called upon to fight forest fires, an activity that cost forty-seven of them their lives.

The CCC also aided the Forest Service in the vast undertaking of establishing a shelterbelt—a windbreak of trees and shrubs—from the Canadian border to the Texas panhandle. Many scoffed at the idea. If God could not grow trees in this unpromising land, why, skeptics asked, did anyone suppose that Washington could? But Roosevelt persisted, despite obdurate resistance in Congress, in nurturing the shelterbelt project and found ingenious ways to finance it. In the end, the government planted more than 200 million trees, many of them in soil where no tree had ever grown before, with what one scholar has called "astounding results which still affect life on the Great Plains." Hubert Humphrey, the son of a South Dakota druggist, later recalled how, as a young man, he saw the entire population of his small town turn out to watch the tree-planting to halt the devastating dust storms. "I remember—we all remember—what a great day it was for us," he said. "We knew that at last somebody cared."

Federal agencies provided sustenance for drought-stricken farmers in the Dust Bowl, and the Soil Conservation Service, another New Deal creation, instructed growers in methods of cultivation to save the land. Starting in 1937 the government, slowly at first but with greater momentum later, covered the nation with more than two thousand soil conservation districts, new units of local government with the capacity to engage in land-use planning. As Alistair Cooke later said, the favorite of the New Dealers was the farmer with the will to "take up contour plowing late in life."

These activities on behalf of farmers represented only a small part of the government's program, for it is not too much to say that in the New Deal years the business of agriculture was revolutionized. Roosevelt took office at a time of mounting desperation for American farmers. In one month in 1932 twenty thousand farmers had lost their land because of inability to meet their debts in a period of collapsing prices. On a single day in May 1932, one-fourth of the state of Mississippi went under the sheriff's hammer. The Farm Credit Administration of 1933 came to the aid of the beleaguered farmer, and within eighteen months, it had refinanced one-fifth of all farm mortgages.

The Rural Electrification Administration literally brought the American countryside out of darkness. At the beginning of the Roosevelt era, only one farm in nine had electricity; not long after his death, only one in nine did not have it. Electricity lit up farm houses, made possible modern plumbing and heating, and powered equipment from milking machines to chicken brooders. Pupils in twelve thousand rural schools could for the first time read their texts in brightly lit rooms on dark winter afternoons, and farm women, who for years had eyed appliances at county fairs knowing they had no way to plug them in, now raced out to buy washing machines and irons. The Electric Home and Farm Authority, though it operated on a small scale, enabled thousands of consumers to take advantage of new patterns of cheap installment credit to purchase refrigerators that, by making it much easier to store perishables, markedly improved nutrition. In generating and distributing cheap, abundant electric power, something the utilities were reluctant to do, the government showed the initiative that theorists allotted exclusively to the private realm.

But more important than any of these developments were the series of enactments, starting with the first AAA (Agricultural Adjustment Act) of 1933, that began the process of granting large-scale subsidies to growers and lending them billions of dollars. One of the foremost authorities in the field, Theodore Saloutos, while writing that "the efforts of the New Deal to control production . . . can hardly be adjudged a success," nonetheless concluded: "The New Deal with all its limitations and frustrations, by making operational ideas and plans that had been long on the minds of agricultural researchers and thinkers, constituted the greatest innovative epoch in the history of American agriculture." As William Faulkner later said, "Our economy is not agricultural any longer. Our economy is the federal government. We no longer farm in Mississippi cotton fields. We farm now in Washington corridors and Congressional committee rooms."

The New Deal, especially after the creation of the Farm Security Administration in 1937, also reached out to the tenant farmer, again something no other American government had ever done before. Operating on a woefully small budget, the FSA carried out its mission with bold imagination. In addition to assisting in land purchases, it set up medical services, including screening for infectious diseases, for the more than a million migrant farm workers, while hundreds of thousands of small farmers, actively encouraged by the agency, took part in purchasing and marketing cooperatives. One historian has concluded that though "the effort was pitifully inadequate," the FSA and its predecessors, notably the

Resettlement Administration, "represented the greatest innovation in agricultural policy since the passage of the Homestead Act."

X

At the same time that it vastly extended the parameters of government, the
New Deal changed the composition of its personnel and of its beneficiaries. Before 1933 the government had paid heed primarily to a single
group—white Anglo-Saxon Protestant males. The Roosevelt administration, however, recruited from a more ethnically diverse medley, symbolized by Ben Cohen and Tommy Corcoran, the Jew and the Irish Catholic.
Jews such as Henry Morgenthau were prominent among the President's
advisers, and though, in the entire history of the republic of nearly a century and a half before 1933 only four Catholics had ever served in a cabinet, FDR, in choosing his first cabinet, named two. The Federal Writers'
Project turned out books on Italians and Albanians, Armenians and
Norwegians, while the Federal Theatre staged productions in Yiddish and
wrote a history of the Chinese theater in Los Angeles.

For the first time also, women received more than token recognition.
FDR as governor had demonstrated that he was comfortable with women
in positions of authority. He had named Frances Perkins the Industrial
Commissioner of the state of New York, and when he was elected president, he appointed her Secretary of Labor, the first ever female cabinet
member. In his first three years in office, Franklin Roosevelt selected more
women for Senate-confirmed posts than his Republican predecessors had
in twelve years. He named eleven women to high positions no woman had
ever held before, including the first woman envoy (Minister to Denmark),
the first female Assistant Secretary of the Treasury, and the first woman
Director of the United States Mint. He chose Florence Allen as the first
woman judge of the U.S. Circuit Court of Appeals, Hallie Flanagan of
Vassar to head the Federal Theatre Project, and Ellen Sullivan Woodward
for the Social Security Board. "At times Washington seemed like a perpetual convention of social workers as women from the Consumers League,
the Women's Trade Union League, and other reform groups came to
Washington to take on government assignments," the historian William
H. Chafe has written. "Mary Anderson, director of the Women's Bureau,
recalled that in earlier years women government officials had dined
together in a small university club. 'Now,' she said, 'there are so many of
them they would need a hall.'"

Women not only constituted a much larger presence in Washington, but also benefited directly from federal policies to a far greater extent than they ever had in the past. When the Women's Division of the Democratic National Committee sponsored a banquet in 1940, seventy women at the speakers' table held high posts either in the national government or in the party. "My heart filled with pride at that long line of intelligent, competent, well-balanced women . . . who represented Roosevelt's confidence in our ability," the first full-time director of the Women's Division of the Democratic National Committee, Molly Dewson, said. "The opportunities given women by Roosevelt in the thirties changed our status." Though women never got their fair proportion of places, the WPA at one point had more than four hundred thousand women on its rolls, and programs such as aid to mothers with dependent children under the Social Security Act targeted women as beneficiaries.

As First Lady, Eleanor Roosevelt symbolized for millions of women their newly won power in government. Before she arrived, most First Ladies had been content to preside over the social functions of the White House. But by 1940 Mrs. Roosevelt had traveled more than a quarter of a million miles, written a million words, and made a greater impression on the popular imagination than had any of her predecessors. No one knew where she would turn up next. In West Virginia an unidentified "tall woman . . . wearing a dark blue skirt, white blouse, and a white ribbon around her hair" visited the scabrous hovels beside foul Scotts Run, where she heard the tales of miners' wives while she held their babies on her lap. In a famous cartoon of the decade, a begrimed coal miner in the bowels of the earth cries out in astonishment to a fellow digger, "For Gosh Sakes, Here Comes Mrs. Roosevelt!" Admiral Byrd, it was said, always set two places for dinner at the South Pole "in case Mrs. Roosevelt should drop in." She was renowned for her informality. When the King and Queen of England visited America, she served them hot dogs and beer, and when during World War II, she traveled to Australia and New Zealand, she greeted her Maori guide by rubbing noses.

While eschewing some of the notions of the radical feminists, she used her influence in the White House to see to it that the neglected—especially blacks, women, and unemployed youth—got attention in the councils of power. "For some time I have had a collection of statesmen hanging upon my wall," the pioneer suffragist Carrie Chapman Catt wrote her, "but under the new administration, I have been obliged to start a new collection and that is one of stateswomen. Now it is ready and you are the very center of it all."

"You see, I think you are a kind of genius," the novelist Dorothy Canfield Fisher told her. "Out of your personality and position you have certainly created something of first-rate and unique value—not a book or statue or painting—an example." According to Rex Tugwell, "No one who ever saw Eleanor Roosevelt sit down facing her husband, and holding his eyes firmly, say to him 'Franklin, I think you should' . . . or, 'Franklin surely you will not' . . . will every forget the experience." She became, as one columnist said, "Cabinet Minister without portfolio—the most influential woman of our times."

Although the New Deal's performance with regard to blacks added to the sorry record of racial discrimination in America, there were also some important gains. African Americans, often excluded from relief in the past, now received a large share, nearly 30 percent, of WPA jobs, three times their proportion of the population, while the PWA under Ickes introduced a quota system to insure the employment of black craftsmen. Blacks moved into federal housing projects; government funds went to schools and hospitals in black neighborhoods; and New Deal agencies such as the Farm Security Administration enabled some 50,000 black tenant farmers and sharecroppers to become proprietors. "Indeed," one historian has written, "there is a high correlation between the location of extensive FSA operations in the 1930s and the rapidity of political modernization in black communities in the South in the 1960's." Roosevelt appointed a number of blacks such as Robert Weaver, destined to be the first black cabinet member, to high posts in the government, and when in 1937 he named the NAACP counsel William Hastie to a U.S. district court, it marked the first time an African American had ever been chosen for a federal judgeship. In the South, African Americans who were disfranchised in regular elections voted in AAA crop referenda and in NLRB plant elections, and the first step was taken toward restoring constitutional rights when Attorney General Frank Murphy set up the Civil Rights Section in the Department of Justice.

The pattern of Jim Crow in national government offices, which had begun under Roosevelt's Democratic predecessor, Woodrow Wilson, was broken by Secretary Ickes, who desegregated cafeterias in the Department of the Interior. Ickes also had a part in the most dramatic episode of the time, for when the Daughters of the American Revolution denied the use of their concert hall to the black contralto Marian Anderson, he made it possible for her to sing before thousands from the steps of Lincoln Memorial, and Mrs. Roosevelt joined in the rebuke to the DAR. (Not many years earlier when the Lincoln Memorial was dedicated, black spectators had been herded into a roped off area on the other side of the road from whites.) Henry Lee Moon, a militant advocate of civil rights who noted that "there was just cause for much of the Negro criticism of the Roosevelt regime," nonetheless acknowledged:

> The gains made under Roosevelt were tangible and lasting: the 66,850 new low-rent dwellings made available for low-income Negro families who formerly were compelled to live in slums; the hospitals, schools, and recreational centers built with federal aid; the training of thousands of young Negroes in the programs of the National Youth Administration and the Civilian Conservation Corps; the aid to more than half a million Negro farmers; the opening up of new employment opportunities in government and in private industry; the stimulation of a progressive non-discriminating labor movement; . . . the elimination of Jim Crow in most government cafeterias and bureaus; and, perhaps most important, the appointment of a liberal Supreme Court which vindicated the Negro's basic rights and, by banning the white primary, opened the way to mass Negro voting in the South. . . . Despite the bitter opposition of entrenched reaction, President Roosevelt's program of social legislation contributed immeasurably to the advancement of the common people of this country.

XI

The Great Depression and the New Deal brought about a significant political realignment of the sort that occurs only rarely in party history in America. The Depression wrenched many lifelong Republican voters from their moorings. In 1928 one couple christened their newborn son "Herbert Hoover Jones." Four years later they petitioned the court, "desiring to relieve the young man from the chagrin and mortification which he is suffering and will suffer," and asked that his name be changed to Franklin D. Roosevelt Jones. "The election of 1932 deserves to be called a 'revolution,'" a political scientist has written, "because it destroyed something very much like a permanent Republican lease of power." In 1932 FDR became the first Democrat to enter the White House with a majority of the popular vote in eighty years, and he took advantage of this opportunity to mold a coalition centered in the low-income districts of the great cities that endured throughout his tenure in the White House. In Philadelphia a seasoned politician who for half a century had been rolling up victories for the GOP machine told an interviewer:

> The last two elections I carried the district for the Republican candidates from top to the bottom, but this man Roosevelt could win against the Lord in my division. The people tell me they will vote for anyone for me except any opponent of Roosevelt. . . .
>   They seemed to think he gives you even the air you breathe and it would be a desecration to vote against him.

No less important was the shift in the character of the Democratic party from the conservative organization of John W. Davis and John Raskob to the country's main political agency for reform. "One political result of the Roosevelt years," the historian Robert Burke has observed, "was a basic change in the nature of the typical Congressional liberal." He was no longer a maverick who made a fetish of orneriness, no longer one of the men a Republican Senator called "the sons of the wild jackass," but "a party Democrat, labor-oriented, urban-, and internationalist-minded."

The New Deal transformed the nature of American politics by drastically altering the agenda. When Arthur Krock of the *New York Times* listed the main programmatic questions before the 1932 Democratic convention, he wrote: "What would be said about the repeal of prohibition that had split the Republicans?" "What would be said about tariffs?" By 1936 these concerns seemed altogether old-fashioned, as campaigners discussed the TVA and industrial relations, slum clearance and aid to the jobless. A Little Rock newspaper commented: "Such matters as tax and tariff laws have given way to universally human things, the living problems and opportunities of the average man and the average family." That year the highly critical columnist Dorothy Thompson, who was featured in the country's foremost Republican newspaper, entered in her diary: "Immense uncovering job done in American problems—Housing—Social Security—Labor—Sharecroppers—Agricultural Conditions."

The Roosevelt years changed the conception of the role of government not just in Washington but in the states and cities. To be sure, not even the Great Depression and the New Deal could overcome conservative instincts in many states. The historian James T. Patterson has characterized the governors of the era as "nobodies, moderates, undramatic, yawn-inspiring men with legislative programs as pedestrian as they were unhelpful," and Roosevelt could not be expected to have much impact on a chief executive such as the Democratic Governor of Oregon, who expressed regret that the elderly and the mentally retarded could not be chloroformed. But FDR's policies did encourage the emergence of "Little New Deals" sponsored by executives such as Frank Murphy in Michigan. Under Eurith D. Rivers, an enthusiastic Roosevelt follower, Georgia got its first welfare system, greatly improved medical care, and the first low-cost housing in the country for rural citizens. Pennsylvania's Little New Deal under Governor George Earle abolished the hated coal and iron police, levied stiff taxes on corporations, and enacted a workmen's compensation law so generous in its benefits that the United Mine Workers objected that it might hurt the coal business, while New York's counterpart under Governor Herbert Lehman added a thick sheaf of legislation that the labor leader George Meany called the greatest social program any state had ever adopted.

Instead of always issuing edicts from above, the New Deal invited the cooperation of state governments. In the age of Roosevelt, the economist John Joseph Wallis has written, "everybody got a piece of the action." This "co-operative federalism" resulted in the establishment at the state level of agencies such as departments of social welfare where there had been none before. As one historian has pointed out, "Many counties in Georgia that had never seen a social worker now had one permanently stationed within their borders." The change came astonishingly swiftly. In 1934 only one state had an unemployment compensation law; in 1937, after numbers of governors called special sessions of legislatures to rush through enabling acts, every state and territory did. From 1932 to 1940 state and local spending for public welfare increased tenfold.

Hard times and New Deal pressure also served to bring city and county administrations into the twentieth century. In Boston, noted a study by Charles Trout, city council members in 1929 "devoted endless hours to street paving." After the coming of the New Deal, they were absorbed with NRA campaigns, public housing, and WPA allotment. "A year after the crash the council thought 5,000 dollars an excessive appropriation for the municipal employment bureau," but during the 1930s "the unemployed drained Boston's treasury of not less than 100,000,000 dollars in direct benefits, and the federal government spent even more."

"The New Deal marked a new epoch in American urban history," the historian Mark Gelfand has declared. Prior to the age of Roosevelt municipal governments, which are not mentioned anywhere in the U.S. Constitution, had no place in national policy and existed only at the sufferance of the states. But the creation of the PWA, CWA, WPA, and USHA "opened up new lines of communications between two levels of government that had not previously acknowledged the other's existence." As early as 1934 a Southern mayor was saying, "Mayors are a familiar sight in Washington these days. . . . The destinies of our cities are clearly tied in with national politics." This enlarged role for government at all levels created a sense of excitement about its potentialities. Between 1931 and 1936, the percentage of majors in the Department of Government at Harvard increased nearly two-and-a-quarter times.

The "Constitutional Revolution" of 1937 and the "Roosevelt Court" permanently changed the nature of the governmental process when this exercise of authority by national and local governments was legitimized. Before 1937 the Supreme Court stood as a formidable barrier to social reform. Since 1937 not one piece of significant social legislation has been struck down, and the Court has shifted its docket instead to issues of civil rights and civil liberties.

To British observers, the dimensions of change were unmistakable. In 1957 Sir Denis Brogan contrasted the situation in the post–New Deal era with that when he had first come to America in the twenties:

I hope I arrived in the United States in 1925 less conscious of effortless superiority than the average Oxford man was wont to display. There was much that delighted me, few things that shocked me. But one thing did shock me. This was the prevalence of what the Greeks (and my servant at Balliol) called "idiots"—that is citizens taking no interest in politics. Even then I was far from thinking that politics were all or nearly all. I was quite prepared for poets and scientists to neglect politics for better things. But it was something else again to find historians, economists—even students of government—indifferent. The professionals looked after politics—either because they made a good if shady living that way, or because they had some inexplicable yen for this dull and rather dirty sport.

In 1957, . . . politics are not neglected. Politics as a career attract lots of young men and women, and a sense of the importance of political matters—and of government—is as marked as its absence was in 1925.

XII

This recapitulation of the changes wrought in the 1930s is in no way intended to suggest either that criticism of the Roosevelt administration is inappropriate or that the New Deal was free of fault. In a variety of publications I have pointed out that in 1932 "Roosevelt's campaign did little to reassure critics who thought him a vacillating politician," for "his speeches sounded painfully discordant themes" and "a great deal of what he said was double talk," with "his farm speech at Topeka . . . designed to mean all things to all men"; that "in the main part of his Inaugural Address, his program for recovery, he had little new to offer"; that in his first weeks in office the President "had pursued a policy more ruthlessly deflationary than anything Hoover had dared"; indeed, that "in his circumspect treatment of the banks, in his economy message, in his beer bill, Roosevelt had summed up the program of the arch-conservative du Pont wing of the Democratic party"; that he "frowned on" federal insurance of bank deposits and, until the very end, disapproved of the Wagner bill that resulted in the National Labor Relations Act; that "the NRA overextended itself in trying to regulate small enterprises and it could not muster enough power to discipline the big corporations"; that "the New Deal remained perpetually embarrassed by its scarcity economics"; that "in many respects" the Social Security Act "was an astonishingly inept and conservative piece of legislation" with a system of financing that "did untold economic mischief"; that "much of Roosevelt's tax program was sharply regressive," with the Wealth Tax Act of 1935 doing "little to redistribute wealth"; that "measured by the needs, or by the potentialities, Roosevelt's public housing program could make only modest claims"; that "the HOLC gave no relief to homeowners who were unemployed and . . . foreclosed mortgages on more than a hundred thousand homes"; that in agriculture "New Deal policies made matters worse" when "the AAA's reduction of cotton acreage drove the tenant and the cropper from the land, and landlords, with the connivance of local AAA committees which they dominated, cheated tenants of their fair share of benefits"; that the TVA's model village of Norris and Eleanor Roosevelt's Arthurdale, "the New Deal showplace communities, were Jim Crow towns"; that "'grassroots democracy' frequently meant a surrender of the national interest to local power groups" and interest-group politics "served to make the Roosevelt administration the prisoner of its own interest groups"; that "even the most precedent-breaking New Deal projects reflected capitalist thinking and deferred to business sensibilities"; that "the New Dealers were never able to develop an adequate reform ideology to challenge the business rhetoricians"; that the end of the New Deal found "many Americans—sharecroppers, slum dwellers, most Negroes—outside of the new equilibrium"; that "the New Deal left many problems unsolved and even created some perplexing new ones"; and that "some of the developments of the postwar era that were to be most deplored, such as the military-industrial complex, had their origins in the age of Roosevelt." There were experiments that miscarried, opportunities that were missed, groups who were neglected, and power that was arrogantly used. Over the whole performance lies the dark cloud of the persistence of hard times.

I am not persuaded, though, that the New Deal experience was negligible. It lasted hardly more than six years, and it is difficult to think of another six-year period in the history of the republic that was so fruitful or of a crisis met with more imagination. The spirit of the New Deal at its best is caught in Roosevelt's words in his second inaugural address. "The test of our progress," he said, "is not whether we add to the abundance of those who have much. It is whether we provide enough for those who have too little."

What then did the New Deal do? It gave far greater amplitude to the national state, expanded the authority of the presidency, recruited university-trained administrators, won control of the money supply, established central banking, imposed regulation on Wall Street, monitored the airwaves, rescued debt-ridden farmers and homeowners, built model communities, transformed home-building, made federal housing a permanent feature, fostered unionization of the factories, drastically reduced child labor, ended the tyranny of company towns, wiped out sweatshops, established minimal working standards, enabled thousands of tenants to buy their own farms, built camps for migrants, introduced the Welfare State with old-age pensions, unemployment insurance, and aid for dependent children and the handicapped, provided jobs for millions of unemployed, set up a special program for the jobless young and for students, covered the American landscape with new edifices, subsidized painters and novelists, composers and ballet dancers, introduced America's first state theater, created documentary films, gave birth to the impressive Tennessee Valley Authority, generated electric power, sent the CCC boys into the forests, initiated the Soil Conservation Service, transformed the economy of agriculture, lighted up rural America, gave women greater recognition, made a start toward breaking the pattern of racial discrimination, put together a liberal party coalition, and changed the agenda of American politics.

But even this summary does not encapsulate the full range of the New Deal. It offered Native Americans new instrumentalities for self-government and established the Indian Arts and Crafts Board, taught counterpoint and *solfeggio*, served more than half a billion hot lunches to school children and launched hundreds of nursery schools, refurbished 80 million library books and transcribed volumes into Braille, constructed refuges for migratory waterfowl, filed thought-provoking reports on the Mississippi valley and the Great Plains, put down-and-out architects to work on the Historic American Buildings Survey, built garden ponds in the Dust Bowl, gave Woody Guthrie a job on the Bonneville project, set up birth control clinics for migrant farmers, sponsored baroque ensembles, sent bookmobiles into isolated communities and, where there were no roads, had books carried in by pack-horses. In Mississippi, where there were forty-eight counties with no library services whatsoever, a New Deal agency, the historian Martha Swain has noted, "created libraries in log cabins, community houses, filling stations, country stores, and even on houseboats that plied the backwaters in river counties." (A Neshoba County woman told the state office, "I still get frightened when I get caught off in big rains and have to wade swift water, knee deep, across the swamp, with my basket of books in one hand and my dress tail in the other.") And only a truly merciful and farsighted government would have taken such pains to find jobs for unemployed historians.

For the past generation America has lived off the legacy of the New Deal. Successive administrations expanded the provisions of statutes such as the Social Security Act, adopted New Deal attitudes toward intervention in the economy to cope with recessions, and put New Deal ideas to new ends, as when the CCC served as the basis for both the Peace Corps and the VISTA program of the War on Poverty. The historian Carl Degler has observed:

> Conventionally the end of the New Deal is dated with the enactment of the Wages and Hours Act of 1938. But in a fundamental sense the New Deal did not end then at all. Americans still live in the era of the New Deal, for its achievements are now the base mark below which no conservative government may go and from which all new reforms now start. Not only did the Republican Eisenhower administration accept all the reform agencies and laws of the New Deal, but the reform efforts of the Democratic Truman, Kennedy,

and Johnson administrations have been little more than fulfillments of the New Deal.

The British historian David K. Adams at Keele has pointed out that the philosophy of the New Frontier had "conscious overtones of the New Deal" and indeed that John Kennedy's "New Frontier" address of 1960 was "almost a paraphrase" of an FDR speech of 1935.

Some writers have assumed that the New Deal was an inevitable consequence of the 1929 crash, but that was not the lesson Herbert Hoover drew nor was it a universal experience in other lands. A Canadian commentator remarked:

> In Canada we had no New Deal, no A.A.A. or other measures designed to give agriculture a "parity" with urban industry, no Wagner Act for the trade unions, no great public housing schemes, no C.C.C. camps for unemployed youth, no T.V.A. to reconstruct a vast blighted area, no Federal Writers or Federal Artists Projects, no new parkways about our big cities and no new recreation camps among our lakes and forests; and—last but not least—no fireside chats.

I began by recalling the words of a British historian, and it seems appropriate to end with the words of another British historian from that same Oxford college, who has written of "the reality of a New Deal or Roosevelt 'revolution.'" In a volume edited by the Vice Chancellor, Herbert Nicholas concluded:

> Certain things were never the same again. America, for better or worse, was henceforward a welfare state. In future, in fact and symbol, Washington was the capital of the country. White House and Capitol Hill, not Wall Street or Pittsburgh or Detroit, would decide. And government henceforth would mean, in inescapable degree, experts, even intellectuals. The "Brains Trust" was, in one form or another, there to stay. This went beyond politics and administration. After 1933 (perhaps after 1929) America was never to be so philistine, so Babbittish again.

Moreover the New Deal's positive achievements, standing out in stark contrast to the inertia of Britain, the decline of France, the headlong rush into barbarism of Germany, produced a new creative American nationalism.

It is this awareness of the achievement of the Roosevelt years, of the broad scope of purpose and accomplishment, that I hope my American colleagues will restore to the continuing dialogue over the meaning of the New Deal.

NINE

The "Europeanization" of America, 1929–1950

[In March 1988 scholars from thirty-one nations, including some from behind the Iron Curtain, gathered at the Free University of Berlin for the biennial conference of the European Association for American Studies. In addition to a good many panels, there were three featured talks. On the first day, the British novelist Malcolm Bradbury and the German journalist Josef Joffe made major presentations, and on the final day I gave the summary address on the theme of the meeting. The paper has not been published before save in the conference proceedings, *Looking Inward, Looking Outward: From the 1930s through the 1940s*, ed. Steve Ickringill (Amsterdam: Vu University Press, 1990), a volume of limited circulation riddled with errors. I have revised it to include additional materials, especially from a broadcast on the Great Depression I made for the Voice of America.]

When on March 4, 1929 Herbert Hoover was inaugurated as President of the United States, he took office at a time of the fairest prospect any country had ever known. As Americans never tired of pointing out, though Europeans must have wearied of hearing, the United States accounted for 44 percent of the industrial production of the entire world, and if the wealth of Great Britain, Germany, France, Italy, and every other country in Europe had been put together, it would not have equaled that of America. This economic hegemony was understood to have inevitable cultural implications. "Culture follows money," said F. Scott Fitzgerald. "We will be the Romans in the next generation." In fact, "in the 1920s," as one historian has noted, "American economic, political, and cultural influence washed over Europe," because the United States was perceived to be, for better or worse—and not a few thought for worse—the land of the future. Even Bertolt Brecht concluded that the key to progress was held not by the Soviet Union but by America.

Yet, for all its eminence, the United States seemed, to a remarkable degree, a nation that in 1929 lacked many of the characteristics expected of a world power and associated with modernity. That judgment was borne out in five respects in particular. First, although America had long welcomed the peoples of many countries, its culture was still, in some aspects, insular. It was that perception—the theme of such Sinclair Lewis novels as *Main Street* and *Babbitt*—that drove so many American artists and writers in the 1920s to Europe. Second, the country, if it did not quite think of itself as a classless society, regarded social stratification as alien to republican ideals. Third, the United States, though it found ways to exercise economic hegemony, refrained from exerting a political role in world affairs commensurate with its latent power. Fourth, the United States, to an astonishing extent, had no real military establishment, though it did have a world-class navy. The American army was smaller than that of Greece or Bulgaria, and when, as late as 1939, the Army conducted maneuvers, it used trucks on which were placed cardboard placards marked "TANK." Fifth, and finally, the United States in the 1920s had almost no institutional structure to which Europeans would accord the term "the State." One journalist has commented that "nobody would have thought of calling the sleepy, rather inconsequential Southern town that Washington was in Calvin Coolidge's day the center of anything very important," and an economist has observed: "Before the New Deal, the only business a citizen had with the government was through the Post Office. No doubt he saw a soldier or a sailor now and then, but the government had nothing to do with the general public."

No one better exemplified this anti-statist, individualistic tradition than Herbert Hoover, who had even written a book on American individualism. Like a Horatio Alger hero, he had been born in a small village, orphaned at an early age, and, after going west, had, wholly on his own, unaided by the State, become, by the age of thirty, a multi-millionaire. His ascent to the presidency in 1929 at a time of piping prosperity appeared to be a vindication, almost a coronation, of traditional values and expectations, for Hoover, in his campaign and afterwards, had gone out of his way to identify himself with the perpetuation of prosperity. In his acceptance speech on the Stanford University campus, he had declared: "We in America today are nearer to the final triumph over poverty than ever before in the history of any land. The poorhouse is vanishing from among us. . . . Our workers with their average weekly wages can today buy two or even three times more bread and butter than any wage earner in Europe."

And in his inaugural address, Hoover had claimed, "In no nation are the fruits of accomplishment more secure."

As Nicholas Halasz has written:

It was as if a new paradise had burgeoned on earth for the exclusive benefit of the Americans and that God had blessed them with the perpetual improvement of this providential condition. They began to believe that in this matter of prosperity they were not as other men are, but instead somehow destined by miracle to go on from strength to strength while the rest of the world went under the harrow.

It would require an event of cataclysmic proportions to upset these expectations and to bring into question the values that went with them, and Hoover had been in office hardly half a year when that catastrophic occurrence took place. The stock market crash of 1929 and the onset of the Great Depression detonated a chain of explosions that would catapult America toward modernity. Although the Depression was worldwide, "the violence of the contraction in the United States," as the economist Wladimir Woytinsky pointed out, "was far greater than in other lands. Indeed, of the decline in industrial production throughout the world, more than half took place in the United States." Furthermore, the shock was far greater in America, because, since it had been riding so high in the 1920s, the fall was not only steeper but also more unanticipated.

European travelers to America were stunned by the transformation they witnessed. In 1922 the British journalist Henry Nevinson, in bidding farewell to New York, had written: "Good-bye most beautiful of modern cities! . . . Good-bye to heaven-piled offices, so clean, so warm, where lovely stenographers . . . sit leisurely at work or converse in charming ease! . . . Good-bye to beautiful 'apartments' and 'homes' . . . to central heating and radiators, fit symbols of the hearts they warm! Good-bye to the long stream of motors—'limousines' or 'flivvers'!" But in 1932 another English visitor, Mary Agnes Hamilton, who had arrived in New York on Christmas eve of 1931, reported:

It was the difference from what I had met before that struck me most forcibly. . . . In New York, one has only to pass outside the central island bounded by Lexington and Sixth Avenues to see hardship, misery and degradation. . . . Times Square, at any hour of the day and late into the evening, offers an exhibit for the edification of the theatre-goers, for it is packed with shabby, utterly dumb and apathetic-looking men. In 1932 there are more beggars to be met with in New York than in London [and in America] a dark undergrowth of horrid suffering that is certainly more degraded and degrading than anything Britain or Germany knows.

She added:

The American people, unfamiliar with suffering, with none of that long history of catastrophe and calamity behind it which makes the experience of European nations, is outraged and baffled by misfortune. . . . Misled in the onset by leaders who assured it . . . that American institutions were immune to the ills that had laid the countries of the rest of the world upon their backs, that prosperity was native to the soil of the Union, and all that was needed was to wait till the clouds, blown up by the wickedness of other lands, rolled by, . . . the nation now suffers from . . . despair. . . . The despicable European tragedies of shrinking exports, falling production curves, slumping prices . . . [have] crossed the Atlantic and settled down there with an awful air of perpetuity.

Similarly, another British traveler remarked: "To Americans, it seemed as if the bottom had dropped out of the world; they just could not believe it. France, yes, Germany, yes, England, why not? But America! Jeese!"

Under such circumstances, it is not surprising that many Europeans stopped looking to the United States as the country of never-ending advance or that Americans themselves came to question whether their nation was still the land of promise. To Brecht, America was no longer where the world was going, but where it had been. In 1930 he wrote derisively:

> What men they were! Their boxers the strongest!
> Their inventors the most adept! Their trains the swiftest!
> So we imitated this renowned race of men
> Who seemed destined
> To rule the world by helping it to progress.

Brecht concluded: "It all looked like lasting a thousand . . . but endured a bare eight years." Thirty-six thousand immigrants entered the United States in 1932; 103,000 emigrants departed. The Depression, wrote one British visitor, Sir Frederick Whyte, "revealed the truth of that early conclusion of Henry Adams that America had outlived her institutions, both economic and political," while another, Morgan Phillips Price, M.P., as the R.M.S. *Olympic* sailed into New York harbor, was reminded of George Bernard Shaw's quip—that upon the Statue of Liberty should be inscribed, "All hope abandon ye who enter here!"

In his essay asking "Warum gibt's in der Vereinigten Staaten keinen Sozialismus?" ("Why Is There No Socialism in the United States?") Werner Sombart had replied that the aspirations of radicals had foundered on "shoals of apple pie," but now the apple pie had run out, and the United States no longer constituted an exception. Sherwood Anderson told a journalist that "America is being caught up with," and another writer later noted that in the United States "destiny" had "ceased to be manifest." As far back as 1893 Frederick Jackson Turner had pointed out that the frontier line had disappeared. Now people feared that the United States was finally paying the price. No longer was there an undeveloped West as a place of refuge. America was confronted, as Europe had so long been, by closed space. Archibald MacLeish wrote:

> We wonder whether the dream of American liberty
> Was two hundred years of pine and hardwood
> And three generations of the grass
> And the generations are up: the years over
> We don't know.

Though this traumatic experience led Americans to take a more critical view of their institutions, it also had the effect, in the short run, of reinforcing some of the attitudes of the 1920s, especially the inclination to look inward. Hoover was only one of many Americans who blamed the Depression on Europe, though Europeans arguably had better grounds for finding fault with the United States. Hoover insisted that the "great center of the storm was Europe," with the collapse of the Kreditanstalt in Vienna in 1931 turning what had, until then, been only a "recession" into a worldwide calamity.

For a time, Roosevelt, too, preferred scolding European policymakers to pursuing international cooperation, and his appointees, though deeply influenced by European precedents, self-consciously shaped institutions in an American mold. Given the continental dimensions of the United States and the nature of New Deal intentions, the Federal Theatre Project "could not be modeled on a government-operated enterprise of any other country," its director, Hallie Flanagan, declared. She added:

This was not France or Germany where a galaxy of artists was to be chosen to play classical repertory. Nor was it Russia where the leaders of the state told the theatre directors what plays to do and what not to do. Neither was it Italy where theatre performances took the form of largesse distributed to the people. This was a distinctly American enterprise growing out of a people's need over a vast geographic area.

In the 1930s in America both isolationism and pacifism gained millions of new adherents, as distrust of the governments of Western Europe mounted and World War I was seen as a grim cosmic farce. Princeton University students lampooned the war-makers by forming a Veterans of Future Wars to ask Congress for bonuses for future military service, so that they could spend the sums while they were still alive. Vassar College students organized an "Association of Gold Star Mothers" and requested free voyages to Europe to inspect the graves of their future husbands and sons killed in the next war. Self-styled "slackers" in Los Angeles asked to serve their jail sentences at once in order to be free to roam during the next war, and a Southern Methodist University student proposed to appoint an unknown soldier, "so folks would know who he is before he gets killed."

Even when, to millions of Americans, involvement in the affairs of Europe seemed inevitable, some drew the lesson that this circumstance made looking inward all the more imperative. In April 1940, as the Nazi blitzkrieg was sweeping through the Low Countries, the historian James T. Flexner wrote the novelist and biographer Esther Forbes:

In these days when European civilization is tearing itself apart much of the torch of culture is being handed to us, but we cannot carry it on adequately merely on the basis of the European tradition which has developed such cancers. We must explore our own past to find other, stronger roots based on a continental federation, on a peaceful mingling of races, on a hardy and unsophisticated democracy that grew naturally from the hardy and rough environment. Of course it is possible to overstress the indigenous parts of our tradition, but certainly it is permissible to dwell on them now since they have for so long been neglected. What we need, I feel, is an intelligent patriotism, based not on fear or the desire to hear the eagle scream, but on a factual re-evaluation of our civilization.

In these years, also, hostility toward immigration from overseas became more intense. Why, it was asked, when millions of Americans were unemployed, add new competitors to the job market? Though immigration to the United States, a country no longer of golden streets but of lengthening breadlines, had slowed to a trickle, the Hoover administration enforced restrictions tenaciously to make sure that any newcomers who did arrive would be well-to-do, a policy that persisted until 1937. Even strip tease impresarios asked Congress for protection against "sinister foreign competition." At a Congressional committee hearing, the Minsky brothers declared indignantly, "We in America have devoted seventeen years to developing the strip tease art. Not just any girl can do it right. . . . She needs rhythm and poise, and looks and harmony, and must choose the exact psychological moment to remove each garment." These "hard-working young ladies come mostly from the Middle West," they explained, and it was not fair for them to be undercut by strippers imported from France. Congress should enact a stringent law, since, they maintained, "burlesque is the stronghold of flesh on the American stage."

Intellectuals, too, looked inward and backward rather than outward. During the Depression years, the Brain Truster Rexford Tugwell later said, "there was a kind of homesickness—historic homesickness," when, as the historian Neil Harris has observed, people "turned back into American history for folk motifs, mythic heroes, icons and rituals which formed the useable past that could anchor a drifting society." In a resurgence of cultural nationalism, the WPA program, as one scholar noted, became "a sort of road map for the cultural rediscovery of America from within." WPA muralists frescoed post office walls with celebrations of the American past; employees of the WPA Federal Writers' Project unearthed forgotten bits of folklore; and the reigning triumvirate of American art—Grant Wood, Thomas Hart Benton, and John Steuart Curry—favored a native idiom. Stephen Vincent Benét composed a sonnet in tribute to American place names, and in one of his documentaries, Pare Lorentz made a litany of the names of American rivers:

Down the Judith, the Grand, the Osage, and the Platte,
The Rock, the Salt, the Black and Minnesota,
Down the Monongahela, the Allegheny, Kanawha and
  Muskingum,
The Miami, the Wabash, the Licking and the Green.

The training of the American painter Philip Evergood was so European that he had actually been educated at Eton, but in the 1930s he forsook European art styles as inappropriate for the only contemporary subjects that were worthwhile—"the down-to-earth robust rawness of a steel worker's boot, or his wrinkled salt-caked sweater, or his grimy blue jeans."

No one has described this maelstrom of cultural nationalism more vividly than Alfred Kazin who observed:

Now, as the tide of Fascism mounted higher and higher in Europe, and it looked as if Americans had been thrown back on their own resources as never before, the whole emphasis of the early depression literature on national self-scrutiny became a thundering flood of national consciousness and self-celebration. Suddenly, as if it marked a necessary expiation of too rapid and embittered a disillusionment in the past, American writing became a swelling chorus of national affirmation and praise. Suddenly all the debunkers of the past, who had long since been on relief, became the special objects of revulsion and contempt. Suddenly all the despised catchwords of the democratic rhetoric took on a brilliant radiance.

In this atmosphere, Archibald MacLeish, who had expressed such strong doubts earlier, came to write that Americans were people "who had the luck to be born on this continent where the heat was hotter and the cold was colder and the sun was brighter and the nights were blacker and the distances were farther and the faces were nearer and the rain was more like rain and the mornings were more like mornings than anywhere else on earth—sooner or sweeter and lovelier over unused hills."

Kazin, while acknowledging that at its worst this kind of writing could sink to the maudlin and jejune, also stressed that to view this phenomenon as regressive was to misread it, for the writers seeking a "cultural inheritance" did so in the spirit of André Malraux. Kazin observed:

The most significant aspect of the new traditionalism, whatever its inevitable narrowness or bigotry, was always its insistence upon reclaiming the past for the strengthening of the present.

So far from being merely a blind and parochial nationalism, this experience in national self-discovery was largely shaped by the sudden emergence of America as the repository of Western culture in a world overrun by Fascism. America may have been cut off from Europe after 1933, but the migration of so many European intellectuals to America meant, as John Peale Bishop said, that the European past was now confided to us, since we alone could "prolong it into the future." This was a profound influence on the awakening to America's own tradition, since it meant a study of the national past conducted in the light of the European example in America, in the light of a new—if frantically enforced—sense of world responsibility. In an America which had either received or enrolled among its own so many of Europe's finest spirits from Thomas Mann to Jacques Maritain, from Albert Einstein to Sigrid Undset, the pride of helping to breed a new cosmopolitan culture gave a healthy stimulus to the searching of our own culture.

Though some features of cultural nationalism were more chauvinistic than Kazin acknowledged, he was right in contending that Americans in the 1930s were not only looking inward and looking backward; they were also looking outward—to such an extent that the nation showed itself to be very different from what it had been in the 1920s. In each of the five aspects mentioned earlier, the United States became less an example of exceptionalism. Or, to put it another way—the way that many of the critics of these developments, especially, saw it—America became more "European."

First, under Franklin D. Roosevelt, America developed a collectivity of institutions that for the first time approximated what Europeans meant by the term "the State." The diplomat George Kennan, thinking back on his Midwestern boyhood, has recalled that in those days "when times were hard, as they often were, groans and lamentations went up to God, but never to Washington," and a Chicagoan has said, "Before Roosevelt, the Federal Government hardly touched your life." But starting in the electrifying First Hundred Days of 1933, the Roosevelt administration vastly accelerated the concentration of power in Washington. "The nation or state which is unwilling by governmental action to tackle new problems,"

Roosevelt said, "is headed for a decline and ultimate death from inaction." In England Harold Laski called FDR the first leader "to use the power of the state to subordinate the primary assumptions of that society to certain vital social purposes."

Franklin Roosevelt accrued powers that were often likened to those of a European head of state. Though at times he sought to woo Congress, on other occasions he made clear that he intended to impose his will on the legislative branch. Similarly, he waged open war on the third branch of the government when he launched his plan to "pack" the Supreme Court, a venture that led to the so-called "Constitutional Revolution of 1937." From 1937 on, the Court validated every New Deal experiment that came before it and legitimated the growth of the national state. FDR was the first president, too, to win election to a third term, and, for good measure, a fourth term as well. Only death cut short his long reign. To be sure, Roosevelt had a deep respect for democratic institutions, and those who likened him to despots elsewhere in the world were foolish. But there is no mistaking that the office of the president was very different at the end of the age of FDR from what it had been.

In 1935 the editor of the *Washington Post* wrote a friend that "we are going through what really amounts to a revolution," adding:

> Right here on the scene, and devoting my entire energies to follow-ing what happens, I can scarcely keep up with even the major impli-cations of the major legislation which has been passed. The whole Federal administrative setup, all the relations between the Federal Government and the States . . .—all these and many more funda-mentals are being shifted. If you were to come back to the United States now you would probably feel almost a foreigner. I am absolutely certain that with the best will in the world you can have no idea of the magnitude of the changes which have been taking place since I saw you last.

The editor concluded with an observation that suggested a paradox. One consequence of the pace of events, he concluded, was that "the eyes of America have been turned inwards to an extent obviously unprecedented at any time since the Civil War." The New Deal, then, while coming closer to the European image of what a national state should be, at the same time focused the attention of the people on the United States rather than on the world. Roosevelt himself, though fostering programs such as the reciprocal trade agreements, did not think that the solution to how to get the country out of the Depression lay overseas, as he demonstrated in his "bombshell message" to the London Economic Conference. Yet he was far from insular. As he put together his New Deal, he kept his eye on events overseas, in part because his critics were forever drawing unfavorable comparisons between his activities and those pursued abroad.

Conservatives declared that, instead of embarking on an ambitious program of government intervention, FDR should be emulating the cautious British prime minister, Stanley Baldwin. In a fireside chat in the fall of 1934 Roosevelt remarked: "They point to England. They would have you believe that England has made progress out of her depression by a do-nothing policy, by letting nature take her course." He responded:

England has her peculiarities and we have ours, but I do not believe any intelligent observer can accuse England of undue orthodoxy in the present emergency.

Did England let nature take her course? No. Did England hold to the gold standard when her reserves were threatened? No. . . . Is it not a fact that ever since the year 1909, Great Britain in many ways has advanced further along lines of social security than the United States? Is it not a fact that relations between capital and labor on the basis of collective bargaining are much further advanced in Great Britain than the United States?

As this passage intimates, the President harvested ideas from all over the globe. Even before he took office, while he was still governor of New York state, he had sent Frances Perkins to England to study the advantages of unemployment insurance, and, though most of the New Deal derived from native sources, it also owed a not inconsiderable debt to European experience. After he entered the White House, Roosevelt received digests of what Spain had done with reforestation and Sweden with national conservation of private lands, while the unprecedentedly innovative farm program drew, in part, upon a plan from Weimar Germany. The first legislation to impose federal regulation on Wall Street benefited not only from a Belgian law but even more from Britain's Companies Act. When in 1934 he sent Congress a special message outlining his thoughts about a social security program, he pointed out: "This is not an untried experiment. Lessons of experience are available from . . . many Nations of the civilized world."

The Tennessee Valley Authority, called by the press a way to create "a Ruhr for America," patterned its educational system after Danish folk schools; the first American public housing projects were modeled upon Sweden's; the campaign for rural electrification cited the Netherlands; the farm security experiment bore in mind the Irish example; and as New Deal administrators contemplated what to do about unemployed authors, they were advised to put them to work writing "Baedekers," a suggestion that led to the highly regarded state guides of the Federal Writers' Project. When Roosevelt mulled over how to cope with a fractious Supreme Court, he recalled the British precedent of the threat to pack the House of Lords. In sum, Roosevelt, as the historian Daniel Boorstin has written, did "a great deal to break down the old antithesis" between Europe and America. "In many ways, some intended and some accidental, the New Deal helped assimilate the American to the 'European' political experience."

For many of FDR's critics, that was precisely the trouble. In the 1930s Americans of many political persuasions were haunted by the prospect that, as one constituent wrote a Republican Congressman, "all the New Deal vagaries come from Leftist Europe." Herbert Hoover called Roosevelt's edict closing the banks "the American equivalent of the burning of the Reichstag to create 'an emergency,'" and in the debate in Congress on the National Industrial Recovery Act, the liberal Senator from Alabama, Hugo Black, warned: "This bill will transfer the lawmaking power of this nation from Congress to the trade associations. . . . That is exactly what has happened in Italy, and as a result, the legislation passed by the parliamentary body in Italy . . . has reached the vanishing point." On the other hand, an avowedly standpat Congressman from Pennsylvania saw the legislation as the work of nefarious intellectuals, "fresh from the academic cloisters of Columbia University, and with the added inspiration of all they have learned in Moscow." Most Americans, one liberal acknowledged, "regard the intellectual planner as a strange creature. There is something Russian or Italian about him, something that will not fit Toledo, Ohio, or Cairo, Illinois."

These concerns persisted well beyond the First Hundred Days. When in 1935 the Social Security Act came before Congress, a Senator from Delaware declared, with no indication of intended humor: "I fear it may end the progress of a great country and bring its people to the level of the average European." Toward the end of Roosevelt's first term, one critic of the New Deal charged that it was "infected, if not permeated, by Fabian Socialism," while the former Democratic presidential candidate, Al Smith, told a banquet of millionaires that "there is some certain kind of foreign 'ism' crawling over this country." Herbert Hoover said, "If there are any items in the march of European collectivism that the New Deal has not imitated it must have been an oversight," and in the 1936 campaign, FDR's Republican opponent, in referring to John Maynard Keynes, remarked, "Of course, as a foreigner, he found ardent followers in this administration, although he had none in his own government." The dictatorship Roosevelt had established, Republicans declared, "must have made the noses of Herr Hitler, Stalin, Mussolini, and Mustapha Kemal of Turkey turn green with envy," and an aggressively anti–New Deal attorney wound up a recital of evidence of the subversive aspects of government policy by asking "Delano, Quo Vadis?" When in 1940 New York City's mayor, Fiorello La Guardia, was talked about as a possible GOP presidential candidate, one Westerner protested to a Republican editor, "My God, man, do we not have enough European ideas in vogue in Washington today without electing an Italian to the White House?"

Though some saw FDR as an incipient Duce, far more perceived him to be an agent of the Kremlin. The President was "a blood-brother of Lenin," declared H. L. Mencken, who also likened FDR to Stalin: "The smile of the sonofabitch in the White House and the smile of Holy Joe in Moscow have a great deal in common." The New Deal programs "are in the Russian primer," Governor Eugene Talmadge of Georgia solemnly told the New York Board of Trade, and the President "has made the statement that he has read it twelve times." In the 1936 campaign Colonel Robert McCormick's arch conservative Chicago *Tribune* announced falsely, "Moscow Orders Reds in U.S. to Back Roosevelt" and insisted that an FDR triumph would place "Moscow in the White House." The publisher William Randolph Hearst went McCormick one better. He addressed Roosevelt and his advisers as "you and your fellow Communists," while a poem in one of his newspapers started:

> A Red New Deal with a Soviet seal
> endorsed by a Moscow hand,
> The strange result of an alien cult
> In a liberty-loving land.

R. H. S. Crossman, though, in seeking to place the New Deal in a European context, likened FDR to Joseph Chamberlain, a comparison suggesting that the transformation, which seemed so radical in America, left not a few Europeans with a sense of *déjà vu*. One European traveler wrote that "from the point of view of a European [the New Deal] was a very belated imitation of . . . methods which the advanced democracies of the Old World had put through sixty or even seventy years ago." He added:

> The reforms that seemed so startling to the American people . . . represent issues that have been, for such a long time now, part of the social structure of Scandinavia, Holland, Switzerland, Belgium, France, and pre-war Germany, where the first concessions were obtained as far back as under Bismarck, that it is impossible for a European to become excited. Indeed, the comment that rises most naturally to our lips is: "*What*! Do you really mean to say that you haven't got those elementary regulations yet?"

Americans themselves were not altogether unaware of this shortcoming. After listening to the British Labour M.P. Herbert Morrison, the diminutive La Guardia said, "I am little as it is, but it made me feel very small when he was telling me what London did for housing." Morrison, in fact, pointed out that if the American reformers achieved all they hoped for in the 1930s, they would be abreast of the British act of 1890.

Every country, though, must also be looked at from the perspective of its own history, and within the American historical context, the 1930s were a watershed in the evolution of the national state. The three countries that took the biggest strides toward establishing a welfare state in the 1930s were Sweden, New Zealand, and the United States, but the first two built on a firm foundation while the New Deal created an almost entirely new pattern.

Furthermore, in an unexpected turn of events, Roosevelt's program served as a model for European statesmen. In its issue following the 1936 election, the *New York Times* ran a headline, "Roosevelt Towers in the Imagination of Europe." David Lloyd George called his bid for a political renascence a "New Deal," and that same term was applied to Paul Van Zeeland's proposals in Belgium. Claude Fohlen of the Sorbonne has noted that a "source of inspiration" for the *Front Populaire* "was the American experiment of the New Deal." He points out that one of Léon Blum's advisers visited America in 1934 to examine the New Deal and returned to write *La Révolution Roosevelt*; that H. W. Arndt, in *The Economic Lessons of the Nineteen Thirties*, observed that "the Blum experiment . . . was a repetition, in very much less favourable circumstances, of the American experiment of the New Deal"; and that there is "the personal testimony of Léon Blum himself who, in February 1937, before an American audience, paid his tribute to F. D. Roosevelt."

"Blum never concealed the fact that he was inspired by the American New Deal and Roosevelt," his biographer, Joel Colton, has written. "Not socialism, but a 'French New Deal' was his objective, Roosevelt not Marx his guide." On one occasion Blum said of FDR, "Seeing him act, the French democracy has had the feeling that an example was traced for it, and it is this example that we wish to follow, adapting it to the conditions and resources of our country," and when in the fall of 1936 Blum devalued the franc, he justified his action by saying, "What has been most remarkable about the Roosevelt experiment has been the courage of President Roosevelt to try one method after another, to refuse to take a stubborn stand against experience, to try something else until at last he found the method that succeeded." After Roosevelt won reelection in 1936, the U.S. ambassador to France, William Bullitt, wrote him:

> Blum came personally to express his congratulations. This is unheard of. If you could have seen the manner of his coming, it would have done you good. . . . He entered the front door, flung his broad-brimmed black hat to the butler, his coat to the footman, leaped the three steps to the point where I was standing, seized me and kissed me violently! I staggered slightly but having been kissed by Stalin, I am now immune to any form of osculation, and I listened without batting an eye to as genuine an outpouring of enthusiasm as I have ever heard. . . . Blum himself said to me that he felt his position had been greatly strengthened because he is attempting in his way to do what you have done in America.

And when news of FDR's death reached Blum in 1945, he bemoaned "the turn of fate worthy of the climax of an ancient tragedy that carried the President off on the eve of a victory to which he had contributed so much."

Writing in 1965, Andrew Shonfield of Chatham House commented:

The special virtue of the American reformers was their refusal to accept the simple dichotomy between socialism and capitalism which then dominated European political thinking. The New Dealers—or at any rate the leading group which stayed the course and occupied a political position a very little left of centre, close to that of Franklin Roosevelt himself—perceived the future as a new mixture of public and private initiatives, with the public side very much reinforced but still operating in the framework of a predominantly capitalist system.

He observed: "There were many elements in the early New Deal which pointed, at a time when few of the European politicians of either the Right or the Left were ready for it, in the direction which much of Western Europe has taken since the war."

As the leader of the New Deal, as an outspoken critic of dictatorship in the 1930s, and as head of the most powerful Allied government in World War II, Roosevelt, for all his flaws, came to symbolize the instinct for democracy and freedom. Isaiah Berlin was to write:

When I say that some men occupy one's imagination for many years, this is literally true of Mr. Roosevelt's effect on the young men of my own generation in England, and probably in many parts of Europe, and indeed the entire world. If one was young in the thirties and lived in a democracy, then, whatever one's politics, if one had human feelings at all, or the faintest spark of social idealism, or any love of life, one must have felt that all was dark and quiet, a great reaction was abroad, and little stirred, and nothing resisted.

In these "dark and leaden thirties," Sir Isaiah continued, "the only light in the darkness was the administration of Mr. Roosevelt and the New Deal in the United States."

In like manner, in *Christ Stopped at Eboli*, Carlo Levi observed the way in which FDR was regarded by the inhabitants of an obscure Italian village during World War II:

What never failed to strike me most of all—and by now I had been in almost every house—were the eyes of two inseparable guardian angels that looked at me from the wall over the bed. On one side was the black, scowling face, with its large, inhuman eyes, of the Madonna of Viggiano; on the other a colored print of the sparkling eyes, behind gleaming glasses, and the hearty grin of President Roosevelt. I never saw other pictures or images than these: not the King nor the Duce, nor even Garibaldi; no famous Italian of any kind, nor any one of the appropriate saints; only Roosevelt and the Madonna of Viggiano never failed to be present. To see them there, one facing the other, in cheap prints, they seemed the two faces of the power that has divided the universe between them. But here their roles were, quite rightly, reversed. The Madonna appeared to be a fierce, pitiless, mysterious ancient earth goddess, the Saturnian mistress of this world; the President a sort of all-powerful Zeus, the benevolent and smiling master of a higher sphere.

In these years, America also came to seem more "European" in a second respect—in its new consciousness of the reality of class in a nation that had hitherto preferred to believe that class cleavages did not exist in America and that "class" was not a very nice word. When the French in 1936, in negotiating a tripartite stabilization agreement, wanted a joint declaration to say that the pact aimed at improving the standard of living of all social classes, a U.S. official protested, "We can't talk about social classes in America."

But that very year, Franklin Roosevelt campaigned for the presidency with a naked class appeal. The wife of FDR's press secretary, Stephen Early, noted that "the President liked newspaper or magazine jibes that depicted him as a traitor to his own social stratum." When Early sent him a *New Yorker* cartoon showing a cluster of the well-to-do beckoning their fellows from outside the window of a posh Manhattan club with the words, "Come along, we're going to the Trans-Lux to hiss Roosevelt," the President gave a one-word response: "Grand." In the summer of 1936 Roosevelt told visitors, "I still think that fellow from New Zealand was right who said to me, 'The Pullmans are against you but the day-coaches are with you.'"

The historian Donald McCoy has written:

In effect, civil war raged in the United States in 1936, but it was fought within the confines of the electoral system, and with words and paper instead of gunpowder and steel. It was not a case, as it had been in some earlier elections, of one section of the country against other sections, or of country folk against city-dwellers, or even of the young against the old. It was the closest that America had come to class warfare, as labor was arrayed almost solidly against business, as the poor were pitted against the well-fixed, and as the middle class was split against itself.

During the political contest, every measurement showed that the lower down the income scale one went the more likely one was to come upon Democratic voters. One commentator remarked:

> On almost any train leaving Grand Central Station at five o'clock for Westchester County or Connecticut, you would hear Mr. Roosevelt and the New Deal condemned with an intolerance and bitterness that would astonish any reasonable-minded man. If you took a bus to Jersey at the same hour, you would hear fanatical loyalty to the present administration and a blind acceptance of practically all that Mr. Roosevelt was doing.

A pollster found that of 129 homes in a working-class section of Lansing 116 were for FDR, and Republican surveys of factory workers reported as high as 98–2 for the President. "That's the way it was all over the country," a labor union official wrote in his diary. "The rich were for Landon; the poor backed Roosevelt." In her splendid study of working class culture, Lizabeth Cohen has written that in 1936 "Chicago was polarized into political camps with definite class identities." When a soloist at a wealthy parish got up to sing to a congregation of a thousand, she found: "It was a sea of yellow. Everybody was decorated with large yellow Landon sunflower buttons. Just the impact of the thing suddenly made me realize there is such a thing as class distinction in America." In November Alf Landon won overwhelmingly in elite neighborhoods (leading business executives gave Roosevelt only 32 percent of their ballots), but FDR got 82 percent of unskilled and semiskilled labor votes in the Windy City. After 1936 no one could any longer credibly deny the importance of class. In FDR's second term an English visitor who was a guest at the White House reported on a dinner conversation with Roosevelt:

With zest he told me of his train passing through Chicago and how one of his companions called his attention to the office windows thronged with people. At many of the windows, he said, were clerks and stenographers shouting "Hullo, Mr. President"; at others were the directors, silent and glum. With a sudden seriousness and a quick turn towards me, he added, "You couldn't have a better picture of what things are like here at present."

In 1940 a Detroit auto worker, asked to explain why people like him had voted for Roosevelt despite the taboo against a third term for a president, replied, "I'll say it even though it doesn't sound nice. We've grown class conscious." Similarly, a New Haven worker told a sociologist, "Hell, brother, you don't have to look far to know there's a workin' class. We may not say so. But look at what we do. Work. Look at who we run around with and bull with. Workers. Look at where we live. If you can find anybody but workers in my block, I'll eat 'em. . . . Hell's bells, of course, there's a workin' class, and its gettin' more so every day." Nor did an awareness of class distinctions end with Roosevelt. When in 1948 his successor, Harry Truman, ran for president in a campaign that accentuated class differences, a higher percentage of workers voted for his party than had ever been reported for a left-wing party in Europe.

The United States changed in yet a third important respect when it began to take a much more active part in world affairs. To be sure, at the outset Roosevelt actually reinforced the mood of isolationism when, in a spirit of *sauve qui peut*, he embarked upon a course of economic nationalism. Moreover, for some years he had to cater to the isolationists. Yet even when the United States offered the least reason for optimism, many in Europe continued to look toward it, for as H. G. Wells wrote, "America is still what, in the school geographies of my childhood, used to be called so hopefully the New World." And when Roosevelt did begin to seize the initiative in foreign affairs in his second term, he was hailed by anti-fascists in many lands. "The moral leadership of the world may pass from Europe to the United States," declared an English M.P. in the late thirties. "Already my constituents in lonely farms take the trouble to tune in to Mr. Roosevelt." That impression intensified after Hitler invaded Poland in 1939. "Whenever opinion in this country moved an inch, the President took an ell" in speeding aid to the Allies and preparing the nation for intervention, the columnist Joseph Alsop has written. "No wonder, then, that . . . when Britain was all but hanging on the ropes, Winston Churchill ended a dark and terrible accounting to his nation, on a note of hope: 'But westward, look; the land is bright.'"

Under FDR's leadership, the United States, in marked contrast to its behavior after World War I, did much to create the postwar structure of international collaboration in meetings at such American locales as Bretton Woods and Dumbarton Oaks, and made plans to host the first convocation of the United Nations at San Francisco. By the time the United Nations gathered in the city by the bay, Roosevelt had been succeeded as president by Harry Truman who for years had carried around in his wallet a clipping of Tennyson's "Locksley Hall" with its vision of a Parliament of Man, a Federation of the World.

In the postwar age the American republic appeared to be, in the words of the poet Robinson Jeffers, "heavily thickening into empire." When the American GI was discharged, he received a button with a design modeled on a bas-relief from Trajan's Forum in Rome. The United States, which less than a generation before had eschewed almost all responsibility in world affairs, occupied Japan and Germany, enunciated the Truman doctrine, initiated the Marshall Plan, carried out, in collaboration with the British, the Berlin airlift, and agreed—for the first time in 150 years—to overseas commitments in the North Atlantic Treaty. "As far as the Free World was concerned," the British historian H. G. Nicholas wrote of the United States in this period, "her shoulders held the sky suspended." Moreover, there had been a fundamental change of attitude among the American people. As a woman in a small Indiana town told a reporter in 1947, "Talk about Europe is in every household now."

The United States became transformed in a fourth regard when the country, whose army as late as 1939 had ranked eighteenth in the world, emerged from the Second World War and its aftermath as a major military power. During World War II millions of American men and women saw service in the most remote parts of the globe—from the Aleutians to Tunisia to New Guinea; what would later be called the "military-industrial complex" took shape; and in Virginia the government erected a huge five-sided building called the Pentagon. (People wondered what possible use that building would be after the war, but it was explained that it could be used then to store records.) In the closing months of the war, the atomic bomb was detonated in the New Mexico desert, and the United States entered the Cold War years with a nuclear arsenal.

In this period, the United States changed, too, in a final respect; it became a more cosmopolitan society. In the New Deal years, the seats of power were no longer monopolized by white Anglo-Saxon Protestants. Commentators made much of the closeness to FDR of Jews such as his counselor and subsequently Supreme Court Justice Felix Frankfurter and his chief speechwriter Samuel Rosenman. They also took note that Roosevelt named so many Catholics to high places and that the head of the Democratic party was an Irish Catholic, Jim Farley. Blacks were not nearly as prominent, but they were more conspicuous than ever before and some, such as Mary McLeod Bethune, influenced government policy.

During the 1930s, largely as a reaction against Nazi doctrine, "a major assault on xenophobic and racist traditions" took place, the historian Richard Weiss has noted. "The New Deal," declared FDR's Commissioner of Immigration, "means a more sympathetic and humane consideration" of the problems of the alien "and a spirit of friendliness and helpfulness rather than one of antagonism and persecution." When Roosevelt allotted money to the Office of Education for radio programs, he insisted that some of it go to broadcasts that would show the "rich heritages that have come to us through the many races and nationalities which make up our population," and when during World War II on a visit to the United States Churchill envisioned an "all conquering alliance of the English speaking peoples," the President told him that Americans did not think of themselves simply as Anglo-Saxons.

A more cosmopolitan spirit could especially be discerned in the universe of intellectuals, in no small part because of the influx of European refugees from fascism. The failure of the United States to do far more than it did to offer a haven, especially to Jews, is a shameful chapter in my country's history. The relatively little it did do, though, brought disproportionately rich rewards. As a German writer has noted, "More than a thousand refugee scholars—besides hundreds of other intellectuals—came across the Atlantic from Germany and Austria in these years and fertilized nearly all of the American academic disciplines."

The migration had an incalculable impact on psychoanalysis, on physics, on the concert hall, on painting, on countless other realms. To reckon the influence on the social sciences, one need only recall the names of certain scholars—the economist Joseph Schumpeter, the sociologist Paul Lazarsfeld, the theorist Hannah Arendt, the psychologist Bruno Bettelheim—and to grasp what the migration meant to symphony music one has merely to imagine, in a concert hall in any one of a number of American cities, the house lights darkening and, emerging from the wings, baton in hand, Bruno Walter or Pierre Monteux, Otto Klemperer or

George Szell. If, in the manner of the American documentary film makers of the 1930s reciting the names of rivers, one were to make a tone poem with a libretto composed of nothing save the names of the émigrés—Mies van der Rohe, Vladimir Nabokov, Walter Gropius, Béla Bartok, Artur Schnabel, Billy Wilder, Igor Stravinsky, Kurt Weill, Paul Tillich, Josef Albers, Theodor Adorno, Gaetano Salvemini, Guiseppe Borgese—the resonance would be magisterial.

Given a second chance, the refugees sought, sometimes against heavy odds, to replicate the world they had known. If Manhattan was not quite the same as their favorite quarter in the old country, said one of them, still "one could live like a Berliner there." The historian Anthony Heilbut has written, "The same political and literary issues that aroused the cabaret customers of Berlin and Paris survived transportation to the Deauville Restaurant on East Seventy-third Street in New York or the Eclair on West Seventy-second." Another historian has even claimed that, thanks to the influence of newcomers such as the theater director Erwin Piscator, New York experienced "a Berlinization of sensibility." Not all the lines of force, however, moved in one direction. It was during his brief sojourn in America that Piet Mondrian painted "Broadway Boogie-Woogie." Other migrants preferred California, though Toscanini dismissed it as "Italy without soul," and Thomas Mann wrote of Pacific Palisades: "Here everything blooms in violet and grape colors that look rather made of paper. The oleander . . . blooms very beautifully. Only I have suspicion that it may do so all year round."

As a consequence of émigré influence and other experiences, the sensibility of America in 1950 differed markedly from that in 1929, or even in the early thirties. Americans were much less disposed to look inward and backward, much more inclined to look outward and forward. In the postwar years, Thomas Hart Benton, who epitomized the more nativistic attitude of an earlier day, said, "Wood, Curry, and I found the bottom knocked out from under us," while Jackson Pollock, who had been Benton's pupil, declared, "The idea of an isolated American painting seems absurd to me just as the idea of creating a purely American mathematics or physics would seem absurd."

To foreign observers, the dimensions of change were unmistakable. In contrasting the situation in the post–New Deal era with that when he visited the United States in the twenties, Sir Denis Brogan later wrote:

Think of how little (to put it kindly) President Lowell of Harvard contributed to the public enlightenment! Try to recall the really stifling complacency of Harvard, the House of Morgan, the press, the pulpit in 1925! Even the greatest political figures of that time, like Al Smith, were parochial.

. . . For millions of Americans who were helpless in face of the great concentrations of economic power which dominated a state like Pennsylvania in 1926, . . . the New Deal, the labor union have been liberating forces. If there is more conflict than there was in Coolidge's time, it is because deeper things are being debated, greater issues are involved, and things taken for granted in 1925 are disputed today.

This concatenation of events would appear to compel us to one irresistible conclusion—that the pesky notion of American exceptionalism had finally met its end. But, as Malcolm Bradbury has said of American innocence, its death has been pronounced more than once. And if American innocence did, at long last, succumb, it is less clear that, despite all these changes, the same can be said, even at the end of the age of Roosevelt, for American exceptionalism. As late as 1944 the *Saturday Evening Post* was still saying, "We Americans can boast that we are not as other men are." There was now what could be called "the State" in America, but still something short of what Europeans meant by the State. Andrew Shonfield has characterized the United States in the post-Roosevelt era as "the outstanding laggard in the general movement of the Western world towards the eager acceptance of a vastly enlarged role for the central government in economic affairs." Authority was now much more concentrated in Washington, but federalism continued to be relevant. The United States was now a world power, but the tug of the idea of a separate American destiny had not altogether receded. The nation was now much more cosmopolitan, but provincialism persisted. America was, then, both much more of the world than it had been but not yet wholly of the world, and the perennially controverted question of the nature of American exceptionalism would not cease to command attention.

Notes

ONE   Franklin D. Roosevelt: The First Modern President

1. Fred I. Greenstein, "Change and Continuity in the Modern Presidency," in Anthony King, ed., *The New American Political System* (Washington, D. C.: American Enterprise Institute for Public Policy Research, 1978), p. 45; Robert Murray and Tim H. Blessing, "The Presidential Performance Study: A Progress Report," *Journal of American History* 70 (December 1983): 542.
2. Joseph E. Kallenbach, *The American Chief Executive: The Presidency and the Governorship* (New York: Harper and Row, 1966), p. 266; Carl T. Keller to Albert G. Keller, March 27, 1937, Sumner-Keller MSS, Yale University, New Haven, Ct., Box 21. In the same month a former Hoover official high in the ranks of the Republican party recorded in his diary: "A congressman said to me this afternoon, 'There is just one thing now, as I see it, that will save this country from a major disaster, and that is the death of the President and [John L.] Lewis and Miss [Frances] Perkins. I consider myself a Christian and I am a Christian but I feel so strongly for the nation that if I did not have a wife and children and grandchildren who would feel themselves disgraced I should really make it my business to shoot as large a proportion of the three as possible, beginning of course, with the President.'" William R. Castle Diary, March 19, 1937, Castle MSS, Houghton Library, Harvard University, Cambridge, Mass.
3. George Wolfskill and John A. Hudson, *All But the People: Franklin D. Roosevelt and His Critics, 1933–1939* (New York: Macmillan, 1969), p. 16; William Manchester, *The Glory and the Dream: A Narrative History of America, 1932–1972* (Boston: Little, Brown, 1974), p. 166; Caroline Bird, *Invisible Scar* (New York: McKay, 1966), p. 219; Richard Bissell, "Carefree Harvard Days of Three Presidents," *McCall's* 90 (October 1962): 162. At a memorial service for FDR in 1945, a schoolteacher allegedly said, "For the first time in twelve years I can raise my hand and pledge allegiance to the flag." Clipping from *Seattle Post-Intelligencer*, April 17, 1945, Naomi Achenbach Benson MSS, University of Washington, Seattle, Wash., Box 27.
4. Wolfskill and Hudson, *All But the People*, pp. 123, 15, 16, 14, 18.

5. James MacGregor Burns, *Roosevelt: The Lion and the Fox* (New York: Harcourt Brace Jovanovich, 1956), p. 144; Jonathan Daniels, *The Time Between the Wars: Armistice to Pearl Harbor* (Garden City, N.Y.: Doubleday, 1966), p. 272; Wolfskill and Hudson, *All But the People*, p. 174. In 1944 Clare Boothe Luce called Roosevelt "the only American President who ever lied us into war because he did not have the political courage to lead us into it." Thomas A. Bailey, *Presidential Greatness: The Image and the Man from George Washington to the Present* (New York: Appleton-Century, 1966), p. 155.

6. Barton J. Bernstein, "The New Deal: The Conservative Achievements of Liberal Reform," in *Towards a New Past: Dissenting Essays in American History* (New York: Pantheon, 1968), p. 265; Allan Nevins, "The Place of Franklin D. Roosevelt in History," *American Heritage* 17 (June 1966): 15.

7. Noel F. Busch, quoted in Torbjørn Sirevåg, "Rooseveltian Ideas and the 1937 Court Fight: A Neglected Factor," *Historian* 33 (August 1971): 584; C. Herman Pritchett, *The Roosevelt Court: A Study in Judicial Politics and Values, 1937–1947* (New York: Macmillan, 1948), p. 265.

8. Raymond Moley, *After Seven Years* (New York: Harper, 1939), pp. 369–70; Rexford Guy Tugwell, *The Brains Trust* (New York: Viking, 1968), pp. xxi-xxii; Tugwell, "The New Deal: The Rise of Business," part 2, *Western Political Quarterly* 5 (September 1952): 503; Bernard Sternsher, "Tugwell's Appraisal of F.D.R.," *Western Political Quarterly* 15 (March 1962): 67–79.

9. Thomas Paterson, *On Every Front: The Making of the Cold War* (New York: Norton, 1979), p. 31. See also Ralph B. Levering, *The Cold War, 1945–1972* (Arlington Heights, Ill.: Harlan Davidson, 1982), p. 15.

10. Robert A. Divine, *Roosevelt and World War II* (Baltimore: The Johns Hopkins Press, 1969), p. 97. See also Robert Dallek, *Franklin D. Roosevelt and American Foreign Policy, 1932–1945* (New York: Oxford University Press, 1979), p. 537. For a more critical estimate, see Gaddis Smith, *American Diplomacy During the Second World War, 1941–1945* (New York: Wiley, 1965), pp. 9–10.

11. Foster Rhea Dulles, *America's Rise to World Power, 1898–1954* (New York: Harper, 1955), p. 222; George F. Will, "The Splendid Legacy of FDR," *Newsweek*, February 1, 1982, p. 78.

12. Arnold J. Toynbee in *Survey of International Affairs 1931* (London: Oxford University Press, 1932), p. 1. See also the trenchant observations in Robert H. Ferrell, *American Diplomacy in the Great Depression: Hoover-Stimson Foreign Policy, 1929–1933* (New Haven: Yale University Press, 1957), pp. 1–2.

13. W. Cameron Forbes, Diary, December 31, 1931, Forbes MSS, Houghton Library; Manchester, *Glory and the Dream*, p. 31.

14. Robert M. Collins, *The Business Response to Keynes, 1929–1964* (New York: Columbia University Press, 1981), p. 28. See also George Bernard Shaw, *The Political Madhouse in America and Nearer Home* (London: Constable,

1933), p. 27; Louis Taber, Columbia Oral History Collection (COHC), Butler Library, Columbia University, p. 259; Willis Van Devanter to Dennis Flynn, January 18, 1933, Van Devanter MSS, Library of Congress (LC), vol. 46; James Grafton Rogers to Felix Frankfurter, February 1, 1933, Frankfurter MSS, LC, Box 97.

15. *Sales Management*, March 15, 1933, p. 244; Donald Hiss, quoted in Katie Louchheim, ed., *The Making of the New Deal: The Insiders Speak* (Cambridge, Mass.: Harvard University Press, 1983), pp. 41–42; Walter Millis, "The Roosevelt Revolution," *Virginia Quarterly Review* 9 (October 1933): 481. See also "Hope in the Middle West," *Spectator*, July 14, 1933, p. 44; Emanuel Celler, *You Never Leave Brooklyn: The Autobiography of Emanuel Celler* (New York: J. Day, 1953), pp. 11–12; Charles H. Trout, *Boston, the Great Depression, and the New Deal* (New York: Oxford University Press, 1977), pp. 124–27.

16. Benjamin D. Rhodes, "Governor Alfred M. Landon of Kansas and the Election of 1936 as Viewed from the British Embassy at Washington," *Midwest Review* 6 (Spring 1984): 27; Nicholas Roosevelt to Mrs. J. West Roosevelt, March 22, 1933, Nicholas Roosevelt MSS, Syracuse University, Syracuse, N.Y., ser. 1, Box 7; Hiram Johnson to Katherine Edson, April 20, 1933, Edson MSS, University of California, Los Angeles, Box 3. See also Hiram Johnson to J. Earl Langdon, March 15, 1933, Johnson MSS, Bancroft Library, University of California, Berkeley, Cal.

17. H. G. L., "We Have a Leader," *Forum* 89 (April 1933): 193. See also James R. Garfield MS. Diary, 1933, Garfield MSS, LC; John W. McCormack, Kennedy Library Oral History, John F. Kennedy Library, Boston, Mass.; Charles T. Hallinan, "Roosevelt as Europe Sees Him," *Forum*, 89 (June 1933), 348.

18. T. V. Smith, "The New Deal as a Cultural Phenomenon," in F. S. C. Northrop, ed., *Ideological Differences and World Order: Studies in the Philosophy and Science of the World's Cultures* (New Haven: Yale University Press, 1949), p. 224; Rita Halle Kleeman, *Gracious Lady: The Life of Sara Delano Roosevelt* (New York: D. Appleton-Century, 1935), p. 170; David Potter, "Sketches for the Roosevelt Portrait," *Yale Review*, n.s., 39 (September 1949): 46. See also Frances Perkins COHC, 7: 556–557. In making his comment on FDR, T. V. Smith may have been thinking of the words of Mr. Emerson to Lucy Honeychurch: "By the side of the everlasting Why there is a Yes. . . ." E. M. Forster, *A Room With a View* (London: Edward Arnold, 1977, originally published 1907), p. 49.

19. Richard E. Neustadt, *Presidential Power: The Politics of Leadership from FDR to Carter* (New York: Wiley, 1980), p. 119. See also Thomas H. Greer, *What Roosevelt Thought: The Social and Political Ideas of Franklin D. Roosevelt* (East Lansing, Mich.: Michigan State University Press, 1958), p. 88.

20. Clinton L. Rossiter, *The American Presidency* (New York: Harcourt, Brace, 1960), p. 145.

21. John Gunther, *Roosevelt in Retrospect: A Profile in History* (New York: Harper, 1950), p. 33; T. R. B., "Washington Notes," *New Republic*, November 1, 1933, p. 332; *Time*, June 10, 1940, p. 17.
22. Will, "Splendid Legacy," p. 78.
23. Eleanor Roosevelt, *This I Remember* (New York: Harper, 1949), pp. 69–70. One of his biographers believes that "the most potent of clues to the innermost workings of his psyche" is "the fact that Franklin Roosevelt was a man of great and evidently remarkably simple religious faith" with "the inward certainty that he was a chosen one of the Almighty, his career a role assigned him by the Author of the Universe." Kenneth S. Davis, "FDR as a Biographer's Problem," *Key Reporter* 50 (Autumn 1984): 5.
24. Frank Freidel, *Franklin D. Roosevelt: The Apprenticeship* (Boston: Little, Brown, 1952), p. 5; Henry Fairlie, "The Voice of Hope," *New Republic*, January 27, 1982, p. 17.
25. Frances Perkins, *The Roosevelt I Knew* (New York: Viking, 1946), p. 164.
26. *The Public Papers and Addresses of Franklin D. Roosevelt*, Samuel I. Rosenman, ed., 13 vols. (New York: Random House, Macmillan, Harper, 1938–50), 7: 302.
27. Rexford G. Tugwell, "The Experimental Roosevelt," *Political Quarterly* 21 (July–September 1950): 262.
28. Irving Bernstein, *A Caring Society: The New Deal, the Worker, and the Great Depression: A History of the American Worker, 1933–1941* (Boston: Houghton Mifflin, 1985), p. 307. See also Fillmore H. Sanford, "Leadership Identification and Acceptance," in Harold Guetzkow, ed., *Groups, Leadership and Men: Research in Human Relations* (Pittsburgh: Carnegie Press, 1951), pp. 173–74.
29. Edward S. Corwin, *The President, Office and Powers, 1787–1957: History and Analysis of Practice and Opinion* (New York: New York University Press, 1957), p. 273; John Gunther, *Roosevelt in Retrospect* (New York: Harper, 1950), p. 135; *Time*, January 15, 1934, p. 13.
30. Leo C. Rosten, *The Washington Correspondents* (New York: Harcourt, Brace, 1937), p. 49. Although Roosevelt gave the impression of nonchalance at his first press conference, Jimmie Byrnes, the South Carolina Senator, noted afterward that "his hand was trembling and he was wet with perspiration." The President himself said that before long he was sure to make some damaging slip. Yet Byrnes added: "I saw he liked the conference and found it immensely stimulating. I think that he found in these verbal challenges a substitute for the competitive sports in which he could no longer take part." James F. Byrnes, *All in One Lifetime* (New York: Harper, 1958), p. 74.
31. John L. Blair, "The Clark-Coolidge Correspondence and the Election of 1932," *Vermont History* 34 (April 1966): 111; Rosten, *Washington Correspondents*, pp. 49–50. The correspondent was Henry M. Hyde of the *Baltimore Evening Sun*. Two days earlier, Hyde had noted in his diary:

"Atmosphere of White House loses all formality; becomes easy and friendly." Henry Morrow Hyde MS. Diary, March 6, 1933, Hyde MSS, University of Virginia, Charlottesville, Va.

32. For his experience on the *Crimson*, see Kenneth S. Davis, *FDR: The Beckoning of Destiny, 1882–1928; A History* (New York: Putnam, 1972), pp. 144–148. Reporters did not always agree on the merits of FDR's methods. "Sometimes the 'off-the-record' material is helpful; often it is an embarrassment," wrote a correspondent who admired FDR's press conferences. "Many newspaper writers covering the White House would prefer that this relic of Mr. Roosevelt's days as Governor of New York, when he had a small and intimate audience, were done away with." Charles W. B. Hurd, "President and Press: A Unique Forum," *New York Times Magazine*, June 9, 1935, p. 3. But others valued off-the-record information. On one occasion, a newspaperman said, "Off the record, Mr. President, can you fill us in on what the situation is on that? Personally I am as ignorant as a nincompoop of it all, and if I could get a little background or off the record. . . . On inflation and deflation of the dollar and so forth." Elmer E. Cornwell, Jr., *Presidential Leadership of Public Opinion* (Bloomington, Ind.: Indiana University Press, 1965), p. 151.

33. M. L. Stein, *When Presidents Meet the Press* (New York: Messner, 1969), p. 86. Reporters learned to study FDR's mood. One of them recalled: "If the cigarette in his holder was pointed toward the ceiling and his head was thrown back, the news would be good, from Roosevelt's standpoint. If he was hunched over his desk and the cigarette pointed downward, look out, somebody was going to get hell." Jack Bell, *The Johnson Treatment: How Lyndon Johnson Took Over the Presidency and Made It His Own* (New York: Harper and Row, 1965), p. 144.

34. Raymond Brandt, quoted in Joseph A. Califano, Jr., *A Presidential Nation* (New York: Norton, 1975), p. 55; Graham J. White, *FDR and the Press* (Chicago: University of Chicago Press, 1979), p. 12.

35. Thomas L. Stokes, *Chip off My Shoulder* (Princeton, N. J.: Princeton University Press, 1940), p. 367; John Dos Passos, "Washington: The Big Tent," *New Republic*, March 14, 1934, p. 123. See also Mark Sullivan to Ray Lyman Wilbur, April 3, 1933, Wilbur MSS, Stanford University Library; Emile Schreiber, "A travers l'Amérique de 1934," *L'Illustration*, August 18, 1934, pp. 504–9.

36. *Literary Digest*, January 5, 1935, p. 6; Raymond Clapper, "Why Reporters Like Roosevelt," *Review of Reviews and World's Work*, June 1934, pp. 15, 17. See also Graham J. White, *FDR and the Press* (Chicago: University of Chicago Press, 1979).

37. Erwin D. Canham, "Democracy's Fifth Wheel," *Literary Digest*, January 5, 1935, p. 6; Douglass Cater, *The Fourth Branch of Government* (Boston: Houghton Mifflin, 1959), pp. 7–17; Elmer E. Cornwell, Jr., "The

Presidential Press Conference: A Study in Institutionalization," *Midwest Journal of Political Science* 4 (November 1960): 370–89.

38. *St. Louis Post-Dispatch*, May 31, 1935; Baltimore *Evening Sun*, May 31, 1935; *Washington Post*, June 1, 2, 1935; James T. Williams to his father, May 31, 1935, Williams MSS, University of South Carolina, Columbia, S. C.; Edward Keating MS. Diary, May 31, 1935, Keating MSS, University of Colorado.

39. Perkins, *The Roosevelt I Knew*, p. 72; Robert West, *The Rape of Radio* (New York: Rodin, 1941), pp. 421–22; David Halberstam, *The Powers That Be* (New York: Knopf, 1979), p. 15.

40. Wilfred E. Binkley, *President and Congress* (New York: Knopf, 1947), pp. 274–75; William J. Hopkins, Kennedy Library Oral History, p. 6. At a dinner party Roosevelt boasted, "Hoover got 400 letters a day. I get 4000"; Dorothy Thompson MS. Diary, 1936, Thompson MSS, Syracuse University.

41. Ira R. T. Smith with Joe Alex Morris, *"Dear Mr. President . . .": The Story of Fifty Years in the White House Mail Room* (New York: Julian Messner, 1949), p. 156. Roosevelt, noted a veteran newspaperman, could not hope to read all the bales of letters of some one hundred each, "but frequently he would order half a dozen bundles sent to his desk. Thus he kept a highly sensitive and extraordinarily long index finger on the public pulse." Charles Hurd, *The White House, a Biography: The Story of the House, Its Occupants, Its Place in American History* (New York: Harper, 1940), p. 306.

42. John C. Donovan, *The Politics of Poverty* (New York: Pegasus, 1967), p. 18; John H. Clarke to Franklin D. Roosevelt, September 18, 1937, Clarke MSS, Western Reserve Historical Society, Cleveland, Ohio, file 2, folder 17.

43. Alf M. Landon to Roy M. Howard, June 13, 1938, Landon MSS, Kansas State Historical Society, Topeka, Kans., Box 89; Edward Keating MS. Diary, November 15, 1936; clipping from Pittsburgh *Press*, June 7, 1936, Mary Van Kleeck MSS, Smith College, Northampton, Mass., Box 71.

44. Bernard F. Donahoe, *Private Plans and Public Dangers: The Story of FDR's Third Nomination* (Notre Dame, Ind.: University of Notre Dame Press, 1965), pp. 6, 8; Grace Abbott, "My Vote Goes to President Roosevelt," typescript, Abbott MSS, University of Chicago Library, Chicago, Ill.

45. E. Pendleton Herring, "First Session of the 73rd Congress," *American Political Science Review* 27 (February 1934): 82.

46. Robert Rienow and Leona Train Rienow, *The Lonely Quest: The Evolution of Presidential Leadership* (New York: Follett, 1966), pp. 186–87; Arthur M. Schlesinger, Jr., *The Coming of the New Deal* (Boston: Houghton Mifflin, 1959), p. 557.

47. Godfrey Hodgson, *All Things to All Men: The False Promise of the Modern American Presidency* (New York: Simon and Schuster, 1980), p. 60.

48. Wilfred E. Binkley, *The Man in the White House: His Powers and Duties* (Baltimore: Johns Hopkins Press, 1959), p. 180; Harold M. Barger, *The*

Impossible Presidency: Illusions and Realities of Executive Power (Glenview, Ill.: Scott, Foresman, 1984), p. 101.

49. Erwin C. Hargrove, *The Power of the Modern Presidency* (Philadelphia: Temple University Press, 1974), p. 53.

50. George C. Robinson, "The Veto Record of Franklin D. Roosevelt," *American Political Science Review* 36 (February 1942): 76; Samuel and Dorothy Rosenman, *Presidential Style: Some Giants and a Pygmy in the White House* (New York: Harper and Row, 1975), pp. 345–46; George W. Robinson, "Alben Barkley and the 1944 Tax Veto," *Register of the Kentucky Historical Society* 67 (1969): 197–210; Polly Ann Davis, "Alben W. Barkley's Public Career in 1944," *Filson Club Quarterly* 51 (April 1977): 144; Leon Henderson, Diary Notes, February 24, 1944, Henderson MSS, Franklin D. Roosevelt Library (FDRL), Hyde Park, N.Y., Box 36; Marcus Cunliffe, *American Presidents and the Presidency* (New York: American Heritage, 1972), p. 267.

51. Raymond Clapper, "Resentment Against the Supreme Court," *Review of Reviews* 95 (January 1937): 38; Representative Charles Gifford in *Congressional Record*, 78th Cong., 1st sess., p. 56.

52. James T. Patterson, "American Politics: The Bursts of Reform, 1930s to 1970s," in Patterson, ed., *Paths to the Present: Interpretive Essays on American History Since 1930* (Minneapolis: Burgess, 1975), pp. 62–63; Bruce Collins, "Federal Power as Contemporary American Dilemma," in Rhodri Jeffreys-Jones and Bruce Collins, eds., *The Growth of Federal Power in American History* (De Kalb, Ill.: Northern Illinois University Press, 1983), p. xiv; V. O. Key, Jr., *The Responsible Electorate* (Cambridge, Mass.: Harvard University Press, 1966), p. 31; Morris Sheppard to H. B. Prother, [misdated] January 3, 1937 [1938], Box 118, Sheppard MSS, University of Texas, Austin, Tex.; "Richard Russell: Georgia Grant," typescript of Cox Broadcasting Corporation broadcast, February 12, 1970, Richard B. Russell MSS, University of Georgia, Athens, Ga.

53. *Public Papers*, 13: 40–41.

54. Ralph F. De Bedts, *The New Deal's SEC: The Formative Years* (New York: Columbia University Press, 1964), pp. 195, 205.

55. Clipping from Detroit *News*, November 7, 1936, Blair Moody Scrapbooks, Moody MSS, Michigan Historical Collections, University of Michigan. One analyst called him the country's "chief economic engineer." Sidney Hyman, *The American President* (New York: Harper, 1954), pp. 263–64.

56. James MacGregor Burns, *Presidential Government: The Crucible of Leadership* (Boston: Houghton Mifflin, 1966), p. 200.

57. William E. Leuchtenburg, "Franklin D. Roosevelt's Supreme Court 'Packing' Plan," in Harold M. Hollingsworth and William F. Holmes, eds., *Essays on the New Deal* (Austin, Tex.: University of Texas Press, 1969); Bernard Schwartz, *The Supreme Court: Constitutional Revolution in*

Retrospect (New York: Ronald Press, 1957), p. 389; Marriner S. Eccles, *Beckoning Frontiers* (New York: Knopf, 1951), p. 336.

58. Eccles, *Beckoning Frontiers*, p. 336.

59. Schlesinger, *Coming of the New Deal*, pp. 534–35.

60. Ibid., p. 528. See also Neustadt, *Presidential Power*, pp. 156–58.

61. Barger, *Impossible Presidency*, p. 205; Neustadt, *Presidential Power*, pp. 115–16.

62. Burns, *Presidential Government*, p. 152; Grant McConnell, *The Modern Presidency*, 2d ed. (New York: St. Martin's, 1976), p. 96; Hodgson, *All Things to All Men*, pp. 58–59. One observer noted "national figures using the same washroom, shoulder to shoulder, and pretending not to see each other." Russell Lord, quoted in Stephen Hess, *Organizing the Presidency* (Washington, D. C.: Brookings Institution, 1976), p. 30.

63. Stanley High MS. Diary, October 19, 20, 1936, High MSS, FDRL.

64. Richard E. Neustadt, "Approaches to Staffing the Presidency: Notes on FDR and JFK," *American Political Science Review* 57 (December 1963): 855; Arthur M. Schlesinger, Jr., *The Imperial Presidency* (Boston: Houghton Mifflin, 1973), p. 409; Louchheim, *Making of the New Deal*, p. 225

65. Hugh S. Johnson, "Profile of a President," *Ladies Home Journal* 55 (March 1938): 103; Jack Bell, *The Presidency: Office of Power* (Boston: Allyn and Bacon, 1967), p. 26.

66. Raymond Moley, *After Seven Years* (New York: Harper, 1939), pp. 128–30.

67. Otis L. Graham, Jr., *Toward a Planned Society: From Roosevelt to Nixon* (New York: Oxford University Press, 1976), p. 50; Lester G. Seligman and Elmer E. Cornwell, Jr., *New Deal Mosaic: Roosevelt Confers with His National Emergency Council, 1933–1936* (Eugene, Ore.: University of Oregon Books, 1965); Peri E. Arnold, *Making the Managerial Presidency: Comprehensive Reorganization Planning, 1905–1980* (Princeton, N. J.: Princeton University Press, 1986); Marion Clawson, *New Deal Planning: The National Resources Planning Board* (Baltimore: Johns Hopkins University Press, 1981); Lester G. Seligman, "Developments in the Presidency and the Conception of Political Leadership," *American Sociological Review* 20 (December 1955): 706–12.

68. Kallenbach, *American Chief Executive*, p. 256; Luther Gulick, quoted in Rossiter, *American Presidency*, p. 129; Burns, *Presidential Government*, p. 73. See also Barry D. Karl, *Executive Reorganization and Reform in the New Deal* (Cambridge, Mass.: Harvard University Press, 1966).

69. Robert E. Sherwood, *Roosevelt and Hopkins: An Intimate History* (New York: Harper, 1948), pp. 72–73; see also Charles E. Jacob, *Leadership in the New Deal: The Administrative Challenge* (Englewood Cliffs, N.J.: Prentice-Hall, 1967), pp. 33–34.

70. Hugh Gregory Gallagher, *FDR's Splendid Deception* (New York: Dodd Mead, 1985), p. 160. Stanley High, "The White House is Calling," *Harper's*

175 (November 1937): 585; Moley, *After Seven Years*, p. 393. See, too, Stuart Gerry Brown, *The American Presidency: Leadership, Partisanship, and Popularity* (New York: Macmillan, 1966), p. 46.

71. Burns, *Roosevelt: The Lion and the Fox* p. 155; J. David Stern COHC; George Creel, *Rebel at Large: Recollections of Fifty Crowded Years* (New York: G. P. Putnam's Sons, 1947), p. 293; *Time*, June 10, 1940, p. 17; George W. Anderson to Louis D. Brandeis, February 12, 1937, Brandeis MSS, University of Louisville Law Library, Louisville, Ky., Supreme Court Box 19, folder 1. See also Raymond Clapper MS. Diary, May 10, 1938; Ellen S. Woodward MSS, Mississippi Department of Archives and History, Jackson, Miss., Box 8.

72. Speech by U.S. Senator Alan Cranston, Commonwealth Club, San Francisco, June 15, 1973. The ensuing discussion draws upon my reply to Cranston, published as an op ed piece in the Los Angeles *Times*, September 18, 1973.

73. Raymond Price, *With Nixon* (New York: Viking, 1977), pp. 228–29, 235, 246, 285–86. Maurice Stans has commented: "New developments of recent years are making some of Nixon's actions less discreditable than they were once made to appear. In the House Judiciary hearings in 1974 there was strong contention that he had misused the forces of government agencies for political purposes, by getting them to spy on and punish enemies of his regime, and this became one of the counts of impeachment. It was not publicly known then, but subsequent revelations have established, that Presidential use of the FBI, the CIA, the IRS, and the Postal Service to exercise surveillance over radical and revolutionary groups dangerous to the nation extended at least as far back as Franklin D. Roosevelt. Employing these agencies to target political adversaries was no less common, and in some instances much more frequent and intensive. As author M. Stanton Evans has written, 'In the light of these disclosures it is plain that Nixon, whatever his sins, was hopelessly outclassed in public infamy by the likes of Franklin Roosevelt, John Kennedy, and Lyndon Johnson. Yet it was Nixon who caught and continues to catch the brickbats, while these Democratic heroes have somehow avoided media censure.'" Maurice Stans, *The Terrors of Justice: The Untold Side of Watergate* (New York: Everest, 1978), pp. 455–56.

74. In 1948 one former FDR cabinet official wrote to another: "I suppose Roosevelt will go down in history a great man, certainly he was a ruthless politician. With it all, he was most attractive personally. In the last analysis, he must have considered himself especially annointed [sic]. In my view, when he found what he could do with the radio, he made up his mind to stay President as long as he lived, if possible, and to take such course from time to time, as seemed most likely to achieve this objective." Jesse H. Jones to James A. Farley, March 10, 1948, Box 7, Jones MSS, LC.

75. Binkley, *President and Congress*, p. 238; Herman Finer, *The Presidency: Crisis and Regeneration, an Essay in Possibilities* (Chicago: University of Chicago Press, 1960), p. 78.

76. Edwin S. Corwin and Louis Koenig, *The Presidency Today* (New York: New York University Press, 1956), p. 34; Arthur M. Schlesinger, Jr., "Congress and the Making of American Foreign Policy," in Rexford G. Tugwell and Thomas E. Cronin, eds., *The Presidency Reappraised* (New York: Praeger, 1974), pp. 94–95.

77. Binkley, *Man in the White House*, p. 237; *Congressional Record*, 77th Cong., 2d sess., p. 7044; Cunliffe, *American Presidents*, p. 267.

78. Quoted in Richard Polenberg, *Reorganizing Roosevelt's Government: The Controversy Over Executive Reorganization, 1936–1939* (Cambridge, Mass.: Harvard University Press, 1966), p. 27.

79. Robert S. McElvaine, *The Great Depression: America, 1929–1941* (New York: Times Books, 1984), pp. 119–20.

80. Emmet Hughes, *The Living Presidency: The Resources and the Dilemmas of the American Presidential Office* (Baltimore: Coward, McCann, and Geoghegan, 1973), pp. 140–41; Binkley, *President and Congress*, pp. 248–51.

81. Rossiter, *American Presidency*, pp. 149–50.

82. Ibid., p. 152. Another prominent British official recorded similar thoughts: "On the midnight news last night I hear that Roosevelt is dead. Parliament to-day will adjourn. He should have lived even a few weeks longer, to see the full light of victory in Europe. But he has seen the dawn and, but for him, there would have been no dawn. Only a long darkness for us all; an eternal night for most of us." Hugh Dalton MS. Diary, April 13, 1945, Dalton MSS, British Library of Political and Economic Science, London School of Economics and Political Science, London, Eng.

83. Schlesinger, *Imperial Presidency*, p. 409.

84. McConnell, *Modern Presidency*, p. 15; Corwin and Koenig, *Presidency Today*, pp. 86–87; E. S. Corwin, "Some Aspects of the Presidency," *Annals* 218 (November 1941): 128. Corwin did, though, see two novel aspects: "Roosevelt's consistent championship of the demands of certain groups, especially Agriculture and Labor," and "the dissolving effect" of FDR's legislation on the principles of separation of powers and dual federalism.

85. Forty years later the vitriolic columnist Westbrook Pegler wrote, "It is regrettable that Giuseppe Zangara hit the wrong man when he shot at Roosevelt in Miami." Quoted in Cunliffe, *American Presidents*, p. 147.

86. Greenstein, "Change and Continuity," p. 48. See also Otis L. Graham, Jr., "1933: What Would the 1930s Have Been Like without Franklin Roosevelt?" in Morton Borden and Otis L. Graham, Jr., eds., *Speculations on American History*, (Boston: Heath, 1977), pp. 119–38.

87. Sidney Hook, *The Hero in History: A Study in Limitation and Possibility* (New York: John Day, 1943), pp. 151–83; John Kenneth Galbraith, "Revolution in Our Time: Marx and Lenin; Lloyd George and Roosevelt; John Maynard Keynes," *Bulletin of the American Academy of Arts and Sciences* 40 (December 1986): 9; "Transcript of Shorthand Notes taken at a Conference of young Liberal Delegates of Caernarvonshire, held in the Guild Hall, Caernarvon, on Saturday afternoon and evening, the 16th of October, 1937," David Lloyd George MSS, G/22/3/12, Beaverbrook Library, London. See also Typescript [1937?], H. A. L. Fisher MSS, Bodleian Library, Oxford University, Box 9; R. H. Pear, "The Impact of the New Deal on British Economic and Political Ideas," *Bulletin of the British Association of American Studies* 4 (August 1962): 24.

88. Christina Stead, *The Man Who Loved Children* (New York: Simon and Schuster, 1940), p. 291.

89. H. G. Nicholas, "Roosevelt and Public Opinion," *Fortnightly* 163 (May 1945): 304; Califano, *Presidential Nation*, p. 8; Rossiter, *American Presidency*, p. 151.

90. See especially the reservations of Theodore J. Lowi in *The Personal President: Power Invested, Promise Unfulfilled* (Ithaca, N.Y.: Cornell University Press, 1985).

Two   The New Deal and the Analogue of War

1. *Magazine of Wall Street* 45 (December 14, 1929): 264, cited in J. Kenneth Galbraith, *The Great Crash* (Boston: Houghton Mifflin, 1955), p. 143.

2. Hoover, observed Gilbert Seldes, "repeatedly used the figures of speech of war in his description of the depression. It was a skillful association of ideas, for the war was a difficult time which ended happily; it was exciting, and it was the last time the whole nation was united." Seldes, *The Years of the Locust: America, 1929–1932* (Boston: Little, Brown, 1933), p. 258. The conviction of political leaders and publicists that reference to the war would evoke a favorable response suggests some modification of the view that the "pacifist thirties" thought of World War I only with abhorrence. Though they viewed war as a wasteful, inhuman social institution, many progressives also recalled World War I as an ennobling experience of sacrifice for the national welfare and as a time of economic advance. In 1931 Richard T. Ely wrote: "A marked difference between the general situation in the World War and our situation during Hard Times must be noticed. A war may at first be attended by a good deal of economic confusion and distress, but very soon the wages and profits mount upward and people are apparently more prosperous than ever. Returns of capital in many lines of activity are large and

wages are apt to mount up to levels heretofore unknown." Ely, *Hard Times—The Way In and the Way Out, with a Special Consideration of the "Seen and the Unseen"* (New York: Macmillan, 1931), p. 110.

3. *Literary Digest*, September 10, 1932, pp. 4–5; *New Republic*, September 7, 1932, p. 86; Theodore Joslin, *Hoover Off the Record* (Garden City, N.Y.: Doubleday, Doran, 1934), p. 63. "Fighting this depression is becoming more and more like waging a war," Hoover observed. "We have the combats, if against an unseen foe of inestimable strength. We have our men and we have our casualties among them." Ibid., p. 182.

4. Henry Stimson MS. Diary, June 15, 1931, Stimson MSS, Sterling Memorial Library, Yale University, New Haven, Ct. For similar assessments of the Depression, see *Report of Proceedings of the Fiftieth Annual Convention of the American Federation of Labor* (Washington, D. C., 1930), p. 366; Henry Morrow Hyde MS. Diary, December 17, 1931, Hyde MSS, Alderman Library, University of Virginia, Charlottesville, Va.; Justice Brandeis's dissent in *New State Ice Co. v. Liebmann*, 285 U.S. 306 (1932); *Rocky Mountain News*, March 1, 1933.

5. Otis L. Graham, Jr., *Toward a Planned Society: From Roosevelt to Nixon* (New York: Oxford University Press, 1976), p. 23.

6. One cannot, of course, distinguish sharply between the relative influence of World War I and progressivism since the war mobilization was, in some respects, a logical outgrowth of the progressive movement. (There were, too, other antecedents of the New Deal, notably the experiments of the 1920s.) Some historians, it should be noted, were sensitive very early either to the indebtedness of the Roosevelt administration to the war mobilization or to the use the New Deal made of war imagery. See, especially, Frank Freidel, *America in the Twentieth Century* (New York: Knopf, 1960), p. 312; Arthur Schlesinger, Jr., *The Crisis of the Old Order* (Boston: Houghton Mifflin, 1957), pp. 37–39; Schlesinger, *Coming of the New Deal* (Boston: Houghton Mifflin, 1959), p. 176; Paul Conkin, *Tomorrow a New World: The New Deal Community Program* (Ithaca, N.Y.: Cornell University Press, 1959), pp. 50–54, 67; Gerald Nash, "Herbert Hoover and the Origins of the Reconstruction Finance Corporation," *Mississippi Valley Historical Review* 46 (December 1959): 455–68. Most narratives, however, have not only ignored this relationship but also minimized the significance of the political and economic events of the war years. With respect to the war, historians have been chiefly interested in what happened *before* our intervention (the submarine crisis) and what happened *afterwards* (the League of Nations fight), not with the substance of the war experience itself.

7. David Brody, *Steelworkers in America: The Nonunion Era* (Cambridge, Mass.: Harvard University Press, 1960), p. 206; *Iron Age*, May 9, 1918, pp. 1206–13. If, by later standards, the experiment in controls was embryonic, it nonetheless represented an unprecedented degree of government

intervention. In the immense literature on the war mobilization, see Benedict Crowell and R. F. Wilson, *How America Went to War: An Account from Official Sources of the Nation's War Activities, 1917–1920,* 6 vols. (New Haven: Yale University Press, 1921); Bernard M. Baruch, *American Industry in the War* (New York: Prentice-Hall, 1941); Woodbury Willoughby, *The Capital Issues Committee and War Finance Corporation* (Baltimore: The Johns Hopkins Press, 1934); Mê Hsin Chiang, "The United States War Industries Board, 1917–1918," M.A. essay, Stanford University, 1937; William Clinton Mullendore, *History of the United States Food Administration 1917–1919* (Palo Alto, Cal.: Stanford University Press, 1941); Waldo G. Leland and Newton D. Mereness, *Introduction to the American Official Sources for the Economic and Social History of the War* (New Haven: Yale University Press, 1926).

8. See, for example, George E. Mowry, *The California Progressives* (Berkeley and Los Angeles: University of California Press, 1951), pp. 294–99. The most ambitious federal program was the investigation conducted on the eve of World War I. Graham Adams, *Age of Industrial Violence, 1910–15: The Activities and Findings of the United States Commission on Industrial Relations* (New York: Columbia University Press, 1966).

9. "Springfield and Bridgeport," *New Republic,* June 8, 1918, pp. 185–86; Henry F. Pringle, *The Life and Times of William Howard Taft: A Biography,* 2 vols. (New York: Farrar and Rinehart, 1939), 2: 921; "Snubbing the War Labor Board," *Survey,* June 8, 1918, pp. 292–93; "The Western Union and the Government," *New Republic,* June 8, 1918, pp. 163–64; Pringle, *Life and Times of William Howard Taft,* 2: 919–20. For the wartime labor experience, see "Final Report of the Chairman of the Labor Division, War Industries Board, 1919," John P. Frey MSS, Library of Congress (LC), Box 15; Brody, *Steelworkers in America,* ch. 10; U.S. Department of Labor, Bureau of Labor Statistics, "National War Labor Board," in *Bulletin No. 287* (Washington, D. C., 1922); Gordon S. Watkins, *Labor Problems and Labor Administration in the United States During the World War* (Urbana, Ill.: The University of Illinois, 1920); Felix Frankfurter, "New Labor Ideas Taught by War," in Edwin Wildman, ed., *Reconstructing America: Our Next Big Job, the Latest Word on the Vital Subjects of the Hour, the Views on Reconstruction and Readjustment* (Boston: Page, 1919), pp. 239–44.

10. Gordon Hall Gerould, "The Professor and the Wide, Wide World," *Scribner's Magazine* 65 (April 1919): 465–66.

11. Bourne, *Untimely Papers,* ed. James Oppenheim (New York: B. W. Huebsch, 1919), p. 129.

12. "The Uses of an Armistice," *New Republic,* November 16, 1918, p. 60; Charles Hirschfeld, "American Reform and World War I," paper delivered at the convention of the Mississippi Valley Historical Association, Denver, Col., April 25, 1969, pp. 3, 12–13.

13. John Dewey, "What Are We Fighting For?" *Independent* 94 (1918): 480, reprinted as "The Social Possibilities of War," in Joseph Ratner, ed., *Characters and Events*, 2 vols. (New York: Holt, 1929), 2: 555; John Dewey, "A New Social Science," *New Republic*, April 6, 1918, p. 293; David Riesman, *Thorstein Veblen: A Critical Interpretation* (New York: Scribner, 1953), p. 119; Joseph Dorfman, *Thorstein Veblen and His America* (New York: Viking, 1934), pp. 380–95; Curtice N. Hitchcock, "The War Industries Board: Its Development, Organization, and Functions," *Journal of Political Economy* 26 (June 1918): 566; Irving Fisher, "Some Contributions of the War to Our Knowledge of Money and Prices," *American Economic Review* 8 (March 1918), Supplement: 257–58; Joseph Dorfman, *The Economic Mind in American Civilization*, 5 vols. (New York: Viking, 1946–59), 3: 485–94; Walter Weyl, *The End of the War* (New York, 1918), pp. 303–4. Cf. Sidney Kaplan, "Social Engineers as Saviors: Effects of World War I on Some American Liberals," *Journal of the History of Ideas* 17 (June 1956): 347–69. The war experience casts doubt on the familiar generalization that war is always fatal to reform. In some ways, the war dealt a severe blow to the progressive movement; in other ways, it opened up new possibilities. No doubt the war resulted in more harm than good for progressivism, but it was not the totally unusable experience it has frequently been represented to be.

14. "The Demobilized Professor," *Atlantic Monthly* 123 (April 1919): 537. In the months after the armistice, economists such as Wesley Mitchell sought to preserve the activities begun during the war, and men like Senator William S. Kenyon of Iowa attempted to keep alive and even expand the work of war agencies, but in vain. See Dorfman, *Economic Mind*, 4: 9–11, 365; Lucy Sprague Mitchell, *Two Lives: The Story of Wesley Clair Mitchell and Myself* (New York: Simon and Schuster, 1953), p. 303; Wesley C. Mitchell, *The Backward Art of Spending Money and Other Essays* (New York: McGraw Hill, 1937), pp. 42–57.

15. Rexford G. Tugwell, "America's War-Time Socialism," *Nation*, April 6, 1927, pp. 364–65. Cf. Donald Richberg, *Tents of the Mighty* (New York: Willett, Clark, and Colby, 1930), p. 82. Even the social security movement of the 1920s was affected by the wartime precedents of government insurance and of the care and rehabilitation of veterans. Clarke Chambers to the writer, June 23, 1962. The Railroad Administration was to provide the model for the New Deal's Coordinator of Transportation.

16. In some respects, this relationship had even earlier antecedents, for example, in the special place that Lincoln and the Union cause had in the hearts of postbellum reformers. It might even be traced back as far as the congruence of reform and imperialism in the Jefferson administration.

17. Herbert Croly, *The Promise of American Life* (New York: Macmillan, 1909), p. 139. Croly rejoiced that the Spanish-American War and the subsequent imperial expansion had given "a tremendous impulse to the work of nation-

al reform." Ibid., p. 169. See William E. Leuchtenburg, "Progressivism and Imperialism: The Progressive Movement and American Foreign Policy, 1898–1916," *Mississippi Valley Historical Review* 39 (December 1952): 483–504.

18. Baruch, *American Industry in the War*, p. 29; Stuart Chase, *A New Deal* (New York: Macmillan, 1932), pp. 84–85; Tugwell, "America's War-Time Socialism," p. 365. See, too, J. M. Clark's perceptive article, "The Basis of War-Time Collectivism," *American Economic Review* 7 (September 1917): 772–90.

19. Stuart Chase, "The Heart of American Industry," in Fred J. Ringel, ed., *America as Americans See It* (New York: Literary Guild, 1932), p. 30; George Soule, *A Planned Society* (New York: Macmillan, 1933), pp. 184–87. See, too, J. Russell Smith, "The End of an Epoch," *Survey*, July 1, 1931, p. 333.

20. Swope to Hoover, October 2, 1930, Gerard Swope MSS, Columbia University, New York; Ely, *Hard Times*, pp. 103–6.

21. Raphael Herman to William McAdoo, June 10, 1931, McAdoo MSS, LC, Box 359; Charles A. Beard, "A 'Five-Year Plan' for America," *Forum* 86 (July 1931): 5. Beard also proposed gigantic agricultural and housing programs to be "financed by Freedom Bonds and sold with the zeal of war issues." Ibid., p. 11.

22. Representative Chester Bolton to Walter Gifford, August 24, 1931, Newton D. Baker MSS, LC, Box 192; J. George Frederick, ed., *The Swope Plan: Details, Criticisms, Analysis* (New York: Business Bourse, 1931); Gerard Swope, Columbia Oral History Collection (COHC); "A Plea from 123 Representatives of Independent Industrial Units and of Labor for the Trial of a Two Years' Truce in Destructive Competition" to Herbert Hoover, February 11, 1932, copy in Harvey Williams to Robert Wagner, March 24, 1932, Wagner MSS, Georgetown University, Washington, D. C.

23. For the wariness of businessmen about using the War Industries Board as a model, see U.S. Congress, Senate, *Establishment of a National Economic Council*, Hearings before a Subcommittee of the Committee on Manufactures, U.S. Senate, 72d Cong., 1st Sess., on S. 6215, October 22 to December 19, 1931 (Washington, D. C., 1932), p. 174. William Appleman Williams saw men like Gerard Swope as representative of a new group of corporation executives who came out of the war with a more sophisticated approach to industrial problems and viewed Herbert Hoover as their most important spokesman. Williams, *The Contours of American History* (Cleveland and New York: World, 1961), pp. 425–26. Though this judgment seems valid for the 1920s, especially during Hoover's tenure as Secretary of Commerce, it is not pertinent for Hoover's presidency. The differences between Swope and President Hoover, sharply revealed by their divergent evaluations of the relevance of war to the Depression, were more significant than their area of agreement.

24. Mallery had headed a division of the War Labor Policies Board charged with developing public works during the postwar transition. For the proposals of Mallery and Father John O'Grady, see the *New York Times*, December 30, 1931. The economist Arthur Gayer recommended profiting from the Liberty Bond example by floating bonds for public works "in a war on growing suffering and distress." Arthur D. Gayer, "Financing the Emergency Public Works Program," *American Labor Legislation Review* 22 (June 1932): 75.

25. Dorfman, *Economic Mind*, 4: 7. Moreover, Hoover had stepped up public works right after the crash. Still, this represented far less than the progressives demanded.

26. Dorfman, *Economic Mind*, 5: 672. During the fight over the sales tax in 1932, an Oklahoma Congressman hooted at the idea that budget-balancing was a patriotic duty. "Those who are so anxious to balance the budget at this time either forget or ignore the fact that we have in times past raised vast sums in emergencies to carry on wars without resorting to the general sales tax," he noted. "Soak the Poor," Wilburn Cartwright MSS, University of Oklahoma, Norman, Okla.

27. William Trufant Foster, "When a Horse Balks," *North American Review* 234 (July 1932): 10. John Maynard Keynes wrote: "I hope that in the future we shall . . . be ready to spend on the enterprises of peace what the financial maxims of the past would only allow us to spend on the devastations of war." Keynes, "The World's Economic Outlook," *Atlantic Monthly* 149 (May 1932): 525. See, too, Lewis Kimmel, *Federal Budget and Fiscal Policy, 1789–1958* (Washington, D. C.: Brookings Institution, 1959), pp. 170–72.

28. White to David Hinshaw, August 10, 1931, William Allen White MSS, LC, Box 135.

29. Baker to Representative Chester Bolton, August 26, 1931, Baker MSS, Box 192; U.S. Congress, Senate, *Unemployment Relief*, Hearings before a Subcommittee of the Committee on Manufactures, U.S. Senate, 72d Cong., 1st Sess., on S. 174 and S. 262, December 28–30, 1931, and January 4–9, 1932 (Washington, D. C., 1932), p. 327. A year later, when Baker was named to head the National Citizen's Committee for the Welfare and Relief Mobilization of 1932, the *Literary Digest* explained: "The concentrated effort is under the direct command of Newton D. Baker, who, as Secretary of War under President Wilson, mobilized the forces of the country for the war in Europe. The campaign is to be the Armageddon of the Great Depression." *Literary Digest*, October 8, 1932, p. 20.

30. Robert Higgs, *Crisis and Leviathan: Critical Episodes in the Growth of American Government* (New York: Oxford University Press, 1987), pp. 164–65; William Starr Myers, ed., *The State Papers and Other Public Writings of Herbert Hoover*, 2 vols. (Garden City, N.Y.: Doubleday, Doran,

1934), 2: 6. Accounts of the origin of the RFC vary in detail. Cf. Eugene Meyer COHC, pp. 612–13; Jackson Reynolds COHC, pp. 152–53; Louis Wehle, *Hidden Threads of History: Wilson Through Roosevelt* (New York: Macmillan, 1953), p. 77; U.S. Congress, Senate, *Creation of a Reconstruction Finance Corporation,* Hearings before a Subcommittee of the Committee on Banking and Currency, U.S. Senate, 72d Cong., 1st Sess., on S. 1, December 18, 19, 21, 22, 1931 (Washington, D. C., 1932).

31. Eugene Meyer COHC, p. 613. Meyer's initiative, and the WFC model, is also stressed in Nash, "Herbert Hoover and the Origins of the Reconstruction Finance Corporation."

32. W. Randolph Burgess, "Plans for Financial Reconstruction," Address at the Century Association of New York, April 7, 1932, Ogden Mills MSS, LC, Box 9; J. Franklin Ebersole, "One Year of the Reconstruction Finance Corporation," *Quarterly Journal of Economics* 47 (May 1933): 468; Wehle, *Hidden Threads of History,* p. 77.

33. *Literary Digest,* February 13, 1932, p. 9. Congress, reported the Philadelphia *Record,* had given the new agency "two billion dollars' worth of ammunition. The people are waiting to see how straight it can shoot."

34. For the determination during the war to refrain from interference with business, see Randall B. Kester, "The War Industries Board, 1917–1918; A Study in Industrial Mobilization," *American Political Science Review* 34 (August 1940): 683; and Herbert Stein, *Government Price Policy in the United States During the World War* (Williamstown, Mass.: Williams College, 1939), p. 13.

35. The integrative function of war is explored in W. Lloyd Warner, *American Life: Dream and Reality* (Chicago: University of Chicago Press, 1953), p. 20.

36. *Official Report of the Proceedings of the Twentieth Republican National Convention, 1932* (New York, 1932), p. 89.

37. Philadelphia *Record,* May 22, 1932, reprinted in Jordan Schwarz, *1933: Roosevelt's Decision: The United States Leaves the Gold Standard* (New York: Chelsea House, 1969), p. 26; Mark Gelfand, draft of Ph.D. dissertation, Columbia University, on the federal government and the cities.

38. As the country entered the election year of 1932, the tempo of demands for a return to the war spirit quickened. See Baker Brownell to Gifford Pinchot, January 10, 1932, Gifford Pinchot MSS, LC, Box 320; John J. Pershing, "We Are at War!" *American Magazine* 113 (June 1932): 15–17, 72, 74; *B. E. F. News,* July 2, 1932.

39. *The Public Papers and Addresses of Franklin D. Roosevelt,* Samuel I. Rosenman, ed., 13 vols. (New York: Random House, Macmillan, Harper, 1938–1950), 1: 624–25. At a Roosevelt rally in Salem, Massachusetts James Michael Curley, the Mayor of Boston, made effective use of the war analogue to berate Hoover. *Salem News,* April 6, 1932, Curley Scrapbooks, Holy Cross College Library, Worcester, Mass.

40. Roosevelt, *Public Papers*, 1: 631–32.

41. Rexford G. Tugwell, *The Brains Trust* (New York: Viking, 1967), p. 527; Thomas L. Stokes, *Chip Off My Shoulder* (Princeton, N.J.: Princeton University Press, 1940), p. 312.

42. Carl Brent Swisher, *American Constitutional Development* (Boston: Houghton Mifflin, 1943), p. 878. The rather conservative Senator from South Carolina, James F. Byrnes, later remembered his attitude during the interregnum: "In our efforts to find a remedy for this situation, we had no guideposts. I recalled that when I went to the House of Representatives I had firm convictions about federal-state relations and the wisdom of preserving local governments, the necessity of maintaining a balanced budget, and like subjects; but when we entered World War I in 1917, I recognized that, in a war emergency, principles as well as policies had to be temporarily subordinated to the necessity of some experimentation in order to preserve the government itself. The economic crisis now demanded a similar attitude. . . . I felt the emergency situation now called for an unusual concentration of power in the White House, however temporary that concentration might be." Byrnes, *All in One Lifetime* (New York: Harper, 1958), pp. 69–70.

43. The President's Research Committee on Social Trends pointed to the "surprising energy and efficiency" that had emerged in 1917 and noted the explanation for this "development of governmental art": "the subordination of private to public interest, the facility in recruitment of the necessary talent when the boycott on government service was lifted, the indifference to established precedent in administrative or other method, the freedom from hairsplitting judicial restraint, the unification of leadership." The President's Research Committee on Social Trends, *Recent Social Trends in the United States* (New York: McGraw-Hill, 1933), p. 1539. Cf. Max Lerner, "The State in War Time," in Willard Waller, ed., *War in the Twentieth Century* (New York: Dryden, 1940), pp. 409–28.

44. Daniel Roper to William Dodd, November 16, 1932, Dodd MSS, LC, Box 41; Daniel C. Roper to William E. Dodd, February 17, 1933, Roper MSS, Box 15.

45. Key Pittman to FDR, June 16, 1932, Pittman MSS, LC, Box 16; Henry Morrow Hyde MS. Diary, January 4, 1933; *New York Times*, February 8, 1933; Willis Thornton, *The Life of Alfred M. Landon* (New York: Grosset and Dunlap, 1936), p. 84.

46. Paul Shoup to Hale Holden, February 27, 1933, Shoup MSS, Stanford University, Stanford, Cal., Box 2; Goldthwaite H. Dorr to Henry L. Stimson, February 14, 1933, in Dorr to Harlan Fiske Stone, February 14, 1933, Stone MSS, LC, Box 11.

47. Raymond Moley, *After Seven Years* (New York: Harper, 1939), pp. 22–23; Tugwell, "Notes from a New Deal Diary," January 4, 1933, February 27,

1933, Tugwell MSS, Franklin D. Roosevelt Library (FDRL), Hyde Park, N.Y.; Key Pittman to Roosevelt, February 28, 1933, Pittman MSS, Box 16; Ernest K. Lindley, *The Roosevelt Revolution: First Phase* (New York: Viking, 1939), p. 78; Rexford Tugwell COHC, pp. 37–40.

48. Ruth McKenney, *Industrial Valley* (New York: Harcourt, Brace, 1939), p. 71; *New York Times*, March 5, 1933.

49. *Public Papers*, 2: 1–15.

50. Schlesinger, *Coming of the New Deal*, p. 3. "It was like a war," James MacGregor Burns has written. "In the White House—now a command post to handle economic crisis—sat the new President." Burns, *Roosevelt: The Lion and the Fox*, pp. 165–66. One periodical noted: "The country was in an exalted mood. It rose to greet the new President as if to support him in the repulsion of invading armies." *Review of Reviews and World's Work* 87 (April 1933): 10. In April 1933 a Democratic Senator completed a volume that was a sustained use of the war as a parable for the Depression. Millard E. Tydings, *Counter-Attack: A Battle Plan to Defeat the Depression* (Indianapolis: Bobbs-Merrill, 1933).

51. Rexford G. Tugwell, *The Battle for Democracy* (New York: Columbia University Press, 1935), pp. 75, 296. Thurman Arnold noted that in war democracies "achieve unity to an extent which seems extraordinary to one viewing the wartime economy from the tangled confusion of peacetime values." He added: "Thus, in peacetimes, when the lack of cooperation between men is distressingly evident, and when the endless argument about the contradictions involved in our symbols seems to have no hope of ending, we look back to the unity of the time when nations were drawn up in battle lines and we demand a moral substitute for war." Arnold, *The Symbols of Government* (New Haven: Yale University Press, 1935), pp. 243–45.

52. The words are Tugwell's. Tugwell, *The Industrial Discipline and the Governmental Arts* (New York: Columbia University Press, 1933), p. 100. See, too, Soule, *Planned Society*, pp. 196–97.

53. Beard, "A 'Five-Year Plan' for America," p. 11; George N. Peek, with Samuel Crowther, *Why Quit Our Own* (New York: Van Nostrand, 1936), p. 123. Raymond Moley, it might be noted, had directed Americanization activities in Ohio under Governor James Cox during World War I.

54. Alfred C. Oliver, Jr., and Harold M. Dudley, *This New America: The Spirit of the Civilian Conservation Corps* (London: Longmans, Green, 1937), p. viii. See, too, the reference to "nation-building" in John L. Christian, "America's Peace Army," *Current History* 49 (January 1939): 43.

55. *Public Papers*, 2: 18. Tugwell, who worked on the banking proclamation, referred to it as "this rather doubtful executive act." Tugwell, "Notes from a New Deal Diary," March 31, 1933. See, too, Rixey Smith and Norman Beasley, *Carter Glass: A Biography* (New York: Longmans, Green, 1939), pp. 341–42.

56. *New York Times*, March 10, 1933 (dispatch of March 9); *Congressional Record*, 73d Cong., 1st Sess., p. 70. *Business Week* called the 1933 Congress a "War Congress." James E. Sargent, *Roosevelt and the Hundred Days: Struggle for the Early New Deal* (New York: Garland, 1981), p. 2. Roosevelt's new banking act was deliberately framed to use the "war power" to overcome possible objections to its constitutionality. The President's extraordinary powers were granted "during time of war or during any other period of national emergency declared by the President." Gustav Cassel, *The Downfall of the Gold Standard* (Oxford: Clarendon, 1936), p. 117.

57. Tom Connally, as told to Alfred Steinberg, *My Name Is Tom Connally* (New York: Crowell, 1954), p. 148; Schlesinger, *Coming of the New Deal*, pp. 9–10.

58. *Congressional Record*, 73d Cong., 1st Sess., pp. 201, 209.

59. Wingate F. Cram to White, March 18, 1933, Wallace White MSS, LC, Box 1; *New York Times*, March 11, 1933. "The President has been elected as Commander-in-Chief to pull us out of this financial crisis and it is my purpose to stand by him," agreed Rep. Sam McReynolds of Tennessee. McReynolds to George Fort Milton, March 27, 1933, Milton MSS, LC, Box 13. At a homecoming meeting for the Nevada Congressional delegation following the historic session of the Hundred Days, Senator Pat McCarran stated: "On March 9 of this year, to the astonishment of many, war was officially declared. . . . The war was against fear, fear that the entire government would go into bankruptcy." Clipping, n. d., Scrapbook 44018, James Scrugham MSS, Nevada State Historical Society, Reno, Nev.

60. *Public Papers*, 2: 122. Cf. Sarah Elizabeth Boseley Winger, "The Genesis of TVA," Ph.D. dissertation, University of Wisconsin, 1959, pp. 580–81; Judson King, *The Conservation Fight: From Theodore Roosevelt to the Tennessee Valley Authority* (Washington, D. C.: Public Affairs Press, 1959), chs. 7–8; Norman Wengert, "Antecedents of TVA: The Legislative History of Muscle Shoals," *Agricultural History* 25 (October 1952): 141–47; Kenneth McKellar to George Fort Milton, May 17, 1933, Milton MSS, Box 13. The special form of the TVA—the government corporation endowed with many of the powers and much of the flexibility of a business corporation—had first found wide acceptance in the war.

61. Tennessee Valley Authority, *To Keep the Water in the Rivers and the Soil on the Land* (Washington, D.C.: Government Printing Office, 1938), p. 44; *Ashwander et al., v. Tennessee Valley Authority et al.*, 297 U.S. 288 (1936); Joseph C. Swidler and Robert H. Marquis, "TVA in Court: A Study of Constitutional Litigation," *Iowa Law Review* 32 (January 1947): 296–326. In arguing the case for passage of the Taylor Grazing Act, a former Senator claimed: "The remaining public domain is vital to the nation from a standpoint of national defense. . . . Without an adequate supply of meat and wool the nation would be considerably handicapped in case of war." Holm

Bursum to Charles McNary, April 16, 1934, Bursum MSS, University of New Mexico, Albuquerque, N. M., Box 1. The public power reformers of the New Deal were schooled in wartime agencies like the Power Section of the Emergency Fleet Corporation. Morris L. Cooke, "Early Days of Rural Electrification," *American Political Science Review* 42 (June 1948): 437; "U.S. War Industries Board, 1918" folder, J. D. Ross MSS, University of Washington, Seattle, Wash. One conservationist commented on his work on the Mississippi Valley Committee with Morris Cooke: "To all of us it was a great experience . . . epoch-making. . . . The exper. was as valuable to me as to you; it was similar to an enriching exper. I had under the same leadership back in 1917–18, during the war." Harlow Person to Donald Bower, December 9, 1935, "Quasi Official and Personal Correspondence of Morris L. Cooke," REA Files, National Archives (courtesy of Jean Christie).

62. Timothy L. McDonnell, S.J., *The Wagner Housing Act: A Case Study of the Legislative Process* (Chicago: Loyola University Press, 1957), pp. 7–9; Curtice N. Hitchcock, "The War Housing Program and Its Future," *Journal of Political Economy* 27 (April 1919): 241–79; Miles Colean, *Housing for Defense: A Review of the Role of Housing in Relation to America's Defense and a Program for Action: The Factual Findings* (New York: Twentieth Century Fund, 1940), ch. 1; Robert D. Kohn, "Housing in a Reconstruction Program," *Survey*, May 31, 1919, p. 341. The most intense interest in government housing, however, came not so much in the war as in the reconversion period, although it was triggered by the war experience. McDonnell, *Wagner Housing Act*, pp. 12–15.

63. Conkin, *Tomorrow a New World*, pp. 50–54, 67; Roy Lubove, "Homes and 'A Few Well-Placed Fruit Trees': An Object Lesson in Federal Housing," *Social Research* 27 (Winter 1960): 469–86; Lubove, "New Cities for Old: The Urban Reconstruction Program of the 1930's," *Social Studies* 53 (November 1962): 205.

64. James Shideler, "Wilson, Hoover, War and Food Control, 1917–1918," paper delivered at the convention of the Mississippi Valley Historical Association, Denver, Col., April 25, 1959; Grosvenor Clarkson, *Industrial America in the World War: A Strategy Behind the Line, 1917–1918* (Boston: Houghton Mifflin, 1923), p. 239; Gilbert Fite, *George N. Peek and the Fight for Farm Parity* (Norman, Okla.: University of Oklahoma Press, 1954), p. 32; George Peek to Earl Smith, October 18, 1932, Peek MSS, Western Historical Manuscripts Collection, University of Missouri, Columbia, Mo.

65. Thomas H. Coode, "Georgia Congressmen and the First Hundred Days of the New Deal," *Georgia Historical Quarterly* 53 (June 1969): 132–33. During the debate, Senator Smith Wildman Brookhart of Iowa advocated a "war emergency" plan in which the surplus would be "commandeered" by the government. Jackson (Miss.) *Daily Clarion Ledger*, January 23, 1933. When Roosevelt sent his farm message to Congress, Secretary of Agriculture

Henry Wallace announced: "In no case will there be any gouging of the consumer. We hope to revive the Wartime spirit in everyone to put this thing across." *Time*, March 27, 1933, p. 12. A study of Wallace's oratory has noted his fondness for military terminology in his speeches. Robert Gene King, "The Rhetoric of Henry Agard Wallace," Ph.D. dissertation, Department of Speech and Drama, Teachers College, Columbia University, 1963. The rural protest movement employed similar metaphors. One farmer told an Iowa county agent bluntly that "the World War [had] its slackers" and that, sixteen years after the war, the country was plagued by "yellow pups running around in the shape of nincompoop-flatheaded County Agents." Jesse Sickler to Milo Reno, April 16, 1933, Reno MSS (privately held).

66. Roosevelt had first offered the post to Peek's "boss," Bernard Baruch, who, as head of the War Industries Board, was regarded as the most important of the war administrators. J. F. T. O'Connor MS. Diary, May 13, 1933, O'Connor MSS, Bancroft Library, University of California, Berkeley, Cal.

67. Georgia Lindsey Peek MS. memoir, "Early New Deal," Peek MSS. For Jerome Frank's first experience with farm issues in the United States Food Administration, see Jerome Frank COHC, pp. 52–53. "It was the greatest thing that ever happened when the government took charge of the wheat situation and told the big and little barons what price the farmers should get for their wheat," a Florida newspaper stated that summer. "Everyone knows what the government was able to do with the price of wheat during the war." "Why Not Government Control of Citrus Fruit?," Lakeland (Fla.) *News*, July 1, 1933, clipping, Spessard Holland MSS, P. K. Yonge Library, University of Florida, Gainesville, Fla., Box 52.

68. There had been widespread agitation for offering such an alternative to groups like "the wandering boys of the road" and the bonus marchers. George Rawick, "The New Deal and Youth," Ph.D. dissertation, University of Wisconsin, 1957, p. 40; Pelham Glassford, "Training Camps for the Unemployed," Glassford MSS, Institute of Industrial Relations Library, University of California at Los Angeles, Los Angeles, Cal., Box 1; James Harvey Rogers, "Sound Inflation," *Economic Forum* 1 (1933): 127.

69. *Public Papers*, 2: 238. Schlesinger points out that Louis Howe's original plan for the CCC called for "a large-scale recruiting effort, bands playing and flags flying, leading to a mass exodus of the unemployed to the forests." Schlesinger, *Coming of the New Deal*, p. 337. See, too, "Memorandum for the Secretary of War: Subject: Civilian Conservation Corps," April 3, 1933, Louis Howe MSS, FDRL, Box 59. The Third Corps Area, it was observed, enrolled the first recruit in the "peace time army" on the anniversary of America's entrance into World War I. Charles Price Harper, *The Administration of the Civilian Conservation Corps* (Clarksburg, W. Va.: Clarksburg Publishing Co., 1939), p. 24.

70. Harrison Doty, "Our Forest Army at War," *Review of Reviews and World's Work* 88 (July 1933): 31. "It represented the greatest peacetime demand ever made upon the Army and constituted a task of character and proportions equivalent to emergencies of war," Chief of Staff Douglas MacArthur wrote in a communiqué to all Army Corps Area Commanders. "It was well done, Army. MacArthur." Rawick, "The New Deal and Youth," p. 66. See, too, "Extracts from Address of Honorable George H. Dern, Secretary of War," n. d., Dern MSS, LC, Box 1.

71. To quiet fears of military control, Roosevelt named as CCC Director the union leader Robert Fechner whom he had first encountered when both were engaged in determining war labor policies. The real control of the camps, however, lay with the military. Tucker Smith to Jane Addams, March 8, 1933, Jane Addams MSS, Swarthmore College Peace Collection, Swarthmore, Pa., Box 22; "Unofficial Observer" [John Franklin Carter], *The New Dealers* (New York: Literary Guild, 1934), pp. 163–65; Rawick, "The New Deal and Youth," chap. 5.

72. Charles W. B. Hurd, "The Forestry Army at the Front," *Literary Digest*, September 9, 1933, pp. 5–6; Joseph Cream, "The Genesis of the Civilian Conservation Corps," M.A. essay, Columbia University, 1955, pp. 45ff.; Oliver and Dudley, *This New America*, p. 133.

73. *Happy Days*, May 20, 1933, p. 8; June 3, 1933, p. 2; June 24, 1933, p. 3; July 1, 1933, p. 1. Cf. Levette J. Davidson, "C. C. C. Chatter," *American Speech* 15 (April 1940): 210–11.

74. Christian, "America's Peace Army," p. 43. Cf. Tulsa *World*, April 10, 1933, clipping, W. A. Pat Murphy MSS, University of Oklahoma, Norman, Okla.; Ferdinand Silcox, "Our Adventure in Conservation: The CCC," *Atlantic Monthly* 160 (December 1937): 714. Moley recalled that when the question of James's influence was raised, Roosevelt conceded there might be a relationship, but he had no conscious awareness of one. Then the President added: "But look here! I think I'll go ahead with this—the way I did on beer." Moley, *After Seven Years*, p. 174.

75. A Detroit *News* cartoon which bore the title, "The Old Veterans of the Conservation Army Will Have Something Worth Bragging About," showed an elderly man holding a little boy by the hand and pointing with his cane to a great forest. The caption read: "In 1933 I planted all of these in the great war against depression." Hurd, "The Forestry Army at the Front," p. 6.

76. Henry T. Rainey to K. G. Baur, March 13, 1934, Rainey MSS, LC, Box 1. Yet another New Deal agency had a World War I counterpart. The Securities and Exchange Commission (SEC) had a forerunner in the Capital Issues Committee, a precedent, William O. Douglas said, that the Administration should be "astute enough to follow." Jordan A. Schwarz, *The New Dealers: Power Politics in the Age of Roosevelt* (New York: Knopf,

1993), p. 165. See, too, Edward N. Gadsby, "Historical Development of the S. E. C.—the Government View," *George Washington Law Review* 28 (October 1959): 7. For the impact of World War I on the Reorganization bill, see "Minutes of Meetings of Members and Staff of President's Committee on Administrative Management, May 9–10, 1936," Charles Merriam MSS, University of Chicago, Chicago, Ill., Box 260.

77. *New York Times*, April 29, 1933; Rexford Tugwell, "Notes from a New Deal Diary," May 30, 1933; Jerome Frank COHC, p. 27. An article which appeared after my essay on the analogue was written amply demonstrates the importance of the war precedent: Gerald D. Nash, "Experiments in Industrial Mobilizations: WIB and NRA," *Mid-America* 45 (July 1963): 167–74.

78. Meyer Jacobstein and H. G. Moulton, "A Plan for Economic Recovery," Wagner MSS; Moley, *After Seven Years*, p. 188. A study he had done for General Pershing, Johnson said, had provided "the whole basis" for the wartime agencies "and of not a little of NRA." Hugh Johnson, *The Blue Eagle from Egg to Earth* (Garden City, N.Y.: Doubleday, Doran, 1935), p. 72.

79. *Public Papers*, 2: 252.

80. Matthew Josephson, *Sidney Hillman: Statesman of American Labor* (Garden City, N.Y.: Doubleday, 1952), p. 357. Hillman had been a member of the Board of Control and Labor Standards for Army Clothing during the war.

81. "Docket—Coal & Stabilization," April 24, May 6, May 23, 1933, W. Jett Lauck MSS, National Recovery Act file, Alderman Library, University of Virginia; *Business Week*, May 24, 1933, pp. 3–4; Edwin E. Witte, "The Background of the Labor Provisions of the N.I.R.A.," *University of Chicago Law Review* 1 (March 1934): 573.

82. Gerald Nash, "Franklin D. Roosevelt and Labor: The World War I Origins of Early New Deal Policy," *Labor History* 1 (Winter 1960): 49. See, too, Frank Freidel, *Franklin D. Roosevelt: The Apprenticeship* (Boston: Little, Brown, 1952), pp. 328–32.

83. Nash, "Franklin D. Roosevelt and Labor," p. 51; Irving Bernstein, *The New Deal Collective Bargaining Policy* (Berkeley and Los Angeles: University of California Press, 1950), pp. 19–20; "Address by Milton Handler, General Counsel of National Labor Board, before the Legal Division of the National Industrial Recovery Administration," n.d., Leon Henderson MSS, FDRL, Box 6; Robert Wagner to Rep. William Ashbrook, April 24, 1935, Wagner MSS.

84. Homer S. Cummings, "The Department of Justice and the New Deal," radio address, June 10, 1933, in Harold Ickes MSS, LC, Box 205.

85. *Wall Street Journal*, March 9, 1933; *Business Week*, May 31, 1933; *American Bankers Association Journal*, June 1933, all quoted in seminar paper by Jonathan Houghton, University of North Carolina at Chapel Hill. The

NRA, noted a journalist, "was a sort of Selective Service Act for industry."
The Unofficial Observer [John Franklin Carter], *American Messiahs* (New
York: Simon and Schuster, 1935), p. 223.

86. Sargent, *Roosevelt and the Hundred Days*, p. 129; Frank Freidel, *Franklin D.
Roosevelt: Launching the New Deal* (Boston: Little, Brown, 1973), p. 249.

87. Henry Steele Commager, "Farewell to Laissez-Faire," *Current History* 38
(August 1933): 517; "Unofficial Observer" [John Franklin Carter], *New
Dealers*, p. 5. "To a large degree," Robert Nisbet has written, "the so-called
New Deal was no more than an assemblage of governmental structures
modeled on those which had existed in 1917." Robert Nisbet, *Twilight of
Authority* (New York: Oxford University Press, 1975), p. 184. See, too,
Nash, "Experiments in Industrial Mobilization," p. 158.

88. *Survey for International Affairs for 1933* (London: Oxford University Press,
1934), pp. 15–16. At times, Roosevelt also employed the martial analogue
to allude not to World War I but to the American Revolution and the early
Republic. Torbjørn Sirevåg, "Franklin D. Roosevelt and the Use of History,"
in Sigmund Skard, ed., *Americana Norvegica: Norwegian Contributions to
American Studies* (Philadelphia: University of Pennsylvania Press, 1968),
p. 310.

89. *Public Papers*, 2: 300; Dale E. Soden, "The New Deal Comes to Shawnee,"
Chronicles of Oklahoma 63 (Summer 1985): 120; James Ware, "The Sooner
NRA: New Deal Recovery in Oklahoma," *Chronicles of Oklahoma* 57 (Fall
1976): 346; Charles H. Trout, *Boston, the Great Depression and the New
Deal* (New York: Oxford University Press, 1977).

90. *Time*, January 15, 1934, p. 25; Irving Bernstein, *A Caring Society: The New
Deal, the Worker, and the Great Depression* (Boston: Houghton, Mifflin,
1985), p. 307; *New York Times*, November 17, 1934; Richmond *Times-
Dispatch*, July 12, 1935, clipping, David J. Lewis Scrapbooks, Lewis MSS,
Duke University, Durham, N.C.; F. W. Foote to C. Blankenship, February
5, 1937, copy in William M. Colmer MSS, University of Southern
Mississippi, Hattiesburg, Miss., Box 113. See, too, *Literary Digest*, May 11,
1935, p. 12; Harry Hopkins, "The War on Distress," *Today*, December 16,
1933, Hopkins MSS, FDRL, Box 8; "Someone the Tenth District Needs,"
Radio Address, former State Senator Fleetwood Richards of Lockhart,
KNOW, Austin, 7:15–7:30, April 1, 1937, Lyndon B. Johnson Library,
Austin, Tex. In the 1936 campaign Harold Ickes, noting that in 1933 Alf
Landon had pledged "enlistment" under FDR "for the duration of the war"
against hard times, gibed, "It would appear that Candidate Landon has
gone A.W.O.L. from the war." Donald R. McCoy, *Landon of Kansas*
(Lincoln, Neb.: University of Nebraska Press, 1966), p. 274.

91. Johnson, *Blue Eagle from Egg to Earth*, p. 96. "Now the battle for recovery
has shifted from the stage of map work at GHQ to the firing line of

action," wrote Raymond Clapper. Administrators like Peek and Johnson were "the top sergeants of recovery." Clapper, "Top Sergeants of the New Deal," *Review of Reviews and World's Work* 88 (August 1933): 19.

92. The idea of an NRA insignia had been suggested by Bernard Baruch in a speech in May. He based the proposal on a War Industries Board notion. Bernard Baruch, *The Public Years* (New York: Holt, Rinehart, and Winston, 1960), pp. 73, 251. In his speech, Baruch had declared: "If it is commonly understood that those who are cooperating are soldiers against the enemy within and those who omit to act are on the other side, there will be little hanging back. The insignia of government approval on doorways, letterheads, and invoices will become a necessity in business. This method was a success in 1918." Johnson, *Blue Eagle from Egg to Earth*, p. 251.

93. *Public Papers*, 2: 301.

94. Schlesinger, *Coming of the New Deal*, p. 113.

95. Johnson, *Blue Eagle from Egg to Earth*, p. 264. Johnson used many of the techniques of World War I draft registration in administering the NRA. Peek, *Why Quit Our Own*, pp. 122–23; Russell Owen, "General Johnson Wages a Peace-Time War," *New York Times Magazine*, July 30, 1933, p. 3; Division of Press Intelligence, "Memorandum on Editorial Reaction Week from April 30 through May 6," May 7, 1935, Louis Howe MSS, Box 85. Ruth McKenney observed of Akron: "Precisely like the old draft board, a local N.R.A. Compliance Committee was set up, its members the very 'best' people in town." McKenney, *Industrial Valley*, p. 107.

96. *Public Papers*, 2: 345.

97. NRA Speakers' Bulletin, Portland, Oregon, Release No. 2, n.d. [September 1933], Burton Lee French MSS, Miami University, Oxford, Ohio.

98. Cooke to Louis Howe, July 3, 1933, Morris Cooke MSS, FDRL, Box 51. "57 varieties" was the well-known slogan of Heinz food products. Russell Leffingwell of the House of Morgan observed later: "Just as the war tore us all up by the roots, and made us seek such opportunity as there might be to serve our country in its need, so every man of good-will, every man of imagination and understanding has been struggling these last four and one-half years to find out how the human agony of the deflation could be stopped." Leffingwell, "The Gold Problem and Currency Revaluation," Academy of Political Science, March 21, 1934, FDRL PPF 866.

99. The New Deal agencies reminded one European visitor of the "War Bureaus of 1914 to 1918." Odette Keun, *I Think Aloud in America* (New York: Longmans, Green, 1939), p. 175. Political scientists had been disappointed by Hoover's failure to name social scientists to government agencies. "During the World War," wrote Arthur Holcombe, "economists and sociologists and statisticians were found to be very useful in Washington and were employed in large numbers. They should be used also in times of

peace." Holcombe, "Trench Warfare," *American Political Science Review* 25 (November 1931): 916.

100. Barbara Blumberg, *The New Deal and the Unemployed: The View from New York City* (Lewisburg, Pa.: Bucknell University Press, 1979), pp. 301–2; Jane De Hart Mathews, *The Federal Theatre, 1935–1939: Plays, Relief, and Politics* (Princeton, N.J.: Princeton University Press, 1967), p. 250. One commentator noted that General Williams, as "an old army man, could think in terms of the government interest." "Unofficial Observer" [John Franklin Carter], *New Dealers*, p. 47. For the high incidence of army officers in New Deal agencies, see John D. Millett, *The Works Progress Administration in New York City* (Chicago: Public Administration Service, 1938), p. 221.

101. Joseph Guffey, *Seventy Years on the Red-Fire Wagon: From Tilden to Truman* (Lebanon, Pa.: n.p., 1952), p. 46. The New Deal's oil controls as well as the coal agencies Guffey helped establish rested, in part, on the precedent of the wartime Fuel Administration. Swisher, *American Constitutional Development*, p. 661.

102. Lubin to Louis Brandeis, August 25, 1933, Brandeis MSS, University of Louisville Law Library, Louisville, Ky., G5. Lubin, United States Commissioner of Labor Statistics, had served as Thorstein Veblen's assistant in the Food Administration and later under Wesley Mitchell with the War Industries Board.

103. Hugh S. Johnson to Jerome Frank, January 9, 1934, Frank MSS, Series II, Box 12; Matthew Josephson, "The General," *The New Yorker*, August 25, 1934, p. 23.

104. Russell Lord, *The Wallaces of Iowa* (Boston: Houghton Mifflin, 1947), p. 346; Joseph P. Lash, *Dealers and Dreamers: A New Look at the New Deal* (New York: Doubleday, 1988), pp. 102, 111; Felix Frankfurter to Donald Richberg, April 4, 1933, Frankfurter MSS, LC, Box 96; William O. Douglas to Leon Henderson, October 5, 1937, Douglas MSS, LC, Box 17. Corcoran had been a law clerk for Justice Oliver Wendell Holmes.

105. Holger Cahill COHC, p. 340; Frank R. McNinch to Sanford Martin, August 28, 1937, Martin MSS, Duke University, Durham, N. C., Box 4. Roosevelt told Carter Glass it was a "war duty" to accept the post of Secretary of the Treasury. Daniel Roper to Edward House, January 24, 1933, House MSS, Sterling Memorial Library, Yale University, New Haven, Ct. Note, too, his attitude toward Chicago Mayor Anton Cermak's assassination in Zangara's attempt on Roosevelt's life in Cordell Hull, *The Memoirs of Cordell Hull*, 2 vols. (New York: Macmillan, 1948), 1: 158. Tugwell commented on his appointment as Assistant Secretary of Agriculture: "F.D.R. marshalled me into service." Tugwell, "Notes from a New Deal Diary," February 18, 1933. That fall, George Creel pledged his

"continued devotion to NIRA as soldier in the ranks." George Creel to Roosevelt, September 23, 1933, Creel MSS, LC, Box 4.

106. William Dow Boutwell, "The War on Want: How It Is Being Fought—and Won!" *School Life* 19 (October 1933): 31; Louise Armstrong, *We Too Are the People* (Boston: Little, Brown, 1938), pp. 435, 465. The columnist Heywood Broun wrote: "Blow, bugles, blow, and let us put a ribbon with palms upon the breast of Travis Harvard Whitney. No soldier could have been more gallant than the man who crumpled at his desk in the Civil Works Administration." Heywood Broun, "Paper Work," in Louis Filler, ed., *The Anxious Years* (New York: Putnam, 1963), p. 118. See, too, Memorandum from Louis Brownlow to John Winant, Brownlow MS. Diary, August 3, 1935, Charles Merriam MSS, Box 164.

107. *Public Papers*, 5: 236. In 1938 Roosevelt stated, "Talking in fighting terms, we cannot capture one hill and claim to have won the battle, because the battlefront extends over thousands of miles and we must push forward along the whole front at the same time." *Public Papers*, 7: 465.

108. *Literary Digest*, February 13, 1932, p. 9; Leon Henderson noted a meeting with Hugh Johnson: "I asked—'who does your work of tieing into the adm. whole plan?' He said 'I do—but there isn't much done. There is no plan: not like old War Ind. Bd. We've got to have one soon. Walker runs too easy. The super-cabinet is just a lot of prima donnas sitting around—can't please 'em'" Henderson MS. Diary, February 20, 1934, Henderson MSS.

109. One writer noted that "the New Deal legislation was heavily garlanded with 'emergency clauses' describing the dire national peril. This was because the Court had decided during the World War that war powers were supreme." "Unofficial Observer" [John Franklin Carter], *New Dealers*, p. 394. See, too, Jane Perry Clark, "Emergencies and the Law," *Political Science Quarterly* 49 (1934): 268–83. Cf. Justice Sutherland's dissent in *Home Building and Loan Association v. Blaisdell*, 290 U.S. 471 (1934). In his press conference after the adverse ruling in the *Schechter* case, Roosevelt protested the Court's failure to recognize an emergency in view of "those war acts which conferred upon the Executive far greater power over human beings and over property than anything that was done in 1933." *Public Papers*, 4: 206.

110. Schlesinger, *Coming of the New Deal*, p. 498.

111. *Public Papers*, 5: 407. Cf. Kimmel, *Federal Budget and Fiscal Policy*, pp. 190–92.

112. *Congressional Record*, 73d Cong., 2d Sess., p. 2174; "Not Back to Hoover, Please!" *Nation*, March 28, 1934, p. 346.

113. Edwin F. Gay, " The Great Depression," *Foreign Affairs* 10 (July 1932): 529; Johnson, *Blue Eagle from Egg to Earth*, p. 222; Freidel, *America in the Twentieth Century*, p. 312.

114. John M. Clark, *Social Control of Business*, 2d ed., (New York: McGraw-Hill, 1939), pp. 424–25. The New Deal theorists were captivated by the idea of "balance." They sought to redress the imbalances between supply and demand, just as the war mobilizers had done. But they lacked the ingredients the war mobilizers could count upon: ample purchasing power and massive federal spending.

115. Paul H. Douglas, "The New Deal After Ten Weeks," *The World Tomorrow* 16 (June 1933): 419.

116. Schwarz, *New Dealers*, p. xiii.

117. David M. Kennedy, *Over Here: The First World War and American Society* (New York: Oxford University Press, 1980), p. 141; Robert D. Cuff, *The War Industries Board: Business-Government Relations During World War I* (Baltimore: The Johns Hopkins University Press, 1973), p. 7.

118. It was not merely that Johnson had the temperament of a war administrator who turned naturally to the tactics of social coercion, but also that he had well-founded doubts about whether the Supreme Court would sanction government edicts. Schlesinger, *Coming of the New Deal*, pp. 108–9. Schlesinger also suggested that Johnson decided on this course because Harold Ickes moved so slowly in spending for public works. This seems unlikely. Johnson made this decision almost as soon as he took office, well before the outlines of Ickes's operation had become clear.

119. Lucy Sprague Mitchell, *Two Lives*, p. 303.

120. *Report of Proceedings of the Fifty-third Annual Convention of the American Federation of Labor* (Washington, D.C., 1933), p. 307. In the summer of 1933 the President had made a "no strike" appeal. He said of it: "It is a document on a par with Samuel Gompers' memorable war-time demand to preserve the *status quo* in labor disputes. . . . It is an act of economic statesmanship." *Public Papers*, 2: 318.

121. AF of L, *Proceedings*, 1933, p. 359; Frances Perkins COHC, 7: 139–40; *Public Papers*, 2: 302.

122. In a capitalist society, bluster frequently serves as a reform government's alternative to institutional rearrangements that would give government a direct share in corporation policy-determination. President Kennedy's role in the 1962 steel-price-hike incident is a case in point.

123. Clarkson, *Industrial America in the World War*, p. 99; Edgar Eugene Robinson and Paul Carroll Edwards, eds., *The Memoirs of Ray Lyman Wilbur, 1875–1949* (Stanford, Cal.: Stanford University Press, 1960), p. 264.

124. Ronald Schaffer, *America in the Great War* (New York: Oxford University Press, 1991), pp. 216–17.

125. *Time*, June 19, 1933, p. 12. "Hoarders are at heart cowards," declared Chandler Hovey, senior partner of Kidder, Peabody. "The government

should declare that to hoard at this time is unpatriotic, destructive and against the public interest." Clipping, David I. Walsh MSS, Holy Cross College Library.

126. "Unofficial Observer" [John Franklin Carter], *New Dealers*, p. 178; Hugh Johnson to Carter Glass, December 4, 1933, Glass MSS, Alderman Library, University of Virginia, Box 4; Donald Richberg, *The Rainbow* (Garden City, N.Y.: Doubleday, Doran, 1936), pp. 288–89; T. R. B., "Washington Notes," *New Republic*, August 9, 1933, p. 340. Erich Ludendorff was the principal German strategist in World War I; Bergdoll was the most notorious "draft dodger" during the war. See, too, George B. Tindall, *The Emergence of the New South, 1913–1945* (Baton Rouge, La.: Louisiana State University Press, 1967), p. 436.

127. Carter Glass to Walter Lippmann, August 10, 1933, Glass MSS, Box 4; Lewis W. Douglas, "There Is One Way Out," *Atlantic Monthly* 156 (September 1935): 267. Walter Lippmann was troubled by the frequent use the planners made of the war analogy. Lippmann, *An Inquiry into the Principles of the Good Society* (Boston: Little, Brown, 1937), pp. 89–105. Cf. Clark, *Social Control of Business*, pp. 463–64. For disapproval of FDR's unwillingness to relinquish the emergency powers of 1933, see Irving Fisher to FDR, February 14, 1937, Fisher MSS, Yale University, Box 19; Edward A. Rumely to William E. Borah, August 7, 1937, Amos Pinchot MSS, LC, Box 60. For objection to FDR's Court-packing plan on the grounds that accepting appointment to a reconstructed Supreme Court could not "help but imply an offer of service as a disciplined soldier" and "an agreement to march wherever the *General* commands," see Raymond Moley, Address, NBC, February 12, 1937, Moley MSS, privately held.

128. "Memorandum on Proposal for Blanket-Code," July 18, 1933, George Peek to Frank Walker, July 18, 1933, Peek MSS (letter not sent).

129. Criticism of the New Deal as fascist was common, and not limited to concern over Johnson's predilections. A radical commentary on Tugwell's *The Industrial Discipline and the Governmental Arts* noted: " The really ominous word which Mr. Tugwell has spoken in his volume lies in his assumption that government in a capitalist society may be imbued with an essentially social aim that is *inclusive*, and may, therefore, in a grave emergency find it necessary to 'compel or persuade a higher co-operation for a national purpose.' The analysis is *liberal*—the solution is essentially *fascist*." J. B. Matthews and R. E. Shallcross, "Must America Go Fascist?" *Harper's* 169 (June 1934): 12.

130. Schlesinger, *Coming of the New Deal*, p. 339; H. H. Woodring, "The American Army Stands Ready," *Liberty*, January 6, 1934; Henry Wallace, *New Frontiers* (New York, 1934), p. 21.

131. Frankfurter to Brandeis, August 2, 1933, Brandeis MSS, G6.

132. "The Crisis of the N.R.A.," *New Republic*, November 8, 1933, p. 349; Richard P. Adelstein, "The Nation as an Economic Unit: Keynes, Roosevelt, and the Managerial Ideal," *Journal of American History* 78 (June 1991): 162; Conkin, *Tomorrow a New World*, p. 130. Cf. Arthur Schlesinger, Jr., *The Politics of Upheaval* (Boston: Houghton Mifflin, 1960), pp. 395–98. General Pershing was suggestive when he wrote in a national magazine in 1933: "In recent months we have been faced with an emergency just as real as that of 1917. More serious, indeed, because in war we at least know who our enemies are." Freidel, *Franklin D. Roosevelt: Launching the New Deal*, p. 248.

133. Doughton to Henry Baker, July 15, 1935, Doughton MSS, Southern Historical Collection, University of North Carolina, Chapel Hill, N.C., Drawer 7; *Public Papers*, 5: 522–23. Among countless examples of war rhetoric, see *Public Papers*, 5: 207, 475, and 7: 228, 545; Address of Governor George H. Earle, Wilkes Barre, Pa., March 16, 1935, Speech and News File No. 68, Earle MSS, Bryn Mawr, Pa. (privately held); Donald McCoy, *Angry Voices: Left-of-Center Politics in the New Deal Era* (Lawrence, Kan.: University of Kansas Press, 1958), p. 166.

134. Victor E. Cappa, "Two Studies of Certain Constitutional Powers as Possible Bases for Federal Regulation of Employer-Employee Relations," Office of National Recovery Administration Division of Review, *Work Materials No. 68* (Washington, D.C., March 1936), mimeographed, copy in Leon Henderson MSS, Box 17.

135. R. G. Tugwell, "After the New Deal," *New Republic*, July 26, 1939, p. 324. Three years later, Stuart Chase wrote: "Nothing in the agenda of the New Deal was as radical as the war agenda of 1917 in respect to the government control of economic activity." Chase, *The Road We Are Traveling, 1914–1942: Guide Lines to America's Future* (New York: Twentieth Century Fund, 1942), p. 42.

136. Tennessee Valley Authority, *To Keep the Water in the Rivers and the Soil on the Land*, pp. 43–44. After the Second World War, Judson King claimed: "TVA and the Columbia River dams 'saved our lives' in World War II. They made possible production of phosphorus, nitrates, light metals and other war materials, including materials for the atom bomb." King, *Conservation Fight*, pp. 280–81.

137. *New York Times*, August 19, 1934; Wallace to Roosevelt, August 26, 1939, FDRL, President's Secretary's File 27. Such observations may suggest that, from the beginning, the New Deal was bent on war, and that the intervention in World War II was the inevitable culmination of Roosevelt's policies, or that there was a symbiotic relationship between war and the New Deal species of reform. Nothing I have found in my own research would support the conclusion that the New Dealers conspired to involve the nation in war, and very little would suggest an inevitable marriage of New

Deal reform with war. Yet the relationship between progressivism and war in the twentieth-century state, it should be added, is a subject which is imperfectly understood and one that deserves more exploration and illumination.

138. Eliot Janeway, *The Struggle for Survival* (New Haven: Yale University Press, 1951), p. 20. Although proud of the achievements of the New Deal, Morris Cooke nonetheless believed that what had been done was inadequate. "I am convinced," he wrote in 1938, "that we have to arouse something akin to a war psychology if we are really to make this a permanent country." Cooke to W. C. Lowdermilk, June 30, 1938, cited in Jean Christie, "Morris L. Cooke," draft of Ph.D. dissertation, Columbia University, 1963.

139. Harry Slattery, Administrator of the Rural Electrification Administration, reported: "I told the Secretary that I was special assistant to Secretary Lane during the war period when he was Vice Counsel of the National Defense Council; . . . and that finally I was assigned to handle a plan for granting of land for returning soldiers and had that especially under me." "Memorandum of conference with Secretary Henry Wallace, October 11, 1939," Slattery MSS, Duke University, Durham, N.C.

140. Kenneth Holland and Frank Ernest Hill, *Youth in the CCC* (Washington, D.C.: American Council on Education, 1942), p. 184; H. S. Person, "The Rural Electrification Administration in Perspective," *Agricultural History* 24 (April 1950): 79–80; Harold Ickes, *Autobiography of a Curmudgeon* (New York: Reynal and Hitchcock, 1943), chap. 15; Frances Perkins COHC, 7: 776 ff.; Janeway, *Struggle for Survival*, p. 161; Matthew Woll to W. Jett Lauck, December 20, 1940, Lauck MSS, Correspondence; Schlesinger, *Coming of the New Deal*, p. 176. Tugwell wrote later: "New agencies were multiplying as they had not since 1933; and in a way this period was much like that of the earlier one when the enemy had been the impalpable but terrifying depression. Franklin had, indeed, used the analogy of war at that time." Tugwell, *The Democratic Roosevelt* (Garden City, N.Y.: Doubleday, 1957), p. 600. "The New Deal was some preparation for this upheaval," observed a columnist. "It was a kind of war." Marquis Childs, *I Write from Washington* (New York: Harper, 1942), p. 3. Frances Perkins reflected that the New Deal had, unconsciously, prepared the nation to meet the demands of war. Perkins, *The Roosevelt I Knew* (New York: Viking, 1946), pp. 349–51. From the very beginning, however, Roosevelt, who wished to maintain personal control of the mobilization, shied away from proposals to reconstitute a War Industries Board. "Meeting with the Business Advisory Council," May 23, 1940, FDRL PSF 17. There were numerous observations, though, on how World War I could serve as a useful precedent. See, e.g., Maxcy R. Dickson, "The Food Administration-Educator," *Agricultural History* 16 (April 1942): 91–96.

141. John Maynard Keynes, " The United States and the Keynes Plan," *New Republic*, July 29, 1940, pp. 156–59. Morris Cooke, writing in the same issue that he did not think war orders as such would necessarily end unemployment, added: "But I do feel that in executing billions in war orders we may learn a technique for deploying American manpower in such a way as to change, radically and permanently, our unemployment outlook." Cooke, "Can We Afford the New Deal?" *New Republic*, July 29, 1940, p. 165. Even before the United States entered the war, writers were predicting that the defense program would provide a precedent for new government intervention to secure full employment in the postwar era. *Business Week* commented: "It is inconceivable that, when the defense program ends, . . . the government will stand idly by in the midst of a great unemployment crisis born of nationwide demobilization. . . . The operation of the profit motive will be limited by the dominant requirement of full employment for the people." *Business Week*, August 16, 1941, pp. 36–37, cited in Chase, *Road We Are Traveling, 1914–1942*, p. 98. See, too, Arthur Feiler, "Economic Impacts of the War," *Social Research* 8 (May 1941): 297–309. As World War I provided a precedent for the New Deal planners, so World War II taught lessons in "full employment" to the liberals of the Truman era.

142. Clark, *Social Control of Business*, pp. 782–85.

143. Malcolm Cowley, "The End of the New Deal," *New Republic*, May 31, 1943, p. 729.

FIVE   Roosevelt, Norris, and the "Seven Little TVAs"

1. Samuel I. Rosenman, ed., *The Public Papers and Addresses of Franklin D. Roosevelt*, 13 vols. (New York: Random House, Macmillan, Harper, 1938–50), 2: 123; *Washington Star*, February 5, 1937; *New York Times*, September 29, 1932, April 1, 1937.

2. Press Conferences of the President, 1937, Franklin Delano Roosevelt Library, Hyde Park, N.Y. (FDRL), President's Personal File (PPF), 1-P; *New York Times*, May 15, 1937.

3. Bell to FDR, March 5, 1935, FDRL Official File (OF) 834; FDR letter in William Citron MSS, Middletown, Ct., privately held, FDR to Marion Dickens, March 9, 1936, FDRL OF 834. I am grateful to Congressman Citron for making his papers available to me.

4. *Electrical World*, January 23, 1937.

5. *New York Times*, January 19, 1937; FDR to Delano, January 16, 1937, National Archives, Washington, D. C., National Power Policy Committee, File 55. There had been an earlier National Power Policy Committee under the Public Works Administration with Harold Ickes as chairman, but it had "floundered." Otis L. Graham, Jr., *Toward a Planned Society: From Roosevelt*

to Nixon (New York: Oxford University Press, 1976), p. 60. In a memo of December 31, 1936, Joel David Wolfsohn, Executive Secretary of the old committee, recommended the reconstitution of the committee by executive order. FDRL OF 2575. The executive order and the personnel of the committee grew out of a conference attended by Ickes, McNinch, Cooke, and Basil Manly, a member of the Federal Power Commission. FDRL OF 466-B. Healy's illness prevented him from serving, and he was replaced by James M. Landis, chairman of the SEC and one of the draftsmen of the Public Utility Holding Company Act. On February 11, Dr. Harlow S. Person of the REA took over from Cooke, and Person gave way to John M. Carmody two weeks later. Cooke resigned from the Committee (and as REA Administrator) when the other members resisted his effort to get them to formulate a national policy statement. Morris Cooke to Colleagues, February 3, 1937, James M. Landis MSS, Box 120; Jean Christie, *Morris Llewellyn Cooke: Progressive Engineer* (New York: Garland, 1983), pp. 206–7.

6. Harold L. Ickes, *The Secret Diary of Harold L. Ickes,* 3 vols. (New York: Simon and Schuster, 1953–54), 2: 60–61. Surprisingly, one historian has indicated that the initiative came not from Norris but from the President. Philip Funigiello has written, "The prospect of little TVAs strung across the country, broached originally by Thomas G. Corcoran and Harry Slattery, intrigued Roosevelt and he promptly enlisted the support of Senator Norris, father of the original valley authority." Philip J. Funigiello, *Toward a National Power Policy: The New Deal and the Electric Utility Industry, 1933–1941* (Pittsburgh: University of Pittsburgh Press, 1973), p. 183. The committee had the Bonneville legislation ready by February 9, but with so much to do it abandoned its task of writing a paper on power policy. Only Morris Cooke continued to pursue that assignment.

7. In a memo to Morris Cooke, Dr. Person emphasized the main objections to the bill: "Too much Corps of Engineers, even with respect to up-stream engineering, soil conservation," and "Department of Agriculture left out of the picture." George W. Norris MSS, Library of Congress, Tray 80, Box 6.

8. *Public Papers,* 6: 78.

9. Charles McKinley, *Uncle Sam in the Pacific Northwest: Federal Management of Natural Resources in the Columbia River Valley* (Berkeley and Los Angeles: University of California Press, 1952), p. 542.

10. Herman C. Voeltz, "Genesis and Development of a Regional Power Agency in the Pacific Northwest, 1933–43," *Pacific Northwest Quarterly* 53 (April 1962): 65–70; McKinley, *Uncle Sam,* pp. 158–60.

11. Harold L. Ickes, "Foreword," Arthur Maass, *Muddy Waters: The Army Engineers and the Nation's Rivers* (Cambridge: Harvard University Press, 1951), p. xiv.

12. FDR to Harold Ickes, March 24, 1937, FDRL OF 2575; Ickes, *Secret Diary,* 2: 129–30, 132–35. His conflict with Woodring was long-standing.

"May I say at the outset," Ickes had scolded him as early as 1933, "that I deny the right of anyone to tell me how to conduct the business of this Department?" Eugene Trani, "Conflict or Compromise: Harold L. Ickes and Franklin D. Roosevelt," *North Dakota Quarterly* 36 (Winter 1968): 23. Years afterward Ickes said: "Woodring never was a man of much consequence in the government. Almost from the start, Roosevelt realized that he had made a mistake even in appointing Woodring temporarily." Harold L. Ickes to the writer, January 5, 1951.

13. FDR to Homer Bone, June 7, 1937, FDRL OF 360; McKinley, *Uncle Sam*, pp. 160–62.
14. T. H. Watkins, *Righteous Pilgrim: The Life and Times of Harold L. Ickes, 1874–1952* (New York: Holt, 1990), p. 561; Graham White and John Maze, *Harold Ickes of the New Deal: His Private Life and Public Career* (Cambridge: Harvard University Press, 1985), pp. 160–61; Trani, "Conflict or Compromise," p. 26; A. L. Riesch Owen, *Conservation Under F.D.R.* (New York: Praeger, 1983), p. 177. "Saw Harold," the former Chief Forester Gifford Pinchot jotted in his diary in June 1935, "who is red hot to get Dept. Cons." M. Nelson McGeary, *Gifford Pinchot: Forester-Politician* (Princeton: Princeton University Press, 1960), p. 410.
15. Paul H. Appleby to the writer, August 30, 1950.
16. James F. Byrnes, *All In One Lifetime* (New York: Harper, 1958), p. 106; Richard Polenberg, "Roosevelt, Carter, and Executive Reorganization: Lessons of the 1930s," *Presidential Studies Quarterly* 9 (Winter 1979): 37, 40; Richard Polenberg, *Reorganizing Roosevelt's Government: The Controversy Over Executive Reorganization, 1936–1939* (Cambridge: Harvard University Press, 1966), pp. 100–12.
17. Report of the President's Committee, *Administrative Management* (Washington, D. C.: Government Printing Office, 1937).
18. Ickes, *Secret Diary*, 1: 350.
19. Ibid., 2: 38–45.
20. Ibid., 2: 60–61; National Archives, Agriculture, Secretary's Correspondence, 1937, Meetings.
21. National Archives, National Power Policy Committee, File 55. A draft of the bill in late February provided for eight conservation authorities that were to be "subject to the supervision and control of the Secretary of _____." The agencies were to submit plans which, if they got the approval of the President, would go to Congress. Confidential Draft, February 26, 1937, in Joel David Wolfsohn to James M. Landis, March 1, 1937, Landis MSS, Box 120. The department was left blank not because there was any doubt about where power would be lodged but because Ickes anticipated that by the time the bill was enacted "Interior" might have been renamed "Conservation." Confidential Draft, February 26, 1937, in Joel David Wolfsohn to James M. Landis, March 1, 1937, Landis MSS, Box 120.

22. Ibid. The documents to which he refers are United States National Resources Committee, *Public Works Planning* (Washington, D. C.: Government Printing Office, 1936), and United States National Resources Committee, *Regional Factors in National Planning and Development* (Washington, D. C.: Government Printing Office, 1935). Ickes, too, disliked three-member boards. He later commented: "I could never see eye to eye with Mr. Lilienthal. He was a strong advocate of a three-man board administration. I never was. At least, if I was, it was before I had had any experience with such a set-up and on such a scale that I came to have in Interior. . . . Lilienthal was the John the Baptist so far as board administration was concerned. He spent a lot of government time and a lot of government money crusading in different parts of the country in advocacy of his theory." Harold L. Ickes to the writer, January 5, 1951.

23. Ickes, *Secret Diary*, 2: 114; Press Conference, April 6, 1937, FDRL PPF 1-P; memo on Conference between President and Ickes, Merriam and Ruml, April 6, 1937, National Archives, 104.1.

24. FDRL PPF 1-P; FDRL PPF 1-F; Minutes, Eleventh Meeting, President's Informal Committee on National Power Policy, April 30, 1937, James M. Landis MSS, Box 121. West was Under Secretary of the Interior and an operative on Capitol Hill.

25. Ickes, *Secret Diary*, 2: 130.

26. Henry A. Wallace to FDR, May 8, 1937; FDR to Wallace, May 8, 1937, FDRL OF 1.

27. FDRL PPF 1-F.

28. Memorandum of May 17, 1937, Milton Eisenhower, Director of Information, to Wallace, Confidential, National Archives, Agriculture, Secretary's Correspondence, 1937, Bills, Miscellaneous.

29. Wallace to FDR, May 18, 1937, National Archives, Agriculture, Secretary's Correspondence, 1937, Bills, Miscellaneous.

30. Wallace and Woodring to FDR, May 24, 1937, National Archives, Agriculture, Secretary's Correspondence, Bills, Miscellaneous.

31. Ibid. Will Whittington was a Democratic Congressman from Mississippi.

32. FDR to Wallace and Ickes, May 26, 1937, FDRL OF 1.

33. Benjamin V. Cohen to the writer, November 24, 1950. Meantime, during all of this internal debate, Norris, who had expected to introduce his bill in April, had been left out on a limb. On May 29 the President wrote Norris regretting that "the message on the bill for establishing Regional Authorities has been delayed so many times that it has caused you all kinds of embarrassment." But he pledged that it would go up to the Hill shortly, and on June 3 it did. Richard Lowitt, *George W. Norris: The Triumph of a Progressive, 1933–1944* (Urbana, Ill.: University of Illinois Press, 1978), p. 201.

34. Drafts of the President's message may be found in FDRL PPF 1-F.

35. After a conversation with Ben Cohen, one of Morris Cooke's chief lieutenants informed him: "Apparently the Administration is neutral as between the bills—is promoting the hearings on the Mansfield bill as well—shooting both barrels of its gun." Harlow Person to Morris L. Cooke, July 7, 1937, Cooke MSS, FDRL, Box 146. Person added: "So Ben is considering whether Mansfield's testimony should not be bolstered by other testimony, for Mansfield hasn't Norris' prestige. That is what was in Ben's mind when he said he wished you were here—to give such supporting testimony, or at least to recommend someone who could."

36. FDR to TVA Board, February 25, 1937, FDRL OF 42; *Public Papers*, 6: 119.

37. The ardent public power advocate Judson King recalled some years later a thirty-minute interview with the President a few days after he sent the regional planning message to Congress. "I brought up the opposition of the Army Engineers to public power and TVAs . . . and by a gesture of his thumb he gave me to understand that he was positive he could bring them into line," King said. Judson King to the writer, November 28, 1950. Roosevelt, King also stated, "outlined to me his ideas and they were certainly for the creation of TVA operating agencies." That recollection seems improbable, though FDR was often guilty of telling people, or implying to them, what he knew they wanted to hear.

38. *Public Papers*, 6: 23–24.

39. U.S. Congress, Senate, *Creation of Conservation Authorities*, Hearings before a Subcommittee of the Committee on Agriculture and Forestry, U.S. Senate, 75th Cong., 1st Sess. on S. 2555, June 21 to July 7, 1937 (Washington, D. C., 1937), p. 1; Conference with President at the White House, February 20, 1937, National Archives, 104.1.

40. U.S. Congress, Senate, *Creation of Conservation Authorities*, p. 2.

41. Press Conference, February 9, 1937, FDRL PPF. 1-P.

42. Press Conference, June 4, 1937, FDRL PPF 1-P. In 1936 construction had begun on one of FDR's pet schemes—to harness the extraordinarily fluctuation in the tides at the Bay of Fundy for electric power—but Congress balked at funding the project and it did not survive. Walter E. Lowrie, "Roosevelt and the Passamaquoddy Bay Tidal Project," *Historian* 31 (1968): 64–89.

43. J. G. Pope and G. W. Norris to Senator Ellison D. Smith, August 6, 1937, Norris MSS, Tray 80, Box 6.

44. U.S. Congress, House of Representatives, *Regional Conservation and Development of National Resources*, Hearings before the Committee on Rivers and Harbors, House of Representatives, 75th Cong., 1st Sess., on H.R. 7365 and H.R. 7863, July and August 1937 (Washington, D.C., 1937), pp. 192, 245.

45. Ibid., pp. 179, 234.

46. *Public Papers*, 3: 416–17.

47. *New York Times*, October 13, November 23, 1937.

48. *Washington Star*, November 23, 28, 1937; *Washington Herald*, November 26, 1937.

49. Roosevelt saw Willkie on November 23.

50. Coleman to Norris, November 22, 1937. Norris MSS, Tray 80, Box 6.

51. *Washington Star*, June 22, 1937; *Sacramento Bee*, November 10, 1937; *Washington Post*, November 11, 1937. Citations to newspapers other than in New York or Washington are from the clipping files in the Norris MSS.

52. *Washington Post*, November 22, 1937.

53. *Philadelphia Record*, November 30, December 1, 1937; McCook (Nebr.) *Daily Gazette*, November 30, 1937. Three weeks later, the columnists Drew Pearson and Robert S. Allen reported Norris's protesting to Roosevelt at the White House: "The attitude of the utilities reminds me of the burglar who was caught red-handed and then offered to bargain just before the judge sentenced him. There isn't anything they have to offer, Mr. President, that is worth accepting. When they talk compromise they mean surrender by the government. You cannot do that." "I have no intention to, George," Roosevelt is quoted as replying. "You remember I said at Madison Square Garden before election, 'We have just begun to fight.' I meant that. We have just begun to fight." Madison (Wis.) *Capital-Times*, December 23, 1937.

54. Honeyman to FDR, December 10, 1937; Delano to James Roosevelt, December 15, 1937, FDRL OF 834.

55. *New York Times*, December 16, 1937.

56. Cohen to FDR, March 2, 1938, FDRL OF 834. James F. Byrnes was Senator from South Carolina.

57. Ibid.; *New York Times*, March 26, 1938. The final form of the Mansfield substitute was influenced by a bill introduced by Senator Carl Hayden of Arizona on December 10, 1937. Mansfield's new bill was a caricature of his own original proposal. It provided for an eleven-member National Resources Board, eight to be appointed by the President (one at large and one from each of seven regions) and three to be named by the Secretaries of War, Interior, and Agriculture, respectively. However, the regional members could vote only on issues affecting their region, giving the real power to the three men picked by cabinet officials, rather than to the men chosen by the President. The regional committees would also be dominated by federal departmental representatives and could have no power to do anything but recommend. Moreover, they would not even make recommendations without the approval of the appropriate federal agency; no regional committee could recommend a flood control or navigation project to Congress unless the Corps of Engineers consented.

58. For the postwar effort to create more valley authorities, see the survey by Wesley Clark in the *American Political Science Review* 40 (February 1946): 62–70.

59. Barry D. Karl, *Charles E. Merriam and the Study of Politics* (Chicago: University of Chicago Press, 1974), pp. 247–48.

60. Eric A. Nordlinger, *On the Autonomy of the Democratic State* (Cambridge: Harvard University Press, 1981), p. 1. One of the foremost theorists on the New Deal has written that "neo-Marxists of all varieties have so far given insufficient weight to state and party organizations as independent determinants of political conflicts and outcomes." Theda Skocpol, "Political Response to Capitalist Crisis: Neo-Marxist Theories of the State and the Case of the New Deal," *Politics and Society* 10 (1980): 155–201.

61. Ickes, "Foreword," in Maass, *Muddy Waters*, pp. x–xi.

62. Paul H. Appleby to the writer, August 30, 1950. "The genius of Norris was agitational—but he got a good many bricks laid, for a brick-thrower!" Appleby wrote in that same letter, "The design was poor, however."

63. Marguerite Owen to the writer, November 24, 1950; Ickes, "Foreword," to Maass, *Muddy Waters*, p. ix; James A. Farley Oral History, University of Kentucky, Lexington, Ky. I appreciate the courtesy of Bill Cooper in granting me access to this last document.

64. C. Herman Pritchett, "The Transplantability of the TVA," *Iowa Law Review* 32 (January 1947): 327.

65. Lowitt, *Norris*, pp. 201–2*n*.

66. Funigiello, *Toward a National Power Policy*, p. 193; Benjamin V. Cohen to the writer, November 24, 1950.

67. Judson King to the writer, November 28, 1950; Paul H. Appleby to the writer, August 30, 1950; Benjamin V. Cohen to the writer, November 24, 1950.

68. Benjamin V. Cohen to the writer, November 24, 1950.

69. Maass, *Muddy Waters*, pp. 87–93.

70. Owen, *Conservation Under F.D.R.*, p. 61; Joseph O'Mahoney to William C. Snow, November 29, 1937, O'Mahoney MSS, University of Wyoming, Laramie, Wyo.; John Braeman, "The Collapse of the Liberal Consensus," *Canadian Review of American Studies* 20 (Summer 1989): 67.

71. The quotations come from the draft of a manuscript by Alan Brinkley, "The Transformation of New Deal Liberalism," that I was privileged to read. "Naturally Senator Norris was deeply disappointed that the President did not give his exclusive support to the Norris bill," Cohen later said. "I do not think Senator Norris felt that he was ever betrayed by the President." Benjamin V. Cohen to the writer, November 24, 1950. Indeed, Norris placed such trust in Roosevelt that when, in the following year, he learned that under the pending reorganization legislation his beloved TVA might lose its independent status and be placed in Interior, he still opposed all exemptions, even for TVA, and went down the line for FDR's scheme. Polenberg, *Reorganizing Roosevelt's Government*, pp. 141–42.

6. HURRICANE POLITICS

1. Bernard De Voto, "Paradox on Betelgeuse," *Harper's* 178 (December 1938): 111.

2. The description of the hurricane is based primarily on newspaper accounts, notably those in the *New York Times*, the Springfield *Republican*, and the *Hartford Courant*. The best single summary of the storm is F. Barrows Colton, "The Geography of a Hurricane," *National Geographic* 85 (April 1939): 529–52. The most vivid personal account of the impact of the hurricane is Frances Woodward, "Wind and Fury," *Atlantic Monthly* 47 (December 1938): 749–757. The recollection is in Jan Myrdal, *Another World: An Autobiographical Novel* (Chicago: Ravenswood, 1994), p. 146. The book was originally published in Sweden in 1984. See, too, De Voto, "Paradox," pp. 109–12; John Q. Stewart, "New England Hurricane," *Harper's* 178 (January 1939): 198–204; Stuart D. Goulding, "Neither Storm, Nor Strife . . . ," *Commonweal* 30 (May 26, 1939): 123–25.

3. *Washington Daily News*, May 23, 1936.

4. *Hartford Times*, May 23, 1936.

5. *Merr. River Valley and Conn. River Valley Interstate Flood Control Compacts*, Hearings before the House Committee on Flood Control, 75th Cong., p. 147.

6. *Regional Conservation and Development of the National Resources*, Hearings before the House Committee on Rivers and Harbors, House of Representatives, 75th Cong., 1st Sess. November and December 1937, p. 800.

7. Franklin D. Roosevelt Library, Hyde Park, N.Y., Official File (FDRL OF) 132C, May 20, 1938.

8. *Hartford Courant*, September 24, 1938.

9. Ibid., September 22, 1938.

10. *Hartford Times*, October 6, 1938. Congressman Citron was informed that Governor Aiken had sent an aide down to get statements from Connecticut state officials asserting that the failure to act on the compacts had resulted in the flood damage. William Citron MSS, privately held, Middletown, Ct.

11. Citron to FDR, September 26, 1938, FDRL OF 132.

12. Kopplemann to FDR, September 26, 1938, FDRL OF 83.

13. Owen Johnson to FDR, October 2, 1938, FDRL OF 132.

14. *Hartford Courant*, October 1, 1938.

15. FDR to Seavey, September 30, 1938; Stephen Early to Seavey, Hopkins, and Schley, October 1, 1938, FDRL OF 132.

16. *New York Times*, October 5, 1938.

17. Bulkley Griffin, "New England Secession," *New Republic* 97 (November 16, 1938): 41.

18. *New York Times*, October 6, 1938.

19. *Springfield Republican*, November 10, 1938.

INDEX

Abbott, Grace, 152
Acuña, Rodolfo, 153
Adams, Brooks, 41
Adams, David K., 281
Adams, Henry, 287
Adelstein, Richard, 72
African Americans, 82, 215; discrimination against, 220–21, 273–74, 278, 279; 1936 election and, 16, 113, 127, 129–30, 144, 146, 157; Eleanor Roosevelt and, 122, 130; visibility of, 230–31, 303
Agricultural Adjustment Act (1933), 54, 270
Agricultural Adjustment Administration, 56, 102, 232; blacks and, 220, 221, 273; deficiencies of, 278; Landon program and, 111; military value of, 73, 75; officials of, 70–71; Peek and, 54; Rauch on, 216
Agriculture Department, 230, 341n7; Congressional relations with, 179; Forest Service and, 167–68; proposed Conservation Department and, 169; regional authorities proposal and, 171, 175, 177, 190–91, 193; revised Mansfield bill and, 187
Aid to Dependent Children programs, 254, 272
Aiken, Conrad, 262
Aiken, George D., 206, 347n10
Air Force, 5

Akron (Ohio), 332n95
Akron Beacon-Journal, 49
Alabama Power Company, 166
Alexander the Great, 243
Allen, Florence, 271
Allen, Henry, 106
Allen, Howard, 151
Allen, Robert S., 344n53
Allied Chemical Corporation, 139
Allied Forces, 5, 29, 298, 301
Allswang, John, 101
Alsop, Joseph, 185, 301–2
Amalgamated Clothing Workers of America, 132
American Bankers Association Journal, 58
American Embassy (Britain), 76
American Expeditionary Force, 45
American Federation of Labor, 68, 131
American Historical Association, 35
American Imprints Inventory, 263
American Institute of Public Opinion, 101–2, 119
American Jewish Congress, 148
American Labor party, 16, 133, 134, 149, 153
American Legion, 110
American Liberty League, 104, 112, 123, 124, 217
American Public Welfare Association, 255